Ambiguous Partnership
Britain and America, 1944–1947

WITHDRAWN
UTSA LIBRARIES

Contemporary American History Series
William E. Leuchtenburg, Editor

AMBIGUOUS PARTNERSHIP

Britain and
America,
1944–1947

Robert M. Hathaway

COLUMBIA UNIVERSITY PRESS
NEW YORK   1981

The Andrew W. Mellon Foundation, through a special grant, has assisted the Press in publishing this volume.

Clothbound editions of Columbia University Press books are Smyth-sewn and printed on permanent and durable acid-free paper.

Library of Congress Cataloging in Publication Data

Hathaway, Robert M., 1947–
Ambiguous partnership.

(Contemporary American history series)
Bibliography: p.
Includes index.
1. United States—Foreign relations—Great
Britain.   2. Great Britain—Foreign rela-
tions—United States.   3. World War, 1939–
1945—Diplomatic history.   4. World politics—
1945–1955.   I. Title.   II. Series.
E183.8.G7H35   1981   327.41073   81-6153
ISBN 0-231-04452-6   AACR2

Columbia University Press
New York   Guildford, Surrey

To Susie,
wife, friend, and full partner in this enterprise,
and
in memory of my father

Contents

◇

Acknowledgments

This study, like most such endeavors, is the product of many minds, both inside and outside of academia. A professional historian accumulates a multitude of intellectual debts, most of which, unhappily, must remain unacknowledged. Three individuals, however, played such an instrumental role in shaping my understanding of Anglo-American relations in the 1940s that failure to mention them would be unpardonable. At the very top of this list is Samuel F. Wells, Jr., who provided guidance, encouragement, and keen questioning in precisely the correct proportions during the formulative stages of my investigations. One could not ask for a better dissertation director. Gerhard Weinberg is another to whom I owe much; his critiques were not always painless, but invariably contained erudition and wisdom. My editor, William E. Leuchtenburg, devoted innumerable hours to keeping me from serious errors of style and substance. A literary craftsman of the first order and an unremitting exposer of the dubious assumption, the circular argument, and the unfounded bias, he furnishes new authors with a high standard toward which to strive. To each of these scholars I offer sincere thanks. Others who read some or all of these pages include Professors Terry Anderson, Donald Bletz, Leonard Dinnerstein, Helen Nutting, Joseph Tulchin, and Samuel R. Williamson. None completely accept my conclusions, but I trust all will recognize their specific contributions, for which I am grateful.

Historians are no better than their librarians and archivists, and in this area too, I have been most fortunate. Particular notice should be made of the genuine helpfulness provided by the staffs of the Franklin D. Roosevelt Library, the Harry S. Truman Library, and the Wilson College Library, each of which met my many needs with dispatch and good humor. Aid of another sort was provided by research grants from the Earhart Foundation, the John Anson Kittredge Fund, the Eleanor Roosevelt Institute, the Harry S. Truman Library Foundation, and the Middlebury College Faculty Research Fund. Without these this study would not have been possible.

Others whose willingness to give of their time made my efforts easier or more rewarding include Ambassador Waldemar J. Gallman, Shepard Jones, Robert Pollard, and Joe and Carolyn Jaros. John A. DeNovo was gracious enough to share his unpublished findings with me. Alice and J. L. Wilson provided critical help at a strategic moment. Karen Mitchell contributed ably during the typing and proofing stages while Annabelle Foster deserves special commendation for bringing coherence to very untidy drafts. To all I express my thanks.

Finally, and most importantly, there is the debt I owe my family, but especially my wife Susie. Simply to mention the long hours she put in behind the typewriter, the many nights she cheerfully endured while I was off doing research, or the continual crises involved in keeping three little girls quiet while Daddy was frantically writing is hardly sufficient to express my feelings of appreciation and gratitude. Fortunately, because she is who she is, she already knows these too. To her this book is dedicated, with love.

Ambiguous Partnership
Britain and America, 1944–1947

Introduction

The story of the early Cold War years is not a novel one. Particularly in the past decade the transition from wartime alliance to postwar enmity has been a dominant theme in American historiography, until today an extensive bibliography exists for this period. And yet, only a portion of the tale has been told. For nearly three and a half decades these years have been thought of and written about almost exclusively in bipolar terms: East against West, United States versus Soviet Russia. It is as if the United States had no contact with other nations except in the context of Cold War hostilities. Today it is virtually impossible to look back on the events of 1945 and 1946 without being prejudiced by knowledge of the Marshall Plan, NATO, and successive crises over Berlin. But the national actors of a generation ago did not and could not have had this perspective. To ignore this elementary logic is to simplify, but also to misrepresent the experience of past ages.

Nowhere has the distorting effect of this preoccupation with Soviet-American conflict been more pronounced than in our reconstruction of ties between Great Britain and the United States at the end of the Second World War. Historically, the Anglo-American connection has been far and away the most important factor in Washington's dealings with the world beyond the seas. Whether these relations were characterized by hostility, as was true of much of the nineteenth century, or by a more amiable tone, as became increasingly common as the nineteenth gave way to the twentieth, American diplomats turned first to ascertain Britain's reaction before evaluating matters of international consequence. The Second World War, of course, radically shifted power relationships throughout the globe, and Britain finally and unalterably slipped from the ranks of the leading nation-states into a secondary position. Still, to portray America's relations with the former mother country as trifling or insignificant, or—worse yet—to disregard bilateral matters altogether, is to warp the views of those in both Great Britain and the United States who were chiefly responsible for the conduct of their respective nation's foreign policies. One of the intentions of this study, then, is to correct, at least partially, this myopic picture of the immediate postwar years, with its neglect of practically all questions other than Soviet-American antagonism—in effect, to depolarize these years.[1]

An investigation such as this, however, lends itself to other purposes as well. American historians have a tendency to portray Europe as simply the object of American policies, the recipient of and reactor to United States initiatives.[2] Often there is an assumption, implicit if not explicit, that different attitudes in the United States alone could have altered a given course of events. This parochialism, itself the product of an incredible optimism fostered by the unique American experience, has led many scholars to ignore or discount any significant European contribution to the American policy-making process.[3] Research in the British archives, however, readily demonstrates just how foolish such an idea is. The decision makers in London fully recognized this. "Consciously or unconsciously, willingly or unwillingly," one Foreign Office official wrote shortly after the end of the war, the Americans will "long continue to see many crucial things through the British window."[4] A second focus of this essay, then, is to document the subtle ways by which and the extent to which British desires became translated into United States foreign policy.

Ultimately, to be sure, British-American relations hinged on whatever role in the international arena the leading politicians and statesmen in Washington selected for their country, for the all-important element of power was by 1944 almost entirely on the side of the United States. But historians have not yet been able to agree as to how Americans perceived themselves and their mission in a world in which they found their nation indisputably the strongest and most powerful. Some have written that the people of the United States, tired of depression and war, wanted only to be left alone to concentrate their attentions on long-deferred comforts offered by American technological prowess. Others have described an aggressive, crusading America out to remake the world in its own democratic-capitalist image. As usual, the truth lies somewhere in between. By seeing how Washington looked upon its closest friend and ally, we are afforded some insight into America's perception of itself, and hence, into the dynamics behind much of United States foreign policy in subsequent years.

The starting date for this study, admittedly somewhat arbitrary, was not selected without reflection. In the late summer of 1944, a significant shift occurred in the concerns prominent in both Washington and London. The extraordinary success of the Normandy invasion and the rapid progress of the armies of all three of the major allies in the succeeding months removed all doubts as to the ultimate achievement of total victory over the Nazi foe in a reasonably short time. August 15 saw a second major amphibious invasion of France, and the troops who waded ashore during DRAGOON were soon fanning out from the Mediterranean coastline in every direction. On August 20 the Red Army initiated a powerful offensive into Rumania. Paris and Bucharest both fell to allied armies on the 23d, exemplifying the gigantic pincers tightening around the German jugular. On August 25 the Finns opened armistice negotiations, and the following day Bulgaria withdrew from the war. At the end of the month the Germans found themselves forced to intervene in Hungary in order to prevent that hapless country's surrender. Events in the Pacific, if not as dramatic, were no less promising. On all fronts allied arms were greeted with success.

The second half of August also saw the opening of the Dumbarton Oaks conference, where representatives of the United

States, Great Britain, the Soviet Union, and China gathered for exploratory talks looking toward the establishment of a new world security organization. No visionary pipedream, this new creation was to be, at least in the minds of many, the granite cornerstone of the peace which allied might was bringing ever closer. The convocation of the conference at that particular moment was symbolic of the recently intensified interest in what was to follow the war, for by the end of August questions of the peace had assumed a more pressing interest for many of the policy makers in London and Washington, particularly those concerned principally with European affairs, than matters dealing primarily with how the war was to be won. Consequently, it is at that point that this study commences.

For a number of reasons the late winter of 1946–47 provides a convenient, if again somewhat artificial, termination date for this consideration of relations between the two Atlantic democracies. Shortly after the turn of the year an unusually severe blizzard, the worst in memory, buffeted Britain. Coupled with an acute shortage of coal, it brought the economic life of the country to a virtual standstill and emphasized just how vulnerable the once proud island had become. Prime Minister Attlee's announcement in the House of Commons during the height of the storm of plans for the final British withdrawal from India only reiterated that slide from the pinnacle of power. In February the British government turned the bewildering puzzle of Palestine over to the United Nations, at once admitting it could no longer handle a problem squarely in the middle of an area traditionally considered a British preserve, and also washing its hands of the issue which had been the most divisive in relations with the Americans during the past year. These months also saw the merging of the British and American zones of occupation in Germany, and finally, the formulation and enunciation of what was to become known as the Truman Doctrine, with all its implications of an American assumption of British responsibilities. Many Englishmen, stunned by the momentous import of these events, believed they were witnessing the end of an era.

One of the more fascinating aspects of an investigation such as this is to observe the dissimilar manner in which British and American officialdom went about the process of making policy, and in particular to see the differences with which they viewed each other and their disparate notions of what the relationship between the two nations should involve. One comes away from such a study all the more conscious of the narrow range of choices confronting the harried men and women in the Foreign Office in London and His Majesty's embassy in Washington. In many respects they were fighting a rear-guard action in defense of a position and a prestige which was no longer supported by the requisite power. Lacking this essential component of successful diplomacy, they sought to rely on experience and maturity, only to discover that their erstwhile partners in the Grand Alliance valued tanks and gold over advice. Offering an abundance of the latter, but possessing precious few of the former, British statesmen were often disappointed in their hopes.

An old story which made the rounds in Great Britain in the 1940s goes far in explaining these dashed expectations. The tale told of a young man preparing for a career in the Foreign Service who was asked what he thought were the most important things in the world. Without a moment's hesitation, he replied: "Love, and Anglo-American relations." A good many diplomats in Whitehall would have echoed this response. Such an assessment, however, seldom guided the calculations of their counterparts in the United States. In fact, Washington officials rarely devoted concentrated, systematic deliberation to bilateral ties between their country and the United Kingdom. When one remembers the central place which relations with Great Britain have always held in America's interaction with the rest of the world, it is astonishing to discover the casualness, the ad hoc nature of United States dealings with the British at the end of the war. Anglo-American relations, which one would expect to have been of crucial interest to Washington, were continually subordinated to more immediate but ultimately less significant concerns. It was this cavalier treatment, this apparent indifference to relations with the British that so infuriated, and at the same time perplexed, those in London who were responsible for devising a British policy toward the United States.

Of course, this blitheful attitude displayed by the Americans merely signified the relative importance each nation possessed for the other. The British, dependent upon American goodwill in so many ways, had little choice but to focus on the United States, while the United Kingdom was not nearly so vital to the Americans. Furthermore, London officials frequently assumed an identity of interests between their country and the United States which most Americans were not always willing to concede. As a consequence, British policy makers sought to create, maintain, and expand a special relationship with the United States, even if it were nothing as overt as that suggested by Winston Churchill in his "iron curtain" speech early in 1946. The Americans, on the other hand, sought equally hard to avoid such a relationship. In this antithesis may be found much of the explanation behind the foreign policies of these two nations as they prepared, in 1944 and afterwards, to face a new and in certain respects frightening world.

1

The Equivocal
Backdrop

The autumn of 1939 found the world once more plunged into the maelstrom of war. German panzers tore through Poland, the first act in a conflict that would come to dwarf even the Great War of 1914–1918. Across the Atlantic, Americans gazed wonderingly at the spectacle, fearful lest they be drawn into the hostilities, yet appalled by the prospect that the western allies, without aid from the United States, might be swept aside by the awesome German military machine. Franklin Roosevelt, like his predecessor in the White House a quarter-century earlier, proclaimed his nation's formal neutrality. Unlike Wilson, however, he pointedly refrained from urging his countrymen to remain impartial in spirit, to avoid moral judgments concerning the belligerents. Even a neutral, he observed, could not close his mind nor disregard his conscience. Two months later Roosevelt signed the Fourth Neutrality Act, clearing the way for Britain and France to purchase arms and munitions in the United States for use in the impending clash with Nazi Germany.

During the following two years the American nation inched its way into an active partnership with the foes of Hitlerism. In early 1941, British and United States military officers met for full-scale staff talks in Washington, where they adopted a Europe-first strategy, in the event of American entry into the war. This ABC-1 plan, as it was called, represented an unprecedented peacetime commitment on the part of the United States. The Argentia conference in August reaffirmed the informal alliance between the two nations. Remembered primarily for the Atlantic Charter, this first wartime meeting between the British Prime Minister and the American President fulfilled a more immediate and pressing need in introducing officials of the two democracies to each other and in establishing the beginnings of what was to blossom into a unique camaraderie between Roosevelt and Churchill. Following the surprise attack on Pearl Harbor, Parliament acted even before the American Congress to declare war upon the Japanese Empire.[1]

Churchill is supposed to have once remarked that the only thing worse than fighting a war with allies was to fight one without them. The Anglo-American alliance, particularly as the war progressed, provided ample proof of the wisdom of this witticism. Time and again relations between the two nations were strained by major disagreements over military strategy, the future of the liberated peoples, colonialism, and a host of other issues. Personal animosities among some of the senior military leaders on each side further marred the wartime cooperation. From Washington's point of view, British policy all too frequently displayed shortsightedness, arrogance, even duplicity. Nor was the United States always as tactful as it might have been in employing its vastly superior resources as a lever to force its ally to give way in dispute after dispute. Years later a former British intelligence officer would recall: "I spent forty per cent of my time fighting the enemy and sixty per cent . . . fighting our friends."[2] The mere presence of thousands of American troops in the United Kingdom could not help but produce occasional resentment and ill-feeling on the part of their British hosts, irritation caused by the fact that the Yanks, so the saying went, were "overpaid, oversexed, overfed, and over here."

Still, to emphasize the frictions endemic both to coalition warfare and to continual and intimate contact between two peoples distorts the fundamental significance of the wartime association.[3] Never in the history of international relations had the affairs of two sovereign nations become so thoroughly entangled. The concept of a worldwide system of unified theater commands, whereby a single officer was placed in charge of the military forces of both countries within that theater, was a startlingly successful innovation.[4] The decision to retain the Germany-first strategy even after the humiliation of Pearl Harbor illustrated the similarity of the two nations' war aims. American repudiation of this strategy would have created a crisis of the first magnitude in British-American relations, but in fact neither the military nor the White House seriously considered such a course.[5]

As important as this military cooperation was, however, of even more significance for the future was the partnership which developed between the two allies in the political and economic spheres. Joint committees and combined boards regulated hundreds of everyday activities, both the mundane and the exceptional. Bilateral agencies oversaw the packaging, shipping, distribution, and conservation of food, fuel, and raw materials. Washington and London were each deluged not only with military officers from the other country, but also with civilian experts on everything from petroleum to propaganda. The innovations of lend-lease and mutual aid removed the dollar sign from the conduct of the war, as Roosevelt had desired, and served to integrate still further the affairs of Great Britain and the United States. For many purposes it was not incorrect to speak of the two as if they constituted a single power bloc. Englishmen even took to celebrating the Fourth of July with their American confreres as a demonstration of their good will and affection for the United States.

This merger of the war efforts of the two allies appears all the more remarkable in light of the events of the previous twenty years, a time when indifference, suspicion, and bitterness characterized relations between the two nations. Indeed, a case can be made that one of the fundamental reasons why Hitler was able to lead the world into war in 1939 lay in the extent to which Anglo-American relations had been allowed to deteriorate in the interwar years. The rejection of the League Covenant by a collection of parochial, splenetic United States senators set the tone for the period. Commercial competition, naval rivalry, tariff walls, and war debts combined to produce an atmosphere which virtually precluded the possibility of any meaningful political cooperation against the nations bent on upsetting the new order established at Versailles. The obvious expediency practiced by Britain's leadership in responding to the crescendoing crises of the 1930s troubled many in the United States who might otherwise have been disposed to support Great Britain in shoring up the concept of collective security. Neville Chamberlain's observation that "It is always best and safest to count on nothing from the Americans but words" brilliantly captured the essence of British-American relations in these years.[6] For all who believed, then, that the wartime Anglo-American partnership lay securely in the logic of history, a review of relations between the two in the period after the First World War proved disquieting.

Other factors in addition to abysmal diplomatic relations in the past hampered the creation of a sturdy wartime coalition. On both sides of the Atlantic, but particularly in the United States, large segments of the citizenry were imbued with values and attitudes which predisposed them to unfriendliness and at times outright antagonism toward their ally. Each country not only maintained but seemed to cherish unflattering stereotypes of the other. Of course, the Anglophobes and Americanophobes by dint of sheer obstreperousness received a disproportionate amount of publicity, but feelings of dislike and mistrust permeated a much broader and politically more significant spectrum of both British and American society.

The popular image of the British diplomat neatly illustrates many of the unsavory qualities which millions of Americans were convinced His Majesty's subjects possessed in overabundant quantities. The archetypal English envoy, caricatured in a thousand cartoons, was wily, polished, and thoroughly unscrupulous, repeatedly taking advantage of his innocent, unsuspecting counterpart from the United States. Had realities matched American fears, Great Britain would never have found itself in such desperate straits in 1940. Closely related to this picture was American disdain for and fear of the Old World diplomatic practices which they saw the British as exemplifying: spheres of influence, the balance of power, and Machiavellian power politics. A good many Americans attributed the outbreak of the present conflict to Europe's stubborn retention of these outmoded methods and attitudes.

In nearly all areas Americans compared the United Kingdom with their own country and found the British wanting. Although the king had virtually no political power, this was not nearly as important to people in the United States as was the fact that Britain still had a royal family—and moreover, refused to acknowledge the backwardness inherent in this. Great Britain's politics, it was commonly believed, were more aristocratic than democratic, its society acutely class conscious, its people aloof, arrogant, humorless, entrapped in hidebound tradition. The Commonwealth and Empire, though few in America fully understood what these terms actually meant in the twentieth-century world, provoked widespread feelings of anticolonialism and vocal outpourings of sympathy for the peoples oppressed by invidious British rule. Many Americans of Irish extraction still nursed anger and resentment toward the British with particular intensity. In another vein, London's repudiation of the debts assumed during the previous war had been neither forgotten nor forgiven and cast serious doubt for numerous Americans on the fundamental trustworthiness of the British nation. These suspicions received constant reinforcement throughout the war years from erroneous but widely believed stories alleging British misuse of lend-lease aid for strictly national purposes.[7]

Americans, though more vocal and blatant about it, were not alone in possessing an unfavorable picture of their closest ally. Few important groups in Great Britain looked upon the United States with particular enthusiasm, either. The commercial classes saw America as a dangerous and powerful business rival. Among the working classes and the British Left the United States was the embodiment of laissez-faire capitalism, the land where trade unions had been crushed by selfish monied interests. To many professionals and intellectuals, it represented a place where wealth was the only criterion of success, a country of vulgar materialism and tawdry Hollywood tinsel. Memories of the American withdrawal from Europe after the previous war embittered many; supporters of the League attributed its failure to the United States. The lowly status of the black man in America appalled countless Englishmen, who questioned the sincerity of Washington's oft-repeated democratic exhortations. Other Britishers were offended by what they saw as the conceit and cocksureness exhibited by many Americans, or by the air of moral superiority which the United States found so easy to don.

None of these popular attitudes guided the foreign policies of either Britain or the United States. Yet, because each was a democracy, broad courses of action had ultimately to receive the sanction of the people. As a consequence, these sentiments, though often founded on nothing more than prejudice, did serve to limit the freedom of maneuver enjoyed by the top officials in each country. Particularly in America, just under the conscious level of decision making lay an irrational folk memory prepared to suspect and believe the worst concerning the intentions of perfidious Albion.

Nearly a century earlier, on the eve of the Civil War, the British Minister in Washington had sent London an appraisal of the prevailing attitude toward Great Britain. This assessment appeared equally sound in the middle of the twentieth century. The bulk of the American people, he had written, while not overly hostile to England, "rather enjoy seeing us in difficulties. Those even who are most friendly like to gratify their pride by the idea of our being reduced to straits and of their coming to our rescue."[8] Far less perceptive observers than Lord Lyons have remarked on this peculiar American delight in finding the British in uncomfortable circumstances. Still, it is the last, and not the first half-dozen words of this evaluation which convey the essence of the relationship. For despite the name-calling and the unflattering stereotypes, there existed equally potent forces which worked to moderate the ill feelings which so colored Anglo-American ties. In truth, much of the criticism which traversed the ocean merely reflected the similarities between the two peoples.

The foundation of this similarity, of course, was demographic. Precise numbers are impossible to obtain in estimating the proportion of the American population with British origins, but a figure above 50 percent appears reasonable.[9] This common racial origin was important not only in itself but also because it had given the two peoples their greatest bond, the same language. No linguistic barriers impeded the exchange of ideas or the formation of friendships. The existence of a common tongue was particularly fortuitous with a man such as Winston Churchill at the head of the British government, for the Prime Minister possessed a command of the English language and of the powers of oratory matched by precious few in his or any other age. Americans thrilled equally with their British allies to his moving wartime speeches. His addresses to Congress probably created more good will for Great Britain in the United States than did six years of intense British publicity and propaganda efforts.

These common racial origins had resulted in another important similarity between the two nations, that of a shared culture, a community of ideals and beliefs and values. British and American diplomats spoke the same language figuratively as well as literally. The similar political and legal institutions arising from this common heritage provided another bond between the two. The inhabitants of Great Britain enjoyed many of the same books, plays, songs, and films as their transatlantic partners. Not only ideas but people crossed the ocean, some to visit, others to stay. By one estimate nearly 20,000 American soldiers brought home British wives at the conclusion of the war.[10] Winston Churchill's mother was an American, a fitting example of the social mingling and intermarriage which produced a further link binding the two. Even the traditional Anglophobia of the Irish-Americans no longer carried the force it once did, as the Americanization of the Irish immigrants and the virtual independence of Ireland itself dampened the hatred with which this group had once regarded Great Britain.

The presence of all these factors pointed up an inescapable truth: the two peoples were united by history in no ordinary relationship. Criticism of each other was frequent and vociferous; yet a common bond of tradition linked them in a relationship unlike that between any other two nations in the world. Henry

James' whimsical confession: "Considering that I lose all patience with the English about fifteen times a day, and vow that I renounce them forever, I get on with them beautifully and love them very well" succinctly captures the ambivalence of the ties binding the two peoples. In a sense the free criticism with which each peppered the other was in itself recognition of a kind of bond. American scolding, one Foreign Office official observed, stemmed "only from the fact that in view of our stable position and close relationship, a higher standard is expected of us."[11]

Like the two peoples, the leaders of Great Britain and the United States were also joined in an unusual, even a unique relationship. Between Franklin Roosevelt and Winston Churchill there developed a camaraderie which greatly facilitated relations between Britain and America. Neither the President nor the Prime Minister fully trusted his foreign office, and both by nature relished the stimulation and sense of control which direct contact offered. The correspondence between the two was exceptionally intimate. One Roosevelt letter sounds more like a woman's tender note to an absent friend: "I want you to know that I think of you often and I know you will not hesitate to ask me if there is anything you think I can do. . . . Do let me hear from you." Churchill once told a trusted confidant: "I love that man."[12]

This personal tie was not without its unpleasantries, and it became more and more one-sided as time passed. Once the United States fully mobilized its vast resources, Churchill was increasingly pushed into the position of a junior partner. At one point there were sixty-one American divisions in Europe, compared to but eighteen for Britain and Canada together. When this was combined with the predominance of the United States in providing the essential munitions and supplies, Churchill had little option but to acquiesce when Roosevelt insisted on some course of action. "Up to July, 1944," the Prime Minister later recalled, "England had a considerable say in things; after that I was conscious that it was America who made the big decisions."[13] Even their official positions conspired to emphasize Britain's secondary rank. Roosevelt was head of state, Churchill head only of government. The Prime Minister usually addressed Roosevelt as "Mr. President," whereas FDR called him "Winston." This disparity underlined the essential fact of the Anglo-American relationship by 1944. The United States had become dependent on Great Britain for its safety; but the British were dependent on America for their very survival.[14] Still, even if asymmetrical, the partnership between the two war leaders continued to flourish, uniting them and their nations in a manner quite unlike the relationship either had with Stalin or Soviet Russia, the third great member of the Grand Alliance.

By the latter half of 1944, then, key decisions concerning the nature of future relations between Washington and London remained to be made. The experience of the immediate past, the years of the close wartime association, encouraged those who desired a prolongation of Anglo-American collaboration into the postwar period, a collaboration made all the easier by the racial, cultural, and intellectual ties between the two. Moreover, given the increasing irrelevance to contemporary reality of the traditional antagonisms which had separated the two peoples in the past, there appeared reason to believe that if the national interests of each ran along parallel and not intersecting tracks, these old suspicions would not necessarily impede continued cooperation. However, the examples of earlier wartime coalitions, which had invariably split apart once the common enemy had been destroyed, tempered this hope. Anglo-American partnership was not a natural and inevitable part of the structure of world politics. It was fragile, in constant need of nurture. If relations between the two were allowed to slip back into a state of rivalry, or even indifference, this would inevitably free the subterranean feelings of antipathy. As the war entered its final phase in the autumn of 1944, it was still unclear in which direction future Anglo-American relations would move.

2

The Economics of
Partnership

For senior officials in the American Department of State, the
Second World War represented at once a humiliation and an opportunity. In matters of a political or strategic nature, Roosevelt
repeatedly circumvented his foreign policy advisers, employing
instead a variety of personal envoys and relying upon the military
for much of his counsel. In addition, the war spawned a prolif-
eration of independent agencies which intruded into areas heretofore considered the exclusive preserves of the State Department. On the other hand, the hostilities provided a singular
occasion to further some of the objectives which the American
Secretary of State, white-maned Cordell Hull, had long cherished.
With a proper utilization of the great economic strength of the
United States, Hull and his associates reasoned, they might be
able to use the tragedy of global conflict to create a new international structure that would substantially reduce the likelihood
of a third world war. In so doing, moreover, they would be insuring
America's own well-being and spreading the blessings of a free
and prosperous world order to other peoples.

Unfortunately, the implementation of this new global structure
did not depend upon American efforts alone. Because Hull's pro-
ject involved major alterations in the conduct of international

economic affairs, other nations, with highly different systems and needs, would have to be persuaded to accept his ideas. Great Britain in particular appeared to be the key, for prior to the war the United Kingdom and its Commonwealth and Empire associates accounted, along with the United States, for nearly one-half of the world's total trade. If Britain and America could agree between themselves on a design for the conduct and regulation of international financial transactions, the remainder of the world would have little choice, short of embracing virtual autarky, but to accept this system.[1] But suppose the British chose not to participate with Hull in his grand undertaking? Here, then, was the challenge for American diplomacy: to convince the United Kingdom that its interests would best be served by embracing the American vision of the postwar order.

Hull eagerly accepted this challenge—indeed, found solace for his exclusion from any policy-making role during the war years by immersing himself in planning for the economic arrangements which were to accompany the peace. A true Wilsonian in virtually every sense of the term, the Secretary was a devoted advocate of his political mentor's belief in a liberal capitalist world order of commercial expansion and free trade. Over the course of four decades in public life, he had developed a distinctive set of ideas concerning the proper nature of international economic relationships, a philosophy that came dangerously close to becoming an obsession. By the early 1940s this body of concepts had gained almost universal acceptance in the State Department bureaucracy, providing a backdrop upon which extensive blueprints for the postwar world were drawn.

Two distinct but interrelated strands of thought ran throughout all the planning which Hull superintended. One concerned itself with the establishment and maintenance of worldwide peace, the other with the narrower question of American prosperity. Hull and his colleagues viewed these two issues as essentially opposite sides of the same coin. To work for one while ignoring the other was self-defeating. There was no conscious hypocrisy in this linking of national interest and lofty idealism. As easy as it is in a more cynical age to ridicule such logic, the evidence appears conclusive that virtually all senior officials in Washington sincerely believed that neither could be attained unless supported by the other.

Put most baldly, the men and women who drafted these detailed plans reasoned that if soldiers were not to cross international borders, then goods must do so. The "chief underlying cause" of the First World War, Secretary Hull had written one of his predecessors, lay "in the strenuous trade conquests and bitter trade rivalry" which had characterized the years before 1914.[2] Similar contention, fueled in part by excessive Republican-sponsored tariff walls in the United States, had resulted in the formation of two antagonistic blocs in Europe in the years preceding the Second World War. Only by preventing the recurrence of economic warfare, the Secretary argued, could one avoid the attendant political frictions which led to war. Assistant Secretary of State for Economic Affairs William L. Clayton put it pithily: "Nations which act as enemies in the marketplace cannot long be friends at the council table." This being the case, the economic aspects of the peace were at least as important as the political aspects. Economics, Hull observed, "should be the spear point of the approach to peace." More specifically, in what was the central tenet of Hull's whole *Weltanschauung*, "unhampered trade dovetailed with peace; high tariffs, trade barriers, and unfair economic competition, with war."[3] This conviction that unrestricted trade was a necessary ingredient for peace had by 1944 become an unquestioned assumption governing American thinking in international affairs.

At the same time, unimpeded trade promised material benefits for America's own producers. While the American economy depended upon foreign markets to a much lesser extent than those of Great Britain and many other countries, exports had become, for large segments of American agriculture and industry, the difference between prosperity and depression. In the two years before the war, the United States had sold abroad 31 percent of its raw cotton, 30 percent of its leaf tobacco, 54 percent of its refined copper. By 1945, moreover, with the economic expansion stimulated by the war itself, the United States possessed an industrial plant with a capacity nearly twice as great as before the hostilities.[4]

Postwar exports, the Director of War Mobilization and Reconversion told the House Ways and Means Committee, would have to be double the prewar level if prosperity and full employment were to be attained.[5]

Hull's long years of isolation from the center of foreign policy decision making had afforded him ample time to reflect upon the best methods for encouraging this expansion of international trade. The United States, the Secretary repeatedly insisted, should do everything in its power to encourage the creation of multilateral, nondiscriminatory trade relations. Gradually this goal of multilateralism, indeed the word itself, came to be seen as the very essence of Hull's—and America's—program. And as befitted a policy of global cooperation, the idea of eliminating all forms of discriminatory treatment in international commerce and of reducing tariffs and other trade barriers established itself as the one unalterable principle of United States policy. In a subtle and perhaps unconscious manner many American leaders came to equate economic freedom in the Gladstonian sense with political freedom.[6]

The international financial institutions erected at the Bretton Woods conference in July 1944 nicely illustrate the prevalent thinking within Hull's State Department—and indeed, throughout the American government. Tucked away in New Hampshire's White Mountains, representatives of forty-four nations gathered to establish an International Bank for Reconstruction and Development (more popularly known as the World Bank) and an International Monetary Fund. The World Bank was designed to make funds available for reconstruction projects requiring large sums of capital, a function which by stimulating sound international investment would automatically promote world trade. The Monetary Fund was to provide nations with liquid reserves to assist in maintaining stable currencies without resorting to restrictive exchange practices. In both instances the predominant assumption was that only economic stability and continual development, fostered to a large extent by an ever-increasing world trade, could stave off a third and perhaps fatal global war. At the same time these arrangements could be defended as completely in the national interest. The arguments used to sell the program to Congress and the public emphasized the aid which it would render in increasing American exports. The nation's second largest labor union predicted that Bretton Woods would create five million American jobs because of its stimulus to overseas trade. There was "not one single element of Santa Claus philosophy" in the Bretton Woods agreements, Clayton assured congressional doubters.[7]

Quite clearly then, American postwar objectives for the world economy consisted of a careful amalgamation of visionary concern for the maintenance of world peace and a determination that the nation avoid any repetition of the disastrous economic experiences of the 1930s. Both aims, Washington officials believed, could be best achieved in a multilateral world of freely flowing, constantly expanding trade. The enthusiastic diplomat who likened multilateral, regional, and bilateral trade to using the elevator, the stairway, and the fire escape was merely reflecting this conviction.[8]

American planners devoted long hours to considering how Great Britain fit into this picture. Of one thing they were certain: London's partnership would be every bit as necessary in winning the peace as it had been in winning the war. Anglo-American economic cooperation, observed one of the senior officials overseeing the American wartime economy, could "influence the entire world's pattern of trade" and make it possible to "remove most of the economic frictions that generate wars."[9] The means of obtaining that cooperation, however, and the concessions which the United States might be willing to make in return, were not nearly so apparent. On the one hand, administration policy makers were determined not to be outsmarted by the wily British, as it was widely believed they had been after the previous war. On the other hand, these same officials possessed an uneasy awareness that in the interests of partnership the British would need substantial aid in reconstructing their economy from the ravages of six years of total warfare. To perplexed American authorities the former seemed to preclude the latter, and Washington bureaucrats anguished for many months trying to develop an approach which would enable Great Britain to become a strong partner in a multilateral world while at the same time mollifying fears at home that American tax dollars were being used to bail out profligate Englishmen.

Hull and his colleagues recognized, of course, that the British might simply choose not to go along with all this careful planning. Great Britain had abandoned free trade in 1931, only shortly before the United States under Hull's tutelage began to move in the direction of fewer trade restrictions. At the Ottawa conference in 1932, the nations of the British Commonwealth had established a system of imperial preferences which served to stimulate trade among the member nations, but which placed severe obstacles in the path of American trade not only with Britain itself, but with Australia, India, South Africa, and a number of lesser nations. The embittered Hull termed the creation of this system of imperial preferences "the greatest injury, in a commercial way, that has been inflicted on this country since I have been in public life" and spent much of the 1930s attempting to persuade the British to relax these restrictions. Congressional approval of the Lend-Lease Act in 1941 provided the Secretary a diplomatic lever with which to press the British, and Article 7 of the Master Lend-Lease Agreement signed the following year committed the two nations to do everything possible to promote the expansion of trade and "the elimination of all forms of discriminatory treatment in international commerce," and to reduce tariffs and other trade barriers.[10] Here, so Washington believed, was a concrete promise by the Churchill government to abandon imperial preference and open the Empire to American commerce.

The British for their part wondered if the Americans were not being a bit hasty in demanding an end to London's system of supports and restrictions. Neither Hull nor anyone else in Washington had been able to convince key officials across the ocean that Great Britain could recover its economic balance simply by accepting the American program of multilateralism. It had taken nearly a year of negotiations after enactment of the lend-lease law before the two sides could complete the agreement extending this aid to the beleaguered British. These difficulties indicated the gap which separated the two countries in their ideas on the future of the imperial preference system. Furthermore, Whitehall harbored well-founded doubts as to the willingness of the United States to accept a large volume of imports, an absolute essential if the British were to have any chance of rebuilding their shattered economy. American manufacturers themselves were worried as to how they were going to dispose of the huge quantities of goods which their plants were able to produce, and neither business nor labor was likely to be enthusiastic about sharing the domestic market with foreign competitors. What was much more probable was that fierce rivalry for overseas markets would place an additional burden on Anglo-American relations. Long before the end of the war American missions around the world were warning of increasing British propaganda efforts and preparations directed toward expanding postwar commerce.[11] The prospects of a potentially bitter competition for foreign markets lent credence to the arguments of those within the Churchill government who warned against any precipitant acceptance of the American scheme for achieving a workable, mutually advantageous economic arrangement between the two Atlantic democracies. This caution surfaced, for example, during a 1944 meeting between Henry Morgenthau, the American Secretary of the Treasury, and Sir John Anderson, Britain's Chancellor of the Exchequer. If the difficult financial problems facing the two nations were to be tackled effectively, the ebullient Morgenthau declared, "we should practically have to sleep together." Perhaps so, Sir John primly replied, but he for one would keep his eyes open.[12]

This brief exchange points out a fundamental distinction in the moods prevalent in each of the two national capitals. One of the most remarkable aspects of the American vision of the postwar economic order was its buoyant optimism, its easy acceptance of the idea that with proper planning and skillful management, both largely American of course, the people of the world could enter an era of peace and prosperity where want and insecurity would be abolished. The roots of much of this confidence undoubtedly lay in the nation's past, stretching back to the country's earliest days when it did appear that the land was sufficiently abundant to provide for all who were willing to work hard and live frugally. The more immediate experience of the war years reinforced this optimism, for in contrast to Great Britain, the United States emerged from the hostilities relatively unscathed and infinitely more powerful than it had been in 1939. Defense spending had finally lifted the country out of its decade-long depression and had acted as a stimulant not only for the war industries but for the economy as a whole. Between 1939 and 1944 the nation's gross national product rose from $91 billion to $210 billion. Manufacturing volume nearly tripled; raw material output increased by 60 percent. Moreover, despite the immense war production, the United States was still able to provide the civilian sector of the population with a greater amount of commodities and services than it had enjoyed in 1939; there was no need to substitute "guns for butter." "The American people," War Mobilizer Fred M. Vinson reported shortly after the Nazi surrender, "are in the pleasant predicament of having to learn to live 50 percent better than they have ever lived before."[13]

Such words rang hollow to the inhabitants of Great Britain. The war for them had been a searing experience. Even as late as the end of March 1945, the fiendish V-weapons, the buzz bomb and the still more indiscriminate rocket bomb, devastated their cities and checked the elation which the daily bulletins from the various fronts might otherwise have occasioned. Four million houses were destroyed or damaged by the enemy. After an inspection of London shortly following the Japanese surrender, the new American Secretary of State, James F. Byrnes, concluded that no fewer than fifteen years would be needed to rebuild the smitten city. A White Paper on the British war effort presented to Parliament in November 1944, reported that the country's meat consumption was down nearly one-fourth from prewar levels; butter consumption was off two-thirds; fruit, tea, eggs, and sugar all significantly lower. Perhaps the illustration offered by an Englishman best explains the differing experiences of Britain and the United States: "When you in America hear a plane overhead," he remarked, "you look up into the sky. You are thrilled. An airplane flying is a symbol of progress to you. When we in England hear a plane overhead, we don't look up. We look for the nearest air raid shelter."[14]

Nor did peace promise better conditions. Within days of the German surrender, Britons were warned to expect not an easing of wartime rationing, but further cuts in the quantities of food which each family would be allowed to purchase. By the end of May the amounts of fats, soap, milk, bacon, and meat which an individual could legally buy had all been reduced. It was the prospect of these conditions that had led Churchill long before V-E Day to tell Henry Morgenthau that after the war he, Churchill, would be the most unpopular man in England because it would then become evident that Britain's strained economic condition would prevent the government from providing the amelioration in living standards which the people would inevitably demand.[15]

The Churchill government, in fact, confronted a whole register of difficulties arising from its participation in the war. Raising the austere levels of civilian consumption and rebuilding the miles of drab, scarred, uninhabited streets into usable homes and factories constituted only part of the problem. The allied victory would also bring new obligations: occupation duties in Europe and the Far East, and some degree of responsibility for insuring that the peoples of Europe, which was even more devastated than Britain, did not starve before the economies of the various nations could be reestablished. Equally important, the government faced insurmountable pressures for new domestic programs: an extension of social insurance, a public health service, advances in education, and a guarantee of full employment. If he defied these demands, the Prime Minister knew, he risked political suicide.

Most knowledgeable Britons realized that they could not blame the war alone for the sorry economic plight in which they found themselves by the end of 1944; thirty years of relative economic stagnation prior to 1939 had also played their part. The interwar period had seen a continual downward trend in the volume of the export trade and an increasing dependence on the earnings of overseas investments and shipping, banking, and insurance services. In the three years before the war, the value of British exports was only 55 percent that of British imports. Income from investments abroad paid for another 24 percent of these imports, while most of the remainder were purchased with monies derived from shipping, insurance, and banking.[16] Such a delicate juggling act could not indefinately sustain a nation as dependent upon imports as was Britain.

The long years of fighting, moreover, had caused a dangerous decline in revenues from these increasingly important "invisible" assets. Net income from foreign investments was less than 40 percent of its prewar value, as many overseas assets had been liquidated in order to pay for essential imports and military supplies from abroad, particularly during the eighteen months before the United States made lend-lease available. The British merchant marine had been decimated by German submarines and was in no condition to compete with the larger, more modern American fleet. Similarly, the war had completed the shift of the financial center of the world from London to New York, and the British Exchequer could anticipate only greatly reduced income from banking and insurance services. In addition, Britain had incurred overseas debts of vast dimensions, approaching nearly 10 percent of the country's total prewar national wealth, and had consumed most of its gold and dollar reserves. Thus, having begun the war with a net creditor position of approximately £3,500 million, Britain would end it as a debtor with liabilities of roughly £2,000 million.[17] Though little appreciated by the average Britisher, these stark figures foreshadowed the frustration of many of his hopes, both for himself and for his nation.

Simple logic seemed to dictate that, given this new debtor status and the loss of much of its income from invisible assets, Britain would in the future have to export more and import less in order to earn the revenue needed to pay off its liabilities. Yet, reducing imports would be difficult at best, for prior to the war nearly two-thirds of the food consumed by the British people and virtually all the basic raw materials except coal used in British industry had been obtained from foreign sources. To cut back on these levels, the United Kingdom would either have to reduce its population, or depress its standard of living still further. Not only would the

British have to find a way to pay for their normal imports; they would also need a considerable amount of goods and equipment from abroad to rebuild their damaged cities and factories and to modernize outmoded, inefficient plants, notably in the textile, mining, and electrical equipment industries. Raw materials for industry were required in substantially greater numbers to sustain full employment. American officials estimated that in the 1945–48 period, the British would need to import from the United States alone 319 percent of the agricultural products and related manufactures which they had bought in the equivalent prewar period; 364 percent of the metals and manufactures; 393 percent of the machinery and vehicles.[18] Despite Britain's indebtedness, the British Treasury announced in the spring of 1945, the country would have to incur over the succeeding three years a further trade deficit of £1,500 million, or $6 billion. In part, this increase in imports of industrial and construction materials would be offset by reductions in purchases of luxury and other nonessential goods. Still, by the end of 1944, it was axiomatic in both London and Washington that the British would need to expand their export trade by 50–75 percent after the war merely to maintain their prewar standard of living. This figure did not begin to take into account any new domestic social programs which the British government might feel constrained to undertake.

Many, however, ridiculed this proposed increase as virtually unattainable. Indeed, formidable obstacles lay in the way of any expansion at all. For one thing, some questioned whether British industry could effectively compete in the world market. Even before the war most British manufacturers had failed to modernize their equipment and improve their methods of production sufficiently to keep pace with advances in the United States and other progressive industrial countries. As a consequence output per worker in the United Kingdom lagged far behind that of its chief competitors. In 1938, output per man-shift in coal mining was only about one-fourth as great in Britain as in the United States; in the iron and steel industry, less than one-half; in radio and automobile manufacturing, less than a quarter.[19]

Most doubts, however, as to Britain's ability to raise its export levels so dramatically centered not on the productivity of the British worker, but on the availability of markets where British goods might be sold. Many of the countries which would most need British wares, those in central and eastern Europe for instance, would have no money to pay for them. Other potential markets, such as the Dominions and Latin America, already had sterling balances acquired during the war, so that exports to these nations would only be paying off old debts. Even more alarmingly, the British export trade during the war had, like so much else in British life, been severely curtailed. Exports from the United Kingdom at the end of the war comprised barely one-third of their prewar volume. The United States, in comparison, had during the war years actually maintained the value of its cash exports at their prewar level, in addition to its enormous lend-lease shipments. British textile exports, to give one example, had dwindled to about one-fifth of their prewar level, whereas American textile sales abroad (aside from lend-lease) almost doubled. This disparity reflected the wholesale displacement of British firms by American exporters in a number of markets which had traditionally been theirs in Latin America, the Middle East, and even Australia.[20] Unless the United Kingdom could win back these markets, prospects for any significant increase in exports looked bleak.

Great Britain, in signing the lend-lease agreement with the United States, had promised not to export anything constructed with lend-lease materials or even things substantially similar to materials supplied by lend-lease. Rather than a ploy to limit British exports and thereby move into British markets, this provision was merely a condition the Roosevelt administration deemed necessary to insure domestic support for its program of aid to the United Kingdom. British businessmen, however, complained bitterly that these restrictions were destroying the British export trade and pointed out that the United States, even though it received raw materials under reverse lend-lease, did not have any such limitations on the type of goods it could export. Some industries, particularly those manufacturing steel products, began pressing for cessation of lend-lease imports of their raw materials long before the war's end. In fact, British exports were being curtailed for reasons that had nothing to do with restrictions imposed by the Americans, but which stemmed directly from the great demands placed on the country by the hostilities. Nonetheless, serious doubts existed about the ability of British manufacturers to find postwar markets for their goods.

The Churchill government attempted to counter all these factors with extensive preparations in planning for industrial reconversion, reorganizing the Department of Overseas Trade, and developing informational and other administrative aids for exporters. A White Paper issued early in 1945 urged parliamentary approval of an equivalent of the American Webb-Pomerene Act to enable industry-wide export organizations to canvass the United States in an effort to discover new markets for British goods. Within days seventeen leading companies had banded together to create the British Export Trade Research Organization, a unique research and promotional agency designed to expand postwar export markets. That this new body had the blessings of the government was commonly understood. Yet, despite this recognition of the necessity of increasing sales abroad, British exports continued to run at only a fraction of the 1938 volume.[21]

At the most elementary level, the British leadership faced two alternatives in attempting to resolve the export crisis. On the one hand, it could accept the principles of the American program of multilateralism, thereby hoping to profit from an expanding world economy in which the British share might be relatively smaller than before the war even though larger in absolute terms. Or Britain could use its position as the world's largest market for food and raw materials to conclude bilateral agreements with as many nations as possible. By the end of 1944 most thinking at the expert level in London favored the first option, in principle at least, but the Cabinet had been unable to reach any consensus.

Proponents of the second, more restrictive approach advanced formidable arguments. Britain's technical backwardness and the demands of British labor for a higher standard of living and greater social security, they insisted, had ended Great Britain's reign as a low-cost manufacturer. Rather than attempt to compete solely on the basis of cost, the United Kingdom must depend upon "arranged trade"—that is, the creation of a sterling bloc which might include not only the Dominions but even Africa, the Middle East, and western Europe. Operating behind frozen sterling and most-favored-nation clauses, such a bloc could be virtually self-sufficient. Best of all, British firms, protected by preferential tariff agreements, quotas, licensing controls, and other government-sponsored restrictions, would not have to worry about being undersold by more efficient competitors. Those who endorsed this position maintained that the attraction of this bloc would be so great that a large part of Latin America might even be lured into it.[22]

The very mention of such a plan created tremors of apprehension among American officials. If Whitehall established such an economic grouping, countries that wished to sell to Great Britain would have to take payment in British exports. The nations to which the United Kingdom owed billions of dollars arising from wartime purchases would be compelled to take British goods as payment for these debts. Trade inside the bloc would be encouraged through preferences and licenses, and trade outside the bloc severely hampered by discriminations and controls. In the three years before the war nearly one-half of the total United States trade was with the countries of the sterling area. These nations purchased 88 percent of American leaf tobacco exports before the war; 59 percent of American meat, grain, and other food exports; 49 percent of American raw cotton exports. To lose these markets through the formation of an exclusive economic grouping would be, in the words of the American Secretary of the Treasury, a "body blow to our whole economy."[23]

Such an idea found favor in Britain with an unlikely coalition of socialists and conservative imperialists, including one of Churchill's closest friends and political allies, Lord Beaverbrook. Portions of the Left, mindful of the massive unemployment suffered by the British worker almost from the moment of peace in 1918, opposed any international scheme that might subject the British economy to external influence, particularly to economic fluctuations in the United States. More influential than these left-ists were the financial interests of the City of London, the old-line industrialists who desired protection from newer, more rationally organized competition. But the group which carried the most weight with the British Prime Minister personally consisted of those traditional defenders of the Empire who saw in America's economic designs another clumsy attempt at dismantling Great Britain's imperial domain. Almost unobtrusively, financial arguments became mixed with those of a different nature; advocates of imperial preference came to believe that the elimination of financial restrictions meant the death of the Empire and Britain's decline as a world power.[24]

More moderate opinion as well had reservations about the advisability of tying British fortunes too closely to American ideas for the postwar world. Both Britain's leading daily, the *Times*, and one of its most respected weeklies, the *Economist*, ran a series of articles describing how the benefits of multilateralism might be obtained among a group of countries by means of bulk-purchasing agreements, quantitative import controls, and a comprehensive system of discrimination against goods from the United States.[25] Quite clearly, resistance to the American vision of expanding trade and diminishing barriers to the free exchange of goods was not simply going to evaporate on its own accord.

British observers also complained that American practices often seemed to bear little resemblance to the fine words mouthed about free trade by Hull and his disciples. The Department of Agriculture, for instance, often pushed schemes involving price-fixing and wholesale bulk-purchasing, directly at variance with a policy of multilateralism. In the Middle East, American oil companies entered into cartel agreements with British firms, with Washington's obvious concurrence. Repeatedly, American officials insisted on the economic benefits which a multilateral world would bring to the United States. These statements, though intended only to insure adequate congressional and public support for administration policies, served to frighten the British as well. What, they pointedly asked, did "free trade" and "equal oppor-

tunity" mean in a world in which the United States had no economic peers?[26]

American tariff practices also made the British skeptical of
United States designs for free trade. Washington officialdom believed that in securing renewal of the Reciprocal Trade Agreements Act in the summer of 1945, it was striking a strong blow
for multilateralism and that its actions deserved some significant
British concession in return. The perspective from across the
ocean could not have been more different. The British viewed
this legislation as little more than a token reduction in the American tariff wall and only further reason to resist the elimination
of imperial preference and other protective devices. President
Truman, they undoubtedly knew, had promised members of the
Senate Finance Committee that he did not contemplate wholesale
reduction in tariff rates under the new act and that any agreements
negotiated under his administration would be neither as extensive
nor sweeping as those being proposed by some of the more enthusiastic supporters of free trade. Moreover, America's assertion
that Britain's preference system was inherently more offensive
than its own trade barriers rankled London. Washington viewed
preferences as repugnant because they were discriminatory. Tariffs should be lowered, but they were not in the same category
with preferences, even though they too hampered trade, because
they discriminated equally against all. Whitehall officials, not surprisingly, placed far less emphasis on this distinction between
tariffs and preferences. Why, they asked, should they be compelled to work for the *elimination* of British preferences but only
for the *reduction* of American tariffs?[27]

Public discussion in the two nations also demonstrated that each
had very different conceptions of the role of the Bretton Woods
institutions and the responsibilities which this program placed
upon the individual national governments, a condition which could
only lead to further misunderstandings and friction. Robert
Boothby, chairman of the Monetary Policy Committee in the
House of Commons, wrote the *New York Times* complaining that
Americans had "been led to believe that the Bretton Woods pro-

posals take us all back along the road to a gold standard, currency stability, non-discrimination and multilateral trade." The British, on the other hand, "have been assured, that they constitute the exact reverse of a gold standard, that exchange rates will be flexible and that reciprocal trade agreements involving discrimination will be permissible."[28] The institutions erected at Bretton Woods, charged the London Chamber of Commerce, failed to deal with the essential problem blocking achievement of a satisfactory international trade: the refusal of certain economically powerful nations to buy as much from other countries as they wished to sell to them. Though no names were mentioned, it did not require much acuity to see that the United States was felt to be the principal culprit.[29]

Given these differing perceptions as to the best means of obtaining national and international prosperity, and given the suspicions which were almost inevitably fostered in the minds of many Britishers by American economic might and the contradictions in American policy, it is hardly surprising that irritation and acrimony crept into the transatlantic dialogue. The chairman of one of England's largest banks chided the British government for "excessive tenderness" toward the United States in discussing commercial matters.[30] Reports that American businessmen had traveled to France and China in military uniform to get a head start in the contest for postwar trade circulated extensively and created widespread alarm.[31] The top official of a large British manufacturing company charged that unnamed foreign suppliers were offering electrical plant equipment and machinery abroad at prices below their production costs.[32] American businessmen filed similar complaints. Motion picture executives protested that the British government was deliberately squeezing them out of the United Kingdom. Representatives of Detroit's auto makers pointedly noted that British cars could enter the United States but that American automobiles were barred from British markets.[33] Such accusations merely served to underscore the basic distrust which influential elements in each nation harbored toward the intentions of the other.

Throughout Britain one heard whispered fears of trade war with the United States, or of large-scale dumping on world markets by American firms eager to prevent unemployment at home. One M.P. called for assurances by the United States that it would not engage in a "phoney" export trade financed by credits that could not be repaid in goods because of high American tariff barriers. Another, admitting that Britain was frightened by United States economic might, suggested that Americans deliberately curb their exports after the war to "leave some leeway" for other countries.[34] Foreign trade, the British Ambassador to Washington told a gathering of bankers, was "the most vexing question of all" separating the two nations. The crux of Anglo-American relations, he added, was how to adjust America's need for export markets with Britain's need to obtain the wherewithal to buy imports vital to its national existence.[35]

But while serious obstacles impeded the establishment of any long-term economic partnership between the two, equally potent forces in Great Britain worked in favor of cooperation. At the abstract level practically all important British leaders tended to support the idea of international collaboration. Britain's wartime dependence on the United States for the achievement of its military and political objectives as well as its economic solvency also tended to push Whitehall toward a policy of cooperation. Perhaps most fundamentally, Britain's overwhelming need for overseas supplies of foodstuffs and raw materials and for foreign markets for its manufactures encouraged acceptance of some sort of multilateral world vision. London's desire to retain its place as a leading financier, carrier, and insurer of the trade of other countries provided a further stake in a free and extensive international commerce. In a typically perceptive editorial, the *Economist* seemed to have caught much of official thinking when it observed that as a matter of plain economics, the American vision of the postwar financial order presented serious pitfalls to the British nation. It went on to add, however, that "as a matter of politics or (if the word is taken to imply something sinister) of amicable relations between Governments, there is almost everything to be said in its favour." In concluding it asked, but could not answer, "How much economic hazard is a reasonable price for continued American generosity and friendship—or at least for the avoidance of American disappointment and resentment?"[36]

One further idea permeated official British thinking on the subject: the absolute necessity of retaining the nation's financial independence and power of initiative. "In spite of their genuine good-will and magnanimous aid to us," John Maynard Keynes warned at the end of 1944,

> financial independence of the United States at the earliest possible opportunity should be a major aim of British policy. . . . There are very few objects of policy beyond the demands of victory over the enemy to which that should be subordinated. A might Empire in financial leading strings to others will not be mighty at all, and we shall have sacrificed real power to show and sham.[37]

As a consequence, while the British were not blind to American sensitivities and sought ways to avoid irritating their powerful ally, they also recognized the imperative need to regain their own economic equilibrium, even if this at times created difficulties in relations with the United States. They would have to stand firm on those issues affecting essential British interests and the future prosperity of the nation. At the same time, a Foreign Office paper cautioned, "We must do so in such a way that we do not provoke the United States to withdraw from international economic collaboration; otherwise all our tasks will be rendered infinitely more difficult." The manner in which British relations with the United States were handled, this paper then continued, "will be a key factor in allowing us the freedom we need to go our own way, without giving the impression that we are sacrificing world interests to our own selfish designs."[38]

Brave words, no doubt. Yet it appeared that the British position was more accurately summarized by the succinct if blunt observation of the group of English manufacturers who commented: "Everything depends upon the extent to which the Americans are prepared to cooperate."[39] In late 1944 this question remained unresolved. The economic aspects of the relationship provided indications that could be interpreted in either fashion. The objectives of world prosperity and an expanding international trade were common to both Great Britain and the United States, and there were influential voices in each nation calling for a continuation of the wartime collaboration into the postwar era. On the other hand, there existed powerful disruptive forces and clashing interests that contained the potential for creating much bitterness in relations between the two, frictions which would inevitably spill over into the political and military spheres. In some cases these disputes had already erupted into the public forum and themselves contributed to an exacerbation of ill feelings. Just how much Americans would be prepared to cooperate with their British cousins remained to be seen. The answer, moreover, rested as much on emotion and irrationality as on any cold-blooded calculation of the national interest.

3

"Bricks Without Straw"

The economic exhaustion of the United Kingdom so apparent by 1944 served warning that in the future Great Britain's power of initiative and range of options would be severely restricted. Already dangerously dependent upon the United States for many of life's essentials, the British people faced the prospect only of further sacrifices. Whichever way policy makers turned, they saw insurmountable difficulties blocking their hopes for a return to some semblance of economic and financial equilibrium. Moreover, economic difficulties, grave as they were, comprised only a portion of the problem confronting the British. Equally worrisome were questions of a strategic nature. In truth, victory had brought the United Kingdom not security but anxiety, not safety but unprecedented dangers. "Here in Britain we are passing through a strange phase in public life," Beaverbrook wrote an American friend in October 1944. "For the first time, the English are not sure of themselves. They are anxious about their future."[1] And well they might have been. So while one set of London officials grappled with the formidable economic dilemmas facing their country, a second group turned its attention as the war wound down to the equally perplexing matter of providing for the future security of the island nation.

The obstacles were myriad. In the first place, technological advances during the war years had combined with longer-range developments to redefine Britain's strategic position, both in Europe and throughout the world. The invention of the rocket, jet engines, guided missiles, and by the end of the war, the atomic bomb underscored the reduced defensive value of the English Channel. The power of the British navy, for centuries Britain's chief bulwark against foreign threats, had been profoundly modified by these technical innovations as well as by the development of increasingly sophisticated aircraft. Sea-power had traditionally served offensive as well as defensive purposes for the British. Now, however, against the only likely future foe, the largely landlocked Soviet Union, naval power would be a relatively ineffective instrument for carrying the fight to the enemy. As a consequence, the British Army would have to be maintained at a considerably higher level of strength than had been the practice before the war. This promised a further drain on scarce British resources, as did the occupation duties which followed the war.[2]

If reliance on a strong navy and strategically located bases had constituted a good portion of Britain's basic defense strategy over the centuries, much of the remainder had consisted of pursuing a balance of power in Europe in order to prevent any one state from dominating the continent. Now the reduced protection offered by the channel reinforced the desirability of this traditional policy of opposition to the unification of Europe under one flag. Here again, however, the war had produced new configurations of power unlike anything in Britain's past. Germany, Italy, and France had all been crushed and could not realistically be expected to regain Great Power status for many years. Instead, standing over the prostrate nations of Europe was the Soviet colossus, savagely mauled in the fighting, but all the more conscious of its preeminence because of this. The European balance of power had been shattered, to be replaced by a single, and in many ways enigmatic Russia. This emergence of the Soviet Union, editorialized the *Times* in a passage which undoubtedly reflected official thinking, was "likely to prove as decisive for the future as the establishment of the British command of the seas at Trafalgar or as the downfall of French predominance at Waterloo."[3]

This new strategic situation created obvious problems, the solutions to which rested in good measure on Moscow's intentions. The most amateur of armchair strategists could see that Britain's strength, even with the help of the Empire, would be insufficient to counter any aggressive Russian move in Europe. Unless the United States could be drawn into the reckoning, any combination of powers which the British might be able to assemble would still leave the Soviets preponderant on the continent.[4] Thus, the part which Russia would play in the postwar world was of great interest and no little anxiety to the policy makers in Whitehall. And as was so often the case in matters concerning the Soviet Union, attempts to forecast the future Russian role were based as much on hopeful fancies as on concrete realities.

Few doubted but that friendship with the Soviet Union constituted one of Britain's most pressing requirements. The Churchill government in August 1944 officially adopted the position that "the foundation of our post-war European policy must be the Anglo-Soviet Alliance, aimed at preventing any recurrence of German aggression." For at least five years after the end of the war, London planners predicted, and probably much longer, Russia would need to concentrate on internal rehabilitation and development. As a consequence, the Soviets were expected to follow a policy of collaboration with Great Britain and the United States, eschewing territorial aggression and attempts to enhance their own influence in foreign countries by methods that would antagonize Britain or America.[5] Not everyone, however, felt comfortable with this estimate. Simple prudence, the British Chiefs of Staff argued at one point, dictated that the military at least consider all possibilities, including postwar Russian antagonism. But the Foreign Office stoutly resisted any planning along these lines, fearing that loose talk of a hostile Russia might reach Soviet ears and actually cause Moscow to discount British expressions of cordiality. Great Britain must guard against Germany, not Russia, Foreign Secretary Anthony Eden insisted.[6]

Others echoed Eden in this hopefulness concerning future Anglo-Soviet relations. Though more cautious, the British Ambassador in Moscow, Sir Archibald Clark Kerr, also noted that Soviet propaganda seemed to be preparing the Russian people for continued collaboration with the West. Churchill, too, at times, though he later tried to gloss over this, expressed confidence in the likelihood of postwar cooperation with Britain's great eastern ally. From Moscow in the fall of 1944, he reported to Roosevelt on the "extraordinary atmosphere of goodwill" which he found. At the end of the year he wrote Eden of the respect which he held for "that great and good man," Joseph Stalin.[7] Close associates have pictured Churchill as hypnotized by the Soviet leader, falling under the sway of the premier's charm and convinced that Stalin meant well and that so long as he remained at the head of the Russian government, Anglo-Soviet friendship could be maintained.[8] Returning from Yalta, Churchill categorically stated: "I know of no Government which stands to its obligations, even in its own despite, more solidly than the Russian Soviet Government." Even the normally sensible *Times* assured its readers that essential British and Russian interests in Europe "not only do not clash, but are precisely the same."[9]

As long as relations between London and Moscow remained cooperative, or at least not antagonistic, the military security of Great Britain could not be seriously endangered. This Big Power unity was the key assumption behind all the hopes for the proposed United Nations Organization, the *sine qua non* underlying any system of collective security. If the British and the Russians, along with the Americans, could maintain a working relationship, any peace-keeping machinery would work, but if they could not, then no machinery could possibly be devised that would be of any use. This elementary but nonetheless sound logic guided all British security planning.

Americans as well envisioned a postwar world where Big Power harmony would enable the United Nations to maintain a just and stable global order. American aspirations for the international organization had led Secretary Hull to claim that there would no longer be any need for "spheres of influence, for alliances, for balance of power, or any other of the special arrangements through which, in the unhappy past, the nations strove to safeguard their security or to promote their interests."[10] In their more private moments, of course, Washington officials freely acknowledged that in spite of this high-flown rhetoric, the United States could not safely place all its reliance on an untested and as yet unborn dream. Not even Hull suggested that. Still, wide segments of the American public received the Secretary's words with enthusiasm and were likely to take offense at actions by any of the allies which threatened to undermine these fine hopes.

For senior officials in London, this attitude created special problems. As the weakest of the three major powers and the one occupying a peculiarly exposed position, Great Britain could less afford to rely exclusively on the embryonic peacekeeping structure for its security than its two wartime partners. Whitehall diplomats recognized the necessity of not deliberately sabotaging American hopes for the new international body, but at the same time few top officials expected it to serve as a substitute for traditional means of reconciling interests and disputes. While British policy supported the creation of an international security organization, London authorities showed little disposition to depend on it as their principal means of safety.

In fact, Churchill and Eden both seemed to think of the United Nations Organization primarily as a vehicle for insuring American participation in European affairs after the war. Roosevelt's repeated statements that he expected to withdraw United States troops from the continent as quickly as possible after Germany's collapse left the British with the unpleasant prospect of facing the mighty Red Army alone across the expanses of a wasted Europe. Some of Churchill's darkest moments occurred when he contemplated such a situation. The unhappy example of Wilson and the precipitant American retreat from world responsibilities after the previous war had not been forgotten. Again and again the bitter memories of 1919-20 were dredged up in newspapers and private conversation. There was a certain "agnosticism" among the British public, one of the senior members in the Coalition Government reported, a questioning as to whether the American political mind had matured sufficiently to permit United States officials to embrace worldwide involvements and commitments this time.[11] As a consequence, Whitehall was hardly disposed to rely too heavily on an active American presence in any international peacekeeping body. Neither Churchill nor Eden took much interest in the Dumbarton Oaks conference or the ensuing negotiations looking toward the creation of the world organization. British participation in the talks was left in the hands of their subordinates while the senior figures pursued other methods of insuring the future security of the United Kingdom.[12]

For Eden this entailed a policy of drawing the nations of western Europe into a closer association with the British Commonwealth and, as a corollary, of doing everything possible to help the French regain their military might and prestige as a Great Power. Such a policy could be accomplished politically, by alliances, or militarily, through staff conversations and collaboration in matters such as training and equipment. Conceivably, economic means might also be employed: financial, currency, and trade agreements, perhaps even a customs union. The Foreign Secretary was supported in this proposal for a special regional association with western Europe by the British Chiefs of Staff. Ostensibly, this sharp departure from traditional policy of maintaining flexibility and freedom to maneuver was directed against Germany. Eden probably was being more candid, however, when he told the House of Commons that such a grouping would "give us more authority with the other great Powers."[13]

United States thinking had not coalesced sufficiently by late 1944, either on the military or the civilian levels, to have developed a firm policy toward this idea of a western European bloc, although there was substantial sentiment in favor of a revitalized France. Important elements in Washington, however, felt uneasy about France being drawn too closely to Britain either politically or economically. More significantly, some saw such a proposal as directly clashing with the spirit which was to guide the United Nations. "The whole plan smacks of power politics," fumed one British Commonwealth expert in the State Department. "The clock would be turning backward instead of forward. The policy is indicative of a return to the old system of war and more war."[14]

Of more immediate consequence for the fate of Eden's plan, Churchill held other notions about the best means for insuring British security. Russia, he believed, was anxious to carry the wartime partnership into the postwar period. Because Germany would be under stern allied occupation, no immediate threat faced Britain once the present war was over. London, therefore, should be leery of assuming commitments of the sort Eden proposed, particularly if they might impose heavy military burdens on Britain's already strained economy. "We must be careful not to involve ourselves in liabilities which we cannot discharge and in engagements to others for which there is no corresponding return," he cautioned his Foreign Secretary.[15] Instead, the Prime Minister preferred to rely on naval power and a strong air force to keep any potential invader on the far side of the channel. More fundamentally, he sought to draw the United States into as close a relationship with Great Britain as was possible. The only hope for a durable peace, he reasoned, and not incidentally, the best guarantee of British security, lay in an agreement between Washington and London to use their combined force, if that became necessary, to maintain the peace. Russia, he added, could join this agreement if it so wished, but in his mind it was an Anglo-American partnership which mattered. "Our friendship is the rock on which I build for the future of the world, so long as I am one of the builders," he wrote Roosevelt.[16]

Policy makers in Washington, on the other hand, envisioned no such intimacy. A strong, independent, and friendly Britain was indeed deemed essential for American security. It was universally recognized that the control or neutralization of the United Kingdom by any hostile power would be incompatible with the safety of the United States and that the imminent threat of such an occurrence would in all probability trigger armed intervention by the United States in defense of the British. American military planners, in drawing up their blueprints for the postwar world, at no time seriously considered the British as a military threat to the United States.[17]

Still, very few senior American officials, either military or civilian, desired any binding bilateral alliance with the British of the sort which Churchill would have welcomed. The benefits to be derived from such an association were felt to be negligible because Britain by its geographic position had no choice but to serve as a defender of America from a continental aggressor. Furthermore, Washington policy makers were very conscious of the necessity that the United States not appear to be endorsing British policies, in India or the Middle East for instance, which might be viewed as questionable by the American public. The most important reason for shunning such an intimate relationship with the British, however, was fear that such an alliance might provoke an opposing coalition or at least inhibit full cooperation with the Soviets. "It is clearly the policy of the Department," observed one Washington diplomat near the end of 1944, "to avoid as far as possible any situation in which the United States and the United Kingdom appear to have developed a party line before presenting a proposal to the Russians. The Russians should be brought in at the beginning."[18] This policy was disregarded perhaps as often as it was followed, both in communications between Roosevelt and Churchill and at the working levels of the various departments and agencies dealing with international matters. Still, the idea remained that if the United Nations were to be made a successful peacekeeping organization, the United States must adopt an almost neutral course between its two major allies. Thus, in the fall of 1944, there appeared little likelihood that Churchill's desire for a firm Anglo-American defense structure for the postwar world would be fulfilled.

Still other voices in London argued that rather than relying on any untried international body, or a grouping of west European nations, or a probably undependable United States, Britain should strengthen its ties to the Commonwealth and Empire and make these the center of British defense strategy. Here too, however, serious difficulties arose. In the first place, this far-flung Empire imposed heavy obligations for defense upon the United Kingdom and offered manifold temptations to other nations to nibble away at British power and prestige. Rising nationalism and the initial

Japanese victories over the colonial rulers meant that control of many of these areas would be even more difficult in the future than it had been in the past. If the British were unable to work out some modus vivendi with India, this troubled subcontinent would require the diversion of a considerable number of British troops for garrison purposes. By the end of the war the American navy had expanded to three times the size of the British navy, so that even continued British control of the Empire depended on the friendship or sufferance of the United States, something which, given the American tradition of rabid anticolonialism, could not necessarily be counted upon. The war itself had shown these nations that they would in the future have to look more toward the United States for their safety and less toward the United Kingdom.[19] As appealing as such a strategy might appear on the surface, reliance on traditional bonds of Empire did not offer an adequate basis for defense of the British Isles. Ultimately, this plan, like its alternatives, left the British without a satisfactory means for insuring their security in the postwar world.

Despite its shortcomings as a basis for Great Britain's defense, the Commonwealth and Empire remained of great importance to statesmen in London. It possessed natural resources and strategic materials in abundance and provided a substantial industrial potential. It also offered a vast reservoir of manpower; India alone had provided 2 million soldiers for service during the war, a full third of the Empire's land forces. Certain parts of the Empire, moreover—Canada, Australia, and New Zealand—retained a large British population. To these areas London officials felt a special responsibility as well as strong emotional ties. Many portions of the Empire were important sources of hard currency, particularly of dollars, for the mother country. Britain's pride and prestige, its status as a Great Power, all appeared to be tied in intimate fashion to its position as head of the world's greatest empire.

Unfortunately for the British, their precious Empire also represented a major impediment to the development of closer relations between London and Washington—"the permanent skeleton in the cupboard," the British Home Secretary called it.[20] Anticolonialism was one of America's dearest and most respected traditions. This had not prevented the United States from assuming the role of colonial master itself, but it did mean that Americans virtually without exception believed that their rule over foreign peoples was so benevolent as to constitute a totally different type of relationship from traditional metropolitan-colonial ties. The United States had no narrow grasping desire to exploit other peoples. Fortunately, the true national interest coincided with the dictates of international morality, and lay only in preparing subject peoples for the day when full independence might be granted, a process which was at that very moment reaching its culmination in the Philippine Islands. Never mind that the facts of America's history belied this belief in the disinterested nature of American rule—it was the belief itself, sincerely and universally held throughout the United States, which colored Anglo-American relations.[21]

The contrast with the British position, or more exactly, with British policy as interpreted by Americans, could not have been sharper. Churchill's defiant Mansion House speech in 1942 was well-known throughout the United States and continually repeated in the press. "Let me . . . make this clear, in case there should be any mistake about it in any quarter," the Prime Minister had thundered. "I have not become the King's First Minister in order to preside over the liquidation of the British Empire."[22] To most Americans this represented a repudiation by Churchill of his pledge in the Atlantic Charter promising self-determination to all the peoples of the world. Yet Churchill had been plain enough in saying publicly that the Argentia declaration covered only those territories liberated from the Axis, and not the British Empire.[23] Unfortunately, Roosevelt had then obscured the issue by claiming that "the Atlantic Charter applies not only to the parts of the world that border the Atlantic but to the whole world."[24]

Whitehall, in fact, minimized the differences in the positions of the two nations and discounted—perhaps too casually—American expressions of concern for British actions in the underdeveloped world. Great Britain was no less interested in human freedoms or justice than the United States, protested Lord Halifax; but its statesmen did have a greater awareness of the difficulties involved in guiding to political independence peoples unaccustomed to self-government. If the real interests of the natives were to be served properly, London argued, then freedom from want and fear must be within reach before political freedom could be granted. Economic, social, and political advances rather than independence, with its attendant economic and military dangers, should be the goal for most colonial areas.[25] Of American plans for helping these peoples, one senior Foreign Office diplomat wrote contemptuously: "In the name of benefitting the backward populations and improving standards of life, we will get here a combination of Wallace up-lift and National Association of Manufacturers export drive, much to the detriment of the nations who will be forced to run before they have learnt to walk."[26] As for American professions of disinterest, many in London, including the Foreign Secretary, believed that Washington's moralizing about the iniquities of empire served merely as a cover for its own selfish ambitions. Others noted America's past. "There is no reason why we should apologize too abjectly . . ." argued another Whitehall official, "while the Americans so blandly ignore many much worse items in their own history . . . which gave them such valuable pieces of real estate as their southwestern states . . . and the Panama Canal Zone."[27]

Actually, American authorities did not follow as consistently an anti-British policy in matters relating to the Empire as the bitter protests from London would have led one to expect. Roosevelt and virtually every important official in his administration at one time or another publicly expressed their dismay at the continued existence of colonialism in the twentieth century, but in practice official policy was long on exhortation but short on concrete actions. "The President has been very good to me about India throughout these years," Churchill at one point wired Halifax, "and has respected my clearly expressed resolve not to admit external interference in our affairs."[28] Hull fumed about "troublemakers and extremists" in the American press who wished to rid Britain of its colonies "in complete disregard of the problem which would then face everyone." When confronted by a Texan who urged that Hongkong be returned to China, he retorted that the colony had been British rather longer than Texas had belonged to the United States. Was his interlocutor suggesting that Washington return Texas to Mexico? he inquired.[29] Toward the end of the war, as uneasiness over Soviet might and intentions increasingly came to grip American decision makers, a number of agencies, including the Office of Strategic Services, advised that the United States take positive steps to buttress Britain's colonial position. "The United States should realize . . . its interest in the maintenance of the British, French and Dutch colonial empires," OSS chief William J. Donovan told the President. "[I]t is not in our national interest to lead a crusade for colonial independence . . . . [O]ur interest in developing a balance to Russia should lead us in the opposite direction."[30]

Advice such as this, however, frequently went unheeded in wartime Washington. The American people expected their government to adopt an anti-imperialist stance in matters relating to the colonial world, and this position was both intellectually and emotionally satisfying to practically every upper level official in the Roosevelt administration. American suspicions, as a consequence, formed the background against which British policy in Southeast Asia and the Far East unfolded.[31] Highly placed officials in the War Department felt that British military activities in the Pacific had little to do with the fight against Japan, but rather were directed toward reestablishing Britain's colonial position. Some Americans charged that the acronym for the Southeast Asia Command, SEAC, actually meant "Save England's Asian Colonies."[32] The central issue in the Far East for many years to come, warned one ranking officer, would be "the old conflict between the aspirations of people to be free and the desire of predatory nations to rule." The United States, it was emphasized, must be careful not to become associated in the public eye with the restoration of British rule.[33] The Americans, the head of the Foreign Office Far Eastern Department complained in mid-1945, "are virtually conducting political warfare against us in the Far East."[34]

Differences over the proper course to be pursued vis-à-vis China placed further obstacles in the way of Anglo-American partnership in the Pacific. The British feared that Roosevelt's efforts to make China into a strong international power could not help but threaten their hold on their own Asian possessions. A considerable degree of skepticism, well-founded as it turned out, existed in London about the domestic support enjoyed by the Chinese Nationalists. The government of Chiang Kai-shek, Beaverbrook informed Hull, "was not a real fighting government but was something plastered on top of China like the button on a coat." With these assumptions, it is hardly surprising that the British were not always willing to follow the American lead in matters relating to China. On the other hand, this lack of enthusiasm for building up Chiang's regime irritated American officials. General Albert C. Wedemeyer, the American military commander in China, finally wired Washington in exasperation: "I strongly suspect that their activities may be undermining the very United States policy that I am striving so hard to implement."[35]

Conflicts of a different nature impeded Anglo-American collaboration in another part of the world. Just below the surface of joint strategic action in the volatile Middle East lay a pattern of economic rivalry and competition for postwar influence between the two countries. Prior to the war Great Britain had dominated this area, holding mandates in Palestine and Transjordan and exercising effective control over Egypt, Iraq, and the Red Sea and Persian Gulf. The United States, on the other hand, had possessed no military or political position in the region. After its entry into the war, however, the American presence throughout the Middle East had increased dramatically, in part through conscious design, in part by nothing more than bureaucratic momentum. The vast oil reserves of the area provided incentive enough for an expanded role there, but the authorities in Washington were also interested in postwar military and commercial air rights, communication routes, and the possibility of new trade relationships.

American officials demonstrated great ingenuity in using the ample wealth of the United States to ease their way into the region, and in the process alarmed their less affluent British allies.

The Navy, always hungry for new oil supplies, sponsored the idea of purchasing large petroleum concessions to augment Washington's influence in Jidda and the other Middle East capitals. Other methods employed for the same purpose included the extention of lend-lease aid in quantities far in excess of wartime needs; the purchase of airfield rights and the construction of airports; advances in oil company royalties; and direct credits from the Export-Import Bank and other government lending agencies.[36] These various actions inevitably created fears in Whitehall that American ambitions threatened London's traditional hegemony in the region. British responses soon led to a situation marked by mutual obstructionism and antagonism and which an incensed Hull labeled "a reversion to a dog-eat-dog policy."[37] Quite clearly, the Middle East was a further area in which clashing American and British interests presented the possibility of a serious rupture in the broad fabric of Anglo-American cooperation, if not during the war, then once defeat of the common foe erased the immediate necessity of close teamwork.

Everywhere, then, Britain saw its position challenged, perhaps its very safety threatened, by the two parvenus on the international scene, Soviet Russia and the United States. Despite the imminent defeat of Germany, the critical goal of a Europe free of any possible threat to the British Isles had not been attained. The war had shattered not only Hitler's grandiose dreams, but also any chance of erecting even a tenuous balance of power to prevent the continent's domination by any one nation. British security in Europe now rested in large measure on the hope of retaining Russian friendship. Elsewhere, rising nationalistic feelings and the altered realities of military and economic strength combined to engender centrifugal forces so strong that the Empire's ability to resist them was not at all certain. Forces released by the war jeopardized the British position in India and the Far East, while both the United States and the Soviet Union appeared ready to step in to replace the British in part or all of their once-secure sphere of dominance. Traditional British preserves in the Middle

East were also being subjected to increasing encroachment by the pushy Americans, who did not seem content simply to have driven British interests from much of Latin America. A United States tendency toward assertiveness, even arrogance, did nothing to assuage British sensitivities. London officials complained of an increasing American proclivity to downgrade Great Britain, to act as if British power could simply be ignored or assumed to be an instrument of American wishes. Churchill on more than one occasion decried the paltry coverage which the American press accorded the military contribution of British arms in the common fight. Americans were prone to judge everything statistically, Halifax reported.

> It is contrary to their whole approach to stop to think whether twenty miles achieved by British and Canadians in the Caen Sector was not as good or better than one hundred miles achieved by Bradley or Patton, or, again, to consider whether the relative effort of a population of 40,000,000 does not compare very favourably the world over with the effort of 130,000,000.[38]

As the extent of their decline became more difficult to ignore, officials of the Churchill government tried that much harder to retain their Great Power status, to avoid joining what Halifax contemptuously called "the mendicant queue."[39] Form as well as substance assumed an increasing importance in the calculations of Whitehall policy makers. At Bretton Woods, for example, Lord Keynes, attempting to achieve some semblance of parity with the United States, sought to have either the fund or the bank headquartered in London. To Britons it did not seem fair that precisely because they alone had faced the German menace in 1940, they should now be dependent on and at times pushed aside by the same Americans who in 1940 had appeared to be shirking their responsibilities.[40]

In fact, the prospect of an expanded American participation in international affairs occasioned a decided ambivalence within most British policy makers. They desperately wanted the United States to take its place in the world arena, to act in accordance with its military and economic might, and not to revert to the political isolationism which it had embraced after the last war. Unfortunately, there was a price to be paid for the abandonment of American isolationism. As the United States moved into world affairs, it would demand a greater voice in a variety of matters in which the British in the past had possessed a relatively free hand. "[I]n this global war," Roosevelt had admonished Stalin late in 1944, "there is literally no question, political or military, in which the United States is not interested."[41] Furthermore, American views would not always be the same as those of the British. "American policy, in becoming more positive, will also become more independent and less prepared for compromise or evasion," Halifax predicted. "The firmer it is in purpose, the more comprehensive it is in its range of interest, the firmer it will also be in regard to ourselves. We may expect a more aggressive American diplomacy." The British Ambassador then bravely added, "We need not fear this, but the difficult task of conducting relations between the English-speaking peoples is likely in the days ahead to require not less but more skill, understanding and, above all, patience."[42]

Patience is a difficult cornerstone upon which to build a successful foreign policy, but Halifax's prescription simply acknowledged the stark realities of the British situation. Britain could no longer rely on the weapons of the rich man—credits, loans, and subsidies. Its financial exhaustion, its increased vulnerability to attack, its relative decline in military might and industrial potency vis-à-vis its two major allies all combined to restrict its freedom of initiative and to limit the options before its decision makers. In the future, Whitehall realized, there would have to be a greater reliance on "pure diplomacy"—friendly personal relations, efficiency and expertise, good advice. Or as one Foreign Office official caustically remarked, Britain would need, for some years to come, "to make bricks without straw."[43]

Yet, there remained reason for hopefulness. If America were the stronger, London policy makers reasoned, it was equally certain that Britain was the wiser. Official circles were permeated by the comforting if illusory belief that as the result of their longer experience, they understood world affairs better than the Americans, and so were equipped to guide the United States in international matters. Churchill, in reflecting on how Great Britain could match the power which Russia and the United States would wield after the war, grasped at Britain's "superior statecraft and experience" as the equalizer. The South African elder statesman General Jan Smuts spoke to the War Cabinet of Britain's having "the authority and prestige of its great record in world affairs." Other nations, he assured his listeners, would need the maturity in international affairs which the British Commonwealth possessed. The recent history of Germany and Japan amply demonstrated the dangers of power suddenly acquired, without experience and a sense of responsibility.[44] The question, of course, was whether the Russians and particularly the Americans would appreciate their need for this maturity and wisdom, or whether they would be content to shove Britain into the background and face each other across the expanses of a burned-out, weary world.

At times the Foreign Office exhibited an incredible, almost irresponsible optimism about its ability to manipulate American opinion and actions. As late as March 1944, an official policy paper, which circulated throughout Whitehall, observed that London would be throwing away one of its greatest assets if it were "to credit the people of the United States with having developed their own ideas of the world's future to such a point of clarity that they were uninfluenced by ours. If we go about our business in the right way," this paper continued, "we can help to steer this great unwieldy barge, the United States of America, into the right harbour. If we don't, it is likely to continue to wallow in the ocean, an isolated menace to navigation." Although the Americans possessed enormous power, it was "the power of the reservoir behind the dam, which may overflow uselessly, or be run through pipes to drive turbines. The transmutation of their power into useful forms, and its direction into advantageous channels, is our concern. . . . It must be our purpose," this remarkable document concluded, "to make use of American power for purposes which we regard as good."[45] This seemingly quixotic hope that American might might be harnessed and put to work for British ends comprised an important ingredient of London's policy toward the United States far into the postwar period.

A new confidence on the part of virtually all Americans, however, would make this task a difficult one. The war had proven, to their satisfaction at least, the superiority of their political and economic institutions, just as it had demonstrated the bankruptcy of Europe's politics and diplomacy. Americans had learned the lessons from 1919 and were now prepared to assume their rightful place on the world stage—the preeminent place, of course. Sure of their future, confident of their might, secure in their righteousness, the Americans presented a deep contrast with the British with whom their fortunes were so inextricably tied.

4

The Hollow Successes
of Octagon

In international politics words come at a discount—that is, their sum total frequently is much less than what it would appear to be. Words are used to mask differences as often as to elucidate them, to obscure rather then to clarify. Hence, one learns to look elsewhere for clues as to the real meaning of events. The tiny nuances, the symbolic actions, the subtle marks of deference—these are the indices which the experienced observer seeks out.

The wartime partnership between Great Britain and the United States spawned its share of these delicate and distinctive signals. Roosevelt's use of Churchill's first name while the Prime Minister employed a more formal mode of address was one such indicator. Another was the fact that in every conference between the two, it was always Churchill who crossed the ocean to see the President, and not the other way around. Twice Quebec served as the meeting site, but as Roosevelt's Hyde Park home was only a few hours from the Canadian border, this concession to British sensibilities was more cosmetic than substantive. It was not that Churchill did not desire the American President as his guest, but Roosevelt, though promising an eventual visit to England, always found the Prime Minister's invitations to come at a particularly inconvenient time.

In September 1944, Churchill once again journeyed to Quebec, this time for his eleventh wartime meeting with the President. He had been pressing for a bilateral conference since the previous March, at first suggesting an Easter rendezvous in Bermuda, then renewing his invitation for Roosevelt to come to Britain. Failing to elicit a favorable response from FDR for a bilateral meeting, he had then proposed a full-scale conference with Stalin, such as the three had held at Teheran. In July Roosevelt had finally agreed to a tripartite meeting in September at Invergordon on the coast of Scotland, only to have Stalin veto this idea, claiming that his military responsibilities made it impossible for him to leave the Soviet Union at that time. Unable to persuade Roosevelt to come to Invergordon alone and anxious that a meeting with the President be delayed no longer, Churchill then agreed to sail to Quebec.

Seldom has a wartime conference been held against such an auspicious backdrop of military successes as was Octagon, as this second Quebec meeting was code named. German forces were in disarray throughout Europe, and at times only a shortage of gasoline slowed the allied advance. Brussels, Antwerp, and Le Havre had fallen in rapid succession during the early days of September, and on the day before the conference opened, the first American patrol crossed the German frontier. No one expected the Nazis to resist much longer. Churchill's departure for Quebec, in fact, had been delayed by a rumor that Hitler was suing for peace. Yet, as Robert Sherwood has written, "The Allies were well prepared for war to the death in Europe, but they were very ill prepared for the cataclysm of sudden total victory."[1]

The composition of the delegation which accompanied Roosevelt to Quebec substantiates this observation. The meeting was to be a military, not a political conference, Roosevelt assured Hull as he explained his decision to leave the Secretary behind in Washington. If, the President promised, the British called any political figures to the meeting, Hull would also be asked to come.[2] This decision not to bring Hull to Quebec could only have pleased Churchill, who felt little fondness for the Secretary and his moralizing. The exclusion of another familiar figure, however, pained him deeply. For the first time in years, Harry Hopkins was not to attend an important international conference. Once Roosevelt's alter ego and trusted confidant, Hopkins in recent months had slipped from his unique niche, as the President no longer seemed to feel the need for his counsel or companionship. A steadying hand, and one which had proven itself a good friend to Britain, was thus lifted from Roosevelt's shoulder, for Hopkins had at times acted as a restraint on the often impulsive President. In his stead, the dour Henry Morgenthau, Secretary of the Treasury and Roosevelt's Dutchess county neighbor, emerged as the man with the ear of the President. This substitution, a seemingly insignificant development, was to produce some rather startling, and potentially disastrous results.

Roosevelt had taken his Treasury Secretary to Quebec as an adviser on lend-lease affairs, but Morgenthau arrived with very different purposes in mind. State Department officials, he had convinced himself, were not contemplating a plan of sufficient severity in thinking of the postwar treatment of a defeated Germany. Berlin had instigated not one, but two world wars in the past thirty years and as a consequence, bore the responsibility for millions of needless deaths and untold misery and destruction. Moreover, the country had enthusiastically embraced a Nazi doctrine that violated the very tenets of decency and had perpetrated in its name atrocities the like of which the civilized world had never seen. Surely, the Secretary reasoned, the Germans must not be given a third chance. Yet, this was exactly what he believed the State Department intended to provide. Here, then, was a worthy cause, and Morgenthau, undaunted by either his inexperience or his narrow understanding of the issues, seized it as his own.[3]

The Secretary's sweeping expectations for the conference contrasted sharply with the President's more limited objectives. For the moment Roosevelt's attention was centered not so much on long range occupation policy for a Germany still fielding an army of several million men, but on the presidential election two months ahead. Nor was the tie between diplomacy and garnering votes as tenuous as it might at first seem. There were numerous Americans of Italian descent, many in the critical state of New York, who sought relief for their former homeland from some of the more onerous burdens arising from Italy's past transgressions. A more lenient attitude on the part of the allies might go far in securing the support of many of these voters two months hence. Moreover, the United States Army wished the Italians to receive a greater measure of economic independence so that American occupying forces could be relieved of their civilian supply responsibilities. The State Department also advised a relaxation of the restrictions earlier placed on the Italian government. Roosevelt, therefore, was in the happy position of being able to meet the desires of the State Department and the Army and, at the same time, to satisfy his own political needs.[4] Clearly, an easing of the armistice terms under which Italy labored was one of the President's chief objectives as he anticipated meeting with Churchill once again.

The American military authorities who journeyed to Quebec saw the conference somewhat differently—primarily as an opportunity to resolve two issues which had been holding back their own planning. One of these concerned future strategy against Japan. The Navy desired final decisions on force levels, targeting, and the division of responsibility between British and American forces. The other matter to be decided pertained to European zones of occupation. Americans and Britishers had wrestled with this latter problem for over a year, but had been unable to reach agreement. Preliminary planning had assigned the southwest part of Germany to the United States, with lines of communication running through France, while British forces were to occupy northwest Germany. Roosevelt, however, had subsequently informed the Joint Chiefs of Staff that he wished the northwestern sector for American troops, even though such a change at this late date would disrupt both the occupation blueprints and planning for the invasion of France. The Departments of State, War, and the Navy as well as the British opposed the President on this matter, but Roosevelt, for a mixture of military and nonmilitary reasons, remained adamant. In the meantime neither military nor civilian planning could advance until this issue was resolved.[5]

American officials arrived at Quebec, then, not with any single well-defined agenda or negotiating stance, but with various individuals and groups determined to push specific issues with which they happened to be preoccupied at that particular moment. Moreover, though it was certain that important political questions would be discussed—Mogenthau's concern for the future of Germany was only the most prominent of many possible subjects—the State Department was not even represented. Nor could the President, deprived of Hopkins' support, bridge this void alone, for by this stage of the war he was no longer able to keep on top of all the various issues by himself, if in fact he had ever been able to do so. As the talks opened, Henry Stimson, the Secretary of War and something of an elder statesman in Washington, brooded about the disjointedness of the American approach and particularly about the President's failure to prepare adequately for the negotiations. "I hope," he privately observed, "the British have brought better trained men with them."[6]

Had he been able to peer into the *Queen Mary*, which was carrying Churchill and his staff westward across the Atlantic, Stimson would have been even more thoroughly alarmed. After one particularly stormy session with his military commanders, the Prime Minister complained, "Here we are within 72 hours of meeting the Americans and there is not a single point that we are in agreement over."[7] The occasion for this outburst was a difference of opinion between Churchill and his Chiefs of Staff over the proper theater for the next strike against the enemy. Senior British military leaders were virtually unanimous in advising that Great Britain's air and naval forces now concentrate their full strength in the Pacific against Japan. Throughout the year one had heard repeated whispers that the United Kingdom would contribute only token assistance in the defeat of the Japanese. Yet, to allow the American people to feel that the United States had shouldered the whole burden in the Pacific war would seriously jeopardize the prospects for future friendly relations between the British and the Americans. The American Ambassador in London warned that if Britain limited its active involvement to recapturing those areas that had formerly been part of the Empire, the resulting bitterness in the United States toward the British would create schisms between the two that would destroy any chance for postwar partnership. Foreign Office experts concurred in this advice, and even Churchill half-heartedly acknowledged its cogency.[8] But only when his advisers described Pacific operations as part of Britain's campaign to regain its imperial possessions could the Prime Minister summon up any enthusiasm for full-scale participation in the assault against Japan. Churchill and his military chieftains continued to quarrel over strategy throughout the conference, so much so that General Hastings "Pug" Ismay, the valued Chief of Staff to the Minister of Defence, finally gave up in disgust and submitted his resignation to the Prime Minister. The Chief of the Imperial General Staff, Field Marshal Alan Brooke, confided in his diary, "it was hard to keep one's temper" in the face of Churchill's bullheadedness.[9]

Rather than commit the full force of British arms to the Pacific, the Prime Minister wished to strike in a totally different area—the Adriatic. Military operations in southeastern Europe had exercised a peculiar fascination for Churchill from at least the time of the First World War, and Stimson had felt the need on occasion to caution Roosevelt that the Prime Minister had a chronic addiction to "half-baked" diversionary schemes in the Balkans.[10] Now Churchill was possessed by the idea of landing an army on the Istrian peninsula and seizing Trieste, with the ultimate intention of moving against Vienna or Budapest. Not only would this enable the Allies "to give Germany a stab in the Adriatic armpit," as he somewhat crudely put it, but such an operation "would have an effect far outside purely military values." This latter consideration was in the first instance directed toward the troublesome Yugoslavs, but it was probably also occasioned by apprehensions regarding Soviet intentions, never distant from Churchill's mind (fears which may go far in explaining his labored efforts to convince himself and others of Stalin's trustworthiness). In any event, in contrast to his military advisers who sought greater British participation in the Pacific, Churchill at Quebec was more concerned with obtaining landing craft from the Americans for operations against Istria.[11]

In addition to strategic moves in the Balkans, a second issue preoccupied the doughty Prime Minister as he sailed toward his meeting with the President. In order for the British to begin to plan for postwar reconversion and reconstruction, they had to secure some indication from the Americans about the level of lend-lease aid they could expect from the United States, once Germany surrendered. Great Britain for political reasons could not remain under conditions of full mobilization during Phase II, as the period between the fall of Hitler and final victory in the Pacific was termed. What Whitehall wished to determine was whether lend-lease would continue to supplement London's war effort, while British industries were at the same time gearing up for the postwar period. The Exchequer also sought to minimize during Phase II the restrictions and regulations governing British exports which had characterized previous lend-lease aid. This matter of Great Britain's receiving sufficient help from the United States during Phase II so that some British resources could be released for the production of consumer goods and exportable items was considered, Churchill wrote Roosevelt, "of extreme and vital importance by the British Government, for reasons which are only too painfully apparent."[12] Churchill, then, came to Quebec seeking two things from the Americans: landing craft for use in the Adriatic, and a generous commitment for future lend-lease aid.

The military discussions which took place at Octagon saw few Anglo-American differences of any significance. Perhaps this was only to be expected. The participants, after all, thought they were approaching the climax of a spectacularly successful military partnership. The United States Joint Chiefs proved to be surprisingly receptive to Churchill's request for landing craft for use in Istria once British forces had pushed the Germans out of northern Italy. The Americans also pleased their British colleagues by promising that United States troops would not be withdrawn from Italy for redeployment to the Pacific until General Alexander's offensive had been completed. Toward the end of the conference Roosevelt unexpectedly gave way in the matter of German occupation zones, consenting to accept the southwestern sector for American troops. Evidently, the combined urgings of his advisers and the fact that the British were willing to place the north German ports of Bremen and Bremerhaven under American control, thereby eliminating the need for extended lines of communication through France, persuaded the President that the southwest zone was not an unsurmountable liability. Arrangements for the deindustrialization of the German economy which Roosevelt and Churchill had decided upon during the conference also made the northwest section less attractive to FDR, for occupation authorities in this zone would be responsible for dismantling the heavy industry of the Ruhr and the Saar.[13] And finally, in a decision which would provoke endless controversy in later years, the Combined Chiefs approved Eisenhower's proposals for a broad frontal advance on Germany, rather than the single, piercing thrust toward Berlin advocated by Britain's mercurial Field Marshal Bernard Montgomery.[14]

Discussion of Asian strategy did not engender quite the same unanimity, but here again, all the participants left the conference reasonably satisfied. Churchill dutifully offered the services of the British fleet and air force to take part under supreme United States command in the principal operations against the Japanese. Roosevelt accepted at once, despite the vehement opposition of his senior naval adviser, Fleet Admiral Ernest J. King, who saw the introduction of British forces into the theater more as a complicating than a salutary factor.[15] Although the American Navy was compelled to grant Great Britain a role in the primary operations, King was successful in delaying a decision concerning the method and location of this involvement, thereby leaving open an opportunity to sabotage or circumvent this agreement at a later date. Still, British military officials left Quebec quite pleased with the outcome of the conference. They had, after all, obtained more of a commitment from the Americans regarding British involvement in the Pacific than they had ever been able to get before. The other participants most concerned with the military discussions were equally pleased. Churchill had gotten his landing craft, and the American chiefs had finally secured a ruling on the German occupation zones and a basis for more concrete planning for operations in the Pacific.[16]

Having easily resolved the question of military strategy, Roosevelt and Churchill next turned to the sensitive matter of Germany's postwar fate. The Quebec conference is usually remembered, when it is remembered at all, as the meeting which saw United States and British approval of the so-called Morgenthau Plan for the postwar treatment of Germany. This being the case, it is particularly ironic to see the haphazard way in which this program was adopted. One of Churchill's closest wartime associates has observed that though military detail fascinated the Prime Minister, he was bored by the types of problems which would accompany the peace. As a consequence, he tended, much like Roosevelt, to postpone political planning as long as possible. Thus, Churchill arrived at Quebec with no well-conceived design for the postwar treatment of Germany.[17] Had experts from the American State Department been present, this deficiency might not have been very important. As it was, Morgenthau turned out to be the only person of any influence at the talks who was even interested in the problem. Roosevelt himself participated only sporadically in the discussions on Germany, evidently having given the matter little structured thought, as was often the case in questions pertaining to the postwar world. The result, not surprisingly, did not reflect credit upon either the Prime Minister or the President.

Morgenthau first broached the subject of allied postwar policy toward Germany at dinner on the evening of September 13. The Germans must never again be given the opportunity to bring such destruction upon the world, he earnestly declared. The Allies had a responsibility to insure that Germany's wealth and manpower would be used for peaceful ends. Statesmen after the last war had erred in not seeing to this; the Versailles Treaty had antagonized the German people but had failed to provide for measures that would guarantee German good behavior in the future. The impassioned Morgenthau then outlined his ideas on how this might be accomplished. All Germany's heavy industry should be dismantled, he explained, and severe controls lasting for at least twenty years should be imposed. Perhaps Germany might be partitioned into several different states as well. At any rate, the German people should become "an agricultural population of small land-owners."[18]

Churchill's immediate reaction to these proposals jolted the Treasury Secretary. The Prime Minister labeled Morgenthau's program "unnatural, unchristian and unnecessary" and asserted that Britain would have no part in such a vindictive policy. Morgenthau, however, was able to enlist the aid of Lord Cherwell, British Paymaster-General, one of Churchill's closest advisers, and a man who harbored, according to British authorities, "an almost pathological hatred for Nazi Germany" as well as a "medieval desire for revenge."[19] Cherwell reinforced Morgenthau's initial inclinations to tie the issue of Germany's future to Britain's economic woes, and in subsequent conversations with the Prime Minister, Morgenthau emphasized the expansion of British exports which the elimination of German competition would make possible. What, the Treasury Secretary inquired of Churchill, was to prevent Great Britain from starving if its exports proved incapable of paying for its imports?[20]

This line of reasoning quickly convinced the Prime Minister of the program's merits. The Americans "opened out their plan for expanding the British Export Trade to meet the loss of Foreign Investments," he wired the War Cabinet. "It is proposed that the Ruhr and the Saar steel industries shall be completely dismantled. . . . The consequences of this will be to emphasize the pastoral character of German life and the goods hitherto supplied from these German centres must to a large extent be provided by Great Britain."[21] When he found inadequate the memorandum drawn up by Morgenthau and Cherwell embodying the plan, Churchill himself dictated another, which became the actual text of what was later known as the Morgenthau Plan. This notorious document provided for the dismantling of the German metallurgical, chemical, and electrical industries as part of a program for "converting Germany into a country primarily agricultural and pastoral in character."[22] Anthony Eden, hastily summoned from London, tried unsuccessfully to keep his impulsive chief from committing the

British to such a program, at one point shouting "you can't do this" to an obviously startled Churchill. Eden later remembered this meeting as the only occasion when Churchill ever became angry at him before the representatives of another power.[23]

One can only be amazed at this cavalier manner in which major questions of policy were settled. It was not simply that a sweeping program affecting the lives of millions of people could be approved without even a minimum of consultation with those most knowledgeable on the subject, though this was bad enough. Even more curious, however, was the fact that such a plan could be adopted for reasons that had very little to do with insuring that Germany would not again lead the world into conflict. "The real nub of the situation," Roosevelt wrote Hull in a memorandum on the disposition of German industry, "is to keep Britain from going into complete bankruptcy at the end of the war."[24] This undoubtedly overstated the President's position; harsh terms toward Germany, for instance, might also reassure Moscow that Britain and the United States did not intend to turn German strength against Russia after the war. Still, Germany's future was of enough importance to merit consideration in its own right, a reality which seems to have completely escaped Roosevelt and Churchill. The dismay felt by diplomats in the Foreign Office over this episode was summed up in the permanent undersecretary's observation: "It's quite impossible to do business this way." Hull's reaction was more emotional. "In Christ's name," he cried, speaking of Roosevelt, "what has happened to the man?"[25]

The long-suffering Hull was to receive a further shock when he learned of the decisions taken at Quebec in regard to Phase II lend-lease aid to the British. Washington officials had been considering this problem for some time, but were still of two minds as to the proper shape future lend-lease should assume. One group, mostly State Department bureaucrats at the "expert" level, argued that it was important to the United States, both politically and economically, that Great Britain reestablish its economic stability as soon as possible and, to this end, that American aid should be generous and without strings. Others, however, were troubled that Congress and the public might balk if it appeared that lend-lease was being supplied to the United Kingdom simply to ease British reconversion to civilian production. This group, composed of officials in both the State Department and the Foreign Economic Administration, thought it advisable not only to scrutinize all British requests carefully, but also to make Phase II aid contingent on London's offering concessions in other areas. Hull, for instance, urged that the British be required to join with the United States in pressing for a world-wide program for the reduction of trade barriers, and especially, that they implement the Bretton Woods agreements.[26]

On this issue as on the German question, however, the Secretary of State discovered that Morgenthau's presence at the conference insured a very different resolution. The impressionable Treasury Secretary had only just returned from a trip to Britain, where he had been assiduously wooed by the Churchill government, and from whence he left with the conviction that Washington must act quickly and generously if London were to avoid bankruptcy. The whole question of Phase II had "to be approached from the standpoint that Great Britain made this fight for democracy," he reported upon his return. "Now we have got to help her. She is a good credit risk, a good moral risk, and we have to put her back on her feet . . . for a permanent world peace."[27]

Roosevelt, preoccupied with other matters, felt no more inclined than Morgenthau to press the British very hard in order to extract something in return for American aid. After perfunctory discussion he and Churchill agreed to the creation of a joint committee to work out the details of this problem. This committee was to be guided by a September 14 discussion between the President and the Prime Minister. During that conversation Roosevelt had agreed that lend-lease should continue even if this made possible the release of British manpower for the production of civilian goods and commercial exports. Churchill emphasized Britain's need to rebuild its overseas trade, to which the President responded that it would not be proper for the United States to attach any conditions to the delivery of lend-lease which might jeopardize the recovery of that trade. At no time did he raise questions concerning policies the British should pursue in return for Phase II assistance. Churchill suggested that Hopkins be named chairman of the joint committee, but Roosevelt insisted on designating Morgenthau. The other American members were to be Edward R. Stettinius, the Under Secretary of State and the former head of the lend-lease program, and FEA chairman Leo T. Crowley.[28]

The British made no attempts to hide their elation over these developments, while back in Washington Hull stormed. When Roosevelt and Churchill met to initial the record of their conversation which was to guide the joint committee, the Prime Minister became "quite emotional about this agreement, and at one time he had tears in his eyes," Morgenthau recorded in his diary. "When the thing was finally signed, he told the President how grateful he was, [and] thanked him most effusively."[29] From London the War Cabinet congratulated Churchill on obtaining an agreement "which is more favourable than we could ever have expected." Hull, on the other hand, deprived of his principal lever with which to pry open British preferential restrictions, was furious. "This whole development at Quebec, I believe," he was later to recall, "angered me as much as anything that had happened during my career as Secretary of State."[30]

Having had his desires satisfied so completely in the matters of landing craft and lend-lease aid, Churchill offered no resistance to meeting Roosevelt's needs with regard to Italy. Even before journeying to Quebec the Prime Minister had indicated that he favored tendering some mark of confidence to the Bonomi government in Rome, such as United Nations Relief and Recovery assistance or partial diplomatic recognition.[31] After five days in Quebec, the two statesmen moved on to Roosevelt's Hyde Park estate, where they talked extensively of Italy amidst a scene far removed from London's Hyde Park, with its bomb craters and artillery emplacements. Unencumbered by diplomatic advisers, they easily agreed upon a whole range of political and economic concessions to the Italians. When these proposals were referred to London for Foreign Office approval, Eden quickly intervened, pointing out that alterations of this magnitude ought first to be cleared with the Russians, who after all were parties to the armistice, and with the dominions. Following a further telegraphic exchange and a number of other modifications to tone down the orginal draft, the White House released a statement announcing these changes on September 26. When Roosevelt carried New York six weeks later, the wisdom of American diplomacy seemed vindicated.[32]

During the course of the conference the two statesmen also shared anxieties arising from Russian activities in Yugoslavia, Greece, and Poland, ultimately deciding to send a second message to Stalin along with the official report describing the military conversations. This additional cable would inform the Soviet Premier of the worries which Churchill and Roosevelt harbored concerning political developments in parts of Europe and would contain a specific plea that the Kremlin not place itself in the embarrassing position of recognizing one set of Polish authorities while London and Washington recognized another.[33] To both western statesmen, the Soviet refusal to facilitate the airlifting of supplies to the embattled partisans in Warsaw was a special vexation. The British, after all, had originally gone to war in defense of Polish freedom, and Poland's anguish had become a rallying point to Americans and Englishmen. Were the brave inhabitants of that tortured nation now to be martyred at the very moment of their deliverance simply because their would-be liberators chose not to make the effort to rescue them? Churchill in particular became incensed at the prospect, attempting at one point to persuade his American colleague to drop provisions to Warsaw by using Russian airfields without Soviet permission.[34] Eventually, calmer counsel prevailed, but the very existence of the issue troubled those who hoped for Big Three unity in peace as well as war. Reflecting this concern, Roosevelt and Churchill reaffirmed their earlier decision to regard the subject of atomic energy as of the utmost secrecy, barring any disclosures to the Soviets. Here was a further manifestation of the fact that a more exclusive coterie thrived within the larger Grand Alliance.

Only when the conversation drifted to the British Empire did any serious differences of opinion perturb the harmony of the proceedings. One evening the two leaders spent an hour exchanging rather, talking past each other) about India. Churchill ₋ₚoke heatedly of the difficulties which the British confronted in that troubled region, and of the lack of understanding in America about India. At one point he threatened to give the United States half of India to administer while the British retained the other half, and then to see which country did the better job. On another occasion he proposed a swap: if Roosevelt would leave "his Indians" alone, he would avoid meddling with "the President's Chinese." In discussions on Far Eastern strategy, Roosevelt again incurred Churchill's ire by suggesting an "end run" around Singapore, fearing its capture would prove too costly.[35] These incidents, however, were but minor irritants in what was otherwise a remarkably congenial and mutually satisfying few days.

At first glance, the most noticeable aspect of this conference appears to be that each of the principals, Eden and possibly King excepted, left Quebec fully contented. To the extent that this was actually the case, this indicated not so much an identity of objectives, but a fortuitous situation in which the differing goals of each individual or group were not mutually exclusive. As a consequence, Roosevelt could report to the press on the last day of their deliberations that the conference had been characterized by less argument and had achieved "complete unanimity" in less time than any previous meeting. The talks had been conducted "in a blaze of friendship," Churchill added.[36] Octagon seemed a success, another of those periodic rituals which were apparently needed to reinvigorate the partnership.

Yet, appearances deceived, for the decisions taken were soon reversed and the arguments reached quickly became unraveled. The British military was never to receive a role in the Pacific commensurate to that which it believed it had secured at Quebec; the unexpectedly rapid Japanese surrender saw to that.[37] Nor did Churchill's grand schemes for operations in Istria come to fruition, for the Germans refused to concede defeat in northern Italy, and British forces remained bogged down in that theater. The Phase II arrangements which had brought the Prime Minister such relief were within a month to be the source of friction, due both to disagreement about what Roosevelt had promised, and to American efforts to add conditions to any aid. Unfavorable public reaction to the Morgenthau Plan after it leaked to the press and additional reflection upon its implications caused Roosevelt to draw back from the commitments regarding Germany assumed at Octagon. Anglo-American accord in affairs concerning Italy crumbled almost immediately following the release of the White House statement, and differences over the proper course toward the Italian government led very soon thereafter to a public display of pique and anger between the two allies seldom matched during the war. The discussions on atomic energy were also to be the source of ill feelings in the months ahead. Finally, even what appeared the stablest of the agreements, that concerning occupation zones for Germany, eventually proved undesirable and within two years Washington and London were again negotiating, this time to merge the zones they had previously worked so hard to create. So ultimately, after all the expectations, the anxieties, and the deliberations, the accomplishments of Octagon came to nought. Churchill and Roosevelt had succeeded only in postponing decision and papering over differences. For Britain and America, for battle-weary peoples around the globe, the difficult problems of war and peace remained to be confronted.

5

Coercive
Liberality

Upon his return to London, Churchill moved quickly to implement Roosevelt's promise of generous Phase II assistance, only to find his plans sidetracked by that peculiarly American phenomenon, the presidential campaign. His first act was to appoint a high-powered delegation headed by the distinguished Cambridge economist John Maynard Keynes to negotiate with Henry Morgenthau and the American committee. Keynes and his associates arrived in Washington early in October 1944, discovering their hosts deeply engrossed in the closing weeks of Thomas Dewey's effort to deny Roosevelt a fourth term in the White House. Also being contested were all 435 positions in the House of Representatives and a full third of the seats in the Senate, as well as numerous state and local offices. There is perhaps nothing so wholly a matter of a country's internal affairs as a national election. Yet the British, as befit the intimacy of the relationship which had developed between the two wartime partners, found their thoughts increasingly drawn toward this American spectacle as the initial high spirits occasioned by the Quebec conference receded into the past. And Keynes found his mission relegated to a distinctly secondary position for the duration of the campaign.

The congressional elections two years earlier had seriously troubled those in both Britain and the United States who hoped for

American leadership in the postwar world, and many in London anxiously anticipated the 1944 elections in an attempt to obtain a further reading on the mood of the American populace. In 1942, the Republican Party had scored impressive gains in both houses, giving the GOP its greatest congressional strength in over a decade. Worse yet, only 5 of the 115 congressmen with isolationist records had failed to win reelection. Immediately, flagging memories of 1920 revived in England. The British press openly predicted a "return to Hardingism" in the United States after the war. Unless the 1944 results indicated a reversal of this trend, agreed concerned individuals on both sides of the ocean, prospects for a lasting peace looked dreary.[1]

Though most observers believed that Churchill and the vast majority of his countrymen wished to see a decisive victory for Roosevelt and the Democrats, British newspapers and politicians for the most part maintained a discreet silence in the weeks prior to the voting. This uncharacteristic restraint reflected an awareness of the strong strains of Anglophobia still latent in much of the American public and recognition of the need to exercise extreme care so as to give no cause for offense. Only after the polls had closed and the outcome had been determined did the British demonstrate just how extensive their reliance on and hopes in Franklin Roosevelt had become.

"Thank God all is well," a relieved Churchill wired to Hopkins immediately upon being informed of the results. The *Times*, echoing official thinking as usual, hailed the reelection of "a tried and trusted friend and a great leader and campaigner in the cause of the United Nations." The *Daily Express* called word of the outcome "great and splendid news."[2] Nor was Roosevelt's victory the only reason for rejoicing. The composition of the new Congress was equally pleasing to the British. Five isolationist members of the Senate Foreign Relations Committee had gone down to defeat. The Anglophobic New York congressman Hamilton Fish lost his seat; so, too, did Gerald Nye of Nye Committee fame.[3] The results of practically all the congressional races were "quite remarkably satisfactory both for the bad men turned out and the good men brought in," the former head of the Foreign Office's American

Department observed. With a Democratic Congress, the *News Chronicle* pointed out, Roosevelt would have decisive advantages not enjoyed by Wilson in 1919.[4] The elections "have clearly set the seal of [the] electorate on [the] trend towards participation in world affairs," Ambassador Halifax reported from Washington. Considering the enormous provocation which the tense atmosphere of an electoral campaign provides, Halifax added, Britain had come off exceptionally lightly in another respect. Accusations of British meddling in American affairs had been, for a preelection period, remarkably few.[5]

The *Economist* interjected a sober note of caution, reminding its readers that "this is only the first step, and it is largely a negative step, a decision not to be isolationist." As yet, the journal continued, no important practical commitments had been made by Washington policy makers in the direction of assuming a more equitable portion of the responsibility for insuring international order and stability in the future.[6] London officials, of course, were fully, even painfully, aware of this, but for the moment at least, the atmosphere was one of guarded optimism. Just perhaps, the election results were a harbinger of a greater maturity on the part of the American people. This, at any rate, was the prevalent British reaction in the immediate aftermath of Roosevelt's reelection. As such, it represented one of the few encouraging moments in what was otherwise to prove a dismal and upsetting autumn for Whitehall diplomats.

The outcome of the Phase II lend-lease talks provided practically the only other cheering news for the Foreign Office in the concluding months of 1944, but success on this front was not achieved without a struggle. Keynes had come to Washington with a detailed catalogue of items the British hoped to obtain from the Americans during the first twelve months after V-E Day. Heading this list were nearly seven billion dollars worth of commodities and services, enough so that some British manpower could be diverted from munitions production to the manufacture of consumer and export goods. In addition, they sought American agreement to the removal of all the restrictions on the British export trade which had been imposed at the time of the first lend-lease shipments to England. Finally, Keynes and his colleagues wanted American acceptance of the principle that British gold and dollar reserves should not be allowed to drop below their current levels.[7] Taken as a group these desires entailed a rather sweeping program of American aid. A good argument could be (and was) made, however, that they were actually only the concrete expression of Roosevelt's somewhat breezy promises at Quebec.

Upon arriving in Washington, the British negotiators immediately found themselves caught in the crossfire of an unseemly bureaucratic squabble over who was to represent the United States in conversations with the Keynes delegation. Roosevelt had designated Morgenthau as head of the committee conducting the talks, and the Treasury Secretary had at once set out to insure that he remain in tight control of the negotiations, even enjoining the British representatives to avoid making any contact with the State Department or the Foreign Economic Administration. Only in this manner, he explained, could he guide the talks to a successful conclusion without the inevitable delays and interference from other departments.[8] Hull, however, had had "an all-out" with Roosevelt about being subordinated to Morgenthau and left the White House believing the President had agreed to put the matter back into the hands of the State Department. FEA head Leo Crowley had also complained to Roosevelt and left his conference with the President also assuming that he had been placed in charge of the negotiations. Finally, Admiral William Leahy, Roosevelt's ambitious and irascible chief of staff, took it upon himself to advise the President in this affair, although admitting in private that this "business of lend-lease is entirely outside of my cognizance."[9]

The British had more than a casual interest in the outcome of this jurisdictional dispute, for the various contending factions had very different ideas about both what the President had actually agreed to at Quebec, and whether these promises left the negotiators any flexibility for extracting concessions from the British in return for Phase II lend-lease. During the Octagon conference Morgenthau had mentioned figures of $3.5 billion for munitions assistance and $3 billion for nonmunitions aid, but neither Church-ill nor Roosevelt had spoken in terms this concrete. Morgenthau himself in the following weeks seemed unable to decide if these numbers represented a specific commitment. FEA, Leahy, and a segment of the State Department bureaucracy, on the other hand, were certain that there was no such commitment and that the United States could never provide such a large amount of aid without provoking widespread and intense public and congres-sional dissatisfaction.[10]

One might reasonably ask whether actual political necessity lay behind this deference to "public opinion," or whether American officials simply found such arguments a convenient rationalization for avoiding distasteful policies. Two assertions can be made with confidence. First, real constraints on the administration's freedom did in fact exist. Second, Washington leaders, from Roosevelt on down, never attempted to test the outer limits of American per-missiveness. The historian looking back on these years must not underestimate either the misconceptions about lend-lease which colored public and congressional thinking about the aid program, or the degree to which the British were still distrusted by large segments of the American population. Thus, when assistance to-talling many billions of dollars was extended to a people whose basic intentions were questioned, the inevitable results were ex-aggerations and outright falsehoods about the uses to which Great Britain put this aid. The attitude displayed by the Air Force lieu-tenant who wrote Under Secretary of State Stettinius wondering "why we are suckers again" was not at all atypical. "England is enjoying such prosperity as she hasn't known for generations," he stormed, "yet we continue to give (not lend) to the largest nation in the world *who despises us whenever she doesn't need us.*"[11]

Administration officials tried to rebut the most glaring of the erroneous accusations leveled at the British but met with only very limited success. In late November, just days before the results of the Phase II negotiations were to be made public, the White House issued a report on lend-lease which dealt exclusively with the contributions to the common cause made by reverse lend-lease provided by Great Britain. Without this aid from the United

Kingdom, Roosevelt assured the Congress, the invasion of France would have been delayed by many months. Yet, a majority of American papers on the following day headlined the story with the President's statement that lend-lease would end with the Japanese surrender. The large volume of British assistance definitely received second billing.[12] At the turn of the year, one poll sent by the State Department to the President indicated that only 32 percent of the public was even aware of the reverse lend-lease furnished by Britain.[13]

Amidst this background of confusion and distrust, recent months had witnessed mounting congressional demands for a stricter accounting of the manner in which lend-lease aid was employed and more frequently voiced suspicions that Whitehall was using American lend-lease supplies not to defeat the enemy but to resell to third countries for British profits.[14] Telegrams between the State Department and the American embassy in London repeatedly referred to this growing pressure from Capitol Hill.[15] Congressmen increasingly complained that Washington was not being sufficiently hard-headed in dealing with the British and passed on to Departmental officials vitriolic letters from constituents asking whether it was true that the United States paid exorbitant rates to use the Suez Canal while the Panama Canal remained free to British vessels, or if lend-lease had enabled the United Kingdom to maintain a high level of exports while America's foreign trade had declined, or some similar question.[16] "The time has come," *Business Week* solemnly stated near the end of October, "for plain speaking on the question of British-American economic relations."[17]

Moreover, widespread doubts whether lend-lease could be legally used for rehabilitation purposes created another problem for those who sought a generous program of assistance for Great Britain. Many officials totally dedicated to helping the British regain their economic strength as quickly as possible worried that lend-lease was not the proper vehicle for this objective and urged that extreme care be exercised to insure that American exporters not get the impression they were competing for foreign markets with goods supplied to the United Kingdom under lend-lease.[18]

In the midst of the Phase II negotiations the *Washington Post* editorialized that Congress had authorized lend-lease solely to promote the defense of the United States. It would be a "complete perversion" of its purposes, the *Post* asserted, to employ this emergency device to assist the British in rehabilitating their civilian economy. Leahy has written that he told Roosevelt that he did not "want to go to jail when they begin, after the war is over, to investigate what has been done with this money."[19]

In the final analysis, one simply cannot say with any degree of accuracy whether a determined and forceful administration could have nullified the substantial opposition which existed to anything that could be interpreted as overly lavish aid. What can be confidently asserted is that these pressures were real, and that Washington policy makers, ever mindful of Wilson's failure after the previous war, were acutely conscious of the need, as they saw it, to avoid getting too far in front of what the public would accept.

Partly as a consequence of these uncertainties, powerful figures in Washington insisted that the Morgenthau committee demand some *quid pro quo* from the British in return for that portion of American aid not directly for use against Japan. Hull, as might be expected, urged that the United States not proceed too rapidly with the implementation of plans for lend-lease until the British provided a more definite commitment to adopt "sound economic policies designed to revive the flow of international trade."[20] Others suggested that the British offer concessions in the telecommunications field, that they withdraw their claims to certain Pacific islands or cede various strategic bases to the United States, or that they commit themselves to support American desires more energetically in Argentina and other neutral countries.[21] As Keynes and his colleagues were sailing to America, Hull summed up these arguments for Roosevelt:

> Our guiding thought has been that the problem of provision of financial assistance to Great Britain beyond direct military requirements is an integral part of our most basic foreign policy. Hence I believe that the negotiations . . . should not be divorced from the discussion of other extremely important matters, . . . and that no final decisions should be reached in connection with this aspect of

lend-lease assistance independently of an adequate clarification of these other matters. I am afraid, therefore, that we are courting disaster unless the whole subject is handled as a matter of foreign policy rather than solely or predominantly a matter of finance.

The head of the State Department's Division of British Commonwealth Affairs worried that if congressional and public sensitivities on this score were not adequately soothed, the resulting uproar would "make U.S.-U.K. relations after World War I (and God knows they were bad then) look like a love feast by comparison."[22]

Thus, as the two delegations began their discussions, very different considerations guided their actions. The levels of military aid, it is true, were easily agreed upon, reflecting the similarity of views on the nature of the job ahead and satisfaction with past cooperative efforts. There was no such confluence of opinion, however, concerning nonmilitary assistance. Roosevelt himself increasingly came to act, Morgenthau complained to Stettinius, as though he had never heard of the Quebec agreements on Phase II. The British had hoped to secure a firm commitment on the levels of aid which were to be granted, much like the Russian supply protocols. Instead, Roosevelt, egged on by Leahy, insisted that past procedure be continued—that is, that supplies be apportioned on the basis of the strategic situation at the time rather than as a result of prior agreement. When Morgenthau pointed out that this was contrary to the understanding reached at Quebec, the President blithely told him not to worry, that he would straighten this out with Churchill. Nothing should be made public, he added; there must be no official record, no signed document. The British would have to rely solely on American good will. Any other course, he explained, would create serious political problems.[23]

Officials in Britain became increasingly irritated at what appeared to them as efforts to back out of the agreements so recently concluded at Quebec. London recognized the political difficulties faced by the administration, the Chancellor of the Exchequer wired Keynes, but Whitehall had never been satisfied that there was the same appreciation on the American side of the political difficulties confronting British policy makers. By late 1944, feeling was running high in the United Kingdom for a liberalization of the lend-lease restrictions governing exports, and the government was under mounting pressure to allow a full-scale debate in Parliament on British export policy. Twice the Cabinet had been able to secure postponement of this debate, but in doing so it had been forced to agree that the Commons could discuss the matter no later than November 29. Members of the Churchill government did not find the prospect appealing. In recent months Britishers had shown a rising willingness to attack Washington's economic practices publicly and to characterize American intentions in most derogatory terms. A parliamentary debate was certain to be sprinkled with accusations and recriminations which could only provoke the United States. If, on top of that, the government had to go before the House without substantial concessions from the Americans, concessions which it had thought had been secured at Octagon, the resulting explosion could seriously jeopardize hopes of further Anglo-American collaboration in the economic field. Moreover, the Prime Minister and his associates would appear foolish and incompetent. Thus, as a result of its own domestic problems, Downing Street handed the British negotiators in Washington a deadline which placed a strict time limit on the slow give-and-take which seemed to be the outstanding characteristic of so many of these technical discussions.[24]

To complicate matters still further, the talks became linked with controversies in two other, thoroughly unrelated, areas: Anglo-American policy toward Argentina, and postwar civil aviation. The Argentine issue was a particularly emotional one for Hull, for relations with Buenos Aires had bedeviled his Latin American policy for much of the time he had been in office. The American Secretary was determined to see that the regime of Edelmiro Farrell received no expression of favor, however indirect, from any nation over which the United States had the least degree of leverage. Such an indication of international disapproval, the Secretary hoped, would soon topple the Argentine government and cause it to be replaced by one more willing to support the United

Nations in their fight against Hitlerism. As part of his program for isolating the ruling clique in Buenos Aires, Hull sought to prevent the British, acting either for themselves or as the purchasing agent for the United Nations, from concluding a long-term contract for the purchase of Argentine beef.

The explanation for his intense opposition to the negotiation of this meat contract embraced an unlikely combination of motives. In the first place, Hull had become convinced that the Farrell regime was a fascist, pro-German dictatorship which represented both an ideological and an actual security threat to the United States and the other democratic nations of the western hemisphere. Conclusion of a lengthy contract could not help but bolster the regime against its domestic opponents, Hull reasoned. Also important to the Secretary, though certainly less enunciated than the alleged fascist menace, was the fact that Argentina's refusal to follow the United States lead in dealing with Germany threatened traditional American hegemony in Latin America. Furthermore, there was widespread fear that a long-term bulk contract might result in American firms being frozen out of the Argentine market after the war, or equally serious, that such contracts might retard the achievement of a multilateral world. For all these reasons officials in Washington came to believe that it was essential that British policy closely parallel that of the United States in matters relating to Argentina.[25] To this end they were willing to apply considerable pressure. "To give the United Kingdom $2,700,000,000 worth of non-military lend-lease assistance for 1945," argued the chief of the State Department's Division of British Commonwealth Affairs, "without regard to the way they have frustrated our policy in regard to Argentina is unthinkable."[26]

To the British the Americans appeared both to be advocating an unwise course and to be creating a major issue between Washington and London where none was justified. The Farrell government was not so much a Nazi regime as "a militarised ultra-Nationalist movement, inflamed in this case by continuous chiding and more from [its] North American rival," concluded the Foreign Office.[27] The British embassy in Buenos Aires reported that there was "at present no evidence showing that the Axis war effort is obtaining any specific advantages through the actions or inaction of the Argentine Government," and that the dispute was essentially a conflict between Argentine pride and the United States claim to paramountcy in Latin America.[28] Moreover, British authorities were well aware that United States imports from Argentina in 1944 were reaching record levels.[29] As for the contracts they sought, officials in London believed these were justified by the need to guarantee adequate quantities of foodstuffs then in short supply at stable, reasonable prices. The Ministry of Food was particularly insistent on this point, and given the wartime scarcity of quality meat in the United Kingdom, this issue was a potentially explosive one, should it be learned that the government had jeopardized the Argentine supply to protect Washington's hemispheric supremacy. In addition, Great Britain had huge investments in Argentine railroads and mining, manufacturing, and shipping concerns. To act precipitantly in the matter of the meat contract might endanger these important assets.[30]

Unfortunately for the British, arguments of this sort failed to move the American Secretary of State. Hull viewed London's desire for a firm understanding with the Argentines only as a further manifestation of what he saw as the traditional British affinity for politically conservative, even reactionary leadership. The British had been remarkably tolerant of Franco's fascist leanings, he believed. When faced with the choice between two contending factions claiming to represent the governments of nations overrun by Germany, Whitehall had invariably backed the less progressive of the two. And now Great Britain wanted to buttress another illiberal, repressive regime, this time in America's own backyard. Worse still, Britain's policy smacked of the same appeasement which had so greatly contributed to the present global conflict. The very thought of this reinforced the Secretary in his conviction that no conclusion of the meat contract should be permitted.

The other issue which became entangled in the Phase II talks revolved around what was essentially a dispute over the degree to which the British would be allowed to protect their postwar aviation interests from American competition. On November 1,

1944, the representatives of fifty-two nations gathered in Chicago to draw up rules to govern peacetime international air traffic. The conference quickly stalled when the British and the Americans, as the two parties with the largest interests, were unable to agree on the functions and powers to be assigned a proposed international regulatory body. Essentially, the British desired a strong organization with the power to set rates, distribute routes, and fix schedules, while the Americans wanted these issues settled between individual companies on a competitive basis. The British plan, so the Americans argued, was overly restrictive and represented an attempt to horn in on traffic originating in the United States and built up by American aviation leadership. The British, on the other hand, feared that without some protection they would be entirely pushed from the skies by the United States. Certainly free competition would have greatly benefited the Americans, both because of their prewar leadership in the field, and because British firms during the war had concentrated on building fighters and had, in the interests of efficiency, left the production of transport planes almost entirely to the United States. Now, London officials feared, if these matters were not resolved at the governmental level, British companies would be faced with almost insurmountable obstacles in competing with the Americans. The United States representatives retorted that they were asking for no more than the British had demanded for generations in the field of maritime transport.[31]

During the third week in November, these three totally disparate issues converged to produce a nightmarish dilemma for British officialdom. In all three instances, Whitehall believed that legitimate, long-range British interests were being threatened by a United States preoccupied with narrow, shortsighted, selfish concerns. Moreover, Great Britain found itself in each case in a tenuous position largely because of its vast efforts exerted in the common cause. Now, so it seemed, the ungrateful Americans were bent on taking unfair advantage of Britain's distress for purposes which appeared less than high-minded. An outraged Hull would have replied that British policies regarding Argentina and civil aviation reflected self-interested or insular motives unbecoming

a true partnership. As to their protests concerning American caution in the Phase II talks, he could easily have reminded his British
complainants that in assuming that the United States would furnish
Great Britain with reconstruction aid, they were asking for almost
unprecedented generosity from an America itself only recently
recovered from the ravages of depression. Their successful alliance
notwithstanding, policy makers of the two countries found even
the adoption of a common perspective most difficult.

Shortly after the first of November, renewed reports had
reached American ears that the British were again considering the
conclusion of a long-term contract with the Argentines. Even earlier, John G. Winant, the American Ambassador in London, had
bluntly informed Eden that British actions in Argentina would
inevitably influence Washington's attitude toward British requests
"for our cooperation and assistance on a much more substantial
scale in other areas." Now was the time to implement this linkage,
argued key officials in the State Department bureaucracy.[32] In a
message to Churchill on November 18, Roosevelt warned the
Prime Minister that signing a meat contract would have repercussions in Congress and the press "at a most unfortunate time."
Only direct intervention by Assistant Secretary of State Dean
Acheson prevented a more explicit reference to the Phase II talks.
Another American note sent through lower channels later the
same day was not subtle. In view of London's failure to take steps
to reduce trade contacts with Buenos Aires, the American embassy
informed the Foreign Office, the State Department would find
it necessary to restrict certain key exports from the United States
to Great Britain.[33]

As soon as Churchill had had an opportunity to digest these
statements, Roosevelt applied pressure from another direction.
On November 22, the Prime Minister wired the White House
that British negotiators in Chicago were unable to concede anything more in the aviation talks. If agreement were still not possible, he suggested, perhaps it would be better to adjourn the
conference to allow for additional conversations away from the
glare of the considerable publicity then focused on Chicago.[34] But
from the American delegation at the conference came pleas that

the lend-lease talks be suspended until the British proved more cooperative in Chicago, a tactic endorsed by at least one member of Roosevelt's Cabinet. The President barely hesitated, directing that a more persuasive message for his unfortunate ally be drafted. Acheson again tried to soften the tone of the note, but before Roosevelt's response could be dispatched to Churchill, the FEA's Oscar Cox intercepted it and inserted considerably tougher language. If the conference ended unsatisfactorily, FDR finally wired Churchill on November 24, the repercussions would seriously affect many other things." Dropping all indirectness, he then added, "We are doing our best to meet your lend-lease needs." He observed, however, that Congress would soon have to approve new lend-lease appropriations, and that it would "not be in a generous mood if it and the people feel that the United Kingdom has not agreed to a generally beneficial air agreement."[35]

The President's cable met with a somber reception in London. Winant, who had developed a real fondness for the Prime Minister, could not have enjoyed his role in delivering such a note. One scholar has written that he knows "of no instance where Roosevelt so blatantly waved the club of economic coercion in his dealings with the Russians."[36] Indeed, this was a threat one might make to a ward heeler or a recalcitrant union boss. But to resort to such peremptory tactics toward the leader of one of the world's major powers—and one's most intimate ally at that—Churchill's anguish was hardly feigned. Many years afterward, one of the Prime Minister's intimates would recall this occasion as one of the few times when Churchill's faith in American good intentions was shaken.[37] However, the Prime Minister also realized that Roosevelt held all the cards, that he was strong enough to define and enforce his interpretation of the issues separating the two.

His reply and Roosevelt's further response reflected this reality of British impotence. The United States was using agreements made to further the common fight, Churchill complained, to "dominate and virtually monopolise traffic not only between our country and yours, but between all other foreign countries and British Dominions besides." Britain could not allow itself to be "run out of the air altogether as a result of your flying start," particularly after the other concessions it had already made in Chicago. "I plead" for a temporary adjournment of the conference to resolve these differences, he wrote, a request which, "if asked for by an intimately-allied power like us, ought not to be denied, nor ought we to be confronted with such very serious contingencies as are set out in your message. . . . It is my earnest hope," he continued, "that you will not bring on this air discussion the prospect of our suffering less generous treatment on Lend-Lease than we had expected from the Quebec discussions." Plaintively he closed by observing, "You will have the greatest navy in the world. You will have, I hope, the greatest air force. You will have the greatest trade. You have all the gold." Given American actions in the previous days, Roosevelt's breezy reply: "We have found ways to help you before and I am confident that we can find ways to help you in overcoming this" could have provided little comfort to the British statesman.[38]

But such skepticism, however understandable, underestimated the strong bureaucratic interests in Washington committed to giving Keynes and his associates a generous package of Phase II aid. Even those most conscious of the need to avoid antagonizing fiscal conservatives in Congress—Crowley, Stimson, Cox, and more grudgingly, Leahy—recognized that it was as much in America's interest as in Britain's for the United Kingdom to regain its economic vitality. Once London imposed the November 29 deadline on its delegation, the pace of the talks quickened and the outstanding issues eventually proved amenable to compromise. The final recommendations to Roosevelt called for the United States to provide $5.5 billion worth of aid in the first year of Phase II, as compared with the initial British request for $7 billion. Keynes and his colleagues successfully resisted all efforts to tie this aid to further concessions in reducing trade barriers or other discriminatory practices but had to accept less than they had hoped for in the removal of restrictions on British exports. Publicly, it was announced that no change in policy would occur before V-E Day. Privately, however, the Americans assured Keynes that the United States would, by "administrative arrangements," allow substantial export freedom after January 1, 1945. Moreover, lend-lease deliveries would no longer include certain categories of goods, including metals, minerals, chemicals, and manufactured civilian supplies, so that the British could legally export similar products. Roosevelt for political reasons insisted there be no formal agreement, as this would make it easier for him when renewal of the lend-lease act and then specific lend-lease appropriations came before Congress. Keynes readily admitted there were "sophistries and obscurities" in this sort of method, but added, "We must hope we shall be as safe with moral obligations which have been created as we should be with a formal agreement."[39]

Keynes, in fact, removed as he was from many of the pressures which Roosevelt was bringing to bear on Churchill, returned to London quite sanguine about the results of the Phase II talks. "I never had reason to doubt the basic friendliness, the intention to help and the genuine frankness of advice of all the American officials with whom I was in touch," Keynes reported. Only in the provision forbidding Britain total export freedom before V-E Day was he disappointed, and even of this he could write, "I affirm with emphasis that there is no ground for supposing any desire or policy on the part of the three departments with which we were dealing to hamper our export trade." On the contrary, he added, "they are as conscious as we are that our recovery of trade is the only way out and is almost as necessary to the solution of their problems as of ours."[40] In Whitehall one ranking official hopefully observed, "There seems a good chance that whatever happens now we are successfully clear of the old . . . [restrictive] arrangements."[41]

Ultimately, the British failed to secure the anticipated benefits of these agreements. Roosevelt's refusal to give the arrangements the status of a formal accord made their fulfillment dependent upon the continuation of American good will, the administration's willingness to interpret the lend-lease act loosely, and the Pacific war lasting more than a few months. As it happened, Congress soon amended the lend-lease act to preclude any postwar rehabilitation, and following Roosevelt's death, the new President, highly sensitive to congressional desires, refused to circumvent the intent of the amendment, carefully scrutinizing British requests for items which might serve some other purpose than the speedy annihilation of Japanese soldiers. Tokyo's unexpected surrender then deprived Great Britain of its last opportunity to draw upon American lend-lease bounty.[42] As a consequence, another program upon which London felt it had a firm commitment from the United States would remain unimplemented.

American participants in the Washington talks bear some responsibility for this subsequent breakdown of the agreement, but one may fairly wonder whether British hopes for $7 billion in aid, unencumbered by conditions of any sort, did not indicate a fundamental misreading of the American mood, thereby complicating the negotiations and making their eventual failure more likely. At the conclusion of the discussions with Keynes, the FEA issued a press release assuring Americans that the principle that no articles received under lend-lease would be exported commercially remained unchanged.[43] Yet the British had been given exactly opposite pledges. This blatant distortion of the conditions agreed to by administration officials only succeeded in restricting Washington's ability to fulfill its promises to the British. Still, in all fairness, those who opposed Keynes' requests most resolutely during the Phase II negotiations were in a very difficult spot. Keynes himself would later admit that the obstructionism which he encountered in Washington arose not from American unfriendliness but from fears of raising hostile criticism in Congress.[44] Crowley, for instance, worried that undue liberality in providing Great Britain with postwar assistance might jeopardize other administration programs—renewal of the lend-lease act, enlargement of the lending powers of the Export-Import Bank, the ultimate settlement of lend-lease accounts—which would undoubtedly benefit the British.[45] Keynes' quip regarding the FEA's sensitivity to public opinion—that Crowley's ear was so near the ground that he was out of range of persons speaking from an erect position[46]—appears rather uncharitable in light of the concerns troubling the American. Nor does it accurately reflect the Englishman's pleasure with the terms of the agreement. If the final arrangements did not fully meet London's initial expectations, they nonetheless represented a remarkably generous settlement.

In an important sense, of course, the unpleasantries which dotted Anglo-American relations in the last part of November simply demonstrated just how close the two nations had become. The more intimate the connections between countries, the more numerous the points where friction may develop. Thus, ill feelings arising from the Phase II talks or from American efforts to erect a common Anglo-American front toward Argentina were made possible only because ties between the two were so close in the first place. Certainly Washington would not have attempted such a policy of parallelism toward Buenos Aires with the Soviets. The fact that the British did not insist upon a written, formal Phase II agreement similarly illustrates the nature of the relationship. Roosevelt's word alone was felt to constitute sufficient bond, despite recent disappointments. Certainly it is illustrative to see that Washington decision makers were nearly unanimous in their readiness to extend the concept of American national interest to Britain's postwar economic well-being. Keynes, it appears, was not overstating the case when he explained that the decisive factor in bringing the Phase II talks to a successful conclusion lay in "the ever increasing and ever deepening conviction in the minds of all responsible Americans that a strong Britain after the war is a vital, indeed an indispensable, requirement of American policy. . . . It has become an unspoken premise," he continued

> which, whatever the momentary, superficial reasons to the contrary, cannot be questioned. Further acquaintance with Russia does not increase intimacy or confidence. The illusion of China has faded. Central Europe is a dreaded cavern of misery and chaos. The Governments of Western Europe are wished well but are doubtful quantities. The little Latin nephews are all very well but not what Uncle hoped. There is nothing to be found reliable or homely in the habitable globe outside Britain and the British Commonwealth. This, today, is America's deepest, least alterable conviction.[47]

This assessment would receive a thorough testing much sooner than anyone anticipated or wished. Like the Quebec accords, the Phase II agreements resulted more in a short-lived euphoria than in lasting accomplishments. Whitehall was, for the most part, pleased with the results, but American coercion in the linking of the Argentine and aviation matters to the financial discussions left many British officials troubled. So, too, did Roosevelt's apparent attempts to back out of the Quebec understandings, and the knowledge that the unofficial status of the Phase II arrangements made possible a similar move. In Washington, at least some administration figures were beginning to wonder if the British had not become rather too presumptuous, making demands which were certain to create future difficulties between the two nations. The Argentine and civil aviation issues, for instance, had finally been postponed rather than really resolved, so the potential existed that these questions would again surface to cloud relations between London and Washington. Before that could happen, however, a new crisis in Anglo-American ties erupted in another area. And this dispute, unlike the earlier ones, quickly spilled over into the public arena, engulfing the policy makers of the two allies in a virtual tidal wave of acrimony and public pique.

6

Transatlantic Cacophony

In the waning days of November 1944, as Lord Keynes and his British associates prepared for the return voyage to England, the American people lost the services of one of the most beloved men ever to head the Department of State. Enfeebled by illness and worn down by the humiliating frustrations of continually being bypassed in the formulation and execution of policy, Cordell Hull, after nearly twelve years as his country's chief diplomat, relinquished his post to withdraw from the rigors of public life. Hull's resignation was soon followed by a White House announcement that his successor would be Edward R. Stettinius, Jr., former chairman of the board of U. S. Steel, more recently Lend-Lease Administrator, and currently Hull's Under Secretary. The British, although eulogizing the departing Secretary, could not have been sorry to hear of his retirement, for they often found trying his sermonizing about the merits of free trade and his tendency to equate American desires with divinely-inspired purposes. The appointment of Stettinius as his replacement, Halifax wired London, indicated Roosevelt's intention to remain his own Secretary of State and would have the effect of increasing the influence of Harry Hopkins, who had largely succeeded in regaining his old position as the President's chief confidant. The friendly attitude which Stettinius had displayed during the recent Phase II talks now took on an added significance.[1]

Within days of assuming his new duties Stettinius confronted another crisis in Anglo-American relations. This time the controversy focused on Italy and the degree to which the occupying powers should attempt to control the internal affairs of that unhappy nation. On November 26, the Bonomi government in Rome collapsed, and the British quickly let it be known that they would not endorse any new government in which Count Carlo Sforza served as either prime minister or foreign secretary. Churchill entertained a strong personal antipathy toward Sforza, believing the Italian had broken a solemn pledge he had once given the British Prime Minister. In addition, London's representative in Rome was reporting that Sforza's intrigues were behind much of the current political unrest.[2] Although some American officials in Italy agreed with this assessment of Sforza's role, influential circles in the United States saw the count as a valiant antifascist and accused Churchill of blocking Sforza's appointment solely because of the latter's antimonarchical beliefs.[3] By the time Stettinius had moved into the Secretary's suite, public dissatisfaction with what was viewed as undue British interference in Italian internal affairs was becoming increasingly difficult to ignore. London's action had touched off "widespread critical comment in press and radio," the Secretary cabled Winant on November 30.[4]

Were the Italian situation an isolated case, the public clamor would probably not have been so pronounced. British actions in Italy, however, were mounted upon a background of seemingly similar circumstances in Greece and Belgium. In Greece the German retreat had brought with it the revival of traditional antagonisms within the Greek body politic. These hatreds had remained suspended in uneasy equilibrium for a short while but by early December, when the coalition government fell apart, armed clashes between government-backed forces and their opponents, primarily of the Left, threatened to engulf Athens and the surrounding countryside in civil anarchy. At Quebec earlier in the fall Roosevelt and Churchill had agreed that a small British contingent should occupy Athens once the Germans moved out, so

London found itself the heir of this explosive situation and the allied representative responsible for the maintenance of order. British soldiers were soon drawn into the strife as active participants, employing their superior organization and weaponry against the leftist forces in support of a Greek government widely acknowledged as unrepresentative and insensitive to the needs of a large majority of the population. In Belgium, bloodshed had thus far been avoided, but here, too, British military authorities had become caught up in an internal contest for postwar political advantage. As in Greece, one of the hotly debated questions in Belgium concerned the future of the monarchy.

Americans knew few of the facts involved in either situation. From across the Atlantic it was impossible to determine whether London was using military exigencies to protect its imperial interests and defend the institution of monarchy, or whether British intervention was indeed necessary to prevent the forceful foisting of undemocratic regimes upon the Greek and Belgium peoples. All they saw was that British troops, quite possibly using American lend-lease weapons, were coercing Belgiums and gunning down Greeks who until recently had been gallantly resisting the German foe. British actions in Greece, radio commentator Raymond Gram Swing informed his audience on December 4, were "giving an ugly twist to the word liberation."[5] Moreover, Greece and Belgium, unlike Italy, had been allies. American opinion, therefore, was even more sensitive to any attempt, actual or perceived, to force unwelcome regimes upon the two countries. To many Americans, all three of these cases seemed to underscore the conflict between the ideals of the Atlantic Charter and decadent Old World practices.

London's veto of Sforza, then, came at a particularly awkward time. Moreover, since Italy was a theater of combined operations, the British intervention to some extent also seemed to involve the United States. "Are our liberating armies going to march over Europe putting down popular aspirations for change?" asked the *St. Louis Post-Dispatch*. "The Sforza episode casts a black shadow on the foreign policies of the two leading Western powers," the same paper asserted four days later. "Once again, as in Belgium and in Greece, dangerous Allied interference with the internal affairs of another country frustrates the progress of that very democracy we are supposed to be fighting for." Other papers voiced similar misgivings.[6] By December 4, the State Department, according to one official, was "deluged" with press queries asking whether Washington supported the British veto. H. Freeman Matthews, head of the European desk, urged the new Secretary to rebuke London for its "high-handed and unilateral action" in Italy. "This is a further example of [the] British practice of demanding prior consultation before any action which we propose but in callously refusing to consult us when it doesn't suit their purpose," he angrily wrote Stettinius.[7]

Meanwhile, in response to the incessant questioning of journalists, Homer M. Byington, an aide to Stettinius' special assistant for press relations, worked up a statement disavowing American responsibility for British actions in Italy and presented it to the Secretary for approval. Stettinius' ready endorsement was entirely in character with his conception of the proper nature of American foreign policy. His department would not repeat the mistakes of the past war, among which Wilson's disregard for the nuances of public and congressional opinion loomed large. Now London's *fait accompli* had provoked intense public disquiet, which could not safely go unheeded. Byington's press release, therefore, was good politics. In addition, such a statement promised personal dividends. Although he had been Secretary for less than a week, Stettinius was already under fire for the allegedly reactionary character of his chief appointees. Thus, it was almost inevitable that the new Secretary, an insecure individual somewhat awed by his associates, would attempt to assert himself in these first days, to demonstrate that he was the equal of his Cabinet colleagues and fully capable of defending American interests abroad. The unilateral British action in Italy seemed to offer such an opportunity, to be a good place in which to bolster his stature and prestige without expending much effort.[8]

Consequently, on the morning of December 5, Byington released his statement to the press. "The composition of the Italian Government," it read, "is purely an Italian affair." The United

States had not in any way expressed opposition to the appointment of Sforza, and Washington had reaffirmed to both London and Rome that it expected the Italians to work out their problems "without influence from the outside." Then, in pointed reference to Greece, the statement concluded that "this policy would apply to an even more pronounced degree with regard to governments of the United Nations in their liberated territories."[9]

The British reaction was fierce and instantaneous. Newspapers called the statement "astonishing," "a direct slap." According to the *Manchester Guardian*, seldom had the British Government received "so sharp a snub" as that administered by the State Department. "It is a rude statement and it is meant to be rude," the *Guardian* informed its readers.[10] Churchill fired off to Roosevelt what one White House aide later wrote "may well have been the most violent outburst of rage in all of their historic correspondence." The Prime Minister was already under intense criticism in Parliament and the British press for London's policies with respect to Greece. Churchill thus wrote that he felt "entitled to remind you that on every single occasion in the course of this war I have loyally tried to support any statements to which you were personally committed," even when he did not necessarily agree with them. "I do not remember anything that the State Department has ever said about Russia . . . comparable to this document with which Mr. Stettinius has inaugurated his assumption of office," Churchill snapped. "I am sure such things have never been said by the State Department about Russia even when very harsh communications have been received and harsher deeds done."[11]

The press release's concluding sentence, which implied American censure of Britain's actions in Greece, particularly troubled London. "In Greece the situation is clear enough," retorted the Foreign Office. "Either we support the constitutional Government which till a few days ago contained representatives of all the parties or we yield to mob law." The American statement was "all the more astonishing" when it was remembered how Churchill had supported Roosevelt in his proposals at Quebec for easing Italy's burdens.[12] As a consequence of this loyalty, Churchill emphasized, "I consider we have a right to the President's support in the policy we are following," especially since "our action was fully approved at Quebec" by Roosevelt.[13] (To this the Americans replied that they had agreed that British troops should undertake the liberation of Greece, but that there had been no discussion of the methods which were to be used.) Upset Whitehall officials complained that their actions in Europe were little different from what Washington had repeatedly done in Argentina. How, they asked, did the United States reconcile its demands for nonintervention in the affairs of other states with its refusal to recognize the existing government in Buenos Aires because of its distaste for the men at its head?[14] If officials in Washington felt unable to support British actions, Eden complained, "the least they could have done was to keep silent or to be vaguely noncommital. In my experience this last is a line which American policy seldom has difficulty in finding."[15]

But to ask the Americans to express their disagreement in private missed the whole point of issuing the statement in the first place. It was not so much that Washington objected to British actions in Italy and Greece. Rather, what finally moved the State Department to release its statement to the press were the increasingly sharp editorial comments protesting what was seen as British interference in the internal affairs of the small, newly liberated states of Europe. Columnist Barnet Nover questioned Washington's silence and inactivity and informed his readers that the real reason for London's veto of Sforza lay in the fact that the Italian leader had demonstrated too much independence in the past to suit Downing Street. The issue, Drew Pearson wrote, "boils down to whether the Allies are going to champion kings or republics in Europe under the Atlantic Charter."[16] On the morning of December 5, shortly before seeing Byington, Stettinius thanked Matthews for his note suggesting a reprimand to Great Britain for its unilateral actions in Italy and added, "I will keep this before me and, at the first opportunity, bring it up in conversation with Halifax."[17] Only after learning from Byington later that day the extent to which London had offended American sensibilities did he decide upon a public statement.

Again and again, American officials privately explained that their action did not imply a censure of British policy. Interference was the prerogative of the victorious powers, providing it was discreet enough not to upset Americans accustomed to viewing international relations in simplistic, black-and-white terms. Only shortly before blasting the British for intervening in Italian affairs, the State Department had stipulated its own demands regarding the nature of any government to be formed. There were conditions concerning both the personnel (they were to be "representative") and the policies which the new government was to follow ("friendliness and cooperation" toward the United Nations).[18] Most officials in the Department thought that the British had gone too far by singling out particular individuals for inclusion or exclusion, but this was more a matter of degree than a basic difference over principle. Stettinius' advice to a favorite columnist not to take the December 5 statement too seriously reflects this absence of any fundamental disagreement. So does the response he sent to Senator Kenneth McKellar, who had written to condemn British policy in Greece, Italy, and Belgium. In his reply, the Secretary devoted five and a half single-spaced pages to defending the policy of the United Kingdom, except for the "unfortunate" Sforza affair. More exactly, he exonerated British intentions. There was, he wrote, "no doubt that the British are doing their utmost" to form representative governments in these countries. In short, Stettinius was handed an opportunity to take a strong stand against British "interference" in the affairs of other countries and chose instead to defend London's actions.[19]

Instead, American diplomats felt aggrieved because of the unilateral nature of the British move and the resulting tenuous position in which this left the Department vis-à-vis the public. Had Whitehall consulted with the United States before vetoing Sforza, perhaps a way might have been found to accomplish London's purposes without antagonizing the American people. "The big point I must make in your mind," Stettinius told one British official, "is that it is another case of lack of consultation on your part."[20] To the President Stettinius wrote: "We simply could not understand why the British took the action they did with regard to Sforza without any consultation with us. . . . The basic difficulty in this whole situation is that the British moved without informing us in any quarter in spite of the many points of contact we have and of our joint responsibility in Italy." Because of this combined responsibility, and in light of continuing American silence, the press and the public were drawing the conclusion that the United States backed London's action, a judgment which offended American faith in the right of each people to select its own leaders.[21]

The December 5 statement, however, struck a receptive chord throughout the expanses of America. One columnist characterized it as a "breath of fresh air blowing through a room of stale smoke." Another called it "good, healthy, liberal Americanism." A Michigan paper found the release "a timely and statesmanlike reaffirmation of historic American doctrine," while a St. Louis editor observed that Stettinius could not have assumed his new position in better fashion.[22] James T. Shotwell, the well-known internationalist, wrote Stettinius of his worries about Britain's erecting a new Holy Alliance and praised the Secretary's "splendid" statement, "as wise as it was necessary."[23] In the Senate Tom Connally, chairman of the Foreign Relations Committee, backed Stettinius in his pronouncement and privately complained that British actions in Italy only emphasized London's determination to dominate the European continent. His colleague Hiram Johnson appealed to the Senate to declare America's sympathy for Greece, while in the lower chamber, Representative Emanuel Celler similarly praised the State Department release and labeled British military action in Greece a "horrible spectacle" and a violation of the Atlantic Charter. It was time to "get tough" with Churchill, another congressman told the House.[24] A few commentators did wonder if "shirt-sleeve diplomacy" offered the best means for obtaining results in the midst of coalition warfare (*Time* termed the statement "a bare-knuckle blow" to Britain), but even these protests were objections not to the American policy but to the tactics of publicly rebuking a needed ally.[25] Stettinius, so it seemed, had achieved a substantial triumph, for both American ideals and his own personal stature.

As the days passed, public irritation with Britain failed to abate. If anything, the clamor against what were interpreted as selfish and reactionary British policies rose in intensity. "From this distance, through the haze and blur of Old World political hocus-pocus," reported the *Houston Post*, "the situation has the faint appearance (and odor) of old-fashioned European power politics." British actions in southern Europe constituted "a seven-league stride in the direction of repudiating the Atlantic Charter." "The time has come to speak plainly," editorialized the *Detroit Free Press*. "[G]overnment by foreign bayonet will not do," added the *St. Louis Post-Dispatch*.[26] One opinion survey which Stettinius sent to the President showed that of those dissatisfied with the extent of allied cooperation, 54 percent blamed Britain while only 18 percent held Russia responsible. These figures compared with a 33–44 percent split the previous April. The proportion of people who believed American interests abroad were adequately protected had declined by nearly a fourth since the previous summer, while the percentage of those feeling other nations were taking advantage of the United States had risen by more than 60 percent during the same period.[27]

Angry comment came from all sections of the country and from individuals representing a variety of ideological positions. Columnist David Lawrence complained that the proposed international peacekeeping body was being torn to shreds by political intrigue even before its creation. "Are we about to witness a repetition of what happened after the last war?" a Detroit paper asked. The *Miami Herald's* response was unequivocal: "If we fail this time in establishing a world security organization for a durable peace, Churchill's intransigent imperialism toward liberated countries will be the impediment on which it will crash." The liberal *PM* contrasted Britain's "stakes of power" in Italy with America's "stakes of peace."[28] Even the stodgy *Army and Navy Journal* grumbled that the British and the Russians were "preoccupied with objectives other than the defeat of Germany." Increasingly, demands were heard that the United States withdraw from Europe altogether and finish up the job in the Pacific singlehandedly.[29] In the Senate, debate over British policies in Greece and Italy and

seemingly comparable Russian actions in Poland held up confir-
mation of Stettinius' nominees for the Under Secretary and Assistant Secretary posts. Allen Ellender introduced a resolution
declaring it to be the sense of the Senate that the British were
doing nothing less than promoting disunity among the Allies, and
charged that almost from the day the United States entered the
war, the British had been playing one ally off against the other.
Perhaps most significantly, not one senator rose to defend America's closest friend.[30]

Quite clearly, the scathing denunciations of Great Britain which
filled the American air throughout December represented more
than the rantings of a small minority. Reporting on a trip to the
Far West, an official of the British embassy observed that "this
time *our friends* seem to be angry with us."[31] Polls indicated that
71 percent of the American population believed Britain was actively meddling in the affairs of small European states, and that
of this number nearly three-quarters resented such action. Significantly, substantially fewer people thought Moscow was similarly intervening, and of those who did, a lower percentage objected to Russian policy. The outrage expressed by the American
press led Churchill to make unfavorable comparison with the silence of *Pravda* and *Isvestia*.[32] A *New York Post* columnist remarked, "It is as if all those planets which exert a malign influence
on American-British understandings have come into conjunction."
Another journalist simply wrote, "Everything has gone to hell on
the diplomatic front."[33]

As the indications of rancor and estrangement continued un-
diminished, some American officials became leery of seeming to
collaborate too closely with the British in activities that might
appear questionable to an angry public. Admiral King issued orders that American naval vessels not be used to transport British
troops or equipment to Greece, reversing his earlier approval of
this task. When London protested this action, the American navy
turned over the vessels in question to the British for use under
the Union Jack rather than have it appear that the United States
was in any way involved in the Greek imbroglio.[34] A sharp disagreement between the military chiefs of the two countries over

the distribution of forces in China and Burma further impeded a harmonious partnership in the vital military sphere.[35] Then, at just this moment, the Germans launched a massive counterattack through the Ardennes against the overextended allied lines. Initial enemy successes in the subsequent Battle of the Bulge, coupled with the nasty bickering which enveloped relations between the British and the Americans, made a mockery of the high expectations voiced so recently at Quebec.

Additional revelations aggravated matters still further. Columnist Drew Pearson published the text of a secret State Department telegram containing Churchill's instructions to his military commander in Greece to treat Athens as a "conquered city" rather than an allied capital. Incensed by the embarrassing leak, Whitehall ordered British officials in Italy to cease sharing sensitive messages with the Americans. At a press conference in mid-December, Roosevelt casually admitted that there never had been a formal, signed Atlantic Charter, a disclosure which shook the country and reinforced doubts regarding British intentions in Greece and Italy. A few days later one correspondent was so bold as to suggest to the President that the purposes of the Charter "are slipping away from us." The Protestant weekly *Christian Century* was equally blunt, warning that "another great betrayal is under way."[36] Wherever one looked, the fond hopes of speedy victory and further Anglo-American amity leered derisively at the policy makers in Washington and London.

In the face of these glaring splits in allied unity, State Department officials worried that American disillusionment could have "the most far reaching" consequences.[37] Blighted expectations might endanger the cooperative military effort. An even greater fear was that British actions would lead to a revival of isolationism in the United States and jeopardize the international cooperation which was to undergird the postwar world order. Whitehall officials expressed a similar concern. "The plain fact," warned one of those with the longest experience in dealing with the Americans, "is that the two-thirds interventionist majority in the Senate is a very narrow one, and it w[oul]d be very easy to upset it." Internationalists worried that recent events had given the obstructionists of 1944 far more powerful ammunition than had been possessed by the handful of men who had blocked American participation in the League a generation before. The New York daily *PM* headlined one story: "Isolationist Trend on Upswing Again in the U.S. Senate."[38] Morgenthau cautioned that criticism of the British might "play right into the hands of the isolationists who are only too eager to capitalize on issues of this character."[39]

Such predictions dismayed administration officials. Stettinius, who had never been as upset with the British as his December 5 statement had implied, quickly backed away from his stance of opposition to London. On December 7, the Secretary noted his full agreement with an earlier statement by Churchill pertaining to Greece. Shortly thereafter, Roosevelt sent an extremely friendly message to the Prime Minister on British difficulties in Greece.[40] A number of senators who had earlier questioned London's actions called for allied unity and protested against congressional colleagues "waving a red flag" at the British. Americans must not permit a momentary sense of irritation to overshadow the infinitely more important benefits of partnership, they warned. Quite obviously, Halifax reported to the Foreign Office, Washington would "like to have the Genie back in the bottle" and was "looking with embarrassment for a way to do it without eating" its words.[41]

The British Ambassador then went on to give his assessment of the reasons behind the December 5 rebuke. This was simply another case, he wrote, "of the State Department handling important issues with an impulsiveness and carelessness which gives the impression (in fact a false one) of deliberate unfriendliness."[42] As with so many of his other evaluations, this one by the Ambassador indicated a real understanding of the currents and eddies of Washington officialdom. The initial statement which had touched off the dispute had been hastily drawn up, designed solely to cope with an immediate problem, that of annoying press inquiries, and formulated with little thought to its wider implications. The needs of the moment had won out over long-term Anglo-American relations.

But Halifax missed a crucial point. His analysis ignored any mention of the British actions which had prompted the State Department's press release. Viewing this entire episode only as another indication of American immaturity, British diplomats saw little reason to ask whether their own policies in liberated Europe needed rethinking. Without such a reassessment, however, every likelihood existed that future British measures would again antagonize those very groups in the United States whose support for American participation in an international security organization was absolutely essential if Washington was to play a leading role in postwar affairs. "As I see it," a prominent American progressive wrote that autumn, "most of us know what we don't want: alliances, spheres of influence, imperialism, high tariffs, domination of small powers by great powers, etc. Many of us also know in a general way what we do want: a world organized for peace on internationalist lines, a better world economic order, universal democracy."[43] Almost any American liberal or moderate might have written this statement. Unless Whitehall took sentiment of this sort into account in tailoring its actions, its hopes for a responsible American policy could very easily be defeated.

There should be no reason why Britain and the United States could not work together for the benefit of the whole world, Cherwell wrote Morgenthau at the end of the year. Unfortunately, events in recent weeks had jeopardized such a partnership and, Cherwell noted, "It is easy for a few grains of sand to bring a big machine to a standstill."[44] What Cherwell could not know was that at the very moment he was expressing these hopes to his American friend, the editors of one of the most pro-American journals in all of Britain were preparing an article which would send the current unhappy state of Anglo-American relations into even deeper doldrums.

On the last day but one of 1944, the respected and widely read *Economist* published an analysis of relations with the United States entitled "Noble Negatives." Eloquently and accurately capturing current British frustrations, the article was read and quoted in Whitehall and Foggy Bottom, extensively reprinted and dissected in both the British and the American press, and provoked a further barrage of anti-American and anti-British comment. More importantly, it also prodded many in the United States into thinking more deeply about America's foreign policies, and in a not inconsequential manner, contributed to a new awareness in Washington that great power often necessitated measures which in the recent past would never have been contemplated.

The article opened by noting the current sour relations between the two allies and declared it was time for "some very plain speaking." The only thing new about the present extensive wave of Anglophobia in the United States, it observed, was that some elements in the American government themselves were more eager to "provide ammunition for the malcontents than to correct their wild misstatements." But each "spasm" of anti-British vituperation in the United States only made the ordinary Englishman "one degree more cynical about America's real intentions of active collaboration, and one degree more ready to believe that the only reliable helping hand is in Soviet Russia." Britain should not hesitate to side with the Soviet Union in the game of power politics throughout the European continent when it was to England's advantage. "And, if Americans find this attitude too cynical or suspicious, they should draw the conclusion that they have twisted the lion's tail just once too often."

Current American criticism of Britain, the article continued, was not only unjust, but came from "a source that has done so little to earn the right to postures of superiority." It was rank hypocrisy for the United States to claim that British policy in Europe had killed the Atlantic Charter when both political parties, hoping to secure the electoral vote of New York, were prepared to promise they would "force a wholly Jewish State on the Arab majority" in Palestine. The British desired nothing, after all, "half as dominating and exclusive as the sphere of influence created by the Monroe Doctrine." It was high time, the editors thundered, for Britain to cease sacrificing essential interests "to the dwindling chances of real American co-operation." It was time for an end to Churchill's "policy of appeasement" toward the United States, "with all the humiliations and abasements it has brought in its train." Instead, London's foreign policy should be strictly on a *quid pro quo* basis. "If British policies and precautions are to be traded against American promises, the only safe terms are cash on delivery."[45]

Unqualified approval throughout Great Britain greeted this commentary. Quite clearly, the *Economist* editors had articulated the innermost thoughts of many Englishmen. It was not that differences of policy had developed—this was to be expected. But what the British resented was America's sanctimonious moralizing, coupled with an unwillingness to accept political responsibilities of its own in Europe. "We do not mind being lectured by Americans within reason (since it is an old American custom)," observed the *Yorkshire Post*, "but we want to know how far we can rely on them in the future for the maintenance of peace. . . . They freely tell us what we ought to do. What are they willing to do?" In a similar vein, the *Times* noted that Washington's censures, "untempered by American proposals for constructive action," inevitably led to the belief that the United States was unwilling to accept a leadership role in postwar Europe. Therefore, the British had quite naturally taken steps they had deemed necessary for their own security. The critical need, the *Times* asserted, was for the United States to exert "a bolder and more active . . . lead in world affairs," backed by assurances that Congress and the American public would support such a lead. As long as United States postwar plans remained unclarified, "it would be rash for the European nations to build, either in Europe or elsewhere, a settlement which could be maintained only with the active and continued support of American power."[46]

On the far side of the Atlantic, indignation marked the response of some to this expression of British irritation. The *Washington Post* termed the *Economist* article "intemperate and quarrelsome" and characterized by "exaggerated touchiness," a sensitivity indicative of Britain's weakened position as a military and financial power. A strong nation able to live on its own resources, after all, could be more tolerant of criticism because it was a comparatively free agent in the formulation of its policy.[47] In Congress, Representative Celler observed that the article complained "of our twisting the lion's tail." Now, he asserted, they "make it necessary to pull his whiskers." Why should Americans refrain from criticizing British activities in Europe and India? he asked. "This is Imperialism run riot. We are now bearing the brunt of the fight on the Western Front while Churchill masses British tommies to kill Greek patriots. . . . We are fighting this war to defeat Fascism, and Churchill consistently butters Franco, while Nehru languishes in gaol in India."[48]

Other reaction was more restrained. *PM* applauded the *Economist* and labeled the article "most important, . . . a valid reminder that as a great nation the role we must play in the world must be something greater than that of a mere mud-slinger." The *Wall Street Journal* felt the British criticism timely and justified in asking for clarification of America's policy. Senator J. William Fulbright echoed the *Economist* in assailing America's conduct of foreign affairs as hesitant, timid, and lacking in forthrightness. Until the United States demonstrated more specifically its determination to share in the responsibility of creating a new world order, he noted, "there is good reason for the skepticism of our allies." Republican spokesman John Foster Dulles criticized Washington's "aloofness" in Greece and other areas of Europe as a primary cause of the problems then threatening to overwhelm the allies.[49]

Roosevelt himself indirectly alluded to the article. In a press conference on January 2, 1945, and in his State of the Union message four days later, the President tried to minimize the differences between the two allies. "We have seen already, in areas liberated from the Nazi and the Fascist tyranny, what problems peace will bring . . .," he observed. "The nearer we come to vanquishing our enemies the more we inevitably become conscious of differences among victors." Still, he added, these differences should not be allowed to "divide us and blind us to our more important common and continuing interests in winning the war and building the peace."[50]

Events elsewhere increased this feeling of malaise which engulfed British-American relations as the new year began. In

France, the combined military effort sputtered as the German offensive continued to rip gaping holes in the allied lines before American superiority in men and materials could be brought to bear against the enemy. Portions of the British press questioned Eisenhower's qualifications for leading the final assault on Germany and agitated for the appointment of Montgomery or Alexander or some other British officer to a new post of deputy supreme commander in charge of all ground operations. Other articles criticized the United States for shirking in its mobilization. In a press conference Montgomery, probably unintentionally, employed certain carelessly chosen phrases which carried a patronizing tone toward the Americans and resulted in further recriminations between the two nations.[51] Even the German radio, disguised as BBC, got into the act, belittling the American role in the Battle of the Bulge, in an effort to stir up more dissension.[52]

Events altogether unrelated to the current Anglo-American difficulties came to be seen in light of the rift separating the two countries. Unilateral and heavy-handed Russian actions in Poland, Bulgaria, and Iran deeply troubled officials in both Washington and London, and some worried that differences between the two democracies might have led the Soviets to believe they could employ such tactics with impunity.[53] Others wondered if Roosevelt's action in asking the Senate to return for renegotiation the Anglo-American petroleum agreement signed the previous summer might not further divide the allies. The President had been forced to make this request because of opposition to the pact from powerful oil and congressional groups, but coming at this time, it inevitably seemed to be a further manifestation of the troubled relations between Washington and London.[54]

Thoroughly alarmed by all these developments, informed American opinion gradually turned away from indignant criticism of British actions toward an examination of American policy and of the role which the United States should assume in the postwar world. By the second week in January 1945, demands for a more positive and a more clearly expressed American policy overshadowed angry accusations directed at the United Kingdom. On January 14, the *New York Times Magazine* featured an article by internationalist Senator Joseph H. Ball entitled "There Is No Ivory Tower for Us." In this article Ball, who had recently questioned British actions in Europe, captured much of the introspection which a small but influential segment of the American population underwent for a brief period in these days. Before we castigate Russia and Britain too severely, Ball cautioned, Americans must "look inward. How much of the present situation," he asked, "is due to failure of the United States to formulate a clear and specific policy toward these immediate problems and assume its share of responsibility for carrying out that policy? . . . We have had plenty of statements of American foreign policy objectives," he continued, "all in nice general and harmless terms. We are for international law and order. We are for self-determination for all peoples. We are for no changes in boundaries without the consent of the people involved. We are for a lot of other very fine objectives." There was no controversy over these goals, the senator observed; everyone was for them. The problem, however, was how to achieve these grand hopes, by what means could they best be obtained. "These are the tough questions in foreign policy: the how and what and how far," he wrote. And the United States had not come forth, the senator charged, with any reasonable answers.[55]

Stettinius himself went to the White House and urged Roosevelt to issue a forthright restatement of the country's basic foreign policies. The President's State of the Union message, however, provided little comfort for those on either side of the ocean who sought a clarification or reformulation of United States foreign policy. Roosevelt spoke only in generalities, thereby reinforcing the impression that America had no consistent, well-defined program or plans in international affairs.[56] Four days later, the influential if somewhat pompous Arthur Vandenberg, senior senator from Michigan and ranking minority member on the Foreign Relations Committee, rose to respond to the President's message. Citizens in increasing numbers, Vandenberg intoned, were asking what America was fighting for, but official silence had only "multiplied confusion at home and abroad." Now was the time for "a new rule of honest candor in Washington," for only frankness could dispel the confusion which threatened wartime unity and which hung like a cloud over Dumbarton Oaks. Now was the time to reassert the basic pledges of the Atlantic Charter. "We are standing by our guns with epic heroism," Vandenberg cried. "I know of no reason why we should not stand by our ideals." Most importantly, the administration must come forth with "the earliest possible clarification of our relations" with the British and the Soviets.[57]

Anglo-American differences had arisen in part, it was thought, simply because of faulty communication between the two nations. As a consequence of this belief, various suggestions for the creation of more formal means of consultation were advanced along with the demands for a frank restatement of American policy. Vandenberg in his widely quoted January 10 speech proposed an interim organization to deal with political matters pending their final disposition at the peace conference—in essence, a combined political chiefs of staff. Eden proposed formalized quarterly meetings of the foreign ministers of the three major allies. From other sources came new demands for another meeting of the Big Three.[58]

By the middle of January the passions of indignation and resentment had largely burnt themselves out, both in Britain and the United States. Various segments of the press played a part in this, just as they had in fueling the row in the first place. The *London Daily Mail*, as early as January 5, called for a halt to the bitter denunciations, warning that such actions satisfied no one except the Nazi enemy. The *Sunday Dispatch* reasoned simply that Britain needed its allies and the United States and Russia needed Britain. "That is the bedrock of the situation. Let us all keep it well in mind," it urged.[59] In the United States, Walter Lippmann lent his respected pen to the purpose of reconciliation. Even if no one had all the answers to the troublesome problems of liberated Europe, he wrote, "we can at least be tolerant and charitable and helpful." Wisconsin's Senator Alexander Wiley warned his countrymen it was time to "quit indulging in the folly of ally-baiting" and suggested that both nations "mind their manners."[60]

Yet, one should not simply dismiss the furor of the preceding six weeks as inconsequential. Whitehall policy makers certainly did not. "We should not disguise from ourselves that it was a very near thing," observed one senior Foreign Office official. "[T]he hubbub while it lasted was far more serious than anything, in my experience at any rate, that we have had before." If British-American relations should undergo many more such experiences, he warned, "it *will* become impossible to get anything through the Senate," and London might just as well forget about the United States assuming a responsible role in the postwar world.[61]

Indeed, the angry exchanges did provide a frightening demonstration of just how unstable the public commitment was, particularly in the United States, to close Anglo-American ties. Nor were these discordant tones simply the work of traditional Anglophobes and Americanophobes. The strongest criticisms of British policy came from liberal segments of American society, those who were the warmest advocates of international collaboration. Diplomats in both countries could not help but be alarmed that a simple disagreement over allied policy in an isolated corner of Europe could be magnified to the point where the whole future of American participation in the world security organization envisaged at Dumbarton Oaks was jeopardized. Policy makers in London were not lax in drawing conclusions from this episode for the future conduct of Britain's foreign affairs. "If we want the U.S.A. to be an element of sanity and stability" in the postwar world, cautioned one Whitehall official, Britain would have to pay more attention to the peculiar sensitivities and susceptibilities of American liberals. "If we decide that it's not worth paying that price," he added,

> We sh[oul]d remember that, whether we like it or not, the U.S.A. is coming into the brave new world (there may be a moving back to isolationism but I don't think it will be the old isolationism—it will be an expansionist isolationism of a highly inconvenient character) and that if the U.S.A. is not supporting us it will be a damned nuisance to us—perhaps a fatal nuisance.[62]

American policy makers as well drew lessons from this experience. One would be hard pressed to imagine a more appropriate illustration of the reactive nature of United States policy than Stettinius' December 5 statement rebuking the British for their actions in Italy and Greece. This was unquestionably a case of "instant" American diplomacy, formulated not on the basis of any clearly designed plan, nor even with American long-range interests in mind, but simply as a response to the needs of the moment. Petulance and rancor had been the results. Taken back by the virulence of the exchanges set off by their press release, State Department officials were virtually forced into rethinking some of the fundamentals of America's foreign policy. The old reliance on vague generalizations about "self-determination" and "nonintervention" no longer worked. Criticism of others without a greater willingness to help in maintaining stability in the liberated areas of Europe was no policy at all. Washington statesmen were not always to act on this new realization, but a greater appreciation of the hazards of aloofness and of a refusal to embrace unavoidable responsibilities did at least color thinking in official circles.[63] American diplomats had, in a small but perceptible fashion, inched toward that set of assumptions which two years later gave birth to what came to be called the Truman Doctrine. Thus did the tiny seeds planted in the *Economist's* year-end issue for 1944 bear their fruit.

The public clamor against the British also forced many in Washington to think more deeply about the essential nature of their country's relationship with Great Britain. Out of this came, in spite of the momentary irritation felt by many for what was seen as unilateral British actions endangering the Anglo-American partnership, a greater appreciation of the bonds between the two nations and of the advantages of retaining the close ties which the wartime effort against the common enemy had fostered. Thus, at the very height of the bitterness, Stettinius could inform the President that the difficulties between London and Washington were "more emotional than substantive" and advise that the United States "make allowances" for British sensitivities. "What has impressed me," reported the British consul in Buffalo, "is that practically everyone deplores the situation on the ground that 'we need one another.'" This, he added, was "an immense improvement on former days when there was something like satisfaction in a row with Britain."[64]

Nor did political tensions hamper effective military cooperation. Following the German breakthrough in the Ardennes, Eisenhower transferred command of the United States troops north of the salient to Field Marshal Montgomery. A month later, when the Germans had finally been beaten back, the troops were reintegrated into American command. Behind the lines, Churchill leaned heavily on British journalists not to question Eisenhower's capabilities, and made a special point to correct the prevalent impression that British troops had played the major part in the Ardennes campaign.[65] In the midst of the transoceanic squabbling, Eden was able to tell the Cabinet how satisfactory it was that British and American policy concerning Poland was so closely aligned. Churchill's reaction to the bickering was more curt. The British could not, he remarked, afford to become "rattled over every trashy press article in America."[66]

Thus, by the end of January 1945, an odd lull had settled over Anglo-American relations. Public dissatisfaction and mistrust coexisted uneasily with a heightened appreciation in official circles of the instability of ties which bound the two allies together. Moreover, the events of the past five months, since Churchill and Roosevelt had met at Quebec, had vividly illustrated the different purposes and perspectives which guided policy makers in each of the two nations. Recognition of this fact had sparked new and more pronounced demands for another meeting of the allied leaders.

Unbeknown to the public, another meeting was already in the wind, waiting only for the completion of Roosevelt's fourth inaugural festivities. This time Churchill and FDR were to be joined by the third member of the allied triumvirate, the awesome and mysterious Stalin. As each of the three prepared to embark for this latest rendezvous, Churchill brooded over the state of relations between London and Washington. "This may well be a fateful Conference," he wired Roosevelt, "coming at a moment when the Great Allies are so divided and the shadow of the war lengthens out before us. At the present time I think the end of this war may well prove to be more disappointing than was the last."[67] Not that there was the slightest possibility that Britain and the United States would ever take up arms against each other. But by failing to cooperate, they could easily enough push the world into further turmoil. They might never again be "positively hostile," one advocate of close Anglo-American ties observed, but they could be "negatively stupid." And Providence punishes the latter condition as cruelly as the former.[68] This thought could not have lightened Churchill's dark mood as the indomitable Prime Minister prepared to lead his delegation to the unknown reaches of the Crimea.

7

The Final
Journey

Yalta: the name even today evokes images of a failing Roosevelt, weary from the battles of twelve tumultuous years, and a cunning, grasping Stalin, plotting to seize the spoils of victory and more, and to obtain in addition the dying President's acquiescence in this thievery. For Americans, the conference held at that forbidding spot under conditions of the utmost secrecy has transgressed the bounds of history and entered into the realm of mythology. Skewed by later events and distorted for partisan purposes, America's understanding of the proceedings which took place during those few momentous days has been, at best, partial and imbalanced. Less justifiably, American historians have contributed to this confusion, for until quite recently they have been overly preoccupied with just one aspect of the conference: its role in dividing East and West into bitter cold war antagonism.[1]

One must be careful not to overreact to this bipolar reading of the past. It does, after all, seem indisputable that American officials at Yalta devoted the great bulk of their attention to relations with the Russian colossus, and that they defined the success or failure of the conference by the extent to which Stalin agreed to cooperate with the United States and Great Britain after the war. Matters of a predominantly British-American nature were clearly second-

ary. Yet, to talk about the "hard rock of Anglo-American solidarity," as some scholars have done, or to view the meeting solely
as a tale of incipient East-West conflict, is to impose an order
upon the negotiations which they lacked at the time. Both then
and in later reminiscences, Churchill and the other British officials
present at Yalta bemoaned Roosevelt's unwillingness to hammer
out a common position vis-à-vis the Soviets or even to exchange
views with his British allies.[2]

From the start, Churchill approached this conference with a
certain trepidation. Neither he nor Roosevelt was enthusiastic
about the Crimea as the site for the tripartite meeting, but Stalin
steadfastly refused all enticements to venture abroad. Eventually,
the desire on the part of Roosevelt and Churchill to meet once
again with the Soviet Premier overrode their reservations about
the location, although Churchill grumbled, "We could not have
found a worse place for a meeting if we had spent ten years on
research." He quickly added, however, that he just might survive
the journey by bringing along an adequate supply of whisky.[3]
More disturbing to the peppery Englishman was Roosevelt's insistence that he could not leave the United States to attend a
summit until after his inauguration in late January. This delay,
Churchill feared, might provide the Red Army with sufficient time
to sweep westward and devour huge chunks of eastern Europe.
Stalin's negotiating position would as a consequence be one of
unassailable strength, rendering the Russians that much less willing
to meet legitimate western requests with reasonable compromises.

This preoccupation with the Soviet presence in eastern Europe
helps explain the gradual shift in Churchill's ideas concerning
France and its future role in European affairs. By the first of the
year the Prime Minister had turned his back on his earlier arguments and embraced Eden's concept of a strong grouping of western European states closely knit to Great Britain and headed by
a rejuvenated France. Such a combination might provide the British an extra margin of security, whether the antagonist be Russia
or a German nation bent on revenge. Continued uncertainty about
the future intentions of the United States only increased the appeal
of this proposal. Shortly before departing for Yalta, Sir Alexander

Cadogan, the Foreign Office's permanent undersecretary, observed that Roosevelt still appeared "determined not to get 'entangled' in Europe—which means leaving all the 'headaches' to
us, with the President securely and comfortably ensconced in the
pulpit." If the British could count on nothing but moralizing from
the United States, a revitalized France seemed more and more an
essential ingredient of British security.[4]

London, then, increasingly came to be the spokesman for the
admission of France to the ranks of the Great Powers, just as
Washington throughout much of the war similarly backed China.
In the months preceding the Yalta meeting, Whitehall lobbied
energetically for French equality with the "Big Three" in the proposed world security organization. British officials pushed equally
hard for French rearmament, for the restoration of France's colonies, and for an occupation zone and a voice for France in the
control of Germany. Churchill pressed Roosevelt to invite Charles
de Gaulle, the imperious French leader, to the forthcoming
summit.

But their entreaties failed to elicit much sympathy in Washington. Only in the matter of French equality in the contemplated
peacekeeping body were the Americans receptive. As for the other
requests, Roosevelt, moved by a deep antipathy to de Gaulle and
perhaps by suspicions that Churchill sought to restore French
strength and prestige as part of a program to revive the discredited
European balance of power, proved singularly unhelpful. Having
de Gaulle at Yalta, the President wired Churchill, would "merely
introduce a complicating and undesirable factor."[5] Foreign Office
officials protested without effect. This American opposition to a
restored France, they worried, coupled with the prospect of
United States troops being withdrawn from Europe as quickly as
possible, would "upset the balance between Eastern and Western
Europe to Russia's advantage." With Soviet forces of occupation
up to or west of the Elbe, "with 4 Slav satellites (Poland, Czech-
oslovakia, Yugoslavia and Bulgaria) as an advance guard pointing
westward and southwards," and with no American or French forces
to act as a restraining barrier, "the Russians would have the ball
at their feet." "The future of Europe for some time to come,"

senior foreign affairs experts warned Eden, "may therefore turn on the treatment of France at the present conference."[6]

Troubled London officials found the American reluctance to effect any sort of understanding with the British prior to meeting the Soviets equally worrisome. Churchill's hopes of having Roosevelt stop in England on the way to Yalta eventually met with a polite but firm refusal. Eden, sensing that the President would oppose his wishes for a tête-à-tête with Stettinius, pressed for a meeting of the three foreign secretaries in the days before the Yalta conclave, just as the Moscow conference had preceded the Teheran summit. Roosevelt, however, refused to entrust his Secretary of State with such an important mission and even directed that the exchange of information with the British be kept to a minimum. He did not, he explained, want to go into the conference with his hands tied by an official agenda. Although FDR cabled Churchill several times that he could not spare Stettinius from Washington before Yalta, the persistent Prime Minister refused to give up, noting finally that the time was too short to arrange a meeting of the three secretaries but pleading that Stettinius at least meet with Eden for forty-eight hours on the British redoubt of Malta. His argument was unanswerable. "I do not see any other way of realising our hopes about world organisation in five or six days," he wired. "Even the Almighty took seven."[7] Roosevelt relented enough to permit Stettinius to accompany the Joint Chiefs of Staff, who had already agreed to consult with their British colleagues at Malta, in order for the two secretaries to confer.

Roosevelt for his part saw few advantages and substantial drawbacks in working too closely with the British before meeting Stalin. He was most anxious not to give the Soviets any reason for suspecting the existence of an Anglo-American bloc, a combination which they could perceive only as directed against themselves. Instead, he hoped to assume a more neutral position between Russia and Britain, to help foster a more stable relationship between the two rivals and thereby to lessen the need for the "power politics scramble" which the State Department warned him was rending Europe. In the President's scheme of things, Russian touchiness concerning an Anglo-American entente was deemed of more importance than the establishment of closer partnership with London.[8] Although Churchill hotly ridiculed this reasoning, in truth Roosevelt's analysis of the matter contained much wisdom.

Other considerations also influenced administration officials to deny that a basis existed for any preconference understanding with London. Recent reports from the Far East had warned that the British, in attempting to reestablish their colonial position, were undercutting American policy in China, and told of "bitterness and antagonism" between personnel of the two countries stationed in the Southeast Asia Command, friction "sufficiently serious to be a factor in Anglo-American relations."[9] In an area of more immediate concern, Stettinius had recently informed Roosevelt that London was "still not playing fair with us" in Argentine matters. In addition, various elements within the administration were urging the President to take a firm stand with Churchill at Yalta about the necessity for Britain to reduce its imperial trade barriers.[10] Most importantly, London was not in a position to meet the two major United States needs at Yalta: a firm commitment from the Soviets as to the timing and extent of their participation in the Pacific war, and Russian approval of American plans for the establishment of the United Nations. The British were not really involved in the first of these matters, and the Foreign Office had already indicated British support for the State Department's program for the world security body.

Although the unpleasantries of the preceding months probably had little influence on Roosevelt's determination to steer a neutral course between his two wartime partners, those clashes did serve to place two issues on the loose Yalta agenda. Almost from the moment of Stettinius' abrasive press statement on December 5, Foreign Office officials had set out to arrange some method to improve communications between Washington and London in order to avoid further such occurrences. Gradually this desire for closer consultation had evolved into a proposal for quarterly meetings of the foreign ministers of the three major allies, and by the first of the year the Foreign Office was firmly committed to gaining acceptance of this idea at the forthcoming conference.

The turmoil in Anglo-American relations in December and January also led the State Department to press for the adoption at Yalta of what came to be known as the Declaration on Liberated Europe. As early as January 6, Stettinius, in warning the President of the widespread public disapproval for what was seen as overt interference by Britain and Russia in the internal politics of the smaller continental countries, had called for a new statement on liberated Europe from the White House. Six days later, while discussing the proposed tripartite meeting with a group of senators, Roosevelt indicated that he hoped to reach some agreement to prevent future occurrences such as the recent unilateral actions by Russia and Britain in Poland, Greece, and the Balkans. He specifically mentioned his desire to obtain Churchill's and Stalin's signatures on a reiteration of the Atlantic Charter principles recently being questioned. To Harold Laski, Britain's well-known political theorist and governmental gadfly, the President wrote that he hoped at Yalta to "put things on a somewhat higher level than they have been for the past two or three months."[11]

Meanwhile, in the State Department John Hickerson, who until the end of December had headed the Division of British Commonwealth Affairs, had outlined plans for a Provisional Security Council for Europe to tide matters over until the proposed international organization could be established. This council was to supervise the newly liberated countries to avoid a repetition of the Greek and Polish situations. Only in this way, he reasoned, could the rest of Europe be rescued from "the diplomacy of the jungle."[12] The genesis for this first draft of what eventually evolved into the Declaration on Liberated Europe lay in Hickerson's experience as the State Department official most directly concerned with the British interventions in Greece and Italy. Although the declaration was later applied by the Americans and the British exclusively against Soviet actions in eastern Europe, it was in its inception directed equally at Britain and Russia.[13]

Americans, then, in the weeks before the conference, continued to believe that global stability and their own nation's security depended more upon the establishment of a vigorous international peacekeeping organization than on any exclusive understanding with Great Britain. Still, Roosevelt may have reasoned, a pacified Churchill would be a more congenial companion in the days ahead than a stubborn Englishman with ruffled sensibilities and a resentful disposition. The President thus turned, as he had so many times before, to Harry Hopkins, dispatching his loyal lieutenant to London in an attempt, as a Hopkins aide was recorded, "to promote a more amiable mood prior to the gathering at Yalta." Hopkins spent three days in brutally frank conversations with Churchill, finding the Prime Minister "volcanic" in his remarks on what he considered his shabby treatment by the Americans in recent months. The presidential emissary listened patiently to the fumings of the British statesman and evidently succeeded in allaying some of the Prime Minister's more extreme worries, but he also found Churchill wobbling in his earlier support of the American position on the voting procedures in the proposed United Nations Security Council, news which produced tremors of apprehension in the American delegation then proceeding toward Yalta.[14]

On Jaunary 29, 1945, the military chieftains of Great Britain and the United States converged on Malta, where they were soon joined by Eden and Stettinius and their aides. The Malta conference was largely a military meeting, and its impact on Anglo-American relations must be judged primarily by the success or failure of the talks held by the Combined Chiefs. Here the impression conveyed by the official minutes is misleading, for their bland recordings mask what was one of the more violent military disagreements of the entire war. The point of contention was the strategy to be followed in the final assault on Germany. Underlying this dispute was an almost undisguised British lack of faith in Eisenhower's judgment and fitness to lead such a mighty undertaking. The British Chiefs, who at Quebec the previous September had approved Eisenhower's plans for a broad frontal advance, now sought to scuttle this strategy and pushed instead for a lightning single thrust by Montgomery's Twenty-First Army Group across the Rhine and deep into northern Germany. Ultimately, the American preponderance of power in France forced the British to give way in this dispute, but they did so only with obvious reluctance.[15]

Fortunately for all the participants, agreement proved easier to reach on other matters. The Combined Chiefs reviewed strategy in the Mediterranean and the Pacific and decided upon subsequent allied moves in these theaters. The British, aided by the arguments and political clout of Harry Hopkins, succeeded in securing from the American military a commitment that United States authorities would leave some shipping in the Atlantic after V-E Day to meet the needs of the civilian populations of Britain and Europe, rather than transfer it all to the Pacific. Another long-running difficulty was finally cleared up with an understanding on access rights and control over the North Sea ports of Bremen and Bremerhaven, a dispute which had impeded the signing of the tripartite agreement on German occupation zones ever since it had been thought this issue had been settled at Quebec five months earlier.

While the Combined Chiefs discussed military strategy, Eden and Stettinius conferred on political matters which were likely to be brought up at Yalta. Perhaps to Eden's surprise, the two foreign secretaries found many similarities in their plans and expectations for the summit talks. On the critical question concerning how to approach negotiations with the Soviets, however, they diverged sharply. Eden was acutely conscious that Britain had little to offer the Russians but that London desired a great deal from them. At one point he proposed that he and Stettinius draw up a list of items on which they wanted Soviet agreement and another list of the concessions they were prepared to make. In the Far East, for instance, the Russians would enter the war regardless of what Britain and the United States gave them, if this were deemed in their interests, so there was no need to offer Moscow much for its participation in the Pacific fighting. If the western allies were prepared to meet Russian territorial demands in the Far East, they should see to it that Britain and America obtained a good return from Moscow. The United States was placing too great an emphasis on the world security body, Eden warned. Unless the Russians could be persuaded to act decently in places such as Poland, an international organization would not be worth much. This being the case, Eden continued, Stettinius should shoulder more of the argument at Yalta on behalf of the Poles.[16]

Churchill joined the two foreign secretaries in some of their talks and on the first such occasion lost no time in letting Stettinius know (in "pungent English," the American later recalled) of his continuing anger over the December 5 press statement on Italy.[17] The Prime Minister also complained about what he deemed Washington's casualness toward the Polish question and its implications for Big Three unity. He struck Stettinius as being severely depressed, at one point observing that there was more suffering at that very moment than at any previous time in history and adding that as he looked out into the world, he saw little but sorrow and bloodshed. Everything, he stressed to the somewhat alarmed Secretary of State, depended on Britain and the United States remaining in close harmony at all times.[18]

On February 2, Roosevelt steamed into Valletta harbor aboard the U.S.S. *Quincy*. That evening he and Churchill met in the President's cabin to review the report prepared by the Combined Chiefs of the discussions which had been held during the previous three days. Churchill, never one to let an opportunity slip by, again spoke of his forebodings about the future and pressed on Roosevelt a refrain which was increasingly to be heard from the Prime Minister: the need for Anglo-American forces to advance as far into Europe as possible before the German surrender. It would be undesirable, he told the President, for the Russians to occupy any more of Western Europe than was unavoidable. Roosevelt merely laughed at these fears and in general showed no inclination for the coordination of policy which the British so ardently desired.[19] Eden's anxiety was evident. They were going into a decisive conference, he complained to Hopkins, "and had so far neither agreed what we would discuss nor how to handle matters with a Bear who would certainly know his mind."[20]

Just as had the acrimony of the preceding months, the consultations at Malta between the two nations emphasized the fragile nature of the Anglo-American partnership. With Hitler's ignominious downfall in sight at long last, the military talks should have been an occasion for self-congratulatory celebration. Instead, they were rancorous and divisive. The political discussions held by the civilian leaders of the two countries were somewhat smoother, but they had also warned the apprehensive British that, when relations with the Russians were involved, officials in London could not always expect the support from the Americans to which they believed they were entitled. Some members of the President's party, on the other hand, worried whether Churchill's heightened distrust of the Soviet Union might not undermine the Big Power unity they desired so ardently for the postwar world. Speeding through the night on the long flight from Malta to Yalta, each delegation had much upon which to ponder.

Eden had been prophetic; the Bear unquestionably did know his mind at Yalta. Stalin showed himself a tough and resourceful negotiator. Yet at the same time, he proved to be a not ungenial host. More importantly, he quite frequently displayed a reasonableness and a flexibility which won the gratitude of his British and American guests. There were harsh words and flaring tempers, to be sure. But the predominant impression which the Soviet Premier left with his negotiating partners was one of accommodation and friendliness. Following his return to London, Cadogan reported to Halifax that Stalin was "more genial and more reasonable than I have ever seen him." The impressive Russian military successes, instead of going to his head, "seemed to have given him the added assurance enabling him to take broad views and to be unafraid of making concessions."[21] Another Foreign Office bureaucrat who was at Yalta wrote that the main impression which he and his colleagues took from the Crimea was "the outstanding friendliness of our Russian Allies and . . . the obvious sincerity of their desire to do us well and their wish to be on good relations with us and to co-operate with us after the war."[22] Churchill and Eden both expressed these same sentiments, as did nearly all of the Americans present at the conference.[23] Prospects for the future seemed considerably brighter as a result of the meeting.

In contrast, Roosevelt deeply disappointed the British during the conference, while the Americans felt equally disgruntled at

Churchill's demeanor. Several members of the Prime Minister's delegation were shocked at the President's appearance and feared for his physical and mental health. Churchill's personal physician gave him only a few more months of life. Roosevelt struck Eden as "vague and loose and ineffective." Cadogan wrote Halifax, "I got the impression that most of the time he really hardly knew what it was all about."[24] Churchill complained that Roosevelt no longer took an intelligent interest in affairs. "The President is behaving very badly," he told a close associate. Stettinius, on the other hand, reported that Churchill had aged and grown "more eccentric" during the past year. The British statesman, the Secretary confided upon his return, "was very erratic at Yalta" and appeared "to be going through some sort of a menopause" throughout the conference.[25]

British unhappiness with Roosevelt may reveal less about the President's actions than about the inability of London officials to recognize that American interests did not automatically coincide with their own concerns. On many of the important issues before the three statesmen the Americans adopted an independent, often even an opposing, stand to that which the British thought in the best interests not only of the United Kingdom but of all western civilization. On the crucial issue of restoring France to a position of equality with the Big Three, for instance, the Americans proved to be little more understanding than were the Soviets. Roosevelt acquiesced in Churchill's desire to give the French an occupation zone in Germany but up until the very end of the conference obstinately refused to consider allowing them a seat on the control council which was to supervise the occupation. Eden pressed for French membership on the committee which was to examine the question of German reparations, but the Americans made no effort to support his request.

In matters concerning Germany the United States offered little more help. Stalin early in the conference proposed that a definite decision to dismember the German state be taken so that planning for Germany's future could advance, and in this he received the backing of the President. The British, however, resisted committing themselves irrevocably and sought to substitute some more innocuous term for the word *dismember*. But when Roosevelt refused to lend him any support, Churchill eventually felt he had no other choice than to agree to the principle of dismemberment. On the issue of reparations, the Cabinet had advised Churchill that it wanted no precise figure mentioned in any document, even as a basis for discussion. Roosevelt initially supported the British in this matter, but on the last full day of the conference, the President broke with the Prime Minister and agreed to set a figure of $20 billion "as a basis for discussion."[26] In each of these instances, British officials rather too easily assumed that their positions were best not only for Great Britain, but for the United States as well. American diplomats found such thinking presumptuous or self-serving.

This whole matter of the stance which the United States adopted on issues pitting the British against the Russians greatly irritated Churchill and his Foreign Office colleagues throughout the conference. One senior member of the Churchill government later remembered, "It was two to one against us" throughout much of the meeting. Because of this, "[w]e had to agree to many things we oughtn't to have agreed to."[27] Stettinius has noted that Roosevelt often assumed the role of arbiter or conciliator between the British Prime Minister and the Russian Premier, and that this seemed to dismay the British. "That the President should deal with Churchill and Stalin as if they were people of equal standing in American eyes shocked Churchill profoundly," one participant and close associate of the Prime Minister recalled afterward. Such was the case, for instance, when questions concerning Yugoslavia arose. Nor did the British receive the support they expected from the Americans on the important issue of the composition of a reorganized Polish government. At one point Roosevelt tried to argue that the differences separating the Anglo-Americans and the Soviets on Poland were largely a matter of the use of words. "He was deluding himself" was Eden's acerbic response.[28]

The Foreign Secretary has written that Roosevelt was convinced that he could get more favorable results by dealing directly with Stalin himself than by the three countries negotiating together. FDR was "always anxious to make it plain to Stalin that the United

States was not 'ganging up' with Britain against Russia," Eden adds.[29] Perhaps as a consequence of this desire, Roosevelt when meeting alone with the Soviet Premier on the opening day of the conference went out of his way, according to Hopkins, to inform Stalin of Anglo-American differences over France and the German occupation zones. The British were "a peculiar people" who wanted to "have their cake and eat it too," FDR confided to his Russian host. At times the President seemed almost to be creating a Soviet-American entente against British colonialism. One afternoon during a tête-à-tête with Stalin, Roosevelt informed the dictator of his hopes that Churchill could be persuaded to give Hongkong back to the Chinese at the end of the war and added that he had no desire to invite the British to participate in a trusteeship in Korea. The Russian leader, obviously taken back by this, demurred, saying this would unnecessarily offend Churchill.[30]

Roosevelt's frequently voiced sympathy for colonial peoples led Churchill to fear that the American proposals concerning trusteeships were simply a ploy to dismantle the Empire. When Stettinius at one point suggested that the permanent members of the Security Council consult in order to devise machinery for dealing with territorial trusteeships and dependent areas, the Prime Minister "exploded." Even after he was reassured that the plan applied only to former enemy territory and that the British Empire would remain unaffected, Churchill continued to mutter, "Never, never, never."[31] When Roosevelt informed him that he was flying to Cairo from Yalta to meet with the kings of Egypt, Saudi Arabia, and Ethiopia, Churchill worried that this entailed some plot to undermine the British Empire in those areas.[32]

More significantly, Roosevelt and Stalin excluded the Prime Minister from any role in negotiating the territorial gains which were to accrue to Russia upon its entrance into the Pacific war. The President, no doubt, believed that in matters relating to the fight against Japan, the British military effort had not been sufficiently substantial to merit a voice in the deliberations. Churchill does not appear to have protested his debarment and affixed his signature to the agreement, despite advice to the contrary from the Foreign Office. To do otherwise, he reasoned, would result in the loss of all British influence in Far Eastern affairs.[33]

In other areas as well, British and American policy diverged. For a time Churchill threatened to support the Soviet suggestions on the voting formula in the Security Council in preference to the position so exhaustingly worked out by the State Department. It was Churchill's staunch backing of the Soviet request for membership for two of the Russian republics in the proposed world security organization which finally led Roosevelt to acquiesce in this, even though he realized such an agreement would create political difficulties with Congress and the American public. The Prime Minister also resisted the President's desire to hold a preparatory meeting of the new world body in the near future. Not to be outdone, Roosevelt chose this moment to urge the British to reopen talks on reducing Empire trade preferences, thereby reminding the two delegations of the controversies which still divided them on international financial questions. According to Alan Brooke, the military authorities of the two countries had difficulties of their own coordinating their approaches to the Russians. Even the President's decision to leave Yalta caused consternation in the British camp. By rushing the deliberations, Churchill feared, the Americans would be forfeiting a rare opportunity to resolve all important differences with the Soviets.[34]

Still, there were times, many of them, when the delegations of the two Atlantic democracies walked hand in hand. In spite of a difference in emphasis between Americans and Britons, the important issue of reorganizing the Polish government found both working toward the same objective and in clear-cut opposition to the Soviets. It was this question which raised passions highest during the conference, and over which all three countries agonized the longest. So the fact that Britain and the United States were in essential agreement on the basic goals to be pursued in this matter is not inconsequential. Similarly, the two formed a united front against the Russians over Iran. And in a move which elated the British, Roosevelt near the end of the conference agreed to drop his opposition to seating France on the German control commission. Stalin then immediately added his consent.

The two matters which derived most directly from the Anglo-American bickering of the preceding weeks also found the two nations—indeed, all three—adopting a common position. Eden's desire for periodic meetings of the foreign secretaries was accepted without dissent. The State Department, in the meantime, had advanced a proposal for a provisional commission and an accompanying declaration of the principles which were to guide the major allies in their supervision of affairs in the newly liberated states of Europe. These two documents had evolved from John Hickerson's earlier proposals which British actions in Greece and Italy had led him to draw up. Although the British proved receptive to the idea of the regulatory body, Roosevelt decided during the ocean voyage across the Atlantic that he did not care to create another commission. Like his Secretary of State, the President was not nearly as concerned with British and Russian "interference" in the internal affairs of the small European countries as with the American public's indignant reaction to their actions. Thus, the declaration of principles, which repeated, sometimes word for word, the Atlantic Charter pledges concerning the right of all peoples to choose their own government, was more to his liking. Not only would it reassure the American public that only noble motives were to govern the allies in their supervision of the territories freed from the Nazis, but, equally appealing, it was worded so loosely as to provide him with the maximum freedom of action he found so preferable to ironclad commitments.[35]

The British for their part, once the Americans clearly specified that the declaration did not apply to the Empire, saw no reason to oppose the President's wishes in this matter. Nor did the Soviets, and what became known as the Declaration on Liberated Europe was accepted by the three delegations with a minimum of debate, or for that matter, with little real interest. Cadogan observed that he doubted anyone could be found who would be able to say exactly what the three were agreeing to. Still, he added, the Declaration was to be welcomed, "if only for the fact that it must to some extent get the U.S. off the side-lines and involve them [sic] in some share of responsibility for settling European difficulties."[36]

But if the Foreign Office questioned the applicability of this pious declaration to actual conditions in Europe, public opinion in the two western democracies proved noticeably less discerning. The *New York Times* hailed this new affirmation of the Atlantic Charter as perhaps the most important of all the agreements reached at Yalta. The *Baltimore Sun* wrote that fears of a reversion to power politics could now be discarded. Across the ocean British papers applauded the allied concord which they saw this statement representing and hammered home the theme that if Big Power unity could be maintained, peace would be assured. The American newsweekly *Time* was less equivocal. "All doubts about the Big Three's ability to cooperate, in peace as well as war," it asserted, "seemed now to have been swept away." Opinion polls indicated that public satisfaction throughout the United States with cooperation among the three major powers had increased to a high of 71 per cent in the weeks after the conclusion of the conference, as compared with a figure of 46 percent in January.[37]

In Whitehall, officials looked out upon the world following their return to London with considerably more optimism.[38] Relations with the Russians, while far from being close, at least appeared to be on firmer and more friendly ground. American aloofness had certainly been a disquieting factor in the tripartite deliberations, but part of the explanation behind the disappointment occasioned by American actions at Yalta arose simply from unrealistic hopes that relations between the two would be so much more intimate. Given the lowered apprehensions about Soviet intentions, the instances when the United States did act more as an obstruction than a partner took on a less menacing air, so that on the whole, London felt that an advance in Anglo-American relations had also been achieved. Certainly the plane of the public exchanges between the two countries had been raised considerably from the depths of the previous few months, as the bickering so prevalent in December and January failed to resurface. The way appeared clear for increased and more solid understandings among the three capitals.

Yet, within weeks, the whole edifice of Big Power unity lay in shambles. Actions viewed by London and Washington as Soviet intransigence in implementing the Yalta agreements on Poland created renewed fears about the value of Russian promises. Soviet demands on Rumania called into question Moscow's devotion to the Yalta Declaration on Liberated Europe so recently signed. Military cooperation disintegrated as the Russians denied British and American bombers access to airfields near Budapest and barred officials of the two western nations from prisoner-of-war camps in eastern Europe. Moscow announced that Foreign Minister Vyacheslav Molotov would be unable to attend the United Nations meeting in San Francisco and accused London and Washington of negotiating a separate peace with Germany. Russian demands on Turkey, it was feared, presaged a new campaign of Soviet aggression in that region of the world. Barely a month after exulting over the successes achieved at Yalta, Eden was forced to admit that British foreign policy "seems a sad wreck."[39]

Churchill's reawakened fears of Russian might evoked some sympathy but few concrete actions in a United States less alarmed by Moscow's new incivility and more disposed to allow events to play themselves out before making final judgments. The British Prime Minister pressed Eisenhower to deploy his forces as much with the Soviets in mind as with the Germans. Britain and the United States, he wrote Roosevelt, "should join hands with the Russian armies as far to the east as possible, and, if circumstances allow, enter Berlin."[40] The Americans, however, farther from the scene and not nearly so exposed to Russian power, were less willing to permit considerations of this nature to dictate military strategy and refused to countermand Eisenhower's instructions. In similar fashion, Churchill throughout March urged upon Roosevelt the wisdom of a joint note of protest to Stalin over affairs in Poland. Again, the President held back, agreeing on such a message only after weeks of delay.[41] During a Cabinet meeting on March 16, Roosevelt half-seriously remarked that the British were perfectly willing to have the United States go to war with Russia and that following Churchill's advice would lead to precisely that end.[42]

The month of March saw other indications of Anglo-American differences and a general unwillingness on the part of Washington officialdom to be drawn too closely to the British. Churchill complained that the President was violating recent promises concerning an American aviation agreement with Ireland and requested FDR's intervention to block the proposed pact. Roosevelt refused.[43] On the return voyage from Yalta, the President talked as much of problems with the British as with the Russians. The traditions of British imperialism, he told an aide at one point, were playing too large a part in Churchill's thinking and would probably lead to further friction between London and Washington.[44] From Africa in the following weeks came reports of British authorities blocking American planes from landing in certain cities. The State Department passed to the White House rumors suggesting that the Prime Minister, in an effort to undercut the Americans in the strategic Horn of Africa, had deliberately misrepresented Roosevelt's position in talks with the Ethiopian Emperor.[45] General Douglas MacArthur grumbled about complications created by the British fleet in the Pacific and suggested that if it were action that the British wanted, then suitable employment might be found for them where they could obtain a taste of the Japanese kamikazes.[46] In Washington, State Department officials compared the British to a "beggar who threatened to stop coming to the house unless he were better treated."[47]

Given the continuing decline in the levels of Russian cooperation with the western allies, poor relations between London and Washington took more and more the appearance of a costly luxury. Seeking to halt this deteriorating spirit of accommodation which again threatened ties between Britain and America, Roosevelt in mid-March asked Bernard Baruch to travel to London to attempt to place matters with the British on a more even keel. Baruch had made a career of advising American Presidents (though not with as much impact as he claimed) and, moreover, was a close friend of Churchill's. Still, FDR could have chosen a more sympathetic envoy, for Baruch had made no secret of his belief that the British were seeking to persuade the United States to do things for them which they should be doing for themselves. As to what he should discuss with the Prime Minister, Baruch could elicit no detailed instructions from Roosevelt, except that the President did want him to tell Churchill that it would be a "grand gesture" if the British restored Hongkong to China.[48] The startled Baruch could not help wondering how the introduction of this topic was going to soothe relations between the two countries!

Events, however, outdistanced Baruch and the entire world on April 12, 1945. That afternoon, sitting in a Georgia cottage having his portrait painted, Franklin Roosevelt complained of a headache and slumped to the floor. He was not to rise again. The moment moved men to tears. Even the prosaic Leahy could not resist recording in his diary the despair around him. "The Captain of the Team is gone, and we are all at loose ends and confused. . . ."[49]

Churchill would later recall that the news of the President's death struck him like a physical blow.[50] In spite of the many frustrations and disappointments in working with the American leader, the Prime Minister had always known that in Roosevelt, the British had a friend. It had been Roosevelt who in the darkest days of 1940 had remained constant; and it was Roosevelt who had promised to see Great Britain through the bleak days still to come. Alongside this, the momentary irritations paled into insignificance.

Over all of Britain people mourned his passing as if Roosevelt had been one of their own. Memorial services were held throughout the Commonwealth. The court went into seven days of mourning, a mark of respect paid only to royalty and a very select outside circle. In a moving eulogy for his departed colleague, Churchill's eloquence soared to new heights. In Franklin Roosevelt, he told Parliament, "there died the greatest American friend we have ever known, and the greatest champion of freedom who has ever brought help and comfort from the New World to the Old." The *Daily Telegraph* wrote that he would "be remembered with Abraham Lincoln as a leader who set and kept his country on the path of true greatness with a steadiness of purpose and grandeur of vision unsurpassed in [the] records of mankind." The *Telegraph* then captured the essence of the British sense of loss:

> His passing leaves a gap in all our hearts and in the counsels of the Allies which it will be hard to fill. This country, in particular, owes him a debt which can never be repaid for his understanding, help

and confidence in its darkest hours. When we had few confident friends he was an unremitting and undespairing one. That's why we venture to share with peculiar poignancy in the sorrow of the American people.[51]

Mixed with sadness over Roosevelt's passing was a sense of uneasiness about the future. Many Britishers had always feared, despite myriad American assertions to the contrary, that once the war was won, the United States would again retreat behind its ocean barriers and leave the rest of the world to make do as best it could. With Roosevelt, they felt that Americans had a President who would keep their nation pointing toward Europe, but about his successor they were not so certain. Once the first shock of the terrible news had passed, this foreboding again resurfaced. Thus, the *Economist* could note, "'An indissoluble part of the whole scheme of things' has gone, and one is left wondering what is going to happen now."[52]

8

Change in Command

Harry S. Truman, unlike his predecessor, was not an imposing figure. When he first took office, people even had difficulty in remembering to stand when he entered the room. He was, *Time* observed, "a man of distant limitations,"[1] an evaluation which his own self-deprecating nature did nothing to alter in the early days of his presidency. A failed haberdasher, a small-time politician unexpectedly elevated to the rarified atmosphere of the United States Senate because of his loyalty to a tainted political machine, a hard-working but uncontroversial legislator overshadowed by more flamboyant colleagues: little in this background indicated Truman would be anything more than a caretaker President until the American electorate could select a new Chief Executive three and a half years hence. Only in his widely acclaimed chairmanship of the Senate Committee to Investigate the National Defense Program was there any hint that the new resident of the White House might possess another, more forceful side. The prevailing impression of Truman as he prepared to step into the gaping void left by Roosevelt's death was not one which inspired high hopes. At the time of his nomination as Vice President, a member of the British embassy had described him as "something of [a] light weight." During the subsequent presidential campaign a senior

Whitehall official had written, "The prospect of Senator Truman as heir apparent is not a happy one."[2]

Shortly after the burial services at Hyde Park, Hopkins paid a call on Halifax and reported that Roosevelt's death had created "a completely new situation" in which the British would be "starting from scratch." The embassy in Washington wired London that FDR's White House staff, including the valued Hopkins, would soon all be gone, succeeded by men "of simpler outlook and more homespun texture." The *Economist* voiced the fear that the replacement of the Roosevelt-Hopkins team with a group of less assured and seasoned men would cause American foreign policy to become more nationalistic. It could not resist adding that nothing in Truman's record or character stood out as different from the average.[3]

Press correspondents speculated that Truman would be less inclined to follow London's advice or to work closely with the British. The new President, most thought, was likely to prove more conservative than FDR on issues such as postwar loans and commitments, more the sharp trader, more inclined to follow the path of caution. It was common knowledge that on several occasions he had said privately that the United States invariably gave away more than it received in its dealings with other countries.[4] At the least, embassy officials warned, American policies would no longer be characterized by the same "vast purposes and energetic drive" provided by Roosevelt. "[W]e are likely to witness missed opportunities and neglected acts," these diplomats predicted, not because Truman would deliberately seek to change the policies of his predecessor, but because the new administration "lacks men and ideas large enough to cope with the exacting demands of the time."[5] This assessment of the new American President was nearly universal among informed British observers in the immediate aftermath of Roosevelt's death. "One can only hope that the dignity of his new office will reveal in him hitherto unsuspected qualities which will render him equal to his enormous responsibilities," observed one Whitehall official. "At the same time it would be foolish for us to overlook the possibility that the United States may be riven by chaotic controversies or that at best its contribution to international reconstruction may be as a result stultified."[6]

But much to their pleasure, the British soon found many of their worst forebodings unjustified. "The new President may not be a commanding figure but his feet are firmly planted upon the ground," Halifax informed London on the day after FDR's death. Truman was "a man of solid sense, wholly Rooseveltian views on international affairs, considerable courage and guts and, above all, eminently educable," Halifax continued. "His attitude on international questions is, from our point of view, impeccable." Equally promising, his popularity in the Senate might mean that crucial legislation would be passed more easily than anything introduced by his distrusted predecessor.[7] Eden, in Washington in preparation for the San Francisco conference of the world security organization, reported to Churchill that Truman had made "a good impression" in a meeting between the President and the Foreign Secretary. "He is conscious of but not overwhelmed by his new responsibilities. His references to you could not have been warmer. I believe we shall have in him a loyal collaborator, and I am much heartened by this first conversation."[8] Another Foreign Office official, after his introduction to the President, came away equally impressed. Truman was, he reported, "a commonsense, alert, friendly man who may turn out to be something better than the jog and trot machine created Missouri politician which is all that the more skeptical will admit him to be." Halifax wrote that Roosevelt's death was not a great catastrophe, for FDR had been a failing man and the world could little stand a repetition of Woodrow Wilson's illness and loss of control after the previous war.[9]

These early days of his presidency also saw Truman forming an impression of the British which would shape his future policies. The new President inherited from his predecessor a mixed set of attitudes and policies toward Great Britain. On the one hand, the demands of coalition warfare had drawn the two nations into closer and more frequent contact than at any time since the American colonists had broken away from the Mother Country 170 years earlier. This contact, buttressed by a common language and similar traditions from the past and goals for the future, had fostered a partnership, a camaraderie between the two unlike the bonds that had ever tied allies together before. Indications of this could be constantly seen in the easy, informal manner which characterized relations between officials of each country as they worked on the numerous joint committees and combined boards, in the degree to which each foreign office attempted to coordinate its policies with those of the other in countless matters far removed from the theaters of combat, in the very expectation that such prior consultation and coordination should and would take place. But undoubtedly the clearest acknowledgment of this special affinity between the two nations and their peoples was the lavish pledges Roosevelt had given Churchill at the Octagon conference of extensive assistance to Great Britain in the gigantic task of rebuilding its economy after the war. If further negotiating later in the autumn trimmed back some of FDR's generosity, the fact remained that the Phase II accords reached in November 1944 represented an unparalleled commitment by one nation to the economic well-being of a second, totally sovereign state.

Unfortunately, a less happy side to the pattern of Anglo-American relations also confronted Truman as he reviewed the record of the past. For every instance of collaboration and teamwork, there seemed an episode marred by friction and bitterness. Whitehall's refusal throughout 1944 to follow the American lead in matters concerning Argentina certainly belied the idea that Britain and the United States were locked in a unique partnership. Nor did constant reports of British obstructionism and intransigence in the Middle East or Southeast Asia indicate the existence of any sort of a special relationship, nor London's stubborn refusal to admit the merits of a postwar international economy based on the principles of multilateralism and the free flow of goods and currency. Great Britain's continuing commitment to colonialism could not help but offend Americans dedicated to the concepts of self-government and the free ballot, and Churchill still persisted in his determination that the Atlantic Charter would have no applicability to the empire. Similarly, his seeming inability to free his thinking of old discredited ideas about power politics and the European balance of power, as evidenced during the recent strife in Italy and Greece and the dangerous hostility toward the Soviets which at times obsessed him, made the British leader a serious impediment to the successful establishment of a lasting peace as envisioned by the Americans. As the clamor of anti-British vituperation which had enveloped the country earlier in the year had forcefully demonstrated, the American people were themselves far from convinced that Washington's wisest course necessarily lay in the maintenance of close ties with Great Britain.

Certainly no Anglophobe himself, the new Chief Executive came from the section of the country least inclined to seek particularly close ties with the British, and Truman's own attitudes could not have avoided being influenced by the suspicions of his neighbors. Moreover, Truman had few personal or intellectual connections with that segment of the American population most anxious for closer Anglo-American relations, the liberal Eastern establishment. Nor could he, always keenly attuned to the public temper, have escaped drawing lessons from the anti-British feeling which had surged through the country a few months previously.

This initial disposition to avoid becoming too closely entangled with the United Kingdom received reinforcement when, on his first full day in office, he studied brief reports from the State Department on relations with the major nations around the world. The summary on Great Britain warned the new President that Churchill had recently been showing an increasing apprehension of the Soviet Union and was inclined to press the Russians on the Yalta agreements on eastern Europe with "unnecessary rigidity as to detail." The other point which this report emphasized was the British consciousness of their decline from the pinnacle of power to a position of junior partner among the major allies, and their consequent desire to buttress their position vis-à-vis both the United States and the Soviet Union by closer ties with the nations of western Europe and the Commonwealth.[10] Although Truman could not realize it at the time, these two issues—fear of Russia and British sensitivity to their reduced status—were in one way or another to dominate virtually all aspects of Anglo-American diplomacy in the coming months and years.

Respected advisers from outside the State Department also counseled caution in relations with London. Hopkins, perhaps more aware of Roosevelt's ambivalence toward the British than any other individual on either side of the ocean, left his hospital bed to be at the new President's side in the confusing first weeks. Stimson instructed Marshall to make sure that Truman was informed of past differences between Washington and London.[11] Joseph E. Davies was a frequent White House visitor and added his voice to those urging Truman not to allow Stalin to think the Americans were becoming too cozy with the British. The officious Baruch, freshly returned from his trip to England, warned the President that British officials were gripped with a pessimism about their economic future which was robbing them of their self-reliance and "threatened to leave them clinging upon us for existence." The United States must resolutely resist British pleas for special consideration, Baruch insisted.[12] All these advisers warned Truman of British balance-of-power machinations in Europe and of Churchill's obvious desire to enlist American might in the creation of a solid bloc opposing the Russians. Truman readily accepted their assessment of the world situation. The need, he came to feel, was "to get Churchill in a frame of mind to forget the old power politics and get a United Nations organization to work."[13]

In the meantime, Churchill had not been idle. Sensing inexperience at the helm of the American ship of state, the Prime Minister, within hours of hearing of Roosevelt's death, moved to seize the initiative in the Anglo-American approach to Russia. "It is important to strike the note of our unity of outlook and of action at the earliest moment," he cabled the new President. This could best be done, he advised, by the two governments issuing a joint public statement on difficulties with the Soviets over Poland. In a related matter, Churchill urged repeatedly in the days that followed that political as well as military considerations be taken into account in the determination of Anglo-American troop movements in Europe. Western armies should be the ones to liberate Berlin, he counseled, and Prague and Trieste. American forces should be kept on the farthest advanced lines they had reached, and should not be withdrawn into the agreed upon oc- cupation zones until the Russians proved more amenable in other areas. On May 12, Churchill wrote of an "iron curtain" separating east and west Europe.[14] The British leader maintained that he sought lasting friendship with the Russian people, but added, "I am sure this can only be founded upon their recognition of Anglo- American strength."[15] In a White House meeting ten days after Truman's sudden elevation to the presidency, Eden forcefully argued that in the past there had been a tendency to show excessive concern about not appearing to be ganging up against Russia. Now, however, with conditions as they were, it was easy to ex- aggerate this danger and, in fact, a demonstration of Anglo-Amer- ican solidarity might even produce better results in dealing with Moscow.[16]

Truman, angered by what he saw as blatant Soviet violations of the pledges so recently made at Yalta, was not immune to these arguments, but he hesitated in breaking openly with a Soviet ally still needed in both Europe and the Far East. Moreover, his mil- itary advisers, interested in as speedy a redeployment to the Pacific as possible, resisted having American forces entangled in what were essentially political questions concerning the postwar make- up of Europe. "The single objective," General Marshall had in- structed Eisenhower, "should be quick and complete victory."[17] Other considerations also played a part in the President's refusal to follow Churchill's desires. The American public would never understand or support such a move. Then, too, Leahy pointed out, the United States and the United Kingdom had a combined total of ninety divisions in Europe. How much bargaining power would these have, he asked, against a Soviet force three times that size?[18] When informed of Washington's decision to withdraw its troops to the designated zones of occupation, Churchill could only reply, "Obviously we are obliged to conform to your decision." But he could not resist adding: "I sincerely hope that your action will in the long run make for a lasting peace in Europe."[19]

Still, deteriorating relations with the Soviet Union oversha- dowed what were, after all, essentially differences over the proper tactics which should guide both British and American policy vis-à-vis Russia. Difficulties in implementing the Yalta accords on Poland were a particular source of worry to Washington officials in April and May, and in this matter Britain and the United States, if not entirely agreeing on nuance or timing, worked exceptionally closely in trying to prod the Soviets into adopting what western officials considered a more reasonable position. Foreign affairs experts from the two countries met often and at great length in these weeks searching for a way out of the Polish impasse. To an important extent, issues of a specifically Anglo-American nature were submerged before the more important task of finding a new basis, now that military necessity had largely been removed, on which to conduct relations with the Soviet Union. Truman, and Washington officialdom in general, were becoming accustomed to thinking of Anglo-American unity vis-à-vis the Russians.[20] Averell Harriman, the influential United States Ambassador in Moscow, recommended the patching of all quarrels with the British and the French in order to present a united front to the Soviets. OSS head William Donovan urged upon Truman even before the German surrender the need to create a "West-European-American power system" to serve as a counterweight to Russia.[21] Halifax informed Truman that he and Stettinius kept no secrets from one another and had a "complete brotherly understanding on all matters," implying that the President might care to establish a similar relationship with Churchill.[22] Though Truman shied away from such intimate bonds with the United Kingdom, he unquestionably felt a sense of partnership with the British which had no parallel in his thoughts about the Russians. The different tones of the victory messages which he dispatched to London and Moscow upon the Nazi surrender are illustrative. His wire to Churchill concluded with the words "With warm affection, we hail our comrades-in-arms across the Atlantic." No such personal touch of cordiality was to be found in the cable he sent to Stalin.[23]

A crisis in the Balkans shortly after Truman's succession underscores the differing perceptions of its two allies which Washington officialdom was coming to hold. Venezia Giulia, lying at the northern tip of the Adriatic on the borders of Italy and Yugoslavia, had long been the object of bitter rivalry between its two neighbors. As German control of the province disintegrated in the early spring of 1945, the region became the focus of renewed competition between Yugoslav partisans fighting under the command of Josip Tito and Anglo-American forces assigned to Field Marshal Alexander. Tito's intentions were obvious and straightforward; he sought to use the confusion following the German withdrawal to incorporate Venezia Giulia, with its key port city of Trieste, into Yugoslavia. The motives of his opponents were slightly more complex. Churchill, who took the lead in this matter, ostensibly sought to insure that unilateral Yugoslav action not prejudice the province's ultimate fate, which was to be determined at the postwar peace conference. At times the Prime Minister also used the necessity of maintaining secure supply lines to the British occupation zone in Austria as a justification for his actions. More fundamentally, however, Churchill's concern for the fate of Venezia Giulia stemmed directly from his worries about his Soviet ally. The Tito government was merely a "Muscovite tentacle," he informed Alexander in early May. "If the Western Allies cannot now resist land-grabbing and other encroachments by Tito, . . . this may well breed a danger far greater than we now face at the head of the Adriatic." Moreover, resistance to Yugoslav demands would win Italian favor, "and it would be a good thing to have a settled Government in Italy which was united to the two western democracies."[24]

Accordingly, Churchill sought to have Alexander seize as much of the disputed territory as possible, even to the extent of using force against the Yugoslavs. In this he received the enthusiastic support of the American State Department, and especially of Acting Secretary Joseph Grew. (Stettinius was attending the organizational meeting of the new world peacekeeping body in San Francisco throughout this crisis.) Grew informed the new President that Moscow was "undoubtedly" behind Tito's actions and hoped to use Trieste as a Russian port in the future. Truman, although he had earlier advised Churchill that he did not intend to become involved in Balkan political questions, momentarily allowed this information to sway him and replied that the only solution was to clear Trieste of the Yugoslavs. On May 12, he cabled Churchill that "I have come to the conclusion that we must decide now whether we should uphold the fundamental principles of territorial settlement by orderly process against force, intimidation or blackmail, . . . tactics which are all too reminiscent of those of Hitler and Japan." Britain and the United States must be prepared to consider any necessary steps to effect Tito's withdrawal. "We have had enough of being pushed around," the President told Eden two days later. An elated Churchill termed Truman's message a "most robust and encouraging telegram" and wired the President in reply, "I agree with every word you say."[25]

The Prime Minister's pleasure was short-lived. Truman's May 12 cable had hardly been dispatched before Stimson and Marshall cautioned the President that any confrontation in Europe would slow the transfer of forces to the Pacific. Both military leaders argued that a showdown with Russia was premature and urged their impetuous chief to explore diplomatic channels further before resorting to force. Upon reflection, Truman probably also realized that he would be hard pressed to explain any confrontation in the Balkans to the American people. Consequently, on the 14th he sent a second message to London, this time backing off from his advanced position of May 12. Two days later he explicitly told the Prime Minister, "I am unable and unwilling to involve this country in a war with the Yugoslavs unless they should attack us."[26]

With this the crisis rapidly deescalated. Although Truman allowed the deployment of additional troops to reinforce Alexander, his primary effort consisted of a plea to Stalin for aid in convincing the obstinate Yugoslav to withdraw his forces. Although the Soviet Premier publicly supported Belgrade's claims to the entire region, it appears likely that behind the scenes he pressured Tito into accepting Anglo-American terms, for the Yugoslav leader adopted a more conciliatory tone almost at once. Within a matter of days, Tito had accepted Alexander's supremacy in the contested area and the crisis was over.[27]

Largely forgotten by historians preoccupied with weightier events, this episode nicely illustrates several facets of the Anglo-

American relationship in the spring of 1945. First of all, and most importantly, the two nations found themselves closely linked in opposing what each saw as reprehensible behavior on the part of the third great ally, Soviet Russia. As with Poland, the contest for Venezia Giulia highlighted the increasingly obvious fact that in matters concerning relations with the Soviet Union, the interests of the two Atlantic democracies were in close harmony. But they were not identical, and the May crisis also demonstrated that if the United States and the United Kingdom often shared objectives, their divergent perspectives just as frequently led them to advocate differing tactics or policies. While the British were fairly consistent in espousing a forceful stance against the Yugoslavs (declining even to allow Tito a face-saving retreat[28]), Truman wavered, ultimately deciding against a military showdown. London found this decision a bitter one, the shared objectives of the two nations notwithstanding. Finally, the manner in which the crisis was finally resolved underscored a further aspect of the London-Washington relationship. When differences of opinion did occur, it was the British, not the Americans, who were usually forced to give way. Try as they might, policy makers in Whitehall were seldom able to circumvent the disparity in the raw strength and power of the two countries, a strength which was translated into American diplomatic advantage time and again. Cordiality there was between officials of the two nations—indeed, it was a cordiality of an unprecedented degree—but it was not a partnership between equals.

Other actions by the Truman administration reminded Churchill that this relative congeniality was not a marketable commodity in dealing with the new leadership in Washington. Particularly in the critical area of lend-lease aid, chagrined London officials discovered that declining amity between Washington and Moscow was no guarantee of closer Anglo-American ties. In spite of the Churchill government's belief that it had a firm commitment from the Americans on Phase II assistance, complaints increased in the latter part of April and throughout May that United States authorities were not as forthcoming in providing lend-lease as the British had been led to believe they would be. Though accusations of this sort had also been lodged in the last weeks before Roosevelt's death, their quantity and significance rose dramatically only after the new President took office, giving the impression that the root explanation for what took on the appearance of a massive repudiation of earlier agreements lay with the new occupant in the White House.

Such an assessment was only partially correct. Earlier in the year Congress, acting strictly in accordance with repeated administration pledges, had amended the lend-lease law to preclude any postwar rehabilitation. Vice President Truman, presiding over the Senate, had cast the vote which broke a 39-39 tie to defeat an amendment which would have prevented even the sale of lend-lease supplies to foreign governments for postwar relief and reconstruction. A mere two days later, with this expression of congressional opposition to any postwar role for lend-lease clearly in mind, Truman had succeeded to the nation's highest office. Realizing the magnitude of the tasks before him, and conscious of the problems with hostile Congresses which had bedeviled his predecessor, Truman immediately made it known that he wished to work in close partnership with the legislative branch. To disregard the quite obvious congressional sentiments as to postwar employment of lend-lease would make such a collaboration infinitely more difficult to effect. Domestic shortages of beef, falsely attributed to excessive American lend-lease shipments overseas, and the continued circulation of stories alleging British misuse of lend-lease also contributed to an atmosphere in which the public and the Congress were not disposed to be overly lavish in furnishing postwar assistance.

The death of Roosevelt did result in personnel changes which had an important bearing on the allocating of further aid. Morgenthau, Stettinius, and Hopkins, all strongly committed to helping the British, were soon eased out of positions of trust and influence in the new administration, to be replaced by others more attuned to the public mood and less inclined to be generous or to look for ways in which to help the British. Director of the

Budget Harold Smith warned Truman of an "isolationist spirit" in Congress which would attack any unfounded lend-lease requests. Bernard Baruch was another key figure who advised the President that London should do more to assist itself. "No one need think that by giving too much and weakening ourselves that we can help the rest of the world," he had earlier written. Following his return from Britain in mid-April, Baruch counseled Truman, "Our greatest single weapon in the peacemaking lies in the wise exercise of the priority power allocating our resources."[29] This two-pronged concern for America's domestic economy as well as its world position also shaped Leo Crowley's thinking on further lend-lease assistance—at one point he specifically spoke of the President's "present collection of 'blue chips'" in dealing with nations needing postwar assistance.[30] The FEA director had spent much of the first months of 1945 defending lend-lease before dubious Capitol Hill committees. This often grueling experience had left no doubt in his mind regarding congressional sentiments, which nicely complemented his own economic conservatism. As a result, Crowley, who assumed a key role in advising the President in these matters, spoke more and more of a "business-like manner" when talking of the way lend-lease should be administered.[31]

Such advice met with Truman's hearty endorsement. In a conference with Smith on April 26, he told his Budget Director that any attempt to use lend-lease for postwar rehabilitation would leave the administration open to "a lot of trouble." While discussing the amount of lend-lease to be requested in the coming year's budget, the President demonstrated an interest not in what requirements or commitments existed, but solely in how much he could "safely send up to the Congress." Moreover, the State Department informed him that the British gold and dollar position was considerably brighter than had been anticipated at the time of the Phase II talks the previous autumn. Here then was another justification for restraint in the dispensation of postwar aid.[32] In all likelihood, however, Truman's own experiences in the Senate and back home in Missouri would have led him to adopt similar caution anyway.

Recognizing a new mood in the White House, Crowley during the second half of April reduced the levels of both munitions and nonmunitions that were slated for shipment to Great Britain. By May, only one-sixth of the military supplies programmed for the year had been sent to the British. Then, following the German capitulation on May 8, Truman directed the appropriate agencies to cut back the volume of goods being shipped to all lend-lease recipients still further. In the absence of any pressures for less precipitous action, such an order appeared both logical and politically prudent, and in fact seemed entirely routine.[33] At the same time the army repossessed most of the material scheduled for transport to British forces in Europe. From Washington, British officials reported that a "wave of economy" was sweeping the United States. "De facto and de jure," the embassy cabled London, "we are where we were before the Keynes discussions" the previous fall. Henry Morgenthau, himself a key figure in those talks, was more direct. Truman, he lamented, was "welching" on the earlier agreement.[34]

Normally, one might expect the Department of State to attempt to block this apparent breach of faith on the part of the United States. In actuality, however, the foreign affairs experts in Washington were remarkably ineffectual in presenting the case for a more faithful fulfillment of the aid agreement. Stettinius, never highly regarded in the Truman White House anyway, was by April completely immersed in preparations for the impending United Nations conference in San Francisco. Although lend-lease had been his personal bailiwick earlier in the war, the critical task of guiding the creation of a powerful international security organization drove all lesser concerns from his focus. Instead, lower echelon officers in the Department, led by Dean Acheson and William Clayton, moved to combat these demands for further cutbacks. But in the face of reassurances from Crowley and the War Department that the Phase II figures had been accepted only for planning purposes and in no way constituted a commitment, their efforts met with little success. Acheson and Clayton next enlisted the help of Acting Secretary Grew. In a statement released to the press on May 14, Grew reminded the nation that until

Japan surrendered, America and its allies were still at war. That being the case, Britain and the other nations participating in the Pacific fighting would continue to qualify for lend-lease assistance.[35]

Statements such as this, however, had virtually no effect, and British officials increasingly worried that all their well-laid plans for postwar reconversion were about to be overturned in the face of this wholesale repudiation of the carefully negotiated Phase II program. After lower level appeals had proved fruitless, Churchill himself entered the controversy, cabling Truman on May 28 that "the machine has come to a standstill" and asking the President for reaffirmation that the principles agreed upon at Quebec the previous September were still in effect.[36]

Acheson, Clayton, and Fred Vinson, the newly appointed head of the Office of War Mobilization and Reconversion, immediately set out to secure Truman's consent to the circulation of such a statement throughout the bureaucracy but again ran up against opposition from the military authorities. "Neither the Lend-Lease policy nor the Lend-Lease Act permit supporting [the] British economy," officials in the War Department wrote in reply. The Joint Chiefs of Staff "can recognize no commitments except those relating to war against Japan." If the administration decided that assistance was to be given in support of the postwar British economy, Stimson added, the War Department would have to go back to Congress to request additional funds.[37] This, of course, was precisely what Truman desired to avoid. As a consequence, he decided to do nothing at the moment, but to wait until he could talk to Churchill in person at the new summit meeting which was then being planned. In the interim, the Joint Chiefs informed their British colleagues on the Combined Chiefs of Staff that since Roosevelt had never formally approved the Phase II agreements, they had no legal authority to provide lend-lease materials of any sort except for direct use against Japan. The once surging torrent of assistance had slowed to a trickle.

Even this relative trickle bothered some. Leahy grumbled: "It is very apparent to me that a number of individuals in the Government are desirous of disbursing great sums of lend-lease money on projects that have no bearing whatever on the prosecution of the war." At one meeting he walked out in disgust at the less dogmatic views of Vinson and other administration figures.[38] In Crowley, however, he found a kindred soul, and when the FEA head sought his assistance in securing a positive directive from the President prohibiting lend-lease for any purpose other than prosecution of the war, Leahy was able to use his personal ties with Truman to obtain a statement which satisfied all of Crowley's requirements. On July 5, the White House directed that, "in order to follow accurately the letter and spirit of the Lend-Lease Act," lend-lease aid should be limited "to that which is to be used in the war against Japan, and it will not be issued for any other purpose."[39] With this as a guide, the War Department then proceeded to prohibit all maintenance and military supplies for British occupation troops in Europe, even though these forces made possible American redeployment to the Pacific. The President's directive, Stimson noted in his understated manner, could be construed by the British as reversing previous commitments entered into by the United States.[40] Apoplectic officials in London would hardly have disagreed.

One can only guess what actions Roosevelt might have taken in this matter had he lived. There can be no question but that congressional and public sentiment clearly opposed the employment of lend-lease in the postwar period, and particularly for the purpose of rebuilding the devastated British economy. Perhaps Roosevelt would not have felt as bound by these unequivocal expressions of opinion as did Truman, new in his office and a bit unsure of himself, but it is difficult to see how FDR could have avoided at least substantially meeting these demands for fiscal restraint. It had been Roosevelt, after all, who had earlier refused to give the Phase II arrangements the status of a formal accord. In addition, the first British complaints about American reluctance to implement the November agreements occurred before, not after his sudden passing.

Of course, a more imaginative Chief Executive than Truman might have devised some substitution for the lend-lease cutbacks, but there is no proof that Congress would have accepted such a program. When the Truman administration did, late in the year, seek legislative approval for a package of financial assistance to the British, Congress delayed nearly six months before finally authorizing this aid, and then did so largely because of fears raised by Russian communism, worries less prevalent in mid-1945. Quite clearly, Truman approached matters of this nature in a more business-like fashion than Roosevelt, and was more attuned to the desires of Congress than his predecessor had been. Truman also lacked the personal commitment which Roosevelt had assumed. Still, these facts do not in themselves necessarily prove that FDR's death led to a crushing reversal of American policy with regard to Phase II assistance to the British.

In another respect, however, the change in Presidents did result in a new situation to which London had to adjust. Truman is supposed to have told an old friend, shortly after his elevation to the nation's highest office, that he was "going to clean out that goddamn state department and get some people in there with guts and leadership."[41] It was widely recognized that Ed Stettinius, while a congenial enough individual, had neither the political savvy nor the diplomatic expertise nor the forcefulness of character required of an effective Secretary of State. As long as Roosevelt desired to direct much of the country's international affairs personally, Stettinius served his purposes. But with the considerably less experienced Truman in the White House, a much stronger Secretary was needed. Almost from the moment of Roosevelt's death, rumors of Stettinius' imminent departure, many carrying the authority of sources close to the new President, made the rounds. Finally, following the completion of the San Francisco meeting of the newly created United Nations, the long-anticipated announcement came: Stettinius' resignation had been offered and accepted.

The choice for his successor came as no surprise. The name of James F. Byrnes had been linked with the Secretary's position with monotonous regularity ever since Hull's resignation the previous autumn. A Washington insider for more than three decades, the diminutive South Carolinian had throughout the years built up such a reputation for effectiveness and political adroitness that he was commonly referred to as the "Assistant President" during the war years—a title Roosevelt himself employed. As a legislative horse-trader, Byrnes had few equals. Les Biffle, the Senate secretary and a knowledgeable judge of such matters, called Byrnes "the smoothest, most effective and most unobtrusive operator" he had ever seen in action. One senator is reported to have remarked: "When I see Jimmy Byrnes coming, I put one hand on my watch, the other on my wallet, and wish to goodness I knew how to protect my conscience." Such was Byrnes' influence during the Roosevelt years that, in the words of one of the most perceptive of the Washington press corps, "it became almost axiomatic that if you wanted something done through the administration, get Jimmy Byrnes' help."[42] The Senate, upon learning of Byrnes' nomination by Truman, responded with enthusiasm, suspending its rules, foregoing the customary hearings and debate, and unanimously confirming him by acclamation. The President, so it seemed, had come up with a first-class appointment.

Whitehall, however, was not so sure. Although the *Times* lauded the selection of Byrnes, saying the choice did "full justice to the high importance of the office," the embassy in Washington reported some less complimentary things about the new appointee. He was likely to follow "the Roosevelt-Hull line in foreign policy," but as a man "who is peculiarly sensitive to the opinion of others, Byrnes seems bound to defer in large measure to the prevailing demand that the United States should pursue policies of a recognisably independent, and, above all, American brand." Because he was "temperamentally inclined to follow lines of least resistance towards public pressures," he would probably seek to adopt the role of mediator between Britain and the Soviet Union and was likely to endorse a somewhat tougher attitude in the conduct of bilateral Anglo-American negotiations.[43] Somewhat optimistically, and not a little patronizingly, one senior official in London responded to this assessment by noting, "Both Mr. Truman and Mr. Byrnes are provincial compared to President Roosevelt and Mr. Hopkins. It will be one of our Ambassador's duties to broaden their outlook."[44]

Roosevelt's death did see an elevation in the influence of the State Department vis-à-vis the White House staff and especially the military. With the advent of peace, this development was a largely natural and expected one, however. Of more immediate impact on Anglo-American relations was the eclipse of Hopkins, who had shown himself a friend of Britain on many occasions in the past. It is difficult to say whether Morgenthau could have rebounded from the ignominy of the ill-advised Morgenthau Plan had FDR lived, but to the extent that he would have been able to do so, Roosevelt's death removed the influence of another key individual inclined to view British problems with sympathy.

The succession of new individuals to the top posts in Washington made little difference, however, in the status or effectiveness of the American Ambassador in London, John G. Winant. The added influence of the State Department following FDR's death did not lead to any corresponding improvement in Winant's unhappy position. During the war the former New Hampshire governor had found himself in an increasingly anomalous situation, cut off from the sources and even the channels of power. Because of the personal nature of the Roosevelt-Churchill relationship, many of the most important matters which transpired between Washington and London were handled by the White House staff and the Prime Minister's aides. If the State Department and the Foreign Office were only later informed of significant messages and developments, Winant and, to a lesser extent, his counterpart in Washington, Lord Halifax, often never received any notification of these occurrences. Clark Kerr and Harriman, the British and American Ambassadors in Moscow, had both been at Yalta, but neither Winant nor Halifax had been invited. The same pattern was to recur at the forthcoming summit meeting at Potsdam. Winant's years as Ambassador were a sham, a charade. He enjoyed the trappings of power and influence, but not the substance. "What do they have against me in Washington?" he plaintively asked Joseph Davies at one point. On another occasion he cabled home that the only time he ever met with Churchill was when the Prime Minister called him in to update him on the current state of relations between Britain and the United States. "I have been bypassed continuously," he complained.[45] But his protests did him little good, nor did the change of command in Washington. During the Potsdam conference he had to resort to telephoning the Foreign Office each day to request briefings from Whitehall in order to discover what was happening at the Berlin summit. One will never know what part this constant humiliation and play-acting had in Winant's decision two years later to take his own life. The American Ambassador may have been a war casualty just as surely as the men caught by the German onslaught in the Ardennes.

Neither Roosevelt's death nor Byrnes' appointment as Secretary, however, possessed nearly the significance for the character and style of the Anglo-American partnership as did Churchill's ensuing rejection by the British electorate. Although he had nothing of the personal rapport with Truman which had grown up between himself and FDR, Churchill continued to fill the airways with messages to the American President as long as he remained Prime Minister. In Truman's first month in the White House, he received forty-four wires from the British leader. Truman and Clement Attlee, Churchill's successor as Prime Minister, did not exchange that many cables during an entire year. So while FDR's death may have snapped a unique bond tying the two nations together, it was actually Churchill's subsequent defeat which resulted in the new and less personal tone which came to mark the Anglo-American relationship.

In considering specific policies which the Truman administration followed in the succeeding months, Whitehall officials agreed that the change of command in Washington had brought few substantial differences in matters of a bilateral nature. Typical of opinion in the Foreign Office was the observation early in 1946 that "the Truman Administration are pursuing the Rooseveltian policies clumsily but pretty consistently."[46] Perhaps a shift of emphasis or a reordering of priorities in places had occurred. Certainly Truman was less casual in financial affairs than his predecessor. In another area, the British would find the new administration more receptive to Zionist pressure than FDR's had been. Then, too, Roosevelt had been a leader of American anti-imperialists in a way Truman never would be. But here as well, the differences were more apparent than real, for Roosevelt's hostility toward British colonialism had only rarely been translated into specific policy proposals. Much more significantly, in their fundamental assumptions about the nature of the world and America's proper place in it, and in their ideas on what policies the United States should pursue to insure that a better world followed this war than had come out of the last, the two administrations differed but little.

But, as Gabriel Kolko has observed, if the content of Truman's policies was largely the same, their "style and pronunciation" were different. Truman had little of Roosevelt's grace and charm and was more apt to choose bluntness over tact. Charles Bohlen, who interpreted for both Presidents, characterized the difference in their relations with Churchill in this manner: "Where Roosevelt was warmly friendly with Churchill . . .," he remembered, "Truman was pleasantly distant."[47] At least one Englishman who observed the new American President closely during the Potsdam conference arrived at a similar conclusion. Truman was more decisive and businesslike than FDR, he was later to recall. "His manner was that of a polite but determined chairman of a Board Meeting."[48] Even this difference in presidential styles can be overplayed, though. With the termination of hostilities, the types of issues that inevitably arose would have altered the tone of the communications between London and Washington no matter who was President.

The realities of diplomacy in an unsettled world soon intruded to put an end to idle speculation of this nature by the British. Roosevelt was dead; it was Harry Truman with whom they now had to deal. Already the new President had shown that he would not be intimidated or awed by the almost legendary Churchill. His actions during his first weeks in office demonstrated that he had a will of his own, and more importantly, that he would not hesitate to exercise it in the nation's best interests as he alone saw them. He might have been an accidental President, but he was not going to be a surrogate, a temporary standby to keep the mechanisms of government running until the American people could choose a true successor to the beloved Roosevelt. And so, as the thousand-year Reich disintegrated and men turned their gaze toward the Pacific, British officialdom could not suppress a tinge of anxiety as they prepared for their first summit meeting with the new American leadership.

9

The Big Two
and a Half

For Winston Churchill, the sight of German armies succumbing, one after another, to the overpowering might of the surging allied forces occasioned little exaltation. For five and a half terrible years, the entire British nation had single-mindedly focused on the destruction of the most fearful foe England had ever known in its many centuries of warfare. Now, with the triumphant culmination of this gargantuan effort, the Nazi state lay vanquished. British tommies strode the streets where only yesterday Hitler had reviled the English people as an effete and despicable race. And yet, brooding in his Downing Street offices or amidst the tranquility of his country home of Chequers, Churchill saw little which led him to join in the victory celebrations. Berlin had been crushed, to be sure, but a new and equally ominous power had risen to take its place on the devastated continent, posing a less immediate but ultimately even more serious threat to the British Isles. Across the ocean, Roosevelt's unexpected death had left affairs of state in the less confident hands of one with whom Churchill lacked any memories of shared battles which might be drawn upon when special considerations were needed. The new President, moreover, had not been long in indicating that he viewed neither the growth of Russian power nor British economic troubles with the alarm which these matters raised in Churchill.

The embattled Prime Minister did not have to look beyond the confines of England, however, to find men whose perspectives differed significantly from his. Even before V-E Day, the Labour members of the Coalition government had become increasingly restive under Churchill's domineering leadership. With the German surrender they considered their obligation to stifle party dispute at an end, and before the month of May was out, the resignation of the Labour ministers and their Liberal Party colleagues forced the dissolution of the government and the formation of a new caretaker government. After some weeks of indecision and anxious poll-taking, Churchill called for national elections on July 5.

Much of the ensuing campaign centered around Churchill himself. The Conservative Party repeatedly argued that the Prime Minister's experience and prestige would best serve Britain at the peace table, while the Labourites pointed to the recent civil strife in Greece in answer to the idea that Churchill was indispensable and warned that it would be dangerous to have a Conservative government to face the explosive postwar scene in Europe. In the domestic field, both major parties promised new programs in housing, health care, social insurance, and a host of related areas in response to virtually unanimous demands from the British electorate. Again, Churchill was the predominant issue, as Labour questioned his commitment to sweeping change and pushed socialism as the best way to cope with the complex questions which the new government would have to confront.

Before the war Clement Attlee, the unassuming leader of the Labour Party and Churchill's Deputy Prime Minister in the Coalition government, had written a book, *The Labour Party in Perspective*, in which he had maintained that a Socialist foreign policy would be wholly different from that of the Tories. As the campaign progressed, in fact, Labour's ideas on foreign policy did acquire a flavoring of their own which distinguished them from the Conservative platform. The Socialists did not seem to value full cooperation with the United States as Churchill did, although they professed they would always seek close relations with Washington. As socialists, the Labourites were more likely to distrust American capitalism. Many party members voiced apprehension lest the economic strength of the United States impede British recovery and lower the standard of living in the United Kingdom. Differences regarding relations with the Soviet Union also emerged. An important plank in Labour's foreign policy platform emphasized improving ties between London and Moscow. A socialist government, so the argument ran, would be able to reach a more satisfactory understanding with the Russian leaders. Labour proponents also pledged sympathy and aid to the new democratic movements in Europe and immediate Dominion status for India. On the whole, they tried to convey the impression that a Labour government would be less traditional and less nationalistic in its conduct of foreign relations than the current government.

In a more fundamental sense, however, Labour's foreign policy as enunciated during the campaign differed in few respects from the principal lines which Churchill and the Conservatives espoused. Attlee, Ernest Bevin, Hugh Morrison, and other Labourite leaders had been members of Churchill's government since the dark days of 1940 and had therefore had a hand in formulating the policies which had guided Britain throughout the war. Labour speakers repeatedly pledged to continue the fight against Japan. Attlee had been one of the members of the British delegation at the San Francisco meeting which drew up the charter for the world security organization, and he and his party were in total accord with the idea of a strong, active peacekeeping body. Noting these numerous points of similarity, American newspapers informed their readership that the outcome of the election would make practically no difference in foreign affairs, since both parties agreed on the basics of British postwar policy. Ambassador Halifax gave similar assurances.[1]

American commentators generally called for the people of the United States to refrain from taking sides in the election, but few completely masked their regard for Churchill or their distaste for Labour's alleged leftist economic policies. Thus, the *New York Times* could in the same editorial call for restraint in taking sides and acclaim Churchill as "one of the towering figures of this century—the incarnation of British courage and tenacity, the savior of his nation in its greatest peril, the spokesman of the highest aspirations of a world at war." In the early days of June, pollster George Gallup reported that Americans favored the reelection of Churchill by a margin of nearly five to one. At any rate, few American observers who ventured a prediction expected that any-one but Churchill would be forming a new British government following the election, an assessment endorsed by the staff of the American embassy in London.[2]

Events outside England did not wait for the British to select a new leadership. And with each passing day Churchill grew more openly worried by what he saw happening on the continent. The Soviets, it appeared, had thrown off all restraint and were quite blatantly consolidating their grip on the eastern half of Europe and perhaps preparing to expand further westward, as well. Russian actions in Rumania, Bulgaria, Hungary, and other areas which had been overrun by the Red Army increasingly seemed to be motivated by considerations other than insuring the security of Soviet mil-itary forces.[3] New pressures on Iran and Turkey led Churchill to question whether Moscow's ambitions were as limited as Stalin had heretofore led him to believe. Continuing deadlocks in ful-filling the Yalta agreements on Poland and German reparations prompted doubts about the value of the Russian leader's promises. Yet, in the absense of cordial relations between Great Britain and the Soviet Union, the very security of the British Isles would be brought into question. Moreover, each public display of friction between the two allies further undercut Tory claims that Churchill alone was qualified to lead Britain into the new era of peace.

As he had done many times in the past, the Prime Minister almost instinctively grasped at the idea of a new summit meeting where he could employ his considerable powers of persuasion to reach fresh understandings with his colleagues. Even before the last German armies had laid down their arms, he cabled Truman to urge that a new tripartite conference be called "as soon as possible." "Matters can hardly be carried further by correspondence," he wired. Moreover, until the three statesmen could meet to settle matters currently separating them, all Anglo-American forces should "hold firmly" to the positions they had obtained in central Europe, he advised. Three days later, Truman replied that such a meeting was desirable, but went little further, other than to say that there was "no valid excuse" why Stalin this time should not come westward "toward us." He added that it would be impossible for him to leave Washington before the end of the fiscal year (June 30).[4]

The idea of postponing any meeting until July absolutely dismayed Churchill. Again and again in the following weeks he attempted to convince the President to agree to an earlier date. Time was all on Stalin's side, he argued. A failure to secure firm understandings in the immediate future on a number of crucial issues would give the Soviets an opportunity to "dig in" throughout eastern and central Europe while American and British military forces "melt away."[5] The State Department also advised Truman against postponing the summit until July, as did Ambassador Harriman,[6] but this counsel had no more effect than did Churchill's pleas. Truman was not to be hurried into the meeting. There was the press of domestic business—Truman had told Eden in their first conversation after Roosevelt's death that "my big problems are domestic."[7] Perhaps the new President also desired to get a better feel for matters before going off to confer with two very experienced, crafty negotiators. He may have wanted to wait until he could see how the San Francisco conference came out, or until he had a new Secretary of State to take with him. Perhaps also he wished to learn first whether the atomic bomb, which was scheduled for testing sometime in July, would actually work. Finally, Joseph Davies, who spent several days in lengthy conversations with the Prime Minister near the end of May, reported that Churchill did not give him any compelling reason for his insistence upon an early meeting of the Big Three other than his own domestic political problems.[8] It is not difficult to imagine Truman exclaiming indignantly that he would be damned if he was going to be hurried simply for that!

Stalin, somewhat to Churchill's surprise, proved amenable enough to the idea of another Big Three conference, but steadfastly refused to budge beyond the territory controlled by Russian armies. After further exchanges among the three capitals, it was decided that Potsdam, a relatively undamaged Berlin suburb, would be the site of the next summit, which would begin on July 15. Stalin had gotten his way concerning the location of the meeting, Truman concerning the date. Such were the subtle workings which marked the distribution of power. Churchill was allowed to suggest the code name for the rendezvous: TERMINAL.

During these weeks the Prime Minister resurrected another idea which had been one of his pet schemes since early in the war. Only days after first proposing a new tripartite meeting, Churchill invited the American President to stop in England on his way to the summit. After conferring about matters which would later be discussed with Stalin, the Prime Minister wired, the two could then travel together the remainder of the journey to the site of the conference. Such an opportunity to meet with Truman, Churchill reasoned, would enable him to begin steering the President's thinking about the threat posed by Russia into what the Prime Minister considered more realistic channels. At the same time, this must have seemed to Churchill little more than what was due him for his voyage to Quebec shortly before the American election the previous autumn.[9] But Truman's immediate response was very much what Roosevelt's had been prior to Yalta. He wished to give the Russians no suspicion that Britain and the United States were "ganging up" on them, he replied to Churchill, so it would be better to avoid any bilateral meetings before the conference. To assuage the Prime Minister's sensibilities, Truman added that he would stop in Great Britain on his way home from the summit meeting.[10]

The President did, however, appreciate the cogency of Churchill's argument that matters could not be allowed simply to drift until the three statesmen met together in July. With this in mind, he determined to launch a foreign policy initiative of his own by dispatching Harry Hopkins to Moscow for private talks with Stalin. Churchill did not miss the implications of this unilateral action by the White House: Truman was not going to be maneuvered into any position which might suggest an Anglo-American front against the Soviets.

Almost as an afterthought, the President asked Joseph E. Davies to undertake a similar mission to London. The choice of Davies as Truman's special emissary to Churchill was a peculiar one and aptly illustrates Truman's perceptions about the nature of relations tying the three allies together. A prewar ambassador to Moscow, Davies was notorious for his sympathetic attitudes toward the Russians, an enthusiasm which blinded him to many of the most blatant abuses of the Soviet system. Several times during his first weeks in office, Truman had summoned Davies to the White House for talks on the troubled state of affairs between Moscow and its western partners, conversations in which the former ambassador reassured the new President that the Kremlin leaders harbored no aggressive intentions. "The real root of most of this present trouble," he said at one point, was "the suspicion and fear that they, the Soviets, are being 'ganged up' on." In too many instances, he added, these suspicions had been justified.[11] It seems unlikely that Truman accepted all of Davies' assertions at face value, but the President did find his explanations sufficiently persuasive that he decided Churchill might benefit from hearing this side of the argument. Shortly after asking Davies to travel to London, Truman recorded, "I told him I was having as much difficulty with Prime Minister Churchill as I was having with Stalin—that it was my opinion that each of them was trying to make me the paw of the cat that pulled the chestnuts out of the fire."[12]

Davies arrived in London on May 25 (after a transatlantic flight during which he was somewhat disconcerted to discover that the crew had appropriated the filling cartridges of the plane's Mae West belts in order to make carbonated water for a nightcap), and spent nearly eight hours in wide-ranging talks with the Prime Minister over the next several days. It is a matter of some dispute exactly what Truman instructed Davies to say to Churchill, but there seems little doubt but that the perhaps overenthusiastic envoy told the Prime Minister that the President wished to meet alone with Stalin prior to the Potsdam summit, with Churchill to join them only later. Truman subsequently wrote that he desired only individual personal contacts prior to the formal sessions, not a separate bilateral conference. At any rate, Churchill protested this affront and complained that it was a poor return for his support of the United States. He would never agree, he firmly declared, to attend any meeting which was a continuation of a conference between Truman and Stalin.[13]

Throughout their talks, Davies found himself shocked again and again by the vehemence of the Prime Minister's denunciations of the Soviet Union. On several occasions, he later reported, Churchill spoke "with great emphasis and emotion" of the grave dangers which would follow the withdrawal of American troops from Europe. Even a pullback to the designated occupation zones should be delayed and used for "bargaining purposes." Churchill also inveighed against the "Black Curtain" (as Davies recorded the phrase in his diary) falling over eastern Europe, and the imposition of Gestapo methods by the Soviet secret police. Turning to another subject, the British statesman worried that Truman's refusal to stop by London on his way to Potsdam might be used by his political opponents in the current campaign.

Davies responded by informing Churchill that no American President would be sustained by the public in holding American armed forces in Europe indefinitely. American armies, he insisted, should be promptly withdrawn to their designated occupation zone. Davies suggested that if Churchill's hostile attitude were known to the Soviet government, that in itself might be responsible for much of the aggressiveness and unilateral action taken by the Russians. He then proceeded to give the Prime Minister a lengthy lecture concerning the justified nature of Soviet suspicions and of the need for Washington and London to take action to allay these fears. Did Churchill now believe that Britain had made a mistake in not supporting Germany, he asked at one point, since the Prime Minister was presently expressing the doctrine which Hitler and Goebbels had reiterated for the past four years?[14]

Upon his return to Washington, Davies reported his impressions to the President. Churchill was, he felt, a very great man, "the greatest Englishman of this or any other time. . . . But he is first and foremost an Englishman. He is still the King's Minister who will not liquidate the Empire. He is still the great Briton of Runnymede and Dunkirk." Behind the Prime Minister's hostile attitude to Russia, Davies thought, was Churchill's recognition of the fact that his country no longer occupied the preeminent position of power in the world. As a consequence, he sought to use American might to protect Great Britain's sphere of influence from Soviet encroachment. "I could not escape the impression," Davies concluded, "that he was basically more concerned over preserving England's position in Europe than in preserving Peace. In any event, he had convinced himself that by serving England, he was best serving Peace."[15]

The American impressed his British hosts no more favorably. "He is the born appeaser and would gladly give Russia all Europe, except perhaps us, so that America might not be embroiled," Eden observed at the time. "All the errors and illusions of Neville C., substituting Russia for Germany."[16] Churchill at one point drew up an aide mémoire to summarize his feelings, though he later decided against giving it to Davies. After observing that Great Britain and the United States shared common ideologies and principles, while the Soviet Union was propelled by an entirely different philosophy, he then protested that he could not readily bring himself

> to accept the idea that the position of the United States is that Britain and Soviet Russia are just two foreign Powers, six of one and a half a dozen of the other. . . . Except in so far as force is concerned, there is no equality between right and wrong. The great cause and principles for which Britain and the United States have suffered and triumphed are not mere matters of the balance of power. They in fact involve the salvation of the world.[17]

Yet, in countless little ways Washington authorities did manage, in the weeks between the Nazi surrender and the gathering of the allied leaders outside the German capital, to convey the impression to anxious officials in London that United States policy recognized little difference between the British and the Russians. The American military increasingly came to deny simple British requests for information on the grounds that the desired intelligence was primarily of significance for the postwar period. The fact that the two were allied in a war which was expected to last for many more months was considered irrelevant in these cases.[18] The lend-lease situation seemed another indication of American reluctance to accord Great Britain special consideration. The British Chiefs informed Churchill shortly before the Potsdam conference that the supply situation had reached a critical stage because of continuing cutbacks in the lend-lease schedules and reminded the Prime Minister that, although six weeks had passed, he had still not received a reply from the White House in response to his May 28 cable asking Truman's intervention in the matter. Unless Churchill succeeded at Potsdam in securing a modification of current American policy, they wrote, future British operations against the Japanese would be "gravely prejudiced."[19]

The Americans proved no more accomodating on nonmilitary issues. Truman's action in dispatching Hopkins to Moscow to deal with Stalin in a strictly bilateral resolution of the sticky Polish controversy irritated Churchill, as did the President's refusal to allow Hopkins to stop in London on his way back to the United States, to brief Churchill on his talks with the Soviet Premier.[20] Truman's subsequent decision to recognize the Polish government without first consulting the British further incensed officials in Whitehall. Nor would Washington join with London in a statement supporting Turkey in resisting Russian demands, though the British argued fervently for this action.[21] Once it became obvious that Truman was determined not to meet with Churchill prior to the summit, the Foreign Office proposed that the State Department at least send a low level expert by London on his way to the conference for an exchange of views. Instead, Truman again sent the insufferable Davies. British military authorities, in turn, suggested a meeting of the Combined Chiefs of Staff in London immediately prior to the Potsdam conclave. Once again, Washington turned down their request.[22] The State Department, Cadogan informed Churchill in early July, even declined to comment on British ideas about the topics which might be discussed at the Big Three meeting.[23]

Behind this all too obvious failure to appreciate the merits of close collaboration with the British, the Foreign Office explained, lay a more dangerous attitude. In the minds of the Russians and the Americans, and especially the Americans, there existed the feeling that Britain was now a secondary power and could be treated as such.[24] In fact, one heard this anxiety increasingly being voiced in concerned circles throughout the United Kingdom. Hence, in the midst of the Potsdam conference, the *Economist* complained that London's role in the proceedings was "indefinite, uncertain and in a sense almost secondary." In an article reminiscent of its influential attack on American policy six months earlier, this respected journal protested Churchill's "policy of deference towards the United States, which has so greatly hindered any effort to evolve a separate British approach" to world affairs.[25]

Worries of another sort complicated preparations for the impending conference, for forebodings about the election continually intruded upon Churchill in the days before the summit. While the polling had taken place on July 5, the results would not become known for a further three weeks, due to the large number of soldiers' votes and other absentee ballots. In the interim, both Churchill and Attlee would sit at the conference table, the latter strictly in an observer's role, until the summit recessed for them to fly home to learn the results of their countrymen's deliberations. Thus, although Churchill acknowledged that they would probably be deciding in the next few weeks "the kind of life that would confront several generations to come,"[26] he found it impossible to concentrate on preparing for the approaching meeting. He complained of depression and lethargy, at one point murmuring that the election "hovers over me like a vulture of uncertainty in the sky." On another occasion he told an intimate, "I shall be only half a man until the result of the poll." His personal physician noted in his diary: "The election festers in his mind."[27]

Enveloped in his dark mood, Churchill made few pretenses of preparing for the conference. Foreign Office officials at Potsdam complained that the Prime Minister was not "mastering his brief"; he was simply responding to issues as they cropped up, without adequate knowledge or understanding of the complexities involved.[28] Eden might have minimized the unfortunate effects of this, but the Foreign Secretary himself was able to devote only half a mind to the proceedings. Shortly after arriving at the conference site, he received official notification that his son had been lost in action. His diary documents his depression, for he noted that he could not suppress "an unworthy hope" that the Tories had lost the election and he would be removed from the burdens of high office.[29]

Not all their gloom arose from electoral doubts and private grief, of course. A good deal of the somberness which marked the British preparations for the Potsdam meeting resulted from a fundamental distrust of Soviet intentions and a realization that there was only so much that Britain could do to resist the Russians without much more aid from the Americans than seemed probable at the present time. In a memorandum to Churchill entitled "Tactics at the Conference," the Foreign Office's Alexander Cadogan observed that the British would be holding few cards in the forthcoming talks. It was imperative, he wrote, that these not be squandered. "Even if Stalin's requests are reasonable we should not grant them except in return for his agreement to reasonable requests on our part."[30] A few days later another Foreign Office paper advised Churchill that he must "take the offensive in challenging Communist penetration" throughout eastern Europe. Britain should also be ready to counteract any Soviet attempt to obtain political control over Germany, Greece, Italy, or Turkey. "We must not desist from this course or be discouraged even if the United States give us no help and even if they adopt a policy of appeasement towards Russian domination, as well they may."[31]

The attitude which the United States would assume towards the Soviets provided a constant source of worry to the policy makers in Whitehall as they prepared to depart for Germany. "Every ounce of Anglo-American cooperation will be needed if the Bear is [to be] brought to a halt," John Balfour wrote from the British embassy in Washington. But Halifax's shrewd predictions of what to expect from the Americans did little to reassure them. Truman would be anxious to work with the British, the cagey Ambassador cabled, but the remainder of his wire went on to qualify this assessment. The Americans were likely to assume Russian willingness to cooperate. In dealing with the British, they would probably be more receptive "to arguments based upon the danger of economic chaos in European countries than to *the balder pleas about the risks of extreme Left Governments or of the spread of Communism.*" Halifax went on to report that the State Department and White House officials to whom he had spoken were not responsive to his portrayal of Europe as the scene of an ideological clash between Russian and western values. "At the back of their minds," he continued,

> there are still lingering suspicions that we want to back Right Wing Governments or monarchies for their own sake. This does not in the least mean that they will be unwilling to stand up with us against the Russians when necessary. But they are likely to pick their occasions with care, and are half expecting to play, or at any rate to represent themselves as playing, a moderating role between ourselves and the Russians.[32]

The news that Davies was to accompany the new President to the conference seemed to verify this picture which Halifax had sketched. If the Americans proved unwilling to resist the Soviets, Eden grumbled darkly, then Britain would just have to go its separate way.[33]

Truman's advisers, for their part, despite a growing distrust of the Russians, urged caution upon the President. Many in the State Department worried that Britain might drag the United States into a war with the Soviet Union. American representatives in Europe cabled Washington of British political maneuvering behind the scenes, thereby fostering the idea that British intentions were no purer than Russian.[34] Fresh reports alleging deliberate British efforts to thwart American desires in the Middle East and the Far East strengthened this conviction.[35] Acting Secretary of State Grew informed Truman that London's agenda for the conference was so drawn as to give the appearance of a bill of complaints against the Soviets. Such an attitude, he observed, "seems hardly the proper approach to the forthcoming meeting."[36] The President may also have been alarmed by reports that Field Marshal Alexander was openly talking of building up Germany against the Soviet Union, information that reinforced Davies' prediction that British efforts to regain their lost prestige and power might well contribute to a real threat to peace.[37]

The President responded to warnings from so many different quarters with suspicion and irritation. The difficulties with Churchill, he confessed to his predecessor's widow on May 10, were very nearly as exasperating as those with the Russians. In an off-the-record press conference in June, Truman went out of his way to emphasize that the Soviets had made more concessions than any other nation at the San Francisco conference of the world security organization and added that the United States had "damned near as many differences" with the British as with the Russians.[38] On the day he left Washington for the voyage across the Atlantic, the President confided to several former Senate colleagues that he was more afraid of Britain and France than he was of Russia.[39]

The position paper which the State Department prepared for Truman to study on the way to Potsdam illustrated the thinking which guided American planning for the conference. The possibility of war between the United States and the Soviet Union "would seem in the highest degree unlikely," the foreign affairs experts informed the President. The only conflict involving the United States which could be imagined would be one pitting Britain against Russia, where America entered to aid the United Kingdom. So long as London and Moscow cooperated, there could be no great war in the foreseeable future. Thus, American policy should be to discourage the development of rival spheres of influence, both British and Russian, and to assist its two allies in smoothing out the points of friction between Moscow and London. "The need of the moment," this analysis concluded, "is to promote understanding between Great Britain and Russia on all matters in dispute."[40] Byrnes, Harriman later recalled, arrived at the conference fully expecting his role would be that of mediator.[41]

Most of all, Truman left for Potsdam determined to brook no nonsense from either of his negotiating partners. He was going "to take the offensive," he told Leahy, using the same phrase the Foreign Office had employed in its memorandum to Churchill on relations with the Russians.[42] Another aide got the distinct impression that "the President feels the U.S. is by far the strongest country in the world and he proposes to take the lead at the coming meeting. In this connection he proposes to raise all the controversial questions."[43] Though some of this may have been bluster to cover a nervousness at sitting on equal terms with two of history's greatest statesmen, a larger part stemmed simply from Truman's conception of the nature of the conference. There were no problems which, given the necessary good will among the world's three giants, could not be happily solved. Moreover, the United States, as the most powerful of the three, would in the end be able to insure that these solutions generally took American forms. Any other outcome would be unthinkable. Fresh in the President's mind was the warning from three of his most trusted advisers that, "as a well known Missouri horse trader, the American people expect you to bring something home to them."[44]

The first order of business for the American President after the arrival of the United States delegation at their quarters in the Berlin suburb of Babelsberg was the establishment of personal relationships with the British Prime Minister and the Russian Premier. Churchill's turn came first, as the irrepressible Englishman called on Truman the day after their arrival. Leahy had earlier worried whether the inexperienced Truman would be as successful as Roosevelt had been in "managing" the volatile Prime Minister. He had underestimated his man; Churchill was quickly captivated by the American's directness and simplicity. Perhaps the President recalled a suggestion offered by Eleanor Roosevelt some months earlier. The British statesman was "a gentleman to whom the personal element means a great deal," the former First Lady had written. If "you can get on a personal basis with Mr. Churchill, you will find it easier. If you talk to him about books and let him quote to you from his marvelous memory everything on earth from Barbara Fritche [*sic*] to the Nonesense Rhymes and Greek tragedy, you will find him easier to deal with on political subjects." Whether or not Truman consciously followed this counsel, Churchill emerged from his initial encounter with the President pleased and relieved.[45] "We not only talk the same language," he later remarked, "we think the same thoughts."[46] The President for his part tended to be less euphoric, but he too came away from this first meeting favorably impressed. "I am sure we can get along if he doesn't try to give me too much soft soap," Truman privately observed that evening.[47]

On the following day Stalin dropped in on the President. Again Truman was pleasantly surprised by the manner of the man he had traveled so far to see. Stalin looked the President straight in the eye when he spoke. To Truman this was an important indication of the Soviet leader's trustworthiness, a sign that the two statesmen would be able to come to terms in a mutually advantageous way. Truman persuaded Stalin to stay for lunch, during the course of which the Russian indicated his opposition to British participation in the Pacific war and attempted to raise doubts in the President's mind concerning the reliability of British intentions in the Far East. To the Americans present, this seemed to confirm Davies' earlier suspicions that Churchill's hostility toward the Soviet Union was well known in Moscow.[48]

Truman quickly discovered, however, that the Russian Premier could be both intractable and unreasonable. Indeed, within a few days he was forced to discard much of his original plan to act in a mediating role between London and Moscow and was propelled into a much more active opposition to the Russians than his predecessor had ever taken. At Potsdam the lines were more clearly drawn than they had been a few months earlier at Yalta. During the Crimea conference, the British and the Americans had each found themselves on occasion isolated and resisting a policy on which the other two allies fully agreed. But throughout the much longer meeting in Potsdam, issue after issue saw the Soviets arguing one side of the question, the two western democracies the other. On only a single major subject dividing the three delegations could Moscow count on the firm support of either of its allies. This involved the American desire to replace the Italian surrender terms with a voluntary accord with the authorities in Rome and to lift most of the allied controls which had been imposed on Italy at the time of its surrender. In this one instance Churchill as well as Stalin blocked American wishes, and Truman was compelled to abandon his plans for Italy's early political independence and economic recovery.

On all other major issues, however, when the three erstwhile allies failed to agree upon a question of importance, the Soviets invariably proved unable to gain the support of either the British or the Americans. London and Washington did not always concur on every detail of these issues, but the two were united in clear-cut opposition to the Russian stance. This was the configuration, for instance, on all three of the questions which sparked the bitterest debate during the negotiations: Poland's western boundary, German reparations, and recognition of the governments of the liberated Balkan states. In each case, Churchill noted approvingly, Truman "told the Russians just where they got on and off."[49] Frequently the British opposed the Soviets more forcefully than the Americans thought advisable, and at times Churchill and Eden complained that their colleagues from the United States were not providing the support they should be.[50] Still, the significant fact was that both nations clearly agreed concerning the unjustified or undesirable nature of Soviet demands.

The secondary issues before the three leaders produced this same pattern. In the matter of breaking relations with the Franco regime in Madrid, in disputes over the exclusion of British and American officials and troops from Austria, in judgments regarding the reprehensible character of Soviet actions in eastern Europe, on the problem of seating France on the new Council of Foreign Ministers, on the question of a Russian trusteeship in one of the Italian colonies on the North African coast—on all these issues, the positions adopted by the United States and Great Britain were similar or identical, and in conflict with the Soviet stand. In matters concerning the newly discovered atomic energy, an equal feeling of Anglo-American partnership predominated. Stalin, it was decided, should receive only the vaguest hint about this potentially revolutionary force and need not be consulted about the advisability of employing it against the Japanese. In like fashion, the Russian was excluded from the negotiations leading to the dispatch of the Potsdam Declaration demanding Tokyo's immediate surrender. Molotov at one point telephoned Byrnes to delay delivery of the ultimatum, only to be informed that it had already been sent.[51] The incident was illustrative: the allied coalition which had won the war would not survive the peace.

The British Prime Minister could hardly contain his elation. The atmosphere at Potsdam, he gloated, was entirely different from that of the earlier Big Three meetings, where Roosevelt and Stalin had often joined forces against the British. Truman was something else altogether. He "intends to get to the bottom of things, and when Stalin gets tough Truman at once makes it plain that he, too, can hand out the rough stuff. The Allies are not in the mood to do all the giving." The Prime Minister, one aide reported, "rubs his eyes to make sure that he is not dreaming" when he sees Truman daring to cross the Soviets. "If only this had happened at Yalta," Churchill at one point sadly remarked.[52]

But if the split between Russia and the Atlantic democracies became more difficult to ignore during the two and a half weeks at Potsdam, the inverse of this proposition—an increased cooperation and perceived community of interests between Great Britain and the United States—failed to develop. The Italian question has already been mentioned. In this instance Churchill seems to have been more mindful of the injury inflicted on his countrymen by the Italians than was Truman, who like his predecessor had military, political, and domestic reasons for forgiving past wrongs. The British Prime Minister in opposing Truman's wishes in this regard may also have been nursing resentment at the unilateral manner in which the Americans had approached the whole question of Italy's future in planning for the conference.[53]

In other, less important matters as well, the policies of the two allies diverged. Churchill, registering his longstanding antipathy to Chiang Kai-shek, joined the Russians in blocking China from receiving a voice in European issues before the Council of Foreign Ministers. Nor was the English statesman any more cooperative whenever the President broached his ideas on internationalizing the waterways of Europe. Such a step would establish an unfortunate precedent, the Prime Minister decided, most probably with Suez in the back of his mind. Truman, for his part, vetoed Churchill's desire to bring the contending Yugoslav factions to Potsdam. The Prime Minister's long-windedness and habit of speaking at length for the record irritated the American, and he had no desire to prolong the deliberations further by becoming involved in every political dispute throughout the continent. "I'm not going to stay around this terrible place all summer, just to listen to speeches," the President testily noted in his diary. "I'll go home to the Senate for that."[54] A week into the conference, exasperated by the slow pace of the proceedings, Truman informed the British that he would not, after all, be able to stop in England before returning to the United States.[55] As often as this had happened, Churchill should not even have been surprised.

The American Joint Chiefs of Staff also shied away from a closer collaboration with their colleagues from the United Kingdom. The British had come to Potsdam hoping to secure a greater participation in the Japanese war, and particularly to change the Pacific command from an exclusively American one, as it had been since 1942 when Britain had few forces in the Far East, to one subordinated to the Combined Chiefs. The Joint Chiefs, however, made it clear that the Pacific was to be an American show, and quickly scotched any suggestions that threatened their unilateral control of Far Eastern operations. Nor did they permit the British to participate in the exchange of information with the Soviets about operations against Japan. As Leahy later explained, this "was difficult at best, and to bring in a third party would only complicate matters." Leahy succinctly summarized the discussions of the Combined Chiefs during the conference when he observed, "The British . . . did most of the proposing and the Americans did most of the disposing."[56]

In a more important area, the American refusal to coordinate plans with the United Kingdom proved particularly disturbing to the British. Churchill had arrived in Potsdam determined to extend and strengthen the Anglo-American military partnership, and to this end he proposed to make the Combined Chiefs of Staff a permanent body, a suggestion he had earlier urged upon Roosevelt at Yalta. In the months since then, alarming Russian actions on the continent had greatly intensified his feeling about the advisability of such a move. As the Potsdam summit opened, the British Chiefs of Staff informed the Prime Minister that they would consider it "a retrograde step" if the close collaboration developed between London and Washington during the war were allowed to fall into disuse merely because Germany and Japan had been defeated. There would be great benefits, for instance, in retaining channels for the mutual exchange of information, and in achieving some measure of uniformity in the design of weaponry and in training.[57] When, however, the British raised this question with the American Chiefs, the latter replied that the United States had not yet sufficiently defined its postwar political relationships with other nations to permit them to discuss such matters. Instead, the Joint Chiefs of Staff asked Truman to arrange termination of the Munitions Assignments Board, one of the key agencies which had coordinated the massive military effort since early in the war.[58]

Churchill himself raised the issue of continuing the present military collaboration shortly after the President came to call at the Prime Minister's quarters on July 18. Truman began by bringing up the question of airfields built in British territory during the war by the United States. Churchill replied that it "would be a great pity if the Americans got worked up about bases and air traffic and set themselves to make a win of it at all costs." The Prime Minister then deftly turned the conversation into a discussion of sharing not only civilian but also military bases. Why should an American battleship calling at Gibraltar, he asked, not find torpedoes to fit its tubes, and shells to fit its guns? Truman, sensing dangerous ground, attempted to backtrack by observing that great care needed to be exercised so as to avoid undermining the United Nations. But Churchill was not to be waylaid. "I said that was all right so long as the facilities were shared between Britain and the United States," he later recorded.

> There was nothing in it if they were made common to everybody. A man might propose marriage to a young lady, but it was not much use if he were told that she would always be a sister to him. I wanted,

under whatever form or cloak, a continuation of the existing wartime system of reciprocal facilities between Britain and the United
States.

Taken back by the Prime Minister's vehemence, the President
again emphasized that any arrangements which might be adopted
must not take the form of a crude military alliance.[59]

One additional bilateral issue occupied the attention of the two
western leaders during these summer days in defeated Germany.
On July 11, while sailing toward Europe, Truman received a message from Henry Stimson reopening the troublesome lend-lease
question. The Secretary of War warned the President that his July
5 directive, as currently being interpreted, was impeding redeployment of American forces to the Pacific and recommended
that the order be modified to provide for maintenance and military
needs for British and French occupation troops in Germany, so
that American personnel could be released for transport to the
Far East. Two days later, the newly nominated Secretary of the
Treasury, Fred Vinson, wrote Byrnes that as a result of the President's July 5 directive, American lend-lease authorities were
"utterly confused" and needed a clarification if redeployment were
not to be hampered.[60]

Evidently these messages led the President to reconsider his
earlier rigid position, for when Churchill spoke with him on July
18 of the "melancholy position" in which Britain found itself as
a result of its mighty wartime effort, Truman responded sympa-
thetically. "If you had gone down like France, we might be fighting
the Germans on the American coast at the present time," Churchill
has recorded the President as saying. "This justifies us in regarding
these matters as above the purely financial plane."[61] Some days
later, Truman told his British ally that he was striving to give the
Lend-Lease Act "the broadest interpretation possible" and that he
had no intention of short-changing Great Britain. Churchill must
be patient, he added, for he wished to avoid any embarrassment
with Congress.[62]

In the succeeding days, Stimson, Clayton, and Assistant Secretary of War John McCloy sought to persuade Byrnes and Leahy
of the need for a more liberal lend-lease directive, something

along the lines of the agreement negotiated the previous fall by
the Keynes and Morgenthau committees. Though not totally successful, they did get Byrnes to accept increased aid to the British,
and Leahy, sensing the way Truman was leaning and not wishing
to be the sole holdout, reluctantly went along.[63] On July 29, the
President issued new instructions to the Joint Chiefs which coun-
termanded his July 5 directive and authorized lend-lease for British occupation troops assisting the redeployment of American
forces to the Pacific. In effect, this insured continued funding for
British occupation duties until V-J Day, but failed to recognize
the British contention that all occupation costs should be eligible
for aid.[64]

London officials still believed this represented a step back from
the arrangements of the previous autumn but were disposed to
accept it as the best they could reasonably hope to get. They were
under few illusions, however, about the reason for Truman's shift
in policies. The President's limited perception of a moral obligation, based on Britain's relatively greater wartime effort, had
played only a small role. Nor did Truman's change of heart represent an American acknowledgment that the economic vitality
of Great Britain was a matter of the first importance to the security
of the United States. Rather, the President had opened American
coffers a fraction wider simply because this seemed the most effective method of bringing the full weight of American arms
against the Japanese. In spite of the heightened sense of threat
which American policy makers carried from Potsdam as the result
of first-hand dealings with the Russians, these officials had not yet
embraced the proposition that closer ties and increased collaboration with the British were the obvious antidote.

The qualities which made for a successful war leader and those
which fostered achievement in times of peace, Churchill once
wrote in the more leisurely days before Munich, seldom combined
in the same man. This, ironically enough, had been the overriding
theme of the Labour campaign in mid-1945, and the success of
the Socialists in convincing the electorate of the validity of this

observation surpassed the hopes even of their most optimistic supporters. Churchill and Attlee had returned to Britain after the plenary session on the morning of July 25, to await the verdict of their countrymen. Early on the following day, it became clear that the Labour Party had received a staggering majority in the polls. Churchill promptly resigned. Hours later, the King asked Clement Attlee to form a new government.

Americans greeted this news with incredulity. At Potsdam, Leahy called Churchill's defeat, "in the present unsettled condition of the warring nations, . . . a world tragedy," and worried how the Allies would fare without "the spark of genius" in his leadership. Further progress at the present conference, he predicted, was unlikely.[65] On the far side of the Atlantic, the lead story in the *New York Times* termed this unexpected turn of events "one of the most stunning election surprises in the history of democracy." The *Detroit Free Press* proclaimed that a "revolution has taken place in Britain." That sensitive index of business and financial opinion, the New York Stock Exchange, reeled at the shock. "To those of us who believe in the free market," editorialized the *Wall Street Journal*, the implications of the Labour victory were "disturbing." The *Journal's* editors wondered if the British people had not traded liberty for security. The United States now stood alone, the *Hartford Courant* wrote, as the last of the major powers still adhering to the system of private enterprise.[66] At least one Congressman in Washington asserted that Churchill's defeat indicated "a Communist trend that should be a warning to the American people."[67]

Not all reaction in the United States to the Labour triumph exhibited such alarm. Liberal and labor circles hailed the victory, predicting the emergence of a new Britain in the role of global leader of the world's progressive forces. Others pointed out that Truman had successfully been able to step into Roosevelt's shoes, and in doing so, had demonstrated that there was no such species as the indispensable man. The pronounced failure of the Communists to win many seats in the new House of Commons reassured some who might otherwise have feared a Red Tide. Even the moderately conservative press, once the initial shock had passed, was cautiously friendly to the new government, taking great pains to explain the essentially conservative nature of the British Labour Party. "It is hard to picture the new Prime Minister, temperate, careful Mr. Attlee, launching full-tilt into socialism," observed the *Christian Science Monitor*. At any rate, it added, the desperate economic plight which the Labourites had inherited would probably prohibit this. The new government, *Business Week* soothingly announced, was committed to support all of Churchill's major initiatives in the field of foreign affairs.[68] After their initial plummet, prices on the New York Stock Exchange advanced in each of the next three trading sessions.

The Labour victory, in fact, created far fewer discontinuities in Britain's foreign policy than might have been expected. Immediately upon taking office, Attlee assured the Americans that his government would continue the fight against Japan until Tokyo's unconditional surrender. Labour leaders had had a voice in the determination of Britain's foreign policies throughout the war years and therefore felt no compelling need to rush precipitously off in new directions. Nor was the British position at the conference likely to be weakened by the change in leadership, since Attlee had sat alongside Churchill in the earlier sessions. The Americans at Potsdam were mildly startled to see that Attlee upon his return to Germany retained the same official advisers who had guided Churchill and Eden. Even Leslie Rowan, Churchill's principal private secretary, continued in the same capacity under the new Prime Minister.[69] Truman was thus led to write his mother: "It is too bad about Churchill but it may turn out to be all right for the world." Back home in the Senate, Leverett Saltonstall of Massachusetts remarked, "Whether we have Churchill or Attlee, our job is to continue to cooperate with Great Britain without sacrificing our principles or security."[70]

Of course, the Labour victory did produce one immediate and very marked change in Britain's conduct of its foreign relations: the replacement of the flamboyant Churchill by the infinitely less colorful Attlee. The change could not have been more pronounced. The *New York Herald Tribune* termed the new Prime Minister "one of those quiet, unemphatic, rather neutral characters

whom one . . . associates with returns to calm and 'normalcy.'"[71]
He inevitably attracted adjectives such as "mild-mannered," "in-
offensive," and "unassuming." Even Cadogan wrote that he "re-
cedes into the background by his very insignificance."[72] Possessing
little of the warmth or exuberance of his predecessor, the new
Prime Minister was destined to misunderstanding and obscurity
even at the height of his career, a condition aptly illustrated by
the fact that authors, editors, and proofreaders all continually
misspelled his surname, giving him only one "t."[73]

Returning to Potsdam with Attlee was the new Foreign Secretary, Ernest Bevin. Blunt, direct, and outspoken, Bevin much
more so than the gentlemanly Attlee seemed to fit the stereotype
of a socialist organizer. Having left school at the age of eleven,
Bevin had advanced through the ranks of the labor movement to
such prominence that Churchill had made him Minister of Labour
and National Service in the Coalition Cabinet. Although he had
had no previous experience in international affairs, he brought
with him to the Foreign Office definite ideas about his nation's
role in the world and its relations with its two allies. "I'm not
going to have Britain barged about," he had told Pug Ismay shortly
after arriving at Potsdam.[74] Attlee took his Foreign Secretary to
meet Truman and Byrnes as soon as the two returned from London. Although they were later to appreciate his frankness, the
Americans that evening questioned whether Bevin's refusal to
mask his talk in diplomatic niceties would prove a hindrance in
working closely with him.[75]

With the arrival of the new British leadership, the conference pace
quickened, and agreements or, more often, decisions to postpone
the search for unanimity were reached within a matter of days on
all unresolved issues. By the time of Attlee's return, Bohlen has
remembered, most of the arrangements had been made, "and
Attlee did not attempt to upset matters."[76] Over Cadogan's protests, Truman insisted on a plenary meeting the very night Attlee
and Bevin arrived in Potsdam, instead of allowing them a day to
be briefed and brought up to date by their Foreign Office sub-

ordinates. A few days later, as Bevin was being pressed by a junior member of the British delegation on the advisability of a proposal then being considered by the Big Three, the Foreign Secretary wearily replied that further discussions with the United States were useless. What Truman clearly wanted, he noted, was to make the best bargain he could and terminate the conference as quickly as possible.[77] Attlee himself has written that the United States officials were "inclined to think of Russia and America as two big boys who could settle things amicably between them." After Churchill's departure and his replacement by Attlee, Cadogan bitingly referred to the plenary sessions in the privacy of his diary as the Big Two and a Half.[78]

Neither the Americans nor the Soviets demonstrated such discretion. Attlee later remembered that Stalin had been very blatant in his attitude that the interests of the United States could not be ignored, implying at the same time that Great Britain was of little consequence.[79] This tendency to downgrade the British did not arise simply after the sudden departure of the forceful Churchill. Even before his defeat, Foreign Office officials had complained of the Americans presenting them with proposals "on a more or less take it or leave it basis." The overbearing, slightly patronizing attitude exhibited by many of the Americans present at Potsdam is captured in Leahy's comment on a July 24 conference of the military staffs of the three countries. This was the first such meeting, he noted, in which the British "were permitted" to participate.[80] When Cadogan was asked sometime later if he had received the impression during the summit that either Truman or Byrnes felt a particular warmth for the British, he replied that if they did, it was not very obvious. "The President's slick and snappy manner (whether natural or assumed)," he observed, "is rather inclined to result in quick decisions about which he does not consult us and in which he appears to ignore our interests."[81]

In London, Foreign Office analysts remarked that the Americans were now in "one of their more irritating cockahoop [*sic*] moods." Such judgments reflected impressions which had been gathering for some time. "We must face the fact," a senior British diplomat had written on the eve of the Potsdam summit, "that they will feel that being the richest and strongest Power they must also be the wisest and the most fair-minded."[82] In the week following Truman's return from Germany, Halifax echoed this assessment. The idea had steadily gained ground in the United States in recent months, he explained, that Britain had come to occupy a position on the world stage which was distinctly inferior to that of its two primary allies. Many Americans, conscious of the vast quantities of lend-lease aid which had been shipped to the United Kingdom, had concluded that Great Britain was largely dependent upon United States bounty for its ability to wage effective warfare—perhaps even for its very survival. Americans being a people who had traditionally acclaimed material success as proof of moral rectitude, the Ambassador cautioned, this feeling on their part was likely to make future dealings with Washington as difficult, if not more so, as they had ever been in the past.[83]

That this should have been the case would appear, on the surface at any rate, surprising. Truman and his advisers had left Potsdam deeply conscious of the frustrations involved in reaching agreement with the Russians on even the simplest of matters. Prolonged and exacting negotiations with Stalin had forcefully brought home to the still inexperienced President the gulf between western values and beliefs and those professed by the Soviet Union. By the time the three world leaders said their farewells to one another, Truman had accepted the essential validity of an observation which Stimson had made to him earlier in the conference. With the passing of each month, the elder statesman had written, it was clearer that relations with the Soviets comprised "the great basic problem of the future."[84]

But if Russian intransigence triggered feelings of uneasiness in the minds of American officials, their forebodings had not yet become so pronounced as to lead them to reorient their thinking vis-à-vis the British. The United States, after all, was undoubtedly the mightiest nation in the long history of the world. Americans could surely protect their interests without the help of an enfeebled Britain still living largely in the past. A heightened distrust of the Soviet Union, in short, brought with it little pressure for closer partnership with the United Kingdom. Feelings of kinship with the British or sentiments of warmth induced by past victories and the hope of future collaboration still played only a negligible role in Washington's thinking about the international situation. Indeed, Dean Acheson, the State Department's leading advocate of close ties with London, expressed alarm about the rising number of incidents which indicated to him that his colleagues were building up a hostile attitude toward Britain. Byrnes himself openly wondered whether British devotion to antiquated notions in international affairs might not preclude a long term program of cooperation between the two nations. But without close ties with Great Britain, Acheson warned, the United States might once again find itself drawn into a diplomatic isolation which could be highly dangerous.[85]

British observers as well retained their skepticism about the stability of America's commitment to a program of international collaboration and worried about the future direction of Washington's policy. London must take American condescension with a minimum of annoyance, Foreign Office officials repeatedly emphasized, since it was in Great Britain's interests that the United States "should continue to be conscious of her power" and willing to use it to maintain world peace. "In the light of our greater experience," one bureaucrat wrote, Whitehall must "try to guide them on sound lines without appearing to patronize." "In due course," another predicted, "it will no doubt be borne upon Americans that we, with our long experience can be of some assistance to them in the proper application of their power." Certainly a little unjustified arrogance from United States authorities was not too great a price to pay to insure that Washington not succumb to popular demands, already apparent, for a quicker demobilization and a speedy return to the isolation of the past.[86]

In the meantime, officials in the Foreign Office had their hands full with other, more pressing problems. The most immediate of these was the need to introduce a new Foreign Secretary and a new Cabinet to the complexities of international affairs and to the massive tasks facing a Britain determined to retain its first class power status without many of the essential components which would support that desire.

10

The Politics
of Money

The first half of August 1945 was a frenzied period, as time itself
seemed to have escaped the confines of orderly progression. Mon-
umental events virtually rushed into one another, each crowding
out its predecessor before the public had had time to digest its
import, to be pushed aside in turn by yet another momentous bit
of news. Scarcely had the Potsdam conference adjourned before
word came of a terrifying new weapon which had been unleashed
on Japan. The abrupt entry of the Soviet Union into the Pacific
war increased the swirl of rumors that Tokyo was seeking to end
the hostilities. The explosion of a second atomic bomb destroyed
all remaining doubts that the world was about to enter an era of
unprecedented possibilities for progress and terror. The frantic
scurrying of important leaders in the major capitals around the
globe contradicted official denials that peace feelers had been
tendered. The world appeared to hold its collective breath, waiting
for word that the end had come. And finally, blessedly, it was
confirmed: Japan had capitulated and history's bloodiest carnage
was only a memory.

For planners in Whitehall, ironically, the Japanese surrender
brought new hardships as well as jubilation, for with the end of

the war came a termination of American lead-lease. On August 17, Truman approved a memorandum drawn up in Crowley's FEA that closed off the spigot of American aid, in order, so the directive read, "that the best faith may be observed towards Congress and the Administration protect itself against any charge of misuse of Congressional authorization."[1] In one blow all of London's careful planning, based on American promises of generous Phase II assistance, was overturned.

Some weeks earlier, during the Potsdam summit, Churchill had asked Truman for assurances that, in the event of a sudden conclusion of the Pacific war, there would be no abrupt shutting down of lend-lease until there had been an opportunity for discussion on future arrangements.[2] The President's response had been to send William Clayton to London for consultation with British officials, but the talks had barely begun when word of Tokyo's surrender arrived. The British had realized that the whole question of lend-lease would have to be reconsidered once the hostilities ceased, but had expected in the interim an orderly tapering off of aid extended over a relatively lengthy period rather than the total and abrupt termination with which they were in fact confronted. "This very heavy blow was struck at us without warning and without discussion," Hugh Dalton, the new Chancellor of the Exchequer, was later to write. Now Britain was faced, not with war, but with "total economic ruin," for although American financing had stopped, many of the needs which lend-lease had funded would continue.[3]

Only a handful of American officials actually appreciated the magnitude of the problem which their action created for the British. From London Clayton wired his superiors shortly before Tokyo surrendered to urge that no changes concerning lend-lease be made until he could return to Washington and report on his discussions with the British. The sudden conclusion of the war, he cabled, would worsen London's balance of payments position by at least a billion dollars. Clayton's colleague in the State Department, Dean Acheson, would undoubtedly have urged similar moderation in this matter, but unfortunately for the British, the newly designated Under Secretary was vacationing in Canada when the question was discussed.[4]

Other lower level experts in the foreign policy bureaucracy warned against too hasty action, but this advice clashed with the conviction held by most senior officials that to ignore congressional and popular sentiment would be irresponsible. Opinion surveys indicated that those desiring a speedy termination of lend-lease outnumbered those willing to extend the program to help in the task of reconstruction by a margin greater than three and a half to one. Even for that aid already expended in the common war effort, a large majority voiced the opinion that Great Britain should repay the United States.[5] "The idea that America is used as a Santa Claus by an ungrateful and largely undeserving world still flourishes luxuriantly here," one officer in the British embassy sourly reported, "and the present Administration, which puts such a premium on the harmony with Congress and on carrying public opinion with it, is very sensitive to this accusation."[6]

Accordingly, those closest to the President counseled him to terminate the aid program. Though the Lend-Lease Act permitted the extension of goods and services so long as the President determined that this contributed to the defense of the United States, Crowley informed Truman, lend-lease had been introduced as a wartime measure, and both the Roosevelt administration and his own had repeatedly promised Congress that the program would be discontinued at the end of the war. Congress, moreover, had expressly prohibited the use of lend-lease for postwar rehabilitation. Not to terminate the aid, therefore, would be breaking faith with the Congress and deliberately circumventing its stated wishes. When Byrnes and Leahy joined Crowley in pushing for the end of aid to Britain and most other countries, Truman had no hesitation in doing so. To him this seemed to be nothing more than a routine decision.[7] On August 21, the White House officially announced that no new orders for aid would be accepted. Moreover, those supplies already processed (in the pipeline) and those delivered to foreign governments but not yet consumed were to be returned to the United States unless satisfactory terms for their payment were negotiated.[8]

In Britain reaction to this announcement ranged from surprise to hurt to indignation. Many believed that the expenses of demobilization and of occupying enemy countries should be considered, for lend-lease purposes, as wartime liabilities. At the very least they had expected pipeline goods and inventories already abroad to be covered under the aid program. A stunned Labour Cabinet summoned one of its top Treasury experts home from Washington, but his assessment only added to the gloom. The political climate, he reported, would not enable the administration, even if it could be persuaded to reverse or modify its decision, to do so. Rumors circulated that the American action represented Washington's comment on the recent British election. One paper called the move "a calculated blow against the new Government directed from Wall Street."[9] The assertion that FDR would never have handled Britain so roughly was repeatedly heard. Churchill rose in the Commons to label the decision "rough and harsh." British leaders, one economist observed, should "tell our people to forget about America, to tighten their belts, and to look to empire."[10]

The British, however, found little sympathy in the United States. American journalists, not privy to Whitehall's expectations of generous Phase II assistance, protested with some justification that there was nothing abrupt or surprising about the cancellation and expressed an inability to understand the tone of shocked dismay which prevailed in the United Kingdom, since administration officials had repeatedly assured Congress that lend-lease would cease with the end of hostilities. The *New York Journal-American* wrote that Great Britain had gone to "new extremes of impudence" in its complaints, while another New York daily compared the British reaction to "being mad at your rich uncle, who has been giving you hand-outs, because he died."[11] White House mail was equally opinionated. "Ending lend lease is a real 100% Yankee action," one pleased correspondent claimed. "Let me congratulate you on putting England in her place," wrote another. "Give them the old Yankee hard-driven-bargain treatment and you shall earn the affection and support of the American people."[12]

The new Labour ministers hardly needed the shock of the abrupt termination of American lend-lease to wake them to the critical economic situation which threatened their country. Even before Truman's surprise move, Dalton had circulated in the Cabinet a paper drawn up by Lord Keynes detailing Britain's financial outlook. It proved to be grim reading. The United Kingdom faced a balance of payments deficit in the coming year of £750 million, compared with a 1936-38 average of £43 million. Britain's external liabilities were a full seven times what they had been on August 31, 1939. Yet London economists would be unable to concentrate solely on restoring some sort of external financial equilibrium, because no less pressing demands confronted them at home. Four million houses had been destroyed or damaged by enemy action, to say nothing of the industrial plants bombed and rocketed. Over and above these losses, Britain's industrial capacity had been run down by the deliberate policy of deferring all but the most vital repair and maintenance. Consumer goods were approaching the point of exhaustion for a wide variety of items, while the civilian population, whose needs had for six years been subordinated to the exigencies of war, could not be expected to tolerate such conditions now that peace had returned.[13]

Keynes' recommendations were equally stark. The famous economist, normally something of an optimist, advised the government to assume a state of bankruptcy, initiate a policy of austerity, and postpone its social and economic programs. Without further aid from the United States, along with immediate governmental economies and increased exports, Keynes told the ministers a few days later, Britain faced a financial Dunkirk.[14] The Cabinet, considerably sobered by this bleak picture, took little time in approving the dispatch of a special delegation to Washington to discuss these matters with American officials, an idea which Churchill had first broached to Truman at Potsdam.[15] Again, the ministers turned to the indefatigable Keynes to lead the British mission. September 11 was selected for the opening round of the talks.

In informal discussions with Clayton throughout much of August, Keynes made it plain that he and his colleagues desired much the same sort of economic world as did the United States. Echoing this idea, Ambassador Winant predicted that the British would criticize American proposals for the reduction of trade barriers for not going far enough rather than for going too far.[16] Keynes warned, however, that London could support measures looking toward a multilateral world only if proper financial arrangements to tide Britain through the hazardous next three to five years could be made. "Realistic" minds would not be sufficient in the forthcoming discussions, he observed. What was needed was "crazy" minds, for only this sort would be able to work out an "inspired" solution to the problems confronting the United Kingdom.[17]

Winant also reported some uneasiness in British circles that the United States intended to use London's financial difficulties as a club to force acceptance of American views on commercial policy. Others, the Ambassador later wired, were suspicious that Washington planned to use the negotiations to pressure the Labour government not to go too far in its program of nationalization.[18] Whitehall was firmly determined to resist any such coercion should it appear. To this end Treasury officials sought to separate the talks on financial aid from discussions having to do with commercial policy, a maneuver which the Americans stoutly resisted.[19] At any rate, it quickly became evident that not even a socialist government would be prepared to give any unilateral commitment on imperial preferences in return for financial aid, unless the United States also agreed to a general reduction in tariffs and trade barriers. Americans must quit talking as if Britain were the sole guilty party in placing impediments in the way of a free flow of commerce, wrote London's liberal *News Chronicle* shortly after the Washington negotiations began. "[I]t is really no good America trying to cover up her own economic shortcomings with the white gown of innocence."[20]

Moreover, a general skepticism prevailed among certain groups in Britain—bankers, some labor leaders, financial journalists, and individuals close to the Board of Trade—about the desirability of American financial assistance, particularly if this were to take the form of a loan. Wherein lay the wisdom, critics pointedly asked, of incurring the greatly increased foreign indebtedness which a loan would entail, and especially to a country which might refuse to buy extensively from Britain?[21] In meeting with Clayton in August, Bevin insisted that Britain would not commit itself to any obligations which it would be unable to meet. The United Kingdom must get back its financial independence, he emphasized.[22] During the Phase II discussions the previous autumn, Keynes had indicated that any borrowing London might undertake in the United States after V-J Day would be on a very limited scale. Even as late as July 1945, a Reuters correspondent reported that Britain would almost certainly refuse any loan, "however big it might be or however low the interest rate." Britain had already "drawn on external capital heavily enough to pay for the war," editorialized the *Financial News*. It would be "ironical indeed if we were expected to incur fresh liabilities to pay for the peace."[23]

Repeatedly, comment in Great Britain returned to the belief that the United Kingdom needed aid now only because Britain had held off the common enemy by itself for more than a year before American lend-lease had been made available. It would be fundamentally wrong, ran the popular argument, if as a result of this unequal distribution of sacrifices the United Kingdom emerged from the hostilities heavily indebted to its allies.[24] Moreover, although civilian consumption in Britain was already 15 to 20 percent below prewar levels (while in the United States it was 10 to 15 percent higher), it was obvious that further stringency in food, fuel, and clothing rations would be necessary. Winant predicted that the anticipated fuel shortage for the coming winter would produce greater hardships than at any time during the war and characterized living standards for much of the British population as "scarecrow conditions."[25] Quite clearly, Britons high and low believed, assistance from the Americans was something other than merely a financial question; it also represented partial recompense for their altogether greater privation.[26]

Before leaving for Washington, Keynes was extremely, even irresponsibly, optimistic about getting the Americans to agree that the principle of equal sacrifice should be applied to the 1939-41 period, before lend-lease began. Despite repeated warnings from both Clayton and officials in the British Treasury, Keynes assured the ministers that he could persuade the Americans to offer a $6 billion grant. There would be no question of a loan to be repaid, nor, of course, of interest. Nor did he have much to say about any conditions which Washington might attach to its assistance. Such a grant would have been, in effect, little more than a continuation of lend-lease under another name. Reflecting this sanguinity, one London paper headlined its report of the Washington talks "Free Loan to Britain is Planned by United States." This undue optimism served to predispose the Cabinet against concessions later in the negotiations and made the final agreement that much more unpalatable.[27] In this instance, Keynes clearly did himself, his country, and the cause of Anglo-American cordiality a disservice by his inflated sense of his abilities to mold American opinion into the channels he thought most proper.

Washington officials speedily stripped the Englishman of his illusions. It was not that the Americans were unsympathetic to Britain's problems. They were, however, far more interested in the future than the past. In a September 17 meeting, they explicitly stated that, although the matter of past contribution to winning the war was not to be overlooked, the important questions for the future involved resolving the international debt situation and extending sufficient aid to help the world get back on its feet under conditions which would contribute to long-term stability.[28] These considerations, rather than any feeling of gratitude or obligation arising from British sacrifices prior to the time Congress approved lend-lease, were to guide the American negotiators.

Sometime earlier, Clayton had written Fred Vinson that Britain's financial problems presented the most difficult obstacle which Washington faced to achieving America's desired global order. They threatened "not only delay but, indeed, the ultimate success of our economic foreign program."[29] In preparation for the Potsdam conference, the State Department had informed Truman that unless the United States could soon come to a definite understanding with the United Kingdom regarding Britain's need for financial assistance, a serious danger existed that London policy makers "may not ultimately go along with our program to restore world-wide multilateralism in finance and trade." Credits of some sort would be "essential if we are to obtain satisfactory arrangements with them on trade and commercial policy."[30] Given the belief almost universally held in official Washington that international peace and prosperity were possible only if the American vision of a multilateral world economy were achieved, statements of this nature gave rise to powerful anxieties throughout the administration. Almost inevitably, these worries shaped the manner in which the Americans approached the financial talks with Keynes. In American eyes, the primary purpose of the negotiations was to provide the assistance necessary to lock the British economy into a multilateral system of international finance and trade.

The Americans also recognized, of course, that more immediate and tangible benefits might accrue from a proper arrangement with the British. Fears that the end of hostilities and the consequent cancellation of the vast wartime contracts might touch off another depression still frightened many in American business and governmental circles. Economists hoped that a dramatic increase in domestic spending, funded by the enforced savings of the wartime years, would more than offset this decline in federal expenditures, but the memory of the 1930s, with its massive unemployment and its idle factories, was seared too deeply on the American psyche for many to face with equanimity the prospect of the loss of these lucrative contracts. The proposed aid to Great Britain, on the other hand, promised to provide at least a partial resolution of these difficulties. If American industry met the expected drop in government orders by expanding its foreign trade, ran an argument one heard repeatedly in these months, the United States might be able to escape another economic catastrophe such as had gripped the world throughout the previous decade. To this end, a properly negotiated financial agreement might persuade the United Kingdom to loosen some of its restrictive measures which otherwise would stifle American trade. If the frozen sterling balances in London could be freed, this would make available something on the order of $13.5 billion, which could then be exchanged for American goods. If the British could be induced to make sterling convertible as well, this would open up markets not only in the sterling area, but also in other countries such as Canada, which customarily had a large favorable balance of payments with the United Kingdom. To assist the British in the recovery of their financial equilibrium, therefore, would in effect strengthen America's own economic position as well as promote world stability.[31]

A further factor, however, one which had little to do with international economics, intruded into the talks, limiting American maneuverability in seeking agreement with the British. "It is in our interest from every standpoint to help Britain," one of the State Department experts wrote Clayton as the discussions opened, "but the problem is a political one rather than an economic one."[32] On the same day another official in the Department informed Clayton that a good case could be made for granting Britain quite generous terms. He felt constrained to add, however, that the "fundamental problem is political acceptability. . . . The most important point is the *quid pro quo* we can show in terms of economic, financial and political objectives."[33] Nor was it only State Department officials who emphasized this point. From James Forrestal, the Secretary of the Navy, came the warning that the American negotiators must "be able to say that we have received considerations for what we have done above and beyond the broad, general abstraction that we get the benefits accruing from order, stability and prosperity in the rest of the world."[34] American loans and other economic settlements, one congressional committee pointedly stated in the midst of the negotiations, were "our best bargaining asset in securing political and economic concessions" from other nations. The administration would be seriously derelict in the execution of its duties if it failed to secure comparable benefits for the United States in exchange for any financial agreements it might make with foreign countries.[35]

Walter Lippmann perhaps put it best. The real issue in the current negotiations, he observed in early October, was not "what would be the right and wise thing to do. There are no serious differences of opinion about this. . . . What [the negotiators] are trying to decide, and they are all of them seriously troubled about it, is how far Congress and Parliament, the American public and the British, will permit them to solve the problem."[36] A "grand article," Keynes wrote Lippmann in response. "I wish you had been here in Washington to see yourself what an impression you had made and how it was the general subject of conversation in almost all the quarters I visited during the day." Clayton made a special point of calling attention to the column, Keynes reported, and said how much he had been struck by it. A number of Senators whom the Englishman saw similarly praised the journalist's analysis.[37]

Indeed, American actions during the autumn did reflect this concern with congressional and public feeling to which Lippmann referred. State Department bureaucrats compiled long lists of items which might be asked of the British in return for American financial assistance—"sweeteners," Halifax called them.[38] Departmental public relations experts made an active effort to contact business interests to insure that American officials had excluded nothing from the discussions. Representatives of the American Sugar Refiners Association, the aviation industry, insurance companies, and a host of similar concerns pressed the negotiators to seek wide-ranging concessions from the British.[39] Additional groups and individuals with less tangible motivations, but propelled by a traditional distrust of Great Britain or uneasiness about the new Socialist government, also demanded circumspection on the part of the American delegation.[40] Byrnes approached Bevin about the possibility of the United Kingdom's ceding certain strategic islands in the Pacific to the United States and of granting long-term military base rights to the Americans in other British territories around the globe. Aviation landing rights in Africa and the Near East were requested. All these, of course, were in addition to the fundamental concessions in the international financial and commercial fields which were a *sine qua non* to any assistance.[41] Despite agreement that the British constituted a special case and were entitled to terms which no other nation would receive, American authorities repeatedly told Keynes they could secure congressional approval only for an arrangement "dressed up in business clothes." This administration, top Washington officials were determined, was not going to leave itself open to charges that it had been hoodwinked by the crafty British.[42]

But American caution represented only half the story, for Lippmann's assessment had accorded British constraints a place of equality in inhibiting the negotiators with constraints from American sources. This Keynes largely ignored, as well he might have, since his own casual optimism had played a role in leading the British to totally unrealistic expectations of what the Americans were prepared to offer. Washington officials, for instance, never contemplated extending a free grant to the United Kingdom, but because Keynes himself had predicted exactly this sort of gift, the British resentfully viewed his failure to secure it as a sign of American niggardliness. When had Great Britain—or any other nation in the world's history—displayed such altruism, American officials finally asked in exasperation? Trapped by the inflated hopes of his countrymen—and his own—Keynes could only reply that Britain's particular combination of distress and potential constituted a unique case. If only administration officials were a little more sure of themselves, a little "bigger," one British diplomat lamented. "But unhappily they are not made that way."[43] By placing on the Americans the onus for the protracted nature of the negotiations, London decision makers were able to avoid examining their own assumptions. Such an attitude provided comfort, no doubt, but it was not conducive to progress in the Washington talks. Largely insensitive to American realities and very conscious of the worries nagging at their own public, the Cabinet and the Exchequer continually dispatched instructions to Keynes which were so rigid that they only antagonized the Americans to whom he had to present them.[44]

The course of the discussions reflected this fundamental cleavage in the perspectives of the two delegations. Although Keynes had set out for Washington expecting to find a sympathetic hearing for the British plight, he discovered instead hard bargaining and a tendency to question each and every figure which the Englishman employed in describing Britain's woes. With poignancy, if exaggerated alarm, Dalton captured the situation as it appeared from

London. As the talks went on, he wrote,

> we retreated, slowly and with a bad grace and with increasing irritation, from a free gift to an interest-free loan, and from this again to a loan bearing interest; from a larger to a smaller total of aid; and from the prospect of loose strings, some of which would be only general declarations of intention, to the most unwilling acceptance of strings so tight that they might strangle our trade and, indeed, our whole economic life.[45]

While these fears of conditions insisted upon by the Americans were surely overblown, they did reveal the extent of the anxiety experienced by those watching from afar.

Dalton later wrote that no other negotiator could have obtained a more favorable agreement from the Americans than Keynes did, but his diary entries clearly express his irritation with his chief negotiator at the time. Keynes was becoming "rather sulky," he remarked at one point. It was obvious that, "as must always be the case, following these long negotiations, those who represent us out there and we here at home have drifted into a condition of mutual incomprehension."[46] Increasingly exasperated by Keynes' apparent inability to translate London's wishes into an agreement with the Americans, the Cabinet eventually dispatched Sir Edward Bridges, the Permanent Secretary to the Treasury, in an attempt to secure better terms. He, too, found the Americans unyielding.[47] To complicate matters further, it was only with the greatest effort that Dalton was able, with considerable help from Bevin and Sir Stafford Cripps, President of the Board of Trade, to persuade the Cabinet to approve even those concessions which he was willing to sanction. It was not that the terms being offered were particularly attractive, Dalton explained, but the alternatives were even less so. If they now rejected the American proposals, another minister pointed out, could Great Britain realistically expect the United States to continue for long to shoulder its responsibilities in international political affairs?[48]

As agreement remained elusive, another consideration thrust its way with increasing frequency into the thoughts of all those interested in the outcome of the talks. Congress had made American participation in the Bretton Woods institutions conditional upon the other major signatories joining by the end of 1945. Parliament had not yet ratified the agreement, nor was it likely to do so until it could examine the terms of the financial aid package which was being discussed in Washington. Since Parliament was to adjourn on December 19, and since at least ten days had to be allowed for parliamentary consideration, this presented the negotiators with a deadline which loomed larger and larger with each passing week.[49] On the American side, a consensus existed that, as of early November, sentiment in Congress was running favorably toward the British. It was therefore important, State Department experts advised their superiors, that the loan proposal be put up to Congress as soon as possible, and certainly before the legislators recessed for the Christmas holidays.[50]

Still the discussions floundered, caught between the British conviction that they could afford to make no further concessions and the American worry that if additional benefits were not extracted, Congress and the public would never approve the agreement. As early as October 18, a dejected Keynes had spoken of breaking off negotiations and returning to London. A few days later there was discussion in the Foreign Office concerning the best course to follow if the talks failed, as was considered quite possible. "If only our waistlines could afford it," observed one Whitehall official, "it might well prove better in the long run for Anglo-American relations that the economic negotiations should break down now rather than be concluded unsatisfactorily in the present atmosphere of incomprehension and blackmail."[51] By the end of November Keynes was again talking of resigning. Only three days before the agreement was actually signed, Dalton so anticipated a break that he had begun preparing the speech he would give in the Commons announcing the failure of the talks. "But I was under no illusion as to what would follow if negotiations were not resumed and if we got no Dollar credit," he recorded in his diary.

> We would go deeper into the dark valley of austerity than ever during the war. Less food—except for bread and potatoes—in particular less meat and sugar; little cotton, and therefore, less clothes and less exports; and worst of all from the point of view of public

morale, practically no smokes since 80% of our tobacco costs dollars. Very soon, after a tremendous patriotic up-surge, the tide of public feeling would turn. Everywhere the Tories would exploit the situation, attributing every shortage to the Government's incompetence. We should be on the downward slope, leading towards defeat at the next election.[52]

Such dire consequences, however, were to be averted. As in the case of the Phase II talks the previous autumn, an impending deadline eventually pushed both sides into further concessions which made agreement possible. Considering some of the grumbling heard in London about American blackmail and shylocking, the terms of the settlement were remarkably generous. The United States agreed to extend a line of credit to the British for the amount of $3.75 billion. Interest was set at 2 percent, but since there was to be a five-year grace period before any payments became due, the true interest amounted to 1.63 percent. Moreover, interest charges were to be waived whenever the British trade balance experienced particularly difficult times. In these years Britain would in effect be receiving an interest-free loan. In addition, the Americans completely erased the British lend-lease account, a debit of more than $20 billion, and transferred to the British considerably more than $6 billion in surplus property, goods already in Britain, and pipeline supplies for $650 million, to be paid on the same terms as the $3.75 billion credit. Thus, in a single stroke, the United States removed the possibility of a war debt specter haunting postwar relations as it had a quarter-century earlier.

In return, the British accepted strict limitations on their use of exchange controls and promised not to apply discriminatory restrictions against American goods. Sterling was to become freely convertible within a year, thereby dissolving the sterling area dollar pool. Blocked sterling balances held by other nations were to be scaled down and refunded. Keynes also pledged that the British would accept as a basis of discussion a series of proposals which Washington wanted considered by an international conference on trade and employment, proposals calling for the elimination of discriminatory tariffs. Finally, the British committed themselves to ratifying the Bretton Woods agreements establishing the IMF and the World Bank. Though at first glance these "strings" appeared to entail extensive British concessions, in reality they amounted to little more than the reaffirmation and application of the promises concerning trade barriers made at the time the two countries signed the Master Lend-Lease Agreement. Only in demanding a relatively brief transition period before sterling would become fully convertible can the American conditions be termed stiff.[53]

Obviously, this settlement came nowhere near the original hopes held by Keynes and the more optimistic London officials. The complaints and bitterness which accompanied the negotiations amply testify to this. Still, much of this disappointment—and this is important—arose not from a comparison with the norm in international affairs, but from inflated hopes that the Americans would be more disposed to accord Great Britain not simply special treatment, but a largesse unprecedented in relations between two sovereign states. When measured against less lofty standards, British diplomats were less critical in their assessments. Halifax wrote that the agreements were not unfair and were vastly preferable to the alternative of failure. The Americans, he reported to Eden, now in the Opposition, "have made very genuine efforts to help and to have regard to our difficulties."[54] Keynes agreed completely. "There is no question that we are working in an atmosphere of great friendliness and an intense desire on their part to work something out to our advantage," he wired London after several weeks of meetings.[55] Dalton, too, in his less frenzied moments, admitted that "the Yanks" had valid arguments on some of the issues dividing the two delegations and that many of their disputes seemed rather trivial "against the great background of 4.4 billion Dollars."[56]

So it misrepresents these events to write, as some scholars have done, that the arrangements which were ultimately agreed upon had to be "forced upon the hesitant English." To picture the negotiations in an adversary framework, to paint the two delegations as distrustful antagonists, the stronger out to coerce the weaker, is to distort the dynamics which informed the discussions.[57] There was, to be sure, hard bargaining and, at times, deeply felt resentment. In a process as drawn out and detailed as was this one, such instances are virtually unavoidable when individuals representing two different countries and two varying perspectives come together. What was remarkable, however, was the degree to which the concept of partnership, of a similarity if not identity of interests prevailed.

Time and again American officials argued within their own delegation that a particular United States proposal was too rigid, or that the British position on some issue had merit.[58] Keynes' biographer, himself a distinguished economist, has noted that the Americans went to great lengths to make the burden of the interest payments practically negligible. One less sympathetic member of the American delegation complained that his countrymen seemed intent on finding the most lenient terms of settlement possible for the British.[59] In another instance, one of the American working groups, in discussing how certain petroleum stores should be priced, decided that even though the American figures were justified, this was a place where the British stand could be defended too. Solely for this reason, the British position was accepted.[60] These examples, rather than instances of acrimony, more accurately indicate the attitudes which guided the negotiators. For many ranking American officials, warm feelings of friendship and admiration for Keynes further reinforced the general sense of joint endeavor. There is no denying that the Americans were hard bargainers, or that the economic partnership they sought was to be largely on American terms. Still, this was infinitely preferable in British eyes to outright antagonism.

The disagreements which divided the two delegations during the discussions did not involve basic doctrinal disputes. Both sides agreed upon the desirability of a world economic order based upon freely flowing and constantly expanding trade. The Americans wished to talk of fundamental principles and long-term solutions, however, the British of what it would be possible for their embattled nation to do in the immediate future. Keynes, for instance, rested his case for generosity toward Great Britain on the argument that it was only by this means that the British would be able to enter into international cooperation with the United States on the general principle of multilateralism.[61] "The representatives of the U.K. expressed agreement with the general objectives of the American administration as being in the best interests of both countries and of the world at large," read the principal British document setting forth London's position.

> At the same time the persisting financial consequences to the economy of the U.K., which have resulted from the war, make it impracticable, whatever the Government of the U.K. may wish, to remove or substantially modify the various defensive mechanisms, which have been built up to conserve the national resources under the impact of war, except with assistance from outside.[62]

The Americans, on the other hand, all too confidently assumed that international economic stability—and British recovery—could be achieved merely by reducing trade barriers and other impediments to the unfettered exchange of goods and money. "It should be stressed," an aide wrote Clayton shortly before the talks opened, "that our proposals . . . are in the British interest no less than ours. Britain, as the banking and trading nation par excellence, has the most to gain from measures to assure that the world will not drift apart into permanent trade and financial blocs" as a result of its temporary disequilibrium.[63] Armed with this belief in the essential benevolence as well as wisdom of their policies, and convinced that they more than the British appreciated what the legislatures and publics in both countries would tolerate, these cocksure representatives of history's mightiest nation relentlessly pressed their British visitors into concessions the latter felt unwise and unwarranted. That London's sensibilities were bruised is not surprising, but that hardly negates the unprecedented character of the aid package.

In at least one instance, moreover, British worries about Washington's motivations proved highly exaggerated. There appears to be no evidence that the election of a Labour government made any American official more hesitant in extending assistance to

Great Britain, as some Whitehall analysts had predicted might be the case. To be sure, the various conditions which accompanied the credit, by tying Britain to the Bretton Woods system, might have imposed limits on how far the Attlee government could move toward socialism,[64] but not one concrete piece of evidence has been found to show that this was an active motivation of anyone with influence in the Washington policy-making process. On the contrary, Clayton explicitly stated that there was nothing the United States could or should do to prevent the United Kingdom from adopting any domestic economic policy it wished, and to attempt to do so would entail totally inexcusable interference in the internal affairs of a sovereign state.[65]

Nor does it seem that Washington decided to aid the British as part of an attempt to forge an alliance against the Soviet Union. Ideas of this nature may have occurred to some or all of the Americans, but not a single individual participating in the negotiations offered this as a reason for helping London. Indeed, at least one Washington official closely involved in the talks, Commerce Secretary Henry Wallace, complained often and vociferously of British attempts to ferment distrust between the United States and Russia. In his mind at any rate, the possible repercussions on relations with Moscow of assisting Great Britain represented a liability rather than a benefit.[66] Distrust both of the ruling Labourites and of the Russians permeated the public discussion of the British credit, but neither seems to have been important in the Truman administration's willingness to help the British rebuild their war-torn island.

Of course, successful completion of the negotiations did not insure delivery of the aid. The two delegations had finally come to terms, though only after many weeks of arduous, closely argued discussions. Now each had to persuade its countrymen that that nebulous concept, the national interest, had been amply guarded. Nor was it certain that Parliament would accept the conditions which accompanied the credit, nor that Congress would find them sufficient. Yet, in deciding the ultimate fate of the aid program, British members of Parliament and American congressmen would be determining more than merely the future of the

Anglo-American partnership. Britain's very position in world affairs was at issue. And should relations with the enigmatic Russians continue to deteriorate, a disabled United Kingdom no longer able to assume an active role throughout the globe would leave the United States alone with the Soviets to carve up the world into two gigantic empires staring apprehensively at each other across an abyss of incomprehension and distrust.

11

American Disengagement— British Disenchantment

The financial negotiations in the autumn of 1945 served as a sharp reminder of the fundamental shift which had occurred in Great Britain's position in the international power equilibrium during the long years of war. Despite their proud words, Keynes and his fellow members of the British delegation had come to Washington as supplicants. They would not have admitted this—indeed, Britain still had much to offer in exchange for American aid—but the inescapable conclusion which these discussions made manifest was that the United Kingdom was no longer an independent force in world affairs. Other episodes in the weeks following the Japanese surrender further emphasized this essential fact. In many areas around the globe where the British once held uncontested sway, the United States found itself, as a result of the war-induced power shift, in a position where its most carelessly taken actions dictated the destinies of entire nations.

One early instance of Washington being called upon to exercise this newly acquired influence occurred while the details of the Japanese surrender were still being worked out. With the first word of Tokyo's intention to lay down its arms, Chiang Kai-shek directed that the Japanese forces in Hongkong surrender only to Chinese armies, despite the fact that Hongkong had been a

British possession for over a century. Attlee immediately appealed to Truman, asking the President to overrule Chiang and permit the British to accept the surrender of the city.[1] For Attlee the matter was crucial. To acquiesce in the return of Chinese troops to Hongkong would have provoked a domestic storm of gargantuan proportions throughout Great Britain. Equally important, Hongkong was a major commercial and industrial center for British economic interests and served as a symbol of British strength in the Far East. Although the Labour party did not possess the sentimental attachments to empire which the Conservatives had, personal, political, economic, strategic, and prestige considerations all dictated Attlee's quick response.

To Truman the choice appeared one between "established rights" and America's antipathy toward European colonialism. Roosevelt only a few weeks before his death had repeated his often-voiced desire to see the British return Hongkong to China. Truman himself was later to write: "We, as a people, have always accepted and encouraged the undeniable right of a people to determine its own political destiny. . . . There could be no 'ifs' attached to this right."[2] Here, it appeared, was a splendid opportunity to fulfill the dead President's dream and to demonstrate America's commitment to a new world free of exploitive imperialism.

The State Department, on the other hand, warned that the United States must mesh its desire for increased political freedom for colonial peoples with the necessity of maintaining Big Power harmony. Washington might properly continue to press for a greater measure of self-government for these nations, read one report circulated throughout the bureaucracy, but "it should avoid any course of action which would seriously impair the unity of the major United Nations."[3] Moreover, on any reasonable scale of priorities Great Britain was certainly more important than an exhausted, faction-ridden China. Truman, therefore, instructed General Douglas MacArthur to arrange for the surrender of Hongkong to British authorities, while at the same time sending word to Chiang that this action did not in any way represent American views regarding the future status of the city. In the face of strenuous Chinese protests, the President blithefully reassured

Chiang that the problem was "primarily a military matter of an operational character."[4] Yet Truman was surely aware of the implications of this action for the ultimate status of Hongkong. After all, he had recently received a lecture himself from Churchill, in connection with another city claimed by two disputants, that "Possession is nine points of the law."[5]

If London drew the impression from this episode that the driving anticolonialism which had permeated the Roosevelt administration no longer wielded such influence now that another man occupied the White House, other American actions in the Far East at this time reinforced this feeling. In Indochina United States troops rapidly withdrew following the Japanese surrender, leaving the field to British and French forces. Plans for a four-power trusteeship in Korea moved forward, notwithstanding Roosevelt's earlier suggestion to Stalin that London be excluded from this area. Key officials in the State Department made it clear to their Whitehall friends that visionary schemes of an anticolonial nature were not among Washington's priorities.[6] Particular care must be exercised, one study cautioned, that in the formulation of American policies for the Orient, Washington not take steps which might "undermine the influence of the West."[7]

Paradoxically, these actions indicated neither a declining American interest in the Far East nor a willingness on the part of Washington policy makers to leave Asian matters largely to the British. Hongkong, Indochina, Korea—these areas were more or less peripheral regions, of at best secondary importance in a strategic and economic sense. Years before two unsuccessful wars reinforced this feeling, United States officials had little desire to become involved on the vast Asian mainland. Besides, American interests in the Far East could be adequately protected from other bases of operation. And when matters relating to these areas arose, Washington was not nearly so accommodating in its treatment of its British ally.

American military planners had argued almost since Pearl Harbor that in any postwar settlement the United States must secure control of a large number of strategically located islands scattered throughout the Pacific. Some of these had formerly been Japanese mandates, while others were owned or administered by the British, the French, or one or another of the Dominions. A third group included a lengthy list whose sovereignty was disputed, often between London and Washington. The United States had formally stated that it had "no thought of territorial expansion" at Japan's expense.[8] Roosevelt, moreover, had pledged himself to placing the Japanese mandates under international trusteeship.[9] Yet by mid-1945, despite these commitments, few in official Washington circles opposed plans for the acquisition either of long-term military base rights or of exclusive American control over many of these islands. It was the "firm if unspoken" intention of the United States, according to War Department officers preparing for the Potsdam conference, "to keep the rest of the world militarily out of the Pacific."[10]

"Keeping the rest of the world out of the Pacific" entailed, among other things, some rather extensive demands being placed upon the British. "You certainly can't conceive of a conflict between Britain and [the] U.S.," Byrnes remarked to Halifax at one point. That being the case, the Secretary continued, it would be well for the United States to assume the major security responsibilities in the Pacific.[11] To this end the State Department in November 1945 requested that the United Kingdom withdraw its claims to a number of islands whose sovereignty was contested by the two nations. In addition, London was asked to grant the United States sweeping base rights in many of its Far Eastern possessions.[12] Diplomats in Whitehall were not altogether reluctant to meet the Americans in some of these demands, particularly if cooperation of this sort might induce a more friendly attitude toward the credit to Britain which was soon to be sent to Congress. The British Chiefs of Staff, on the other hand, insisted upon more concrete benefits in the military-security sphere, while spokesmen for Australia and New Zealand flatly vetoed such ideas. Other London policy makers warned of setting a precedent which might give the Soviets an opportunity to demand bases in Denmark or Norway.[13]

American actions in the more immediately important matter of the occupation and control of Japan demonstrated this same singleness of purpose. The handling of Tokyo's offer to surrender in itself warned the British that working with the United States in this area was not likely to be easy. When word that the Japanese had accepted American terms reached Washington on the afternoon of August 14, Byrnes at once arranged a four-way teletype link-up with London, Moscow, and Chungking. After the Secretary had relayed the text of the Japanese reply, there was some discussion whether this constituted full acceptance of allied terms. Byrnes brusquely interrupted to say that the United States regarded the Japanese note as equivalent to unconditional surrender and that Truman was going to announce American acceptance in ninety minutes. He then invited the others to do likewise and broke the circuit.[14]

This inauspicious beginning set the tone for Anglo-American collaboration in most matters concerning Japan. The occupation of the Japanese islands was in theory an allied operation, and MacArthur, as Supreme Commander for the Allied Powers, was actually an international administrator and not simply a United States official. Yet, despite statements in Washington to the contrary, occupation policies remained tightly in American hands.[15] The principal directive governing the postwar treatment of Japan clearly stated American intentions on this score. Every effort would be made, this document observed, "by consultation and by constitution of appropriate advisory bodies," to establish policies which would satisfy the major Allies, but "in the event of any differences of opinion among them, the policies of the United States will govern." Though Washington was perfectly content to have its allies share in the occupation duties, they were to do so only under close American supervision.[16]

A variety of considerations combined to produce this determination to dominate proceedings in Japan so thoroughly. Few policy makers desired arrangements which would permit the same intransigence which American officials had encountered in attempting to work with Soviet authorities in Germany and the

European satellite states.[17] The feeling that American predominance arose naturally from the fact that the United States had
done the major share of the fighting against Japan similarly encouraged this attitude (though Washington did not necessarily see
fit to apply this same criterion in eastern Europe).[18] MacArthur's
irascible nature provides a portion of the explanation, for the
pugnacious general made it clear that he desired help from neither
the British nor the Russians.[19] Finally, Washington officials believed that the war had conclusively demonstrated that the United
States had the "paramount interest in and responsibility for" peace
and security in the Pacific, despite the fact that Averell Harriman
was wiring from Moscow that "Japan as much as Eastern Europe
is in [the] Soviet zone of vital strategic interest."[20]

For whatever reasons, policies drawn up in the State Department's Office of Far Eastern Affairs proved noticeably restrictive
in the degree to which Washington's major partners were accorded even superficial participation in the control processes. China
and the Soviet Union originally accepted the basic American proposal for a Far Eastern Advisory Commission, but the British
objected to any supervisory body with only advisory powers.[21]
"We are quite willing to let [the Americans] take the lead in
controlling Japan," observed one Foreign Office representative as
the occupation began to take shape, "[but] . . . H.M.G. surely
cannot accept the assumption which the Americans appear to be
making that we have given them unlimited power of attorney in
all matters relating to Japan."[22] Under prodding by officials of the
Department's European desk, Byrnes later in the fall agreed to
some limited concessions to assuage British sensibilities.[23] By the
end of the year, however, it was clear that the Japanese occupation
was to be an American operation. Although Byrnes had permitted
the word "Advisory" to be dropped from the title of the allied
body which was to work with MacArthur, the Far Eastern Commission could do little more than discuss and then approve, but
not disapprove, previous American actions. Though the council
was in theory the supreme policy-making body for Japan, with the
right to review all of MacArthur's directives, American veto power

could effectively block any action the FEC sought to take. It held a position, a later American ambassador to Japan would recall, of "pompous futility."[24]

Thus, in matters concerning the crucially important question of the current control and probable future orientation of Japan, Washington displayed little disposition to effect any meaningful collaboration with the British, or even to distinguish between Great Britain and the Soviet Union. Any bipolar analysis in this area would have to pit the United States against virtually all other nations with an interest in Far Eastern affairs. Despite the fact that the interests of the two nations in Japan were largely the same, British policy makers found their American counterparts in both Washington and Tokyo unconcerned with the sort of close collaboration which publicists of both governments were fond of extolling.

To an important degree, international relations in the autumn of 1945 revolved around the question of Moscow's intentions. Following the collapse in early October of the first session of the Council of Foreign Ministers, top foreign affairs experts in both Washington and London devoted more time to finding some way of maintaining at least a modicum of collaboration with the Kremlin than to any other matter. They ultimately failed, of course, but their method of approaching this problem—and particularly the degree to which each set of officials looked to the other for assistance and support—reveals something of the nature of the Anglo-American partnership as it moved beyond the period of wartime cooperation.

Leading statesmen in the two capitals recognized that in matters pertaining to relations with the Soviets, the interests of their two nations, while not identical, ran along parallel lines. Perception of this basic fact was of vital importance, for as the schism between Russia and its erstwhile allies grew and came to be accepted as a part of the international scene in the years after the war, this inevitably drove Great Britain and the United States, despite real differences producing irritation and hostility in many places around the globe, closer together. Thus, Halifax could in all sincerity tell Byrnes, "We have reached the point where every Britisher sleeps better at night knowing you have a strong navy."[25]

Yet Washington policy makers demonstrated remarkably little disposition to translate this awareness of a similarity of interests into any sort of a concerted policy with the British. In part this reflected the still healthy distrust of London's intentions and ambitions which the wartime partnership had failed to erase. Just days before the Japanese surrender, a now-retired Hopkins complained, "To hear some people talk about the British, you would think [they] were our potential enemies." At least one Cabinet officer, Commerce Secretary Henry Wallace, warned Truman that Britain's game had always been one of international intrigue and cautioned the President that London sought to promote an unbreachable rupture between the United States and the Soviet Union. If Wallace's diary is to be believed, Truman agreed with these charges.[26] Lingering suspicions of British imperialism and newly awakened fears of British socialism also contributed to a disinclination to embrace the United Kingdom too closely, as did resentment created by British policies in Palestine. In early 1946, the American Ambassador in Cuba wrote a friend in the State Department, "I sometimes feel that the Mother Country needs to be reminded that the umbilical cord was cut in 1776." The irritation and distrust implicit in this statement accurately captures the lack of warmth toward Great Britain still felt by many American officials, despite mounting apprehensions about the possibility of good relations with the Soviet Union.[27]

Much of the reluctance in Washington to forge a common policy with the British, however, can be attributed to the vacillating nature of American thinking on relations with the Soviets. The idea that the establishment of a lasting peace required continued collaboration with Russia still prevailed in Washington, and there was a real hesitancy to take actions that sensitive men in the Kremlin might construe as directed toward the creation of an Anglo-American bloc aimed at the Soviet Union. Fears of conveying the impression that London and Washington were "ganging up" on Russia still carried weight within American policy-making circles.[28] Furthermore, neither official nor public opinion had yet crystallized into an attitude of antagonism toward the Soviets which might propel the administration into a more forceful position.[29]

This feeling of uncertainty about the Russians also characterized the thinking of the new Attlee government. On the one hand, the British Prime Minister could write Jan Smuts, "We believe that the only road to safety lies in the maintenance of trust and understanding between the Great Powers," in order that an effective peace-keeping organization, "on which our hopes for the future are based," could be established. "I think we must at all costs avoid trying to seek a cure [for Anglo-Soviet friction] by building up Germany or by forming blocs aimed at Russia."[30] Yet at the same time, the Labourites were forced to admit the mistaken nature of their initial hopes that their socialist sympathies might enable them to work more easily with the Kremlin than the Tories could have done. By October, Foreign Office officials had concluded that the Labour victory had produced just the opposite result, since the Soviets feared that a successful Labour Party in the United Kingdom might strengthen the moderate socialists on the continent against the Communists. By mid-December, officials in the British embassy in Washington were complaining of the Truman administration's unwillingness to stand up to the Russians. "In spite of accumulating evidence of Soviet intransigence," Halifax cabled London, "there is a stubborn determination in responsible quarters to rationalise the actions of the Soviet Union wherever possible and to make conciliatory moves as and when the opportunity presents itself."[31]

As a consequence, although Whitehall officials resisted the idea that further collaboration with Moscow could be attained only on terms dictated by the Soviets, they fought equally hard American worries of "ganging up" on the Russians. Instead, they argued that the Kremlin was likely to become more cooperative only when presented with concrete evidence of Anglo-American unity. Hence, they were gravely concerned, even resentful, at Washington balkiness in coordinating approaches toward the Russians. Harriman remembers that Bevin as early as September 1945 was quite openly bitter about Byrnes' unilateralism in dealing with the Soviets. Even a return to the tactics of Hull and Stettinius, the Foreign Secretary hinted, would be preferable to Byrnes' attitude.[32] Particularly galling to the Foreign Office was the lingering tendency in some American circles to paint the international scene as a clash between the rival imperial interests of Britain and Russia, in which it behooved the United States to act as a mediator or conciliator. This type of wishful thinking, one Whitehall official bitingly observed, was never applied to the Far East, where American interests were unmistakable.[33]

Notwithstanding British hopes, however, the formal machinery of the wartime partnership gradually dissolved over the course of the fall. A good illustration of the prevailing disposition in Washington to play a lone hand in international affairs is provided by the alacrity with which the bilateral bodies and committees spawned in the years after Pearl Harbor were dismantled. On September 25, 1945, Truman approved a statement calling for the early abolition of the Anglo-American combined boards. In response to a suggestion from Attlee that this matter be carefully examined before precipitant action was taken, the President wrote that such a study would serve no useful purpose.[34]

A more significant question concerned the future of the Combined Chiefs of Staff. At both Yalta and Potsdam the British had argued for its continuation for a number of years after the war. As one British officer remarked, "It seemed perfectly obvious that the British nations [*sic*] and the United States were in the same boat and if our way of life were going to continue we would have to defend it together against any eventual threat." There was also some sentiment on the American side—from Secretary of the Navy James Forrestal and Henry H. Arnold, the commanding general of the Army Air Forces, for example—for a continuation of close military collaboration with the British.[35] But the predominant feeling in both civilian and military circles was that political decisions concerning the goals of the two countries must precede any action in the military sphere. As one top-level memorandum in the War Department observed, "Since U.S. and British aims may very well be in conflict, particularly in the western hemisphere, it would . . . seem desirable not to be confined at present by the requirement for such military collaboration."[36] Washington was eventually persuaded to retain the CCS until the peace treaties were signed, a day which was not thought to be far off. But a growing reserve on the part of many United States officials, anticipating this termination, impeded the exchange of information and generally reduced the efficacy of the collaboration.[37]

If concern over relations with the Soviet Union formed one recurring strand in the thinking of statesmen in London and Washington throughout the autumn months of 1945, the future of the recently discovered atomic energy furnished a topic of equal importance occupying leadership circles in the two nations. In the first years after its inception the atomic bomb was looked upon not as merely another and more powerful weapon but as "a discovery more revolutionary in human society than the invention of the wheel, the use of metals, or the steam or internal combustion engine."[38] One chairman of the Atomic Energy Commission later recalled that in the period immediately following the Japanese surrender, the United States was in "the uniquely favourable position of being the sole possessor of a weapon that was almost universally credited with a capacity to destroy cities on a ratio of one bomb per city, and to end wars on a ratio of two bombs per war."[39] In a message to Truman shortly after the Hiroshima explosion, Attlee solemnly, almost reverently, wrote, "A new factor pregnant with immense possibilities for good or evil has come into existence." Several weeks later he told the President that this extraordinary discovery called for "very far-reaching changes in the relationship between States . . . and a new valuation of what are called national interests."[40]

The Prime Minister would discover, however, that the Truman administration reacted to the harnessing of this mighty force in very predictable, timeworn ways. Despite his own admission that "the release of atomic energy constitutes a new force too revolutionary to consider in the framework of old ideas,"[41] the President personally saw to it that American policy was guided largely by traditional concepts of the national interest. The discussion of atomic energy in governmental circles in the months after Hiroshima and Nagasaki fell into two categories: the possibility of international control, and the future of the wartime Anglo-American cooperation which had so greatly facilitated the invention of the atom bomb. In considering both these issues, Washington officials viewed this new power as a national treasure, to be carefully hoarded until such time as the rest of the world proved itself worthy of sharing in the responsibilities and benefits widely expected to accompany further development of atomic energy. This insured that the American reluctance to move in concert with the British would also manifest itself in this area, to the disappointment and alarm of London policy makers.

Collaboration in the field of atomic energy had proved difficult even at the height of the war, primarily because of American hesitancy in accepting scientists from the United Kingdom as full partners in the vast undertaking. The American general who directed the entire research and development program later admitted that his policy during the war had consistently been to tell the British as little as possible.[42] Finally, in order to secure Roosevelt's assent that the wartime research effort would function on the basis of equal partnership, Churchill had agreed, during the first Quebec conference in August 1943, that the United States President alone would have the authority to determine what rights in the postwar industrial application of atomic energy the British would possess.[43] A year later, as the two allied statesmen conferred at Hyde Park following the Octagon meeting, they initialed a revised agreement on the subject which read in part: "Full collaboration between the United States and the British Government in developing TUBE ALLOYS [the code name for atomic energy] for military and commercial purposes should continue after the defeat of Japan unless and until terminated by joint agreement."[44]

Roosevelt's actual intentions in signing this Hyde Park aide-mémoire provoked considerable subsequent disagreement. Leahy informed Truman that his predecessor had made no promise about sharing details concerning the manufacture of atomic bombs, and this was the position which Truman took in all his dealings with the British.[45] On the other hand, Vannevar Bush, one of the scientists most involved in the development of this new and frightening force, reported that Roosevelt had said that he had talked with Churchill along the lines of a complete interchange with Great Britain after the war on all phases of atomic energy.[46] At any rate, it seems clear that Churchill thought he had secured a promise of total postwar collaboration, a pledge which implied a continuation of the current military partnership.[47] Like many of the understandings between Roosevelt and Churchill, however, this agreement was only an informal arrangement and in no way bound the new White House occupant.

Following FDR's death, Truman was from the first predisposed to deal with atomic energy on a unilateral basis. In the days after the Hiroshima explosion Attlee suggested that he and the President issue a joint statement to assure the world of their good intentions with respect to the bomb. Truman instead went ahead with his prior plans to send his own message to Congress on the subject. Much more alarming to the British were indications that the diminished need for security precautions accompanying the end of the war brought with it no increase in the flow of information concerning atomic energy from the Americans. Truman quickly made it clear that he distinguished between basic scientific principles, which were widely known, and the actual manufacturing processes involved in the production of an atomic bomb, the "practical know-how," he called it.[48] This latter category of information was not to be shared with Britain or any other country, "any more than we would make freely available any of our trade secrets."[49] He was fortified in this distinction by advice from the State Department, the military, and many of the leading scientists, though each counseled this course for different and often contradictory reasons.[50] As had happened many times before, this matter had also become embroiled in a domestic controversy, in this case a desire on the part of Congress to reassert its authority over the conduct of foreign affairs which it had largely let slip during the hostilities. By bowing before congressional demands that no information be shared without legislative consent, Truman hoped to defuse this issue and thereby retain control of this new force in the executive branch.[51]

On the other side of the atomic energy question, that concerning international control, less marked differences separated Washington and London. During the second week in November, Attlee flew to the United States, where he, Truman, and Canadian Prime Minister William L. Mackenzie King, the third member of the wartime triumvirate which developed the bomb, conferred for several days. The ideas each of the three held relating to the steps which should be taken to insure that atomic energy was not misused were for the most part comparable, and those disagreements which did arise proved amenable to compromise. On the most important matter before the three statesmen, Attlee showed himself no more willing than Truman to share detailed information with the Russians without a great deal more evidence than had lately been received concerning the peaceful intentions of the Kremlin. On November 15, the three statesmen released a Joint Declaration announcing they intended to keep detailed knowledge regarding the practical application of atomic energy to themselves, and proposing the establishment of a United Nations commission to examine the whole problem in greater detail.[52]

A second, considerably less publicized aspect of the November talks in Washington concerned the future of the bilateral atomic partnership. London officials had been disappointed and angered by indications that the Truman administration had no intentions of sharing its expertise with the United Kingdom, a proficiency acquired with the help of British brainpower and research activities. By October 1945, the British had decided to set up their own atomic research plant at Harwell, a decision in effect to produce their own bomb. This decision was the result of a combination of security and prestige considerations, hopes that research might produce important industrial and commercial applications, and sheer bureaucratic momentum.[53] If, however, the Americans refused to share the knowledge they had gained during the common wartime effort, the British task would be both much longer and more costly.

Thus, Attlee journeyed to Washington in part to secure a continuation of that complete cooperation which Roosevelt had promised Churchill at Hyde Park the previous autumn. The Prime Minister's worst fears about American intransigence were never met, and on the surface at least, it appeared that he had achieved total success in this mission. On November 16, Truman, Attlee, and Mackenzie King signed a brief memo which called for "full and effective cooperation in the field of atomic energy" among the three nations. There were no conditions or exceptions mentioned in this short statement. Attlee left Washington confident that all difficulties in the way of peacetime collaboration had been removed.[54]

He should not have been so sanguine, for in the absence of any clarifying or qualifying clauses, a certain degree of legalistic legerdemain might suffice to interpret this broad injunction in a number of different ways. Indeed, discussion among lower level experts from the two nations demonstrated that a certain disparity still existed regarding the exact meaning of those crucial words "full and effective." Ultimately, General Leslie Groves for the United States and Sir John Anderson for Great Britain signed a Memorandum of Intention which was to serve as a guide in implementing the simple directive of their superiors. This document recommended that all uranium and thorium supplies which might be acquired by either country should be held jointly, a proposal extremely favorable to the United States since it was anticipated that South Africa would soon produce large deposits of uranium. The memorandum also called for complete cooperation in the exchange of information on basic scientific research. In the field of development, design, construction, and operation of atomic plants, cooperation was recognized as desirable in principle, but at American insistence, it was stipulated that the sharing of information in this area would be regulated by ad hoc arrangements.[55] London officials, on the basis of painful experience, should have immediately been alerted by this hedging on the part of the United States.

The end of the war also loosened restraints in the Middle East which during the hostilities had more or less muffled the resentment which the close Anglo-American partnership had inevitably engendered. Officials in both Washington and London increasingly vocalized their dissatisfaction with the behavior of the other nation in this oil-rich region. Few had doubts about the justice of their complaints. "I do not think we want a preeminent position over the British, either political or economic," one State Department bureaucrat wrote as the fighting in the Pacific sped to its abrupt conclusion. However, "[w]e do want them to stop obstructing our legitimate requests."[56]

The British for their part thought that American definitions of "legitimate requests" often proved rather too sweeping. "Diplomatic gangsterism," a British official in Jidda termed American practices.[57] Foreign Office representatives welcomed United States interest in the Middle East as part of their continuing desire to secure American participation in world affairs, but were at the same time determined to maintain Britain's predominant political and commercial position in the region.[58] Out of this mixed bundle of motives and perspectives came increasingly frequent accusations of economic discrimination and political back-stabbing. "British obstructionist tactics in the Middle East" became a stock phrase within the State Department bureaucracy. Employing similar descriptions, officials in London worried about Washington's "obstructive and disapproving attitude, the basis and reason of which remained obscure."[59] Diplomats in both capitals expressed concern that if the United States and Great Britain competed against each other too vigorously in the region, the Russians might, in the words of one State Department expert, "find it easier to throw us both out."[60]

Disputes over oil concessions and aviation rights contributed to the atmosphere of suspicion which generally enveloped British-American relations in the Middle East, but ill-feelings growing out of differences on another matter poisoned ties between Washington and London to an even greater extent. Of all the questions confronting the foreign affairs experts of the two nations in the autumn of 1945, the perplexing problem of the future of Palestine was the most emotional and least reasoned-out. To complicate matters further, the issue was, for millions of Americans and a good number of Britishers as well, a visceral one. As such, mere rationality counted for little. Passion, not reason, was to be the controlling factor in Anglo-American exchanges on this issue. And passion is hardly conducive to a friendly adjustment of honestly held differences.

The problem of Palestine was not, of course, a new one. During the First World War the British government had opened a Pandora's box of trials and grief by endorsing with the controversial Balfour Declaration the concept of a Jewish national home in Palestine. Not surprisingly, the Arab inhabitants of that land had reacted strongly against any such proposal, and as they increasingly recognized the need for Arab good will in the late 1930s, London authorities backed off from the idea. With the publication of the 1939 White Paper, the British promised to place strict limitations on future Jewish immigration and prohibited the sale of land in certain areas to Jews. The situation had seethed without actually erupting throughout the years of war, but with the termination of hostilities, British officials in Palestine found themselves faced with a growing number of Jews immigrating illegally into the country as well as a mounting Jewish campaign of terrorism within Palestine.

When Truman stepped into this thicket on April 12, 1945, he found few certainties to guide his policy. From his predecessor he inherited a legacy of incompatible assurances to Arab and Jew. With characteristic caution, Roosevelt had managed to placate both sides with sweeping generalities and ambiguous banalities without committing himself to any particular course of action.[61] Forced to strike out without clear precedents, Truman soon confronted a further difficulty when he discovered that the advice offered by his foreign affairs experts conflicted with his humanitarian impulses and his political instincts. The State Department, the military, and the OSS all cautioned him to avoid making commitments which might inflame the Arabs in the Middle East or lead to developments which would require the commitment of American troops or resources in that region. Viewing the issue largely from the perspective of America's role in international affairs, these groups all argued that Arab friendship was more important to Unites States interests in the Middle East than was a Jewish state.[62]

From the vantage point of the White House, however, other considerations had to be taken into account. Zionist feeling was very marked in the United States, and not merely because of the many Jews there, nor even because of the appalling horrors suffered by the Jews in Hitler's Europe. The concept of a Jewish national home appealed to the idealistic, humanitarian, and liberal beliefs of the American people, to their sense of justice and fair play. Powerful organizations propelled by various combinations of these factors coalesced to create great pressures on Truman to take some action to express his sympathies for the plight of the Jewish displaced persons in Europe and to facilitate the entry into Palestine of as many of these DPs as desired to immigrate. The President was so besieged with letters, petitions, pleas, and offers of advice from Zionist groups that one White House secretary finally quipped, only half-humorously, "If this keeps up, he will be an honorary Rabbi before we are out of this place."[63] Congressmen were themselves the objects of intense lobbying, providing in turn further pressure on the President. On July 3, as Truman prepared to embark for the voyage to Potsdam, he received a letter signed by 54 senators and 250 members of the House (a majority of each body) demanding unrestricted Jewish immigration and colonization and urging that the United States take the lead in establishing Palestine as a free and democratic Jewish commonwealth.[64]

Yet to say that domestic pressure groups alone molded Truman's attitudes toward the Palestine issue would be unjust. Certainly their potential political clout would have made implementation of a pro-Arab policy more difficult, but fortunately for the President, the requirements of practical politics meshed nicely with his own highly developed sense of right and wrong. To Truman the question of Palestine was inseparable from that of the fate of those Jewish victims of Hitler's madness still surviving in Europe. Although both Attlee and his own advisers tried to divorce the two issues, Truman obstinately refused to permit this. Perhaps the severe illness of his childhood, which left him paralyzed for some months, fostered in him a compassion and an understanding for others who had been subjected to suffering and torment. For whatever reason, his strong if somewhat simplistic concept of morality led him to sympathize with those Jews desiring to immigrate to Palestine. Basic human decency required this, he believed; Arab rights would have to be subordinated to this imperative. Besides, the Arab world had largely forfeited its claims for consideration, for during the war it had been only lukewarm at best in its support of the Allies, and many Arabs had been openly pro-German. As a consequence, the arguments of his advisers that Arab good will had to be carefully cultivated had little impact on a President more attuned to the fate of the Jewish displaced persons wandering throughout central Europe.[65] In the midst of the Potsdam conference he wrote Churchill expressing the hope that Britain would find it possible to lift the White Paper restrictions on Jewish immigration into Palestine.[66]

Great Britain, on the other hand, with substantial interests in the Middle East, could not afford to view the Palestine question as primarily a moral one. Situated on the Suez life line to India and the Pacific and next door to the Mideast's vast oil deposits, Palestine was of paramount strategic importance to the United Kingdom. A Foreign Office study in 1944 likened the significance of the eastern Mediterranean for the British Commonwealth to that of the Caribbean and the Canal Zone for the United States.[67] This being the case, London authorities were bound to resent Washington's criticism of British policy, particularly when the Americans made it obvious they had no intention of accepting any of the military or political responsibilities for maintaining order in the region. Churchill soon after Yalta publicly invited the United States to play a larger role in Palestine, an offer that was studiously ignored in Washington.[68] Reduced to its lowest level, the Palestine question for the British revolved around the central fact that the Americans, as Attlee bluntly put it, "had no obligations there. We had."[69]

Given these contradictory perspectives, little reason existed to hope that Anglo-American initiatives and responses over the coming months would contribute to an alleviation of the dangerous tension that was rising almost daily in the Middle East. The most noticeable result, in fact, of the policies which London and Washington followed with respect to Palestine was to embitter relations between the two and, at one point, to endanger congressional passage of the credit which Keynes had worked so hard to obtain.

Shortly after his return from Potsdam, Truman, without waiting for a response to his note to Churchill, publicly committed himself to supporting entry into Palestine for as many Jews "as it is possible to let into that country." A week later Earl G. Harrison, whom the President had asked to look into the problems of the displaced persons, submitted his report to Truman. It told a story of shocking proportions, vividly detailing the miserable conditions under which European Jews still labored. Harrison frankly stated that if "there is any genuine sympathy for what these survivors have endured, some reasonable extension or modification of the British White Paper of 1939 ought to be possible without too serious repercussions." For some of the DPs, the presidential envoy added, "there is no acceptable or even decent solution for their future other than Palestine." Perceptibly shaken, Truman sent a copy of Harrison's report to Attlee and suggested that the British government immediately issue an additional 100,000 permits for immigration into Palestine.[70] Again, Attlee attempted in his reply to separate the problem of aid to the Jews in Europe from consideration of the future of Palestine. In a passage of revealing candor, he worried about setting "aflame the whole Middle East" and alienating India's 90 million Moslems.[71]

The State Department's Middle East experts sought to restrain the President, writing him that "No government should advocate a policy of mass immigration unless it is prepared to assist in making available the necessary security forces, shipping, housing, [and] unemployment guarantees."[72] Attlee later recalled that the State Department's position was very similar to that held by the British. Harold Laski captured London's viewpoint perfectly when he wrote a United States correspondent to deplore the American habit of offering advice by resolution rather than sharing in the difficult responsibilities of governing the country. "5,000 American troops in Palestine," he observed, "are worth 100 resolutions from the United States Senate."[73] The British suspected Truman's actions were purely "a result of domestic political pressure." Moreover, Attlee lamented, "Americans are always having elections."[74] Officials in the Foreign Office caustically noted "the rather shabby record" of the United States itself in admitting Jewish refugees over the preceding dozen years.[75]

Perhaps, but Whitehall again deluded itself in assuming that Americans should be ready to equate British objectives in Palestine with their own. London authorities, in fact, fully understood just how extensively their Palestine policy served national ends. "Our whole military position in the Middle East depended upon the cooperation of the Arab states," Lord Tedder, the Chief of the Air Staff, would tell the Cabinet at one point. Should British preeminence be undermined, the defense structure for the entire empire would be threatened. The Foreign Office view was summed up in the judgment that if Great Britain lost Arab good will, "the Americans and the Russians will be on hand to profit from our mistakes." If London forfeited its leading role in the region, many would regard this as "symptomatic of our abdication as a great power."[76] That it actually furthered the national interests of the United States for Washington blindly to follow the British lead in Palestine was an article of faith in Whitehall—but not a demonstrated fact.

Bevin had devoted little thought to the issue of Palestine prior to becoming Foreign Secretary. Almost inevitably, he came to rely heavily for advice on the careerists in the department, men deeply concerned that Britain not antagonize the Moslem world. According to the recollections of one official, this Foreign Office caution simply "absorbed" the new Foreign Secretary in his first months in office.[77] In later years Bevin would be charged with anti-Semitism. The accusation is probably unfair; he was not unsympathetic to the plight of European Jewry. He never succeeded, however, in understanding the intensity of the feeling harbored by many Jews that they must be allowed a refuge in the Middle East in order to insure that never again would they be exposed to another Hitler. Bevin failed to comprehend that for large numbers of Jews, the alternative of continued existence in Europe was simply intolerable. Thus, he quite wrongly came to blame a small group of Zionists, supported by American agitation, for the discontent in Palestine. If London and Washington could agree upon a common policy, he believed, the problem would quickly resolve itself.

Finally, in an attempt to enlist the United States into taking a more active role in Palestine, Attlee formally proposed the creation of a joint committee of inquiry to look into the question of possible areas where the European refugees might relocate, including of course, Palestine. The President found himself in a predicament. If he refused this latest offer for United States participation, it would appear that his oft-voiced concern for the fate of the displaced persons was nothing more than sham. The United States would have no further grounds for expressing any complaints about British actions in Palestine. If, on the other hand, he accepted Attlee's recommendation, powerful blocs of Jewish voters, who viewed the British suggestion as merely a substitute for action, would be alienated only weeks before a crucial mayoral election in New York, the nation's largest city and home to well over a million politically conscious Jews. Samuel Rosenman, Truman's top aide in matters concerning Palestine, advised the President to reject Attlee's proposal. "Why in the world there has to be a statement on October 25th, ten days before the election in New York," he complained, "I cannot possibly imagine."[78]

Truman ultimately responded to Attlee's suggestion with the demand that the committee focus primarily on Palestine, and specifically, on determining how many new immigrants Palestine could realistically absorb each month, a reply that Rosenman had worked out in advance with important Zionist leaders. Whitehall resisted assigning the committee such a narrow scope of inquiry, but failing to persuade Truman to permit other places to be studied as potential settlement areas, eventually accepted these terms of reference as the only way to obtain any American participation at all.[79] During Attlee's visit to Washington in mid-November, safely after the New York election, the two statesmen announced the establishment of a twelve-man committee. Lest Jewish voters get the impression he was backing off from his earlier promises of full support for the cause of Jewish immigration, Truman shortly afterwards wrote Eleanor Roosevelt that he intended "to continue to do what we can to get as many Jews as possible into Palestine as quickly as possible." This hardly promised an open-minded readiness to reevaluate American policy in light of the report submitted by the Inquiry. Moreover, in a statement to the House of Commons, Bevin described the joint committee in a fashion that emphasized the possibilities of finding suitable homes in Europe for the DPs while downplaying further immigration to Palestine. Even before their investigations had begun, members of the Inquiry found themselves pulled in contrary directions.[80]

When Edward Stettinius arrived in London in early autumn of 1945 to take part in the preparations for the first session of the United Nations General Assembly, he was disturbed to discover that relations between the British and his own country were not nearly so intimate as they had been at Dumbarton Oaks, Yalta, or even as recently as the San Francisco conference. Observing from a far different perspective, the editor of the *New Republic* offered a similar assessment, writing Eisenhower in October of his worries about the "coolness that has recently developed between England and America."[81] Undoubtedly a certain loosening of the bonds was inevitable with the return of peace, but thoughtful observers on both sides of the ocean wondered aloud whether ties between the two nations were being slackened rather more extensively than was either unavoidable or wise. Americans, especially, appeared in an almost unseemly haste to disengage from collective actions and even consultation with their British colleagues.

Policy makers in Whitehall particularly resented Washington's reluctance to confer with London before making decisions or taking actions which inevitably affected Britain as well as the United States. Harriman remembers that the British "were ready to support American policies provided they had a chance to thrash out questions before we took decisions." All too often, however, Washington placed London authorities in the embarrassing position of having "to defend matters with which they did not agree and on which they had not had a chance to express their views."[82] At one point Bevin told Byrnes that he simply refused to attend another conference without knowing in advance the American view of things, only to have the Secretary blandly reply that it was unnecessary and undesirable for the United States and Britain to reach agreement on every detail before meeting with the Soviets.[83] An exasperated Cadogan complained that determining American policy objectives was "like trying to tickle a trout with highly oiled gloves."[84]

As the months slipped by and it became apparent that Washington officials saw no need to keep United States policy closely aligned with Britain's, diplomats in the Foreign Office came more and more to miss Roosevelt's imaginative leadership and dashing flair. The termination of lend-lease, the patronizing attitude sometimes displayed by American negotiators during the subsequent financial talks in Washington, the unilateral and high-handed actions of United States authorities in Japan, Truman's obvious reluctance to treat atomic energy as anything but another force in the American arsenal, the administration's irresponsibility, as they deemed it, in matters relating to Palestine—each incident led the statesmen in Whitehall to forget a little more the frustrations and bitterness which working with FDR had also engendered. Halifax, for instance, compared Roosevelt's "inspired leadership" and "admirable sense of timing" in guiding American opinion with the current administration's disposition to "chart [its] course in the manner best calculated to propitiate what [it conceives] to be the prevailing sentiments of Congress and of important pressure groups." America's foreign policy, the British embassy warned, was in danger of "becoming the shuttlecock of domestic controversy."[85] Even a return of the scorned Hull seemed preferable to matters as they then stood. Secretary Byrnes, Cadogan wrote, was "really rather a disaster. . . . He appears to be shallow and impulsive—and rather slippery!"[86]

Much of British disenchantment with the Truman administration arose from apprehensions that American policies were shortsighted and unnecessarily nationalistic. American unilateralism in matters concerning relations with the Soviets, in Japan, and in the field of atomic energy all appeared likely to exacerbate problems in these areas rather than solve them. Washington's relentless penetration of the Middle East and its particular sensitivity to congressional and public opinion, as illustrated during the financial negotiations and again in matters having anything to do with Palestine, seemed equally unwise. Considerable concern existed in Whitehall over the rapid American demobilization and Washington's reluctance to institute a system of conscription. Without adequate military forces to back its diplomacy, British authorities worried, the United States would find it much more difficult to play a truly active role on the world scene. On practically all issues of international significance, the most discouraged concluded, American policy appeared myopic, arbitrary, or undependable.

These judgments, however, illustrate more about British diplomats than about the American actions they so roundly condemned. The shrill, alarmist tone of some of their assessments—Cadogan's stand out in this regard—bears little relationship to the actual merits of Washington's conduct, but it does clearly underscore Whitehall's consciousness of its own position of inferiority in the face of American might. At times the disparity in resources looked overwhelming. Arriving in New York during the Christmas season, wrote one Britisher, "was really like coming to fairyland." The United States "seems like a dream world it's so different from England."[87] Confronted with daily reminders of America's strength and their dependence upon it, many British officials found comfort in criticizing American policy. Behind London's ill-tempered outbursts, Keynes explained to a friend shortly after the new year, lay an "inner reluctance of England to accept a situation so wholly reversed from what she is used to. . . . I am afraid it is not easy for us to accept the new situation gracefully, and that is what makes sane and acceptable counsel so difficult to give and unacceptable to receive."[88]

In many instances, acerbic British comments reflected resentment not as much at American policies as at the attitude which shaped them. By the second half of the year, few Americans made any attempt to conceal their belief that the pattern of world power had radically shifted in favor of the United States, and even the friendliest of them were inclined to cast Britain in the position of the junior member of the Anglo-American relationship. Cables from the British embassy in Washington repeatedly reported of "the current tendency to ignore our role in world affairs and to represent us as a much harrassed [*sic*] and waning imperial power."[89] Similar complaints came from British diplomats in Moscow. The problem, one official wrote his superiors from the Soviet capital, was not that the British and the Americans risked saying different things when the Americans approached the Kremlin leaders without first checking with the British, but that "the Russians may tend to attribute less importance to our own representations when they appear always to follow at least two or three days after those of the Americans."[90] A short time later the Foreign Office received another wire from its embassy in Moscow warning:

> there is a growing danger that if we leave major negotiations . . . too much to the Americans, we may tend to drop increasingly out of the Soviet picture and thus strengthen the tendency here to substitute a Big Two conception of the world for that of the Big Three.

Such a development would be most unfortunate, this cable continued, for Britain was "in many respects too vulnerable . . . to risk the Russians regarding us as of little account."[91]

London officials were determined to resist any tendency to relegate Great Britain to a position of secondary rank or importance in international affairs. This consideration, more so than fear of Russia or any other specific country, led to the decision to obtain their own nuclear capability. To do otherwise would be tantamount to forsaking great power status. Years later Attlee was to explain the decision to build a bomb by referring not to the Soviet Union but to the United States. "It had become essential," he remembered. "We had to hold up our position vis-à-vis the Americans. We couldn't allow ourselves to be wholly in their hands."[92] Some officials in the Foreign Office protested that those who talked of Britain as a junior partner to the Americans forgot that the United Kingdom had a tremendous advantage over the United States "both in the amount of available and competent leadership which the country possesses and [in] the willingness of the population to be led." Moreover, pessimistic assessments of this sort tended "to overlook the enormous influence which Britain continues to exert upon the ways in which the Americans look at the world."[93]

Although in some respects accurate, such appraisals merely obscured the matter. In fact, the balance of power within the Anglo-American partnership had shifted dramatically since the opening years of the war. Great Britain had become a "harassed and waning" power. In recognizing this altered condition, American officials were simply acknowledging reality, a feat Whitehall appeared incapable of duplicating. Moreover, in any alliance, but especially in one of unequals, strains are inevitable, given the differing needs and expectations of each member. This, too, British statesmen tended to ignore, choosing to interpret Washington's refusal to coordinate all aspects of its policy as proof of American ineptitude. Such an attitude in turn contributed to a further loosening of the wartime bonds and encouraged the United States to play a unilateral role in global politics.

Given these circumstances, officials in the Foreign Office might have marveled that American and British policies did not clash even more than they actually did. That they did not can be attributed to the fact that over much of the world Great Britain and the United States shared a fundamental similarity of interests: to insure that no new aggressor-state rose to continue the ways of Germany and Japan, to resist any violent change in the status quo, to alleviate suffering and poverty, to promote world-wide economic, financial, intellectual, scientific, and cultural exchange. So it is important to remember that the sharp disagreements which punctuated relations between the two countries in these initial months after the return of peace were frictions arising from a basic similarity in goals. Moreover, had relations not been as close as they were, many of these irritations would never have occurred. Had not Britain and the United States shared a special atomic partnership within the anti-Nazi alliance, problems of continued collaboration in the field of atomic energy would not have marred relations between the two in the postwar period. If the policy makers in each of the two countries had not been in fundamental agreement with respect to what relations with the Soviet Union should be, then there would have been no reason for British ruffled sensibilities. While the pattern of relations in this period was one of squabbles and disagreements, the equally significant point is that these arose because of the similar interests and the unusually close ties binding Washington and London.

Perhaps it is easier to appreciate this fact at a distance than it was at the time. Although the statesmen in Washington and London recognized this basic compatibility, acting upon it in the face of intransigence emanating from across the ocean often proved difficult. As a result, as 1945 hurried to its conclusion, officials of the two governments prepared to seek legislative approval for the credit negotiated by Keynes and his associates against a background of apathy, confusion, mistrust, and irritation. Keynes had secured for Great Britain probably the best settlement obtainable. Yet this in itself would not necessarily insure parliamentary approval of the credit if it were felt that the United States posed a threat to essential British interests, whether these be commercial or financial opportunities in the Middle East, development of an atomic bomb, or continued security of the Suez Canal as represented by a stable eastern Mediterranean. Nor did a nearly unbroken pattern of acrimony between the two nations make congressional passage of the credit any more likely, particularly given the lingering distrust of British intentions and renewed resentment occasioned by Britain's cautious policy in Palestine and continuing restrictions on American economic interests. Thus it was not with undue optimism that officials of the two nations turned inward toward the task of convincing ill-humored and flighty legislators neither country had allowed itself to be taken advantage of in the complex world of international finance.

12

Financial Aid and Fraternal Association

Shortly after noon on the eighteenth day of December 1945, John Maynard Keynes rose from his seat in the House of Lords to address an unusually full and attentive chamber. Summoning all his eloquence, he presented a stirring defense of the financial agreements he had recently negotiated in Washington, and by the time he had finished there was little doubt but that the peers would vote to accept the American credit and its accompanying conditions. In the course of his speech, Keynes made an observation the validity of which extended far beyond the matter of a financial aid package to the British. "How difficult it is for nations to understand one another," he remarked, "even when they have the advantage of a common language. How differently things appear in Washington than in London, and how easy it is to misunderstand one another's difficulties and the real purpose which lies behind each one's way of solving them."[1]

In seeking to fathom the British reaction to the financial arrangements agreed upon in Washington, one repeatedly returns to these sentences. Clayton and Vinson and the other American negotiators, though by no means blind to the aspects of this agreement beneficial to the United States, had honestly sought to assist the British in recovering from the disruptions of six years of war to the greatest extent that was politically possible. And in comparison with intergovernmental loans of the past, the terms ultimately agreed upon were anything but beggarly. The total amount was a healthy one, the rate of interest unusually low, and the insertion of the clause providing for the waiver of interest payments in bad years quite unprecedented. Yet the British reception of these arrangements was almost universally one of ill-humor.

"By any computation the bargain is hard," editorialized the *Times* on December 12. Britain had been forced to make "tremendous and shackling concessions involving tremendous risks." The *Economist* found the agreement "cruelly hard," "a bitter pill to swallow."[2] One M.P. termed the aid package "a financial Munich" and complained that Great Britain was being treated like a defeated country. The Labour government, he charged, had sold the British Empire "for a package of cigarettes."[3] A second declared there was neither wisdom nor kindness in the credit; it was "a niggardly, barbaric and antediluvian settlement."[4] The Duke of Bedford called the agreement "the most impudent attempt history has ever known to establish an economic and financial dictatorship," while the respected Viscount Simon observed that the credit had created more anxiety and mistrust throughout the country than any other international agreement ever put before the Parliament.[5] One journalist was reported to have asked Keynes if it were indeed true that Britain had become the forty-ninth state in the American Union.[6]

Behind this widespread reaction of outrage lay the feeling that the United States had taken advantage of Britain's current distress to drive a hard bargain. Officials in both the Roosevelt and the Truman administrations had repeatedly extolled the principle of equal sacrifice in the joint endeavor in public statements and private assurances to their British colleagues. Surely, Englishmen reasoned, interest-free and conditionless American assistance in repairing the dislocations arising from Britain's immense efforts during the war was nothing more than their just due. The *Economist* spoke for many when it noted it was "aggravating to find that our reward for losing a quarter of our total national wealth in the common cause is to pay tribute for half a century to those who have been enriched by the war." The United States, however, was concerned with the future, not the past, Keynes explained. "Our American friends were interested not in our wounds, though incurred in the common cause, but in our convalescence." "We have saved our freedom at a great price," the *Manchester Guardian* grumbled; "the Americans have, materially, saved theirs at a profit."[7]

Both supporters and opponents of the credit emphasized that there would not be the slightest possibility of Britain ever being able to meet either the interest or the principal payments arising from the credit unless a fully functioning multilateral system of trade were established within the next several years. However, no multilateral system could be successfully achieved unless the United States proved willing to take payment in goods by an import surplus. Since Britons of all political hues had serious reservations about the probability of Americans willingly accepting a trade deficit, many thought it wrong for the United Kingdom to assume an obligation it was not likely to be able to honor.[8] Even the Chancellor of the Exchequer confided that his "cynical and secret reflection" on the credit was that "it is quite certain that the conditions will have to be 'revised' long before A.D. 2001 and that, even in the next year or two it may well be that circumstances will require a considerable variation, which might even be 'unilateral.' "[9]

The precipitant manner in which the government rushed the whole package through Parliament did little to help British humor. Whereas the American Congress dawdled over the agreement for a number of months, Parliament was allowed only days to study and debate the settlement. Haste was necessary in order to meet the congressional deadline of December 31 for British membership in the Bretton Woods institutions, but this merely reinforced the impression of American dictation, which was naturally resented.[10]

Vocal elements in both parties threatened to vote against the credit. Segments of the Labour Left feared the arrangements smacked too much of laissez-faire or saw the agreement subordinating Britain's foreign policy to that of the United States.[11] Of more significance was the split in Conservative ranks. Both Churchill and Eden personally favored the credit as the best which was obtainable. Much of the party, however, perhaps even a majority of the M.P.s, worried that the British pledge to work toward the reduction of trade barriers subverted both imperial preference and close ties with the empire. In combination with the other reservations which the settlement engendered, this fear was sufficiently strong so that Churchill and Eden were unable to browbeat the Tories into supporting the aid package. Since the Conservatives controlled the House of Lords, the only way to prevent this chamber from blocking acceptance of the agreement was to adopt abstention as the official party position (to which Bevin rejoined that he had never expected to meet Churchill in the capacity of an abstainer).[12] Even at that, a substantial number of Tories broke with the leadership and voted against the credit. On the far side of the Atlantic, Halifax was incensed when he learned of the Conservative stand. To a close friend he wrote, "I have never felt more humiliated by the Party to which I am supposed to belong, and which I should find it very difficult today to support."[13]

In the end, the arguments of the government prevailed. The entire press, with the exception of the Beaverbrook papers, reluctantly supported parliamentary approval of the credit, as did most of the more informed elements of the public. The Commons passed the agreement by well over 200 votes, but this margin, given the 169 abstentions, gives a misleading picture of the actual divisiveness of the issue. According to the *Daily Telegraph*, the House had "rarely shown itself so uneasy as during the debate." In the upper chamber, the possibility of a Tory uprising persisted until the last moment, but the peers, too, eventually fell into line, pushed no doubt by the government's threat to raise the constitutional issue of the power of the House of Lords.[14]

For most Britons who expressed an opinion, acceptance came not from a sense of free choice, or with relief or elation, but from a feeling of necessity. The government's strategy, in fact, had been to stress the evil effects of rejection rather than any alleged benefits. The financial editor of the *Times* reported that the credit was supported almost unanimously in the business world "simply because most people are appalled at the thought of any practicable alternative." The *Daily Telegraph* remarked that Congress was not likely to approve any arrangements with more favorable terms so "it is this agreement or nothing."[15] Britain's only other option, Keynes reminded the Lords, was to build up a separate economic bloc consisting of "countries to which we already owe more than we can pay, on the basis of their agreeing to lend us money they have not got and buy only from us and one another goods we are unable to supply."[16] Keynes' logic was irrefutable. Britain did have little choice. Recognition of this basic fact, however, made the financial aid package no more palatable. There was, the *Economist* observed,

> one compulsion to which we are not subject. We are not compelled to say we like it. . . . Our present needs are the direct consequences of the fact that we fought earliest, that we fought longest and that we fought hardest. In moral terms we are creditors; and for that we shall pay $140 million a year for the rest of the twentieth century. It may be unavoidable; but it is not right.[17]

British sulkiness did not go unnoticed in the United States. Though it might have convinced a few wavering congressmen that American negotiators had secured real and valuable concessions from Keynes and his associates, this salutary result was more than offset by the realization that the credit had not bought British gratitude. The English "are already beginning to 'shylock' us even before the papers are signed," Vandenberg complained to a Republican colleague. "If we are not going to get good will what are we going to get?" Even as sympathetic an observer as Walter Lippmann confessed that the Conservative abstention forced him to question whether a future Tory government would attempt to implement "the imponderable parts" of the agreement.[18]

Individuals and groups with an incongruous variety of interests and backgrounds joined together in opposition to the British credit. Traditional Anglophobes allied themselves with liberals concerned about Britain's imperialism. The *Chicago Tribune* featured a front page cartoon of John Bull standing at America's back door saying, "Spare a morsel for a poor, weak, sick, hungry, starvin' man, [but] make it sirloin, medium rare . . . and if it isn't done just right, I won't eat it! No use beggin' me!"[19] Walter White, executive secretary of the National Association for the Advancement of Colored People, cabled Truman asking that before any money was made available to the British, pledges be obtained from London that none of it would be used "to perpetuate imperialism or to deny any colonials of British Empire full freedom and justice. Reported use of American war materials by British against Indonesian people," he claimed, "constitutes one of greatest scandals and tragedies of contemporary history."[20]

A variety of other complaints also surfaced. Some analysts worried that the United States had been unduly generous in aiding a commercial competitor, or that good American dollars were being provided to undermine free enterprise and to further socialization in Britain. Fears that the British would never repay the credit were repeatedly expressed. Congressman Roy Woodruff of Michigan reminded his House colleagues that Britain still owed money from the First World War and labeled the arrangements nothing more that a "gift of $4,400,000,000 to finance a Socialist experiment."[21] Emanuel Celler of New York grumbled that the "agreement is so full of escape clauses, weasel words, and abracadabra as to permit Great Britain to do anything she pleases after she receives the money. The promises to pay are loaded with ambiguities."[22] A young judge in Wisconsin, one Joseph R. McCarthy, seeking the Republican nomination for the United States Senate, charged that the credit would be used to build a British trade supremacy over the United States with America's own money.[23] Some of the opposition which developed to the aid program was downright frivolous. In an argument unintentionally illustrating the level of much of the debate, Senator William Langer, North Dakota's anachronistic isolationist, condemned the credit on the grounds that Keynes, in his masterful *Economic Consequences of the Peace* a generation earlier, had been disrespectful to Woodrow Wilson.[24] Another opponent of financial assistance to Great Britain warned that the Gospel of John dictated rejection of the credit.[25]

Still others expressed apprehension lest the agreement further exacerbate international tensions. Many Americans voiced the concern that the United States was setting an unfortunate precedent, particularly with respect to the Soviet Union. Before congressional Republicans considered this aid, John Foster Dulles advised, they should demand clarification from the administration on the total amount of assistance it planned to provide other nations, and on the principles which were to guide allocation of American largesse among the possible recipients.[26] Vandenberg told friends he would have to vote against the credit because there was no way Congress would approve a similar arrangement for the Russians, and such obvious partiality by the United States could not avoid antagonizing the Soviets.[27] Sharing this anxiety about alienating Moscow, Eleanor Roosevelt wrote her husband's successor that the United States should lend equally to all its allies. It would be a sad mistake to provide money only to Britain, she declared, for by doing this America would be entering "into an economic alliance against other nations, and our hope for the future lies in joint cooperation." Reflecting another and somewhat contradictory argument against the credit, she added, "I have a deep sense that we have an obligation, first of all, to solve our own problems at home."[28]

Administration officials, fully aware of the deep-seated opposition which existed to any liberal arrangements for assisting the United Kingdom, aggressively set forth to counter this resistance with a high-powered information program. Convinced that what they had agreed to was defensible, confident that they had left no opportunity for opponents of the credit to charge that American interests had been neglected, and certain that all reasonable men would recognize this if properly instructed, government spokesmen threw aside their customary caution and embarked upon a carefully orchestrated campaign to overpower all doubts about the aid package. Background briefings for the press and for representatives of magazines, journals, and the motion picture industry were frequently held. State Department publicists stayed in close contact with radio commentators and organized special broadcasts by governmental officials. Meetings with the representatives of national groups and organizations were staged, and support was actively sought from labor, women's organizations, agricultural groups such as the Grange, and business and trade associations. The State Department instituted a special speakers program to crisscross the nation. Other federal agencies were enlisted in the effort. The Departments of Agriculture, Commerce, and Labor all cooperated in making material available to the public through their offices scattered around the country. Treasury officials were no less active than State Department bureaucrats in arranging for talks and speeches. The *Federal Reserve Bulletin* lent its pages for an explanation of the credit, together with a statement of support by the chairman of the Federal Reserve Board.[29]

Only with American assistance, ran the recurring theme in the administration's defense of the credit, could Britain embrace economic and financial policies pointing toward a multilateral world. The commitments entered into by Britain in return for the credit, Vinson assured a skeptical House committee, represented "a whole hearted adoption of the letter and spirit" of the American policy of multilateralism.[30] As much as Americans sympathized with the hardships the British had endured, and were still enduring, leading officials remarked, these had "nothing to do with this loan. This loan is not a pension for a worthy war partner. . . . It's not a question of relief. . . . This loan looks to the future, not to the past."[31] Reflecting the confidence which Washington policy makers felt in America's ability to prosper in a world of reduced trade barriers, Vinson unabashedly stated, "The principal purpose of this loan is to increase international trade."[32] Its implementation would "open the markets of England and many other countries to our exporters. This means more exports for our farmers and manufacturers, more jobs for our workers, more profits for business, and a higher income for all our people."[33] The President himself was no less direct. "This agreement is good business," he said, "good business for the industries of America, good business for our farmers, and good business for our workers." It was clearly in America's interest to implement the agreement.[34] Moreover, since a multilateral system would prevent the world from splitting into competing economic blocs, the financial arrangements with the British were in addition an investment in global prosperity and international peace.[35]

In one sense this vigorous publicity campaign was not long in bearing fruit. Numerous organizations representing business, labor, farm, educational, religious, and various other interests quickly lined up behind the credit, although the reasons they gave for their support were often contradictory or based on an inaccurate understanding of the situation. Leadership opinion as expressed in editorials, columns, and radio broadcasts stressed the seriousness of Britain's financial plight and the conviction that a prosperous United Kingdom was a necessary prerequisite for a prosperous America.[36]

These endorsements notwithstanding, it rather quickly became obvious that the administration's economic arguments had failed to evoke enthusiasm for the credit from the public or, more importantly, from its representatives in Congress.[37] Despite widespread support from traditional molders of opinion, the financial agreement providing Britain with much-needed aid appeared, three months after its negotiation and publication, mired in a bog of congressional indifference or outright hostility. A call to the White House from Senator James Eastland's office illustrated the seriousness of the situation. Mail received by senators from the South, the Mississippi legislator reported, was running 100 to 1 against the credit.[38]

Then, in dramatic fashion, a new and potentially explosive issue burst into this situation, introduced by none other than the leader of His Majesty's Loyal Opposition, Winston Churchill. Shortly after the turn of the year, Churchill had come to the United States for some weeks of rest and reflection about the state of world affairs. On March 5, just as the Senate Banking and Currency Committee was opening hearings on the British credit, he and the President traveled together to Truman's home state, where the two world leaders were to be awarded honorary degrees by a small Presbyterian school in Fulton, Missouri, Westminster College.

The Englishman had also been invited to deliver an address in the Westminster gymnasium, and during their train ride across America, in between long sessions at the poker table (where the experienced Truman lifted $100 from his British visitor the first evening), the two reviewed what Churchill expected to say. According to a personal message which the former Prime Minister sent to Attlee and Bevin on March 7, the President expressed admiration for the proposed speech and said he felt it "would do nothing but good though it would make a stir."[39] Leahy, who also read the address before its delivery, indicated similar approval of its contents although he too predicted it would draw unfavorable comment from "vocal communists, 'fellow travelers' and 'pinkies.'"[40] Had either Truman or Leahy known just how extensive this adverse reaction was actually to be, it is unlikely that they would have journeyed to Fulton with such equanimity.

When it came his turn to speak, Churchill proceeded to offer his audience a spellbinding if troubling analysis of the international scene. Surveying the world around him, the indomitable old Tory found that a "shadow has fallen upon the scenes so lately lighted by the Allied victory." It was his duty, he declared, to alert his listeners to certain facts about the present situation in Europe, the chief of which was that from "Stettin in the Baltic to Trieste in the Adriatic, an iron curtain has descended across the continent," enveloping "all the capitals of the ancient states of central and eastern Europe." Churchill specifically absolved the Soviets of seeking a new war, but added, "What they desire is the fruits of war and the indefinite expansion of their power and doctrines."

All of this, however, directed at one so recently a valued ally, was but prelude to "the crux of what I have traveled here to say." Having paid lip service to the United Nations, the Englishman then hammered home his central theme. "Neither the sure prevention of war, nor the continuous rise of world organization," he passionately argued, "will be gained without what I have called the fraternal association of the English-speaking peoples. This means a special relationship between the British Commonwealth and Empire and the United States." Carefully avoiding the term "alliance," Churchill elaborated on the nature of this "fraternal association." Such an arrangement would entail a continuation of the wartime military collaboration, including joint planning, the standardization of weaponry and training procedures, and the sharing of bases. The United States and each of the Commonwealth nations should also establish permanent defense agreements identical to those now tying Canada and the United States. The secret of the atom should be tightly guarded. Eventually, he predicted, taking up an old theme, common citizenship might bind the inhabitants of the two countries but, he magnanimously added, "that we may be content to leave to destiny." Reminding his audience that his had been a solitary voice in warning of the rise of Hitlerism, he exhorted them to act before delay again proved costly. "Beware, I say; time may be short," he cried. "Do not let us take the course of letting events drift along till it is too late."[41]

A storm of public protest broke immediately. Although scattered applause for the speech could be heard in the succeeding days—a columnist for the *Wall Street Journal*, for instance, termed it "brilliant," with a "hard core of indisputable fact"[42]—the overwhelming reaction in all sections of the country and from spokesmen representing all portions of the political and ideological spectrum was one of vehement rejection. Newspapers as different as the *New York Herald Tribune*, the *Chicago Sun*, the *Atlanta Constitution*, and the *Boston Globe* denounced the speech.[43] Internationalists feared that it would only further alienate Moscow and make the tasks of the United Nations that much more difficult. "The notion of close Anglo-American cooperation as the necessary backbone for UNO, which in British eyes is a wholly sensible and reasonable idea, still looks to the American mind very much like the juxtaposition of two contrary ideas," the *Economist* explained. Eleanor Roosevelt publicly worried that such collaboration might induce "other nations" to form similar blocs and move the world back to a balance of power situation.[44] Liberals and conservatives both thought an association of the sort Churchill prescribed bore too close a resemblance to the traditional power politics of a discredited past. Isolationists resisted the extensive entanglement in world affairs such a partnership would entail, while traditional Anglophobes opposed the very idea of intimacy with Great Britain.[45] Others objected to any thought of America being tied to the defense of British colonialism. "Churchill is ready to destroy us all in order that his own brand of tyranny may prevail," one angry correspondent wrote Truman. His "policies in Greece, Indonesia, his country's long history of exploitation of the population of India and Palestine speak far more eloquently than the words spoken at Missouri." Another asked, "Does critisizm [*sic*] of Russia negate the fact that millions of Britain's colonials are living in slavery?"[46] In the Senate, Claude Pepper warned the United States not to become "a guarantor of British imperialism."[47]

In reporting to the Foreign Office in the aftermath of Churchill's address, Halifax tended to underestimate the extent of American resistance to anything resembling an Anglo-American alliance. The widespread critical remarks, he explained, merely evinced an unwillingness on the part of most Americans to face squarely a disagreeable situation. "Comment is disgruntled because the unpleasant facts were stated very bluntly," he cabled, "but few have ventured to deny the fundamental correctness of the analysis." There was undoubtedly some truth in this assessment insofar as it applied to Churchill's description of Soviet actions, but the Ambassador in adopting this tone misled his superiors.[48] Instead, public opinion polls indicated widespread repudiation of closer military ties with the British. An incident two days after the Fulton speech illustrated the prevailing mood. On March 7, the *New York Times* ran a front page story reporting that the Combined Chiefs of Staff, "in an atmosphere of secrecy, enforced by armed guards," were continuing their joint military planning, "although the war they were established to direct has been over for more than six months." Neither country, according to the *Times*, would discuss the nature of this planning, nor reveal how much longer the agency would operate. Later that same day the prominent radio commentator Raymond Gram Swing demanded the abolition of the CCS, thereby registering his response to Churchill's call for continuing collaboration in the military sphere.[49]

Some comment specifically tied Churchill's speech to the financial aid package then before the Senate or, more generally, to Britain's perilous economic state. One indignant editorial observed that when "he suggests a military alliance between the United States and the empire he is not much different from the tramp who presents a button and asks that a shirt be sewed on it." An upset private citizen wrote, "It appears Churchill is willing to stir up another war, if he can't wangle money out of us by any other method."[50] Another told Truman, "Churchill's speech offers the conclusive argument against the granting of the proposed loan to Britain."[51] If the credit were not considered in isolation from the Englishman's proposals, Swing warned, Congress would likely either reject the agreement or accept it for the wrong reasons.[52]

Officials in the Truman administration, obviously surprised by the fervent condemnation which greeted Churchill's remarks, speedily moved to dissociate themselves from the speech, notwithstanding their earlier private endorsements. Truman denied, not only to the press but even to members of his own Cabinet, that he had seen the address before its delivery. He elaborated in great detail to Henry Wallace how he had been "sucked in and how Churchill had put him on the spot."[53] Byrnes claimed he had not been consulted about it, and shortly afterwards, the State Department announced that Dean Acheson was "too busy" to attend a public dinner for Churchill in New York. On March 16, Byrnes went before the Friendly Sons of St. Patrick, an Irish-American fraternal association, to announce that the United States was no more interested in an alliance with Britain against Russia than in an alliance with the Soviets against Great Britain.[54] Churchill himself, though he professed to be pleased with the reaction to his Fulton address, alluded to its chilly reception and adopted a much less combative tone in a speech in Richmond, Virginia, on March 8, downgrading his "fraternal association" to the less ominous sounding "union of hearts."[55]

Realizing that their cause had suffered a serious reversal, proponents of the British credit returned to the offensive. London officials quickly denied that Churchill's words were an expression of government policy, hoping to prevent the unfavorable response to the speech from further endangering the chances for congressional passage of the aid.[56] Churchill sought to rectify the damage he had done by stepping up his own efforts on behalf of the financial agreement. He reassured old friends that Conservative abstention had been necessary for internal political reasons, but that he strongly backed the credit. Speaking before the National Press Club, he stated it would be a "disaster" if Congress turned down these arrangements and strongly denied that American aid would merely subsidize socialism.[57]

In an anxious attempt to prevent the adoption of debilitating amendments to the agreement, Byrnes sought to induce the British to offer further concessions to the United States. Ernest McFarland, Democratic Senator from Arizona, had proposed that Great Britain give the United States additional commercial and military rights on British naval and air bases around the globe in return for American financial assistance, and it appeared there was a good chance the Senate would approve such an amendment. In an effort to forestall this blatant and insulting coercion, Byrnes on April 19 wrote Halifax it would be "of great assistance in pending legislation" if the two countries could quickly come to some agreement on the status of a number of disputed islands dotting the Pacific. His subsequent proposals, however, made it clear that any such accord would be largely on American terms.[58] The State Department was not trying to "high-pressure" them, one Washington official explained to an English friend. It was simply trying to persuade Whitehall of the advisability of moving speedily in order to reap political dividends for actions which it would undoubtedly take in the next few months anyhow.[59]

However advantageous in theory, in practice these arrangements presented obstacles too difficult to overcome in the limited time available. Surprisingly enough, policy makers in the Foreign Office readily accepted Washington's explanation of American motives. Halifax sent a strong wire to London urging his superiors to follow Byrnes' suggestions. Bevin, too, was receptive to meeting United States desires in this matter, but was opposed in this by the Dominions and Colonial Offices, by the British Chiefs of Staff, and by Australian and New Zealand officials.[60] In view of the opinion throughout Britain that the United Kingdom had been the victim of a hard bargain, it is unlikely that the Cabinet could have approved further concessions without antagonizing the public. When the Foreign Office raised the question of reciprocal rights for the two nations at each other's installations, the Americans quickly backed away. In view of Churchill's recent speeches, one Washington diplomat observed, such a subject had embarrassing implications which had best not be raised. The State Department official who reported this conversation then added a significant statement. "It was quite clear as everyone knew," he wrote, "that in case of actual international hostilities involving the Pacific the problem would really solve itself."[61]

Weeks passed, as the Washington decision-making process appeared incapable of resolute action. Finally reported favorably out of committee near the end of March, the bill authorizing aid to Britain languished in a Senate unable to raise a quorum to do business, as several senators staged a quasi-filibuster. "This British loan has perplexed me more than any other problem in all my 18 Senate years," Vandenberg told his colleagues, reflecting the dilemma felt by those lawmakers who wanted to back the administration's efforts to build a stable international order, but who by supporting the bill would be violating many of their deeply held beliefs regarding the foolhardiness of government extravagance and unsecured foreign loans.[62] Nor did it appear that the public's reservations about the agreement had been overcome, as the polls continued to show a substantial majority of Americans opposing the credit. One experienced Washington insider estimated in mid-April that if the Senate did pass the bill, there was only a 30 percent chance that the House would do so.[63] An exasperated Halifax could barely contain his frustration. "Isn't it funny," he observed, "how wrong we have all been in our feeling when F.D.R. died: 'Well at least Truman will get on well with the Congress!!'" In London, the Cabinet began considering what steps to take if the agreement were rejected.[64]

Paradoxically, each week of delay gained the credit a little more support—for reasons which had absolutely nothing to do with the elaborate economic justifications the administration offered in favor of assisting the British. As Russian actions and strident posturing came more and more to arouse a feeling of anxiety in many Americans, proponents of the credit increasingly maintained that financial aid to Great Britain would provide necessary assistance to a valued ally in a disordered world. Though such a rationale was seldom publicly advocated by administration officials, it assumed a mounting importance in the congressional debates. Congressman Christian Herter, himself a future Secretary of State, spoke for many of his colleagues when he wrote Clayton: "I find that the economic arguments in favor of the loan are on the whole much less convincing . . . than the feeling that the loan may serve us in good stead in holding up a hand of a nation whom we may need badly as a friend because of impending Russian troubles." Washington officials deplored the increasingly vocal indications of congressional antagonism directed toward the Soviet Union but were secretly relieved by the added support which accrued to the British credit.[65]

Then, just as it appeared the administration might finally have enough backing to secure passage of the aid, a new crisis erupted. The Senate eventually mustered a quorum and on May 10, approved the agreement by a twelve-vote margin, with sixteen Senators not casting ballots.[66] Attention now turned toward the House. Suddenly, opponents of the measure received unexpected assistance from across the ocean. Angered by what he considered Truman's complete lack of responsibility on questions in which American Jewish voters had any interest, Ernest Bevin bluntly stated that the United States championed a Palestinian home for Europe's Jews because Americans "did not want too many of them in New York."[67] His tactless outburst could hardly have come at a more inopportune moment. Congressmen from New York and other eastern states were swamped with incensed protests, and some who had been considered "safe" on the credit noticeably wavered in their support.[68] One House leader warned that unless the British "put a muffler on Bevin," the aid agreement would lose more votes every time the Foreign Minister opened his mouth, and press correspondents reported the bill was in "grave danger" in the House. It was a sound prediction, one journalist observed as the lower chamber prepared to debate the credit, that the British would be made to feel "they are being handed a cockleburr."[69]

In the end, however, apprehensions about the Soviet Union outweighed all other concerns, and in mid-July, the House passed the bill by a vote of 219–155. The most telling argument in favor of the credit, Majority Leader John McCormack privately stated in explaining the unexpectedly wide margin of approval, had concerned Russia. Willis Robertson of Virginia asked what was the point of the United States spending "billions of dollars and thousands of lives to prevent the world from being engulfed by one form of totalitarianism and then refuse to contribute as much as 2 weeks of the cost of that war to a program to prevent the world from being engulfed by another type of totalitarianism[?]" Passage of this bill, he assured his House colleagues, "will mean the survival in Europe of the last substantial bulwark against the spread of communism."[70] A Republican representative told the House, "War has been declared on Western civilization and we must recognize it. In that sense and that sense alone can this British loan be justified." This statement, wrote the *New York Times*, was illustrative of House sentiment that it was the political importance of Anglo-American solidarity rather than the economic merits of the agreement which eventually compelled congressional approval of the credit.[71]

An analysis of the Senate and House votes revealed significant bipartisan backing for the measure. In the Senate 49 percent of the Republicans joined 66 percent of the Democrats in supporting the bill. Although the percentage of House Republicans favoring the credit dropped to 33 percent, the sixty-one Republicans in the lower chamber casting an affirmative ballot more than offset the thirty-two Democrats who voted against the proposed assistance. In general, big-city Democrats voted for the agreement, big-city Republicans and representatives from agricultural regions opposed it. The Northeast and the South provided the most affirmative votes, the Midwest and sections of the Far West the most negative ballots. In a striking exception to this broad pattern, however, Democratic representatives from New York City, most of whom had rather consistently supported administration desires since before Pearl Harbor, voted against the loan, undoubtedly reflecting the displeasure of their many Jewish constituents with Britain's Palestine policy. As Representative Celler put it: "I shall vote against this loan. I assure you it will give me great pleasure to do so. I shall not vote . . . money for the British that could be used to support soldiers to maim and strafe innocent people in Palestine."[72]

On July 15, 1946, President Truman placed his signature on the legislation putting the Anglo-American financial agreement into effect. With this simple action he brought to an apparently successful conclusion an effort in which countless officials, high and low, had been engaged for many months. It should have been a moment for celebration, for congratulation and unwinding after a most arduous labor. Yet thoughtful observers could not help but be disturbed at the manner in which the two nations had gone about the business of striking a bargain that promised benefits for both.

The whole process, from when the British had first realized that the spigot of lend-lease aid was to be shut off in precipitous fashion until the final vote in the House of Representatives nearly eleven months later, had been characterized by injured sensibilities and ill-tempered exchanges. Though most governmental officials in each of the two capitals approached the problem of Britain's financial distress with honorable intentions and compatible purposes, the procedure of hammering out a suitable arrangement by which to aid the British had often reduced the level of interchange to one of petty bickering and unjustified suspicions. Then, when it came the turn of the two legislatures and their respective publics to pass on the handiwork of the negotiators, the restraints of civility, to say nothing of shared interests, seemed to disintegrate altogether. The debates in both Britain and America only further irritated already raw nerves. In this sense, the British credit, instead of bettering relations between the two western democracies, had only served to separate and alienate them. Moreover, officials, legislators, and the public in each nation had ultimately accepted the agreement for very different reasons. As a consequence, each viewed the future, now that the credit had been approved, with varied and at times contradictory expectations as to what new obligations had been created. Here was to be another source of misunderstanding in the days to come. Repeating the recurrent pattern, British-American cooperation had laid the groundwork for further conflict.

13

The Reign of Ambivalence

The year 1946 was, in many respects, a year of transition in international affairs. Germany, Japan, and Italy—all defeated in battle—entered the year as occupied countries, governed by the caprice of foreign conquerors. Yet before twelve months had passed, the status of each had undergone a subtle but real alteration, as the war's recent victors, already preparing for their own global competition, gradually came to view their erstwhile foes as possible allies in future confrontations. Soon huge quantities of foodstuffs and other essentials replaced the bullets and bombs which, not long before, had been the principal products designated for the peoples of these nations. France, China, Poland, Yugoslavia, and countless other states struggled to make the passage from war to peace in countries ravaged by the frighting and riven by antagonistic factions. The newly created United Nations took its first hesitant steps, provoking immediate speculation whether its vitality would be sufficient to cope with the myriad problems before it.

In Washington, policy makers most directly concerned with Anglo-American relations, reflecting the uncertainties inherent in this process of transition, vacillated for most of the year between two conflicting conceptions of what ties between their nation and the United Kingdom should involve. At times, majority opinion seemed to lean toward the notion that close links with London were little more than plain common sense amidst the turmoil of an unsettled world. More frequently, a chary reluctance to acknowledge the many similar interests binding them to the British appeared the prevalent sentiment in the American capital. Complicating the matter further, individual officials fluctuated from one position to the other, depending upon the nature of the particular issue under consideration, the geographical location of any other nations involved, and whether the question was primarily a strategic, political, or economic one. Ambivalent at the best of times, American thinking about Great Britain in 1946 exhibited even more indecision than usual.

The three remaining major powers spent much of the year searching for a new basis upon which to conduct their affairs, now that the cohesive force of a common enemy had been removed. The most conspicuous aspect of international relations in 1946 was the continuing decline in cordiality between the Soviet Union on the one hand, and the United States and the United Kingdom on the other. This troubling development had by midsummer come to dominate any discussion of world affairs, providing the mark against which all other events were measured. Fear of Russian ambitions had tipped the balance in Congress in favor of the British credit, and relations between the two Atlantic democracies were, as the months passed, increasingly influenced by the widening split in the ranks of the former allies. In fact, Soviet actions had, by the end of the year, pushed Washington officials, almost in spite of themselves, into a much closer partnership with the British than even the most enthusiastic advocate of firm Anglo-American ties would have dared predict twelve months earlier.

As the first session of the United Nations General Assembly opened in January, key American officials, including the Secretary of State, still viewed international relations primarily as a series of conflicts between Great Britain and the Soviet Union. The proper role for the United States in these clashes was one of mediator, being careful not to appear to be siding with either disputant too often.[1] And because British and American interests frequently led to the adoption of similar policies, in opposition to the Soviets, officials in the State Department on occasion deliberately provoked public disagreement with London. As one American representative who followed this tactic explained, "[I]t would be healthy to have a little rowing between the two of us with the Soviets as observers." Otherwise, the apparent similarity in the policies pursued by the two western nations would unavoidably foster the impression of an Anglo-American bloc.[2] Even as late as June 1946, State Department officials spoke of achieving a "general understanding on objectives" with the British but sought to stop short of measures which "would give the appearance of joint action."[3]

Nonetheless, British and American policies did increasingly develop along parallel if not identical lines. In the recently liberated nations of southern and eastern Europe, diplomatic representatives of the two countries discovered themselves agreeing again and again on the unacceptable nature of Soviet actions and the need for a resolute Anglo-American response. British and American troops remained under combined command in Italy and Venezia Giulia, and fears that Tito's forces were about to move on allied positions around Trieste prompted worried consultations between military officers of the two nations. In Iran, in Manchuria, on questions concerning Franco's Spain, on the future of the United Nations—in all these areas involving relations with the Soviet Union, American officials found themselves through force of circumstance working closely with their British colleagues. And gradually, Washington came to replace London as the chief proponent of a firm stance toward the Russians.[4]

"Americans have learnt rapidly in the school of realism," a satisfied Foreign Office official wrote in mid-May. A month later the British embassy's John Balfour advised London that there was no further need to be unduly disturbed by American fears of "ganging up" with the British against the Russians, although when given the alternative, the State Department would still prefer parallel action rather than joint representation.[5] On May 31, the *New York*

Times' respected James Reston concluded that the consensus in Washington was that there was "no future in trying to break up the Anglo-American bloc or denying that it exists." Reston's article, the British embassy cabled home, closely reflected the State Department's point of view.[6] Even formerly Anglophobic newspapers like the *Washington Times-Herald* found nice things to print about Great Britain as relations with the Soviet Union continued to deteriorate. One heard fewer and fewer references in Washington to "power politics" or a mediator role for the United States, Halifax reported. Indeed, in a startling reversal of positions, Bevin by the end of the year was publicly explaining that Britain's role was to act as mediator between Russia and the United States.[7]

British officialdom, however, was not wholly satisfied. American policy in Europe tended "to vacillate violently and unpredictably between absolute non-intervention and intervention beyond a point which we think desirable," observed a Foreign Office representative in April. Britain had tried its best to keep in step with American shifts in policy, but "they are undoubtedly awkward as a dancing partner."[8] Other officials fretted about the "practical implementation" of Washington's new, firmer stance toward the Soviets, a worry underscored by the delays in passing the credit and extending conscription.[9] Behind these complaints lay a more nagging concern, for Whitehall recognized that this recent parallelism in policy stemmed from growing apprehensions about the Soviet Union rather than from any fundamental acknowledgment that a similarity of interests linked the United States and Great Britain. An awareness of this same fact led Walter Lippmann to observe that a dangerous tendency existed among Americans "to assume that the British-American partnership is closer than it is." Ties between the two nations, he wrote, were "extremely superficial," held together only by a common fear of Russian intentions. This was hardly the basis on which an enduring peace might be built, he cautioned.[10]

British officials heartily endorsed this warning, for political and military cooperation with the United States ranked near the very top of their catalogue of diplomatic priorities. "Let there be no doubt, . . ." wrote the *Economist* in an article precisely capturing official sentiment, "of the unalterably pro-American bias of British policy. Let it be recited regularly, as a diplomatic litany, that agreement with the United States on the fundamental issues is a first commandment of British policy, with a superiority over all other objects."[11] Though frustrated bureaucrats at times toyed with the idea of playing off, or balancing the United States against the Soviet Union, the political, economic, and strategic realities of the world quickly squashed such suggestions. Extensive collaboration with the United States was, by choice and by necessity, the cornerstone of Britain's policy.

This desire for the closest possible relationship with Washington expressed itself in a number of different ways. It entailed for British military planners a particular concern that the wartime cooperation established by the Combined Chiefs of Staff not be allowed to disintegrate through disuse or indifference. Admiral of the Fleet Sir James Somerville suggested a joint review of naval tactics, battle formations, and cruising dispositions, "with a view to establishing a common doctrine for the two fleets." Other officials pushed for the free exchange of intelligence, for a coordination of training procedures, for a pooling of information on guided missiles and other new discoveries, and for the standardization of weaponry between the armed forces of the two nations.[12] It was not that war with the Soviet Union or any other country was anticipated. Early in 1946, policy makers in London officially adopted a ten year no-war planning assumption. The Air Staff, by opting for a long-term research-oriented program, similarly demonstrated its confidence that no major hostilities would disrupt the world in the immediate future. None of the services devoted much effort to drawing up detailed war plans against a specific enemy. Rather, the desire on the part of London military authorities for the closest of ties with the United States arose more from general anxieties caused by the nation's weakened condition than from a specific fear of war with Russia.[13]

At the same time, as American policy became more openly hostile toward the Soviet Union, civilian decision makers in London took greater care to avoid the appearance of siding with the Americans against the Russians, although they, too, sought to effect an unprecedented degree of peacetime collaboration with the United States. A report circulated by the United States Chief of Naval Operations in February 1947 described the "fundamental tenet" of British policy as intimate cooperation with the United States. London officials did not intend to let Anglo-American collaboration be weakened by any other considerations, this memorandum noted, but they "do not wish this cooperation to appear as directed necessarily at the Soviet Union, and still maintain hope that the common need to contain Germany will form a continuing bond between all 4 Great Powers."[14] The *Daily Herald*, the organ of the Labour Party, responded to Churchill's Fulton speech by observing that while not a single member of the government wanted anything but the closest and friendliest of ties with the Americans, "an overriding condition of such relations is that they shall not become exclusive, shall not be an obstacle to equally good relations with other powers. . . . The aim of British statesmanship is to foster unity between Russia and the United States, not to 'gang up' with one or the other."[15] Even as late as June 1947, both Attlee and Bevin criticized the British Chiefs of Staff for basing Britain's defense policy on the likelihood of Anglo-Soviet antagonism. A resurgent Germany, the Foreign Secretary warned, posed the most serious threat to world peace and England's safety.[16]

Much to this opposition to adopting a more blatantly partisan stance in world affairs can be explained by continuing British hopes for the United Nations and the concept of an international peace-keeping organization. This was ironic, for prior to 1946, American officials had repeatedly voiced skepticism regarding London's commitment to the world body. As it became evident just how weakened the war had left the United Kingdom, however, and particularly after the election of the Labour government, British policy makers came to rely more and more on a strong, effective international security organization. The United Nations must become "the overriding factor in foreign policy," Attlee told the opening session of the General Assembly.[17] The Cabinet ruled that Britain should put all its force behind a vigorous organization, "with power and determination to smash any aggressor by every means, including Atom Bombs."[18] In discussing the question of bases in the Pacific with the United States, officials in the Foreign Office emphasized their desire not to prejudice inauguration of military security arrangements sponsored by the United Nations and insisted that nothing be done that might lessen confidence in the ability of the world body to provide for the security of all nations. The Americans, on the other, hand, breezily assumed that any arrangements pertaining to bases made with the United Kingdom would be compatible with the spirit of a strong United Nations, and moreover, that the world would recognize and acknowledge this. The British for their part were not so sanguine.[19]

To some extent these British hopes for a strong international organization proceeded from the realization that this would inevitably entail an expanded role in world affairs for the United States.[20] A repetition of the 1930s' isolationism must at all costs be avoided. But diplomats in the Foreign Office sought more than simply an active policy from the Americans. They also desired a responsible and ably formulated stance from Washington, and since they defined this largely to mean greater receptivity to British aspirations, they were often disappointed. Moreover, to compound London's unhappiness, American policy, except in those areas where Russian obstinacy forced Washington into close partnership with the United Kingdom, displayed the same chariness toward the British as it had in the years before the war.

United States policy in the Far East, for instance, continued to be characterized more by unilateralism than by any desire for Anglo-American collaboration. In Japan, American authorities insisted upon maintaining their exclusive control over the occupation and rebuilding of that defeated state, despite British hopes that a four-power regulatory body similar in structure (but without the Russian obstructionism) to the Allied Control Commission for Germany might be created. In Korea and in China, the British found themselves being squeezed out of any significant activities, although in the latter case this was at least partially voluntary.[21] The State Department did not hesitate to exert "friendly pressure" at times to insure that it got its way. In May 1946, American officials explicitly told the British they would not press United

States claims to Tanganyika, the Cameroons, and Togoland, if Great Britain gave them in return a free hand with respect to Japan's former mandates in the Pacific.[22] Washington was, in effect, offering to stay out of sub-Sahara Africa, where it had few interests and little inclination to go, if London would agree to American domination of the Pacific, where the British had traditional ties and many important interests.

Diplomats in Whitehall found their counterparts in the United States equally unprepared to establish a close relationship in the southwest Pacific. Commonwealth strategists determined that in light of Britain's reduced capability to play a worldwide military role, it would be advisable for Australia and New Zealand to seek some sort of defensive arrangements with the Americans, perhaps something similar to the current bonds between Canada and the United States, so that the British burden in that area of the world could be lightened. Here was a frank admission of London's reduced status in international affairs. But Washington planners resisted the creation of any firm regional defense network. There was no likely enemy in the southwest Pacific, they explained, and besides, such a grouping would establish an unfortunate precedent for Soviet emulation.[23] British analysts, preoccupied with finding ways to ease the strain on their exhausted country, preferred to ignore the merits of this argument.

In financial matters United States policy makers proved little more accommodating, thereby magnifying the anxieties in Whitehall created by America's economic power and Washington's insistence that it alone understood what was best for Great Britain. Fears of being excluded from world markets by aggressive American exporters, buttressed by deep-rooted opposition in the United States to any substantial lowering of its own import duties, continued to trouble many Britons. The 1946 trade agreement between the United States and the Philippines appeared to the British as wholly at variance with the avowed American policy of eliminating preferential tariffs and absolute quotas, but this did not prevent self-righteous Washington officials from pressing Britain for further reductions in its own trade barriers.[24] American efforts to prevent Whitehall from signing a bulk purchase agreement with Canada for the sale of badly needed wheat also antagonized authorities in London, who felt that the United States did not hesitate in making similar arrangements when it suited American purposes. As the *Economist* noted—with a good deal of justification in this instance—the principles urged by the Americans in the field of international finance exhibited a "failure to realise how much self-interest is wrapped up in the high-sounding moralities."[25]

Two international economic conferences sponsored by the United States reinforced these doubts about the advisability of the American concept of a multilateral world. In March 1946, representatives of the nations which had accepted the Bretton Woods accords gathered in Savannah, Georgia for the inaugural meeting of the World Bank and the IMF. American high-handedness so incensed the British that one daily, despite the fact that current Senate hearings on the credit dictated reticence, irritably complained of the "steamroller tactics" and the "rigidly domineering manner" with which the Americans ran the conference. "[T]he worst fears of those who had always warned us that this was what the United States meant by international economic cooperation were borne out at Savannah," observed the *Manchester Guardian*.[26]

Later in the year, the Attlee government received another reminder of the domestic political liabilities which accompanied continued acceptance of America's program for the postwar economic order. At a conference in London preparing for an international meeting on trade and employment, the United States scored what Washington officials exuberantly called a "tremendous victory" in securing agreement to American proposals.[27] This had been possible, the director of the State Department's Office of International Trade Policy candidly admitted, in part because the United Kingdom had "lived up to the letter of its commitments to us and was scrupulously correct in its public statements of formal support"—in spite of the fact that these actions "are highly unpalatable to important segments of British opinion and that the Government, in living up to these commitments, is having to swim against a strong current of public sentiment."[28] Only because it was so essential to establish an across-the-board cooperative relationship with the United States was the government willing to accept the additional burden which this dissatisfaction entailed.

Events in Germany at first glance appear to comprise an exception to this general pattern. On July 11, 1946, Byrnes announced American readiness to merge its zone with that of any other occupying power in order that the German economy might be treated on a more systematic basis. Shortly thereafter, Bevin declared that Great Britain accepted the principle of fusion, and representatives of the two nations soon commenced formal discussions toward this end.

A closer look into American intentions, however, again reveals this absence of any conscious desire to work closely with the British. Officials in London, increasingly disturbed at the heavy drain on British resources which their occupation duties entailed, had pressed their American colleagues for some months with proposals for pooling food supplies in the two zones. Hugh Dalton came to feel, with understandable resentment, that in feeding the Germans, victorious Britain was being called upon to pay reparations to defeated Germany.[29] In July the Attlee government was compelled to introduce bread rationing in the United Kingdom, a measure which had been avoided throughout the war. At the same time, a governmental investigating committee concluded that the financial burden represented by the German zone of occupation was not likely to lessen appreciably during the coming year.[30] Clearly, London could no longer afford, nor would the British people tolerate, these massive payments. Yet in spite of the obvious British distress, American authorities evinced little interest in creating closer ties between the two zones, although for many of them concern over the wastefulness of the German economy as it was then being run increasingly came to replace their earlier attention to the punitive aspects of the occupation.[31]

Then, in July, a speech by Soviet Foreign Minister Molotov provided the catalyst for a reorientation of American policy in a manner which ultimately moved it closer to Great Britain's. Early in the month, Lucius Clay, the deputy military governor of the

American zone in Germany, met with Byrnes and warned him of the "positive nature" of communist propaganda in Germany and the necessity for an early public statement to "nullify the effectiveness of the Communist appeal." The opportunity for such a pronouncement came perhaps more quickly than either Byrnes or Clay had anticipated. On July 10, Molotov unexpectedly assumed the role of champion of German political unity in an address attacking the level of industry permitted by the occupation authorities. Byrnes speedily replied on the following day with his offer to merge the American zone with any or all others. A resolve to prevent the Soviets from scoring propaganda points had triggered his announcement, although behind this lay an awareness of the disastrous effects which a continuation of the disordered economic conditions in Germany could have on the cost, ease, and ultimate success of the American occupation.[32] Only infrequently did United States officials advocate the idea of merger because it would relieve the British of some of the burden which threatened to overpower them. The benefits which the fusion brought Great Britain were, in fact, little more than the fortuitous byproduct of an action taken largely for other reasons.

The negotiations which followed acceptance of the principle of merger graphically illustrated this point. The deficit for the American zone for 1947 was estimated at $200 million, that for the British zone at $400 million. Bevin asked that the United States agree to assume 60 percent of this combined burden, arguing that during the Washington talks the previous autumn leading to the British credit, London had not counted on having to use its precious dollars to provide food for Germans. The Cabinet was convinced, British officials reported, that the next three years would bring a "financial battle of Britain" in which dollars would be as important as Spitfires had been in 1940.[33] "The stability of our finances, the standard of life of our people and the reputation of our Government will be put in peril unless we make a firm stand now," Dalton wired Bevin at one point in the negotiations.[34] Particularly fearful that they would be obliged to meet food requirements for Germany by further cuts in rations for their own people, the British also asked that the United States accept the principle that derationing of bread in the United Kingdom should be an objective to be achieved as soon as possible.[35]

Their pleas brought consoling words but few concrete actions from the Americans, underlining the low priority which aiding the British occupied in the decision to propose the merger. Byrnes, warned by Secretary of War Patterson that any bizonal financing arrangements had to be justified to Congress "as a good business proposition," resolutely resisted any suggestion that would have obligated America to pay for more than 50 percent of the trade deficit of the merged zones. He later wrote: "I thought it unwise for Britain to be put in the position of a poor relative or a junior partner by contributing less than 50 percent." But in view of a noticeable lack of a comparable sensitivity in other matters, one is left with the suspicion that he was more concerned that the United States not appear to have been outnegotiated by the wily British. Washington's refusal to assume a larger portion of the expense, the Secretary candidly reported to Bevin, "was not a case of lack of goodwill or money but solely the attitude of Congress."[36] American officials readily conceded the desirability of derationing bread in Great Britain as soon as possible, but consistently declined to sign any document formally accepting this as a justifiable goal.[37] Economists in the American Treasury stoutly resisted to the very last minute of the negotiations any acknowledgment that the agreement fusing the two zones should be justified because of the perilous British dollar position. Only Treasury Secretary Snyder's chance absence from Washington and Byrnes' insistence that, having announced the imminent signing of an agreement, no further delays would be tolerated prevented a nasty public debate.[38] As it was, negotiations were not completed until December. During that time officials in London received ample evidence to disabuse them of any misconceptions that American policy in Germany was devised to aid Great Britain.

Nor did Whitehall find the Americans any more inclined to satisfy British desires in the area of atomic energy, despite Truman's

November 16, 1945, pledge of "full and effective cooperation" with the British and the Canadians. When Halifax approached officials in Washington seeking to activate the November 16 agreement, he quickly discovered that the partnership envisioned by the Truman administration did not extend to the sharing of engineering and technical information needed for the construction of an atomic energy plant in England. Truman insisted that, based on the Groves-Anderson Memorandum of Intention,[39] the United States was required to furnish aid only in the field of basic scientific research. Washington was under no obligation to provide assistance to the British to construct their own plant, he wrote Attlee, nor would public sentiment, in view of American advocacy of international control of atomic energy, allow him to do so.[40] The British protested vigorously—but ineffectually. Finally, Acheson shamefacedly told officials of the British embassy that they "must just resign themselves to the fact that, although we made the agreement, we simply could not carry it out; that things like that happen in the Government of the U.S. due to the loose way things are handled."[41]

Technically, Truman was correct in maintaining that he had never promised to provide the British with information to assist them in the construction of an atomic energy plant, but by so interpreting the Groves-Anderson Memorandum of Intention, he directly contravened the spirit which had informed the discussions which he and Attlee had held the previous November. The American argument that such a sharing of information would undermine efforts to secure international control of this frightening new force was sincere enough, at least on the part of some Washington officials. Given other actions by the United States in the 1945-47 period, however, it is doubtful that worries of this nature alone would have deterred Truman from doing something he desired to do.

Other considerations seem to have been of more importance to the Americans in their thinking about the future of the atomic partnership. Groves warned that the full and effective interchange of information would be tantamount to an outright military alliance, a step which few in the American government were prepared to take. There was also some fear that an atomic plant in England would be too vulnerable to Russian attack, should war ever come. The British replied with some heat that this was a danger which London alone had to consider, and that Washington's refusal to share its expertise for this reason constituted an insufferable interference in the sovereign affairs of Great Britain. The Americans pointed in turn to the Soviet espionage ring which had been unearthed in Ottawa in February as evidence of the dangers inherent in the dissemination of such highly classified information. The revelation that atomic secrets had been regularly passed to Moscow for some time had staggered Washington officialdom. No precaution was too extreme, a growing number of key figures in the Truman administration came to feel, to insure that this did not recur.[42]

In May 1946, Halifax, about to retire from the turmoil of diplomatic service and return to England, called on the President to say good-by. Once more he raised the question of the future of the atomic partnership. Truman candidly admitted that his main concern was securing congressional approval of legislation regulating the domestic use of atomic energy, declaring he would do nothing to jeopardize this. Afterwards, he airily remarked, everything would be worked out between the British and the Americans. This response could hardly have reassured his visitor, for the bill to which Truman referred promised to close off bilateral collaboration in the field of atomic energy still further. Whether Truman's comments reflected ignorance of the legislation then pending before Congress or was calculated deception, Halifax was unable to determine. His primary impression was that the President was not very well informed on the whole question.[43]

Congress eventually passed this bill which so preoccupied Truman, and the President signed the McMahon Act into law on August 1, 1946. The struggle to win approval of the legislation had been lengthy and hard fought, pitting Congress against the executive branch and civilian against military. As the price for securing the principle of civilian control over this potent force, the lawmakers had agreed to insert stringent restrictions on the dissemination of information to the nationals of any other country.

Despite the fact that the bill exhibited a total disregard for both the letter and spirit of the 1944 Hyde Park aide mémoire and the tripartite agreement of November 16, 1945, commitments of which the Congress knew little or nothing, neither the White House nor the State Department made any effort to alert the legislators to this situation.[44] An alarmed Attlee wired Truman to protest this apparent repudiation of American promises, but his pleas brought no satisfaction. The Prime Minister pointed out that sharing still continued in the distribution of uranium ore. Why should it be abandoned in the pooling of information, he not illogically asked.[45] But with the passage of the McMahon Act, all exchange of atomic information stopped. The United States had turned its back on collaboration with the British in what was universally felt would be the decisive weapon in any future war.

This action inevitably retarded cooperation in the whole field of strategic planning. Indeed, in this area, perhaps the most crucial of all for a secure America, Washington officials floundered during much of 1946 unable to decide exactly how closely to work with the British. As a consequence, no concerted policy directed the nation's thinking vis-à-vis the United Kingdom. No one, of course, envisioned a return to the deplorable relations of the 1930s. Increasingly, internal documents within the American bureaucracy focused on the interests linking the two countries rather than upon their points of difference.[46] Yet, although this fundamental assumption of shared concerns must form the background in any analysis of the Anglo-American strategic relationship in 1946, time and again Washington officials shied away from translating this underlying conviction of unity into overt action.

But another, more disturbing side to this story exists. Appreciating the considerations which made an open continuation of the wartime collaboration impolitic, American military authorities nonetheless worried that only a public demonstration of British-American solidarity would be likely to have the desired restraining influence on potential destabilizers of the global order. If, however, they were to be denied such a show of friendship with Great Britain, all the more reason remained for establishing the next best thing: covert partnership. And so, working without the knowledge of their civilian heads, even contrary to the desires of these superiors, a small group of officers took it upon themselves to enter into arrangements with the British which had the effect of tying their two countries together far closer than all but a few imagined.

Maintaining the intimate wartime association was, of course, a primary objective of the British military. At Potsdam, it will be remembered, when the British had raised this matter, the Americans had replied that the United States had not yet sufficiently defined its postwar political relationships with other nations to permit such discussions. During his brief visit to Washington in November, Attlee again broached the subject. Truman readily agreed that postwar cooperation for defensive purposes was desirable, but the Prime Minister was unable to coax any specific commitments from the President.[47] If no formal action were taken, however, the CCS organization, having neither legal authorization nor defined duties, would in all probability largely wither away. Indications that this was already occurring were widespread.[48]

Determined to halt this process, Ismay wrote Eisenhower at the end of 1945: "If your armed forces and ours had more or less the same equipment, more or less the same doctrine, more or less the same organization—AND NO SECRETS of any kind between them—they would at once constitute a hard core of resistance to any breach of the peace." Fearful lest this exclusiveness scare the Americans off, Ismay then added, "Thereafter, any other nation that was worthy and willing could join 'The Club.'"[49] Desirous of pursuing this matter further, Eisenhower, the new Army Chief of Staff, and Field Marshal Henry Maitland Wilson, the ranking British officer in Washington, agreed to hold informal talks on the subject. Their first meeting took place on February 8, 1946, when Wilson lunched with Leahy, Eisenhower, and Admiral Chester Nimitz, Chief of Naval Operations. Temporarily freed from the restraining influence of subordinates, the four men spoke candidly and the one record of their conversation offers a fascinating picture of British and American thinking on postwar military cooperation.

Wilson not surprisingly spoke forcefully for a continuation of collaboration in all fields of military interest. The Combined Chiefs of Staff should be maintained despite the existence of any international peace-keeping body, he argued, for a firm demonstration of Anglo-American unity was the best possible deterrent to aggression in a world which would clearly take some years to regain its stability. At a lower level, collaboration should also continue in the field of tactical or operational doctrine: matters such as communication procedure, signal books, techniques in amphibious operations, and air coordination with ground and sea forces. Finally, cooperation in the fields of intelligence, scientific development, and training should be maintained. Underlying all this, Wilson asserted, was the basic principle that "it is unthinkable that there should ever be any grave misunderstanding between our two countries."[50]

The American response revealed a troubling disdain for the traditional arrangements which had in the past served to check independent action by the military. They agreed completely, Eisenhower and his colleagues replied; they wanted collaboration to continue "on exactly the same scale as it had [during the] war and in all the same fields." After much deliberation, however, they had come to the conclusion that it would be impossible to obtain permission from their political superiors to continue this collaboration openly. So much had been said about the new United Nations Organization and the need for cooperation with all nations that the American public simply would not permit a special degree of Anglo-American collaboration. As a consequence, the Combined Chiefs of Staff machinery would "have to go underground" when conditions of peace fully resumed.

The Americans were "equally of strong opinion, however, that ways and means should be found for continuing full collaboration under cover of other activities," Wilson reported to London, and they proposed several methods by which this might be done. "It was obvious that the United States Chiefs of Staff had been thinking over the subject for some time," Wilson added, and were "firmly of the opinion that there was no hope of their getting approval to open collaboration." As the next best alternative, the four officers agreed to establish a combined committee to study the matter further.

Wilson concluded his dispatch with a striking note of caution. He did not believe the Americans

> were speaking on any definite instructions from the President and indeed General Eisenhower emphasized his view that consideration of this matter should for the present be confined to military circles. The United States Chiefs of Staff drew attention to the danger of these proposals leaking out and asked that the results of this discussion and the deliberations of the proposed Combined Committee should be Top Secret and given minimum possible circulation.[51]

Within this one conversation lay the basic pattern of the Anglo-American relationship in strategic and defense matters for much the remainder of the year, as well as the explanation of many of the disagreements which separated military authorities of the two nations. The British strongly resisted the position that the Combined Chiefs of Staff organization should be other than open collaboration and repeatedly pressed their American colleagues to prepare a case for presentation to Truman. It was not that effective subterranean collaboration could not be established and maintained as long as "the value of our [wartime] contacts remains fresh in everyone's mind." Unfortunately, this "would always depend on good will on both sides," Wilson warned, "and with the passage of time this might deteriorate until we found ourselves in a position very little different from that of 1939."[52]

But the Americans stoutly resisted formalizing these or any other arrangements. As long as a combined Anglo-American force existed in Italy and Venezia Giulia, the CCS would continue to function, thereby nullifying the need for any immediate action. In the meanwhile, Wilson informed London, the United States Chiefs of Staff were "anxious to avoid putting anything on paper."[53] Instructions and understandings were to be oral, diplomatic channels bypassed, normal procedures circumvented. In that manner, one American planning group emphasized, if awkward questions about collusion with the British did arise, senior officials could claim they were unaware of such activity and blame subordinates for unauthorized action. "In the present state of international relations," Leahy cautioned Wilson in the aftermath of Churchill's Fulton address, "the American Chiefs of Staff would not have the support of the State Department in raising the issue of permanent military collaboration" with the President.[54]

This determination on the part of the Americans to avoid the appearance of undue cooperation with the British has produced a misleading picture of the degree to which collaboration actually did occur. If one looks at much of the American documentation which survives from this period, dissension and a failure of co-ordination is the predominant image. For instance, Washington comes through as extremely hesitant to exchange classified military information of the sort which is routinely shared among allies. Late in 1945, to give one example, London invited the Americans to send a representative to sit on a British committee studying guided missiles and projectiles. United States officials, fearing acceptance of this offer would obligate them to reciprocate, declined the British invitation, although the field of guided missiles was a new one of great potential, and the Americans would have profited by collaboration with the United Kingdom.[55] Shortly after this episode, the President approved a new and much more restrictive policy governing disclosure of classified military information to foreign nationals. Under the provisions of this directive, the British were no longer to be singled out for special treatment. The United States, senior officials insisted in discussions within the Washington bureaucracy, must avoid any steps which might be interpreted as a military alliance with Great Britain. American authorities took this advice to heart. In the months since V-J Day, one survey revealed near the end of 1946, the British had furnished their American colleagues with fifteen separate military intelligence estimates. During the same period, the United States had provided London with only one—on insignificant Albania.[56]

Careful investigation of the British records, on the other hand, conveys a dramatically different picture. Reporting on developments between V-J Day and the end of 1945, senior British officers in Washington observed that while there was an occasional indication of reluctance from the Americans to maintain the wartime level of collaboration, "the general tendency was to continue the exchange of information on an unofficial basis in anticipation of an agreed post-war policy which would endorse this state of affairs."[57] In April 1946, Field Marshal Wilson again mentioned difficulties placed in the way of collaboration in technical and scientific fields, but then added: "Generally speaking, on the basis of personal contacts established during the war, we still continue to get a great deal of what we want and we should not like to create the impression that there is any serious deterioration in the standard of the wartime collaboration." Officers in the United States Army were particularly cooperative, he noted, and the Navy nearly so. Only the Army Air Force had shown serious reluctance to collaborate.[58] A month later, Foreign Office representatives urged that since the current informal arrangements appeared to be working satisfactorily, the question of more institutionalized collaboration not be raised with the State Department at present.[59]

Occasionally officials of the two nations employed subterfuge or other methods of indirection to foster the idea that nothing out of the ordinary was occurring. At one point during the year Wilson and Eisenhower arranged to have British officers attending the United States Army War College refused admittance to a lecture so that Eisenhower could report to Congress that foreign students operated under restrictions. On another occasion, when a curious M.P. sought to inquire about the present and projected functions of the Combined Chiefs of Staff, the government maneuvered to get his question withdrawn in order to avoid public attention on an issue more comfortably left alone. During a visit to Great Britain in October, Eisenhower arranged to lunch with the British Chiefs of Staff at the American embassy rather than accept their invitation for a formal meeting of the top ranking British military officials, again in the hopes of avoiding questions or embarrassing publicity.

Of course from the British perspective, serious disadvantages accompanied such clandestine collaboration, and grumbling about American intransigence was not infrequent. At midyear, in response to complaints about difficulties in the exchange of certain technical information, the British Chiefs of Staff reemphasized their determination that "every attempt should be made to persuade the United States . . . to keep the doors wide open to all forms of technical and scientific collaboration," and directed Wilson to use less restraint in pressing American authorities on the point.[60] The problem, British officials in Washington explained, was that the wartime officers were being released and the War Department was again becoming staffed with regular army officers, who were more career conscious, more likely to interpret regulations literally, and more reluctant to jeopardize their positions by shouldering avoidable responsibilities.[61]

Only toward the end of the year did cooperation become more open. In mid-September Field Marshal Montgomery, now Chief of the Imperial General Staff, arrived in the United States to inspect various army installations and to discuss, according to the British embassy, "purely technical" military matters. Montgomery subsequently wrote, however, that his conversations went far beyond the technical level. Although London had warned him to confine his talks about military cooperation to the American Chiefs of Staff, since Truman had not yet been apprised of the collaboration which then existed, Montgomery claims to have introduced the subject in a brief interview with the President on September 11 and to have secured Truman's approval for the military authorities of Great Britain, Canada, and the United States to discuss the entire range of matters relating to defense.[62]

Although the reliability of Montgomery's account of his meeting with the President can be questioned,[63] the pace of both covert and open collaboration in military affairs did quicken in the last months of 1946. Naval authorities of the two nations agreed to resurrect the wartime practice which permitted British and American naval vessels to call at each other's bases without prior application through diplomatic channels.[64] While these arrangements rested upon an oral understanding rather than a formal exchange of notes, which would make it more difficult to keep them secret, it was publicly announced in December that officials of the two nations were studying the feasibility of standardizing the weaponry of their armed forces. In another move applauded by London, the War and Navy Departments issued a new directive somewhat liberalizing the requirements which had to be met before any information of a military nature could be shared with the British. On the last day of the year the Army Air Force announced that agreement with the RAF had been reached to continue their wartime cooperation in staff methods, tactics, equipment, and research activities.[65]

Ironically, just as American sentiment showed itself more receptive to open collaboration with the United Kingdom, events in Britain pushed Whitehall in exactly the opposite direction. Throughout much of the year, segments of the Labour Party had become increasingly unhappy with what they saw as the anti-Soviet, pro-American orientation of the government's foreign policies. On October 29, twenty-two Labour M.P.s sent Attlee a letter complaining that Britain's preoccupation with Russian expansionism appeared most one-sided since it was not accompanied "by concern or comment with regard to the extension of United States Military bases from Greenland to the Faroes, from Japan to the Pacific Islands, and in the Mediterranean itself, notwithstanding the United States monoply [*sic*] of the atomic bomb, her inflated military budget, and the capitalist expansionist nature of her economy." The government too often appeared to be infected "by the anti-red virus which is cultivated in the United States of America by forces just as hostile to democratic Socialism as they are to Soviet Communism." The continued existence of the Combined Chiefs of Staff, the dissidents charged, had linked Britain in a de facto alliance with American imperialism. Two weeks later, nearly sixty Labour M.P.s offered an amendment to the King's Address criticizing the government for undue deference to the United States.[66]

A public challenge of this magnitude could not simply be ignored. Stung by the accusations, Attlee denied that Britain had ever been subservient to Washington or had demonstrated insufficient readiness to cooperate with the Soviet Union. Privately he complained that the ensuing debate on British foreign policy could not fail to embarrass the government in its relations with the United States. Collaboration in the military sphere would have to be more circumspect, he directed.[67] Responding to these instructions, Montgomery early the following year coupled his invitation for the United States to send three senior officers to a British training exercise with the plea that his offer "be kept very quiet" and that the visiting Americans wear civilian clothes to avoid identification. In Washington the Chief of Naval Intelligence told a ranking British naval officer that the backbench revolt gave "an alarming indication" of an unfortunate trend in British politics and warned this was likely to have repercussions on the exchange of classified information.[68]

Nonetheless, relations between the British and American military establishments were far closer by the end of 1946 than they had been twelve months earlier. And in comparison with the years following the First World War, the sense of partnership which bound the two nations together in early 1947 was phenomenal indeed. Only in the American unwillingness to formalize the CCS organization for the postwar period was there significant disagreement over a fundamental issue. And even in this case, it was the American conviction that such an action would retard, not accelerate, collaboration that produced this divergence. Moreover, it appears likely that Eisenhower and his American colleagues were correct in their assessment of what was politically possible in Washington.

A revealing memorandum drawn up in September 1946 by White House aide Clark M. Clifford reinforces this judgment. One of the President's most trusted advisers, Clifford sought to provide some larger framework in which to set relations between Washington and Moscow. His analysis focused on the agreements which—in American eyes—the Soviets had broken over the preceding several years. It emphasized the need for a firm policy to counter Russian expansionism. Great Britain was mentioned only in passing. Clifford evidently saw few advantages, despite growing doubts about the Soviet Union, in maintaining close ties with the British.[69] The product of extensive consultation within the executive branch, this document aptly illustrates the administration's preference for a policy of unilateralism, free of entangling commitments to other nations. It was this attitude which convinced Eisenhower and his military colleagues of the absolute necessity for caution before agreeing to arrangements which might be interpreted as evidence of an Anglo-American alliance.

Surveying the broad pattern of Anglo-American relations at the end of 1946, officials in the Foreign Office were not entirely unhappy. Certainly in the troubling area of Big Power politics, Washington had assumed a more forceful position in opposing intolerable Russian actions than Whitehall had ever thought possible a year earlier. A growing willingness on the part of the Truman administration to couple this resistance with concrete expressions of American military power prompted an even greater satisfaction in London. To the British way of thinking, the United States had finally shown itself capable of assuming the burdens and responsibilities of a great power. This was all to the good.

And yet, this review of relations between the two nations also gave the Foreign Office ample reason to lament the fact that many disagreeable aspects of American policy remained. American unilateralism in Japan and the Pacific, the insensitivity to British problems shown by Washington in the negotiations over Germany, the continued arrogance and narrowness of vision which American economic might fostered, Truman's refusal to accord the British special treatment on matters relating to atomic energy, the numerous instances when American military authorities rejected the wholehearted collaboration which London believed the times demanded—all these episodes and others led British officials to complain that the United States still had far to go before achieving the level of competence and political maturity which they all too easily assigned their own actions. Early in 1946, one Whitehall diplomat had described Washington's policy as "at present muddling along, not only torn by conflicting aims, but without any very clear idea of where it wants to go, besides being subject to a great deal of administrative bungling and a fair share of sheer incompetence." Shortly thereafter, Dalton had expressed similar reservations in his diary when he wrote, "The U.S.A. seem to be exactly repeating their post-last-war [*sic*] experience. The little men are nominally in charge and the whole political machine is out of control." In all too many cases, the British unhappily observed, these assessments were just as valid at the end of the year as at the beginning. Sweeping Republican victories in the November elections only added to their gloom.[70]

And it was true: confusion and uncertainty did reign in Washington throughout the year. The American stance in world affairs was guided not by any carefully devised grand strategy, but by daily expedients contrived to cope with current problems. More often than not, relations with the British never appeared so pressing as to demand immediate attention. Except when bilateral matters reached such a critical point as to force themselves upon the Secretary of State, ties with Great Britain received no top level consideration, no closely reasoned deliberation. As a consequence, they were allowed simply to drift.[71] "It would be a mistake to suppose that the Americans have far-sighted plans, whether good or bad," Keynes wrote following one particularly trying conference. Americans as well complained about the "notable lack of any central planning" which seemed the predominant feature of America's posture in the world.[72]

British analysts pointed to this absence of any grand geopolitical view in explaining Washington's stubborn refusal to accept the United Kingdom as an equal partner with shared interests and concerns around the world, but they undoubtedly flattered themselves in thinking that a more calculated American policy would automatically have accorded a greater voice to the British. Nor, though Whitehall officials would have stoutly argued otherwise, is there any reason to think that American interests would have been better served had Washington simply accepted London's prescription of wholehearted and complete partnership in all matters of importance. As much as they scolded American officials for narrowness of vision, policy makers in Great Britain themselves exhibited this same provincialism in thinking of world affairs. Nowhere was this demonstrated more vividly than in London's ready assumption that a responsible Unites States policy would inevitably align itself with British desires. In fact, Washington had good reason to dissociate itself from British actions in the Middle East, in Africa, and in Asia. The demands of British defense planners that the Truman administration openly enter into military arrangements that could only be regarded as an Anglo-American alliance against the Soviet Union were equally unwise. American officialdom by and large accurately perceived these realities; British statesmen did not.

Other considerations as well contributed to this casual American attitude toward collaboration with Great Britain. Traditional suspicions of British intentions and ambitions continued to plague relations between the two countries, despite growing alarm about the Soviet Union.[73] In the aftermath of Churchill's Fulton address and the contentious congressional debate on the British credit, close ties with London did not seem a smart public relations move to politically sophisticated Washington bureaucrats.[74] Disdain for British capabilities, reinforced by the obvious financial distress which Great Britain faced, may have influenced some American officials. More significantly, the United States itself was so strong, so obviously the world's paramount military and economic power, that there seemed little reason to modify American desires to accommodate British needs, as any true partnership would have unavoidably entailed. Even institutional factors retarded cooperation. Bureaucratic routines developed over many years are difficult to break, and in the past, American diplomats had eschewed the close and continuing contacts with representatives of other powers which Whitehall so eagerly sought.

As a consequence, most senior American policy makers harbored a powerful disposition to avoid any binding arrangements or long term commitments to the British. Ambiguity and uncertainty were the distinguishing characteristics of the relationship between Great Britain and the United States throughout 1946. Specific issues were decided as they arose, with no reference to an overall strategic concept or plan. An easy assumption prevailed in Washington that the British could always be relied upon if war ever threatened, but this was as far as official thinking sought to go. As a result, the statesmen in Whitehall, who had neither the financial nor the military resources to base their security upon such a carefree strategy, found themselves in a most equivocal and uncomfortable position: unable to disregard the Americans and strike out on their own, but equally unable to formulate any solid plans for the defense of their homeland and essential British interests around the world.

14

Middle East Morass

Throughout 1946 efforts to promote Anglo-American collaboration in the political and strategic fields ran afoul of difficulties in one additional area: the seemingly insoluble dilemma of Palestine. The issue of Palestine overshadowed all others in relations between Great Britain and the United States during these months, generating as much ill feeling and outright hostility as had British actions in Greece and Italy in the latter part of 1944. And once again American public opinion and domestic politics impinged on matters of the gravest import in international affairs. The predictable result was another nasty dispute which so scarred relations between London and Washington that meaningful communication in matters relating to the Middle East virtually ceased for a time. Ten years later, British-American ties sank to their lowest point thus far in the postwar period, in large part because officials of the two nations still proved unable to confide in one another when Palestine was involved. It would be gratuitous to blame Truman and Attlee for the diplomatic debacle of 1956; quite certainly Eisenhower and Eden showed themselves singularly inept throughout this episode. Still, perhaps it is not too fanciful to suggest that the statesmen of 1956 were also the victims of a pattern of unilateralism and incomprehension which their predecessors had done much to institutionalize a decade earlier.

Attlee had, at the end of 1945, finally convinced Truman to agree to the formation of a binational Committee of Inquiry to examine the deplorable situation still confronting the vast numbers of displaced persons wandering throughout Europe and the capability of Palestine to absorb many of these unfortunates. The committee began its investigation in Washington early in 1946 and then quickly proceeded to London and onto the continent, eventually visiting most of the countries of central Europe and the Middle East. Relations between the British and the American representatives on the committee were at times strained, but by the end of April all twelve members had agreed on a binational state in Palestine with the British mandate to be continued pending the establishment of a United Nations trusteeship. Their report downplayed the possibility of Jewish violence and advocated the admission of 100,000 European Jews into Palestine, observing that "[w]e know of no [other] country to which the great majority can go in the immediate future," a frank admission that this recommendation was based on the appalling conditions in Europe and not on whether Palestine could peacefully absorb such an influx. Significantly, the report focused more on the desired goals than on the means which would be necessary to implement them.[1]

The Inquiry's submission of its conclusions immediately touched off renewed British-American wrangling. As the committee completed its deliberations, Bevin asked that the United States refrain from any action without prior consultation between Washington and London, a request to which Truman gave his assent. On the day the report was released, however, the President publicly endorsed the recommendations on immigration while at the same time reserving judgment on the remainder of the proposals.[2] Bevin was incensed, believing this statement directly violated the President's pledge. The irate Foreign Secretary, in Paris for a meeting of the Council of Foreign Ministers, wired Attlee of his intentions to send Byrnes "a stiff letter."[3] The Prime Minister himself replied to Truman's remarks in a statement to the House of Commons in which he said that the study had to be accepted "as a whole in all its implications" before any particular portions could be put into effect. Britain would not accept the responsibility of carrying out the recommendations alone, he announced, but would consult with the United States to see what additional military and financial liabilities Washington was prepared to assume. There could be, moreover, no large-scale immigration until the underground Jewish armies had been disbanded and Jewish organizations cooperated in suppressing terrorism. Privately, Attlee complained that the report "proposed a policy which would set both the Arabs and the Jews against us," while other officials asserted that the British members of the committee had "sold out" to the Americans.[4]

Conferring with Byrnes in Paris, Bevin voiced his concern about the added financial burden and the additional military forces which implementation of the Inquiry's report would necessitate and urged the American to view the problem in its broadest international context. The United States must be willing to provide troops for duty in Palestine, he insisted, and not merely token contingents. The Foreign Secretary warned Byrnes that Britain had reached the point where it had to consider the possibility of a complete withdrawal from Palestine because of the expense involved in remaining there. Such a pullback would facilitate Russian penetration of the Middle East, Bevin conceded, but he saw little alternative unless Washington accepted a share of the responsibility. Worst of all, he complained, the whole situation was "poisoning" relations between the United Kingdom and the United States.[5] An impartial observer might have replied that the Foreign Secretary's tactless remark a short time later about the Americans supporting Jewish immigration into Palestine because "they did not want too many of them in New York" was not any more likely to improve these ties.[6]

In fact, Bevin had no intention of implementing the Inquiry's recommendations, despite having earlier promised to abide by any report which was signed by all twelve committee members. Now, however, he backed away from that pledge. Instead, he and Attlee imposed new conditions—the suppression of terrorism and the underground armies, the introduction of American troops into the region—which no one believed were capable of fulfillment. Acutely conscious of the possibility of Arab unrest, Whitehall showed itself remarkably oblivious to the likelihood that the Jews already in Palestine would immediately step up their own campaign against British rule. By its scornful disregard of the Inquiry's work, the Attlee government succeeded only in alienating the large numbers of Jewish moderates who up until this moment had resisted open warfare against the British. Nor did London's cool reception of the report make the British-American accord it so badly wanted any more probable.[7]

Truman for his part exhibited less interest in establishing a common position with the British than in other considerations. He remained, not unnaturally, thoroughly aware of the political dividends which might be accrued by a strong stance in favor of increased Jewish immigration. Not long before, an appreciative citizen had written him that Jews throughout the country were delighted that "at long last there is a man in the White House who is really trying to help us, and is not feeding us soft, pretty words intended merely to win Jewish votes."[8] Of even greater importance in Truman's mind was the "desperate situation faced by the remnant of European Jewry," and the conviction, fortified by key advisers, that Britain was stalling on aiding the refugees.[9] Aside from the human tragedy, further procrastination held additional drawbacks. Secretary of the Army Robert P. Patterson was begging the White House to relieve the armed forces of responsibility for the care of displaced persons in Europe since the army's size and effectiveness were decreasing so rapidly.[10] Military intelligence sources, moreover, estimated that the introduction of 100,000 Jews into Palestine would not appreciably increase the military capabilities of the Jewish underground nor require additional British forces to keep order.[11] From almost every perspective important to Truman, there seemed substantial advantages in pressing, and pressing publicly for an additional 100,000 immigration permits.

But the President adamantly refused to listen to British pleas that the United States accept a larger share of the burden in Palestine by providing troops for police duties. The Joint Chiefs of Staff and the State, War, and Navy Departments all urged that in implementing the Inquiry's report, "the guiding principle be that no action should be taken which will cause repercussions in Palestine which are beyond the capabilities of British troops to control." Nothing should be done which might commit American armed forces, endanger western oil interests, or give cause for the Arabs to turn to Russia.[12]

Thus, the Inquiry had failed in its attempt to forge a common Anglo-American position on this volatile problem. Truman persisted in his demand for large-scale immigration while declining to shoulder any of the financial or security burdens this would create. The British just as stubbornly refused to countenance any significant increase in immigration without some commitment from the United States that it would assist in maintaining order in Palestine. Anglo-American diplomacy in this area appeared to have run aground.

Events in Palestine did not wait for the British and the Americans to resolve their differences. Palestinian Jews increasingly turned to terrorist activities, culminating in the blowing up of the King David Hotel in Jerusalem and the death of nearly a hundred persons. Pressure mounted in London for a more forceful response. The senior British officer in the Middle East reported growing concern that British troops might take the law into their own hands if they were unduly restricted in their military actions against the terrorists. Bevin backed the Chiefs of Staff in their pleas for greater latitude in dealing with the guerrillas. Momentarily the Cabinet refused their request, but events in Palestine continued to win new converts for a firmer stance against the Jewish underground.[13] On June 14, Attlee wired Truman, "Tension is mounting in Palestine and we are satisfied that precipitate action on the immigration question alone would provoke widespread violence."[14]

Realizing that the British were not going to be bullied into acting by themselves and under increasing pressure that the United States take more positive measures to secure the 100,000 immigration permits, the President looked for other methods of inducing Anglo-American agreement. In early July he dispatched

Henry F. Grady, a former Assistant Secretary of State and roving ambassador for the administration, to London to discuss implementation of the Inquiry report. On July 24, Grady submitted another set of recommendations, commonly called the Morrison Plan after its British author. These proposals, largely the work of Foreign Office experts, endorsed the creation of a federal state with two provinces, one Jewish and one Arab. Great Britain, as the mandatory power, would continue to control such matters as defense, foreign affairs, taxation, and most importantly, immigration.[15] The British Cabinet approved these suggestions on the following day, but before Truman had time to make any decision on the American response, the plan leaked to the press. Zionists and their allies across the country reacted with shock and outrage, protesting that the proposals represented the negation rather than the fulfillment of the Inquiry's report.[16]

The violence of this response dismayed the President. Although Truman later wrote, "I was unable to see that anything could come out of [the Morrison Plan] except more unrest," diary entries made by Henry Wallace at the time indicate that the President thought the recommendations eminently fair and praised Grady for following his instructions explicitly.[17] Wallace, however, warned that the matter "was loaded with political dynamite" and that the Republicans would certainly make it an issue during the forthcoming campaign if the President accepted the plan. Following one of many telephone conversations with Truman, the Commerce Secretary remarked, "I emphasized the political angle because that is the one angle of Palestine which has a really deep interest for Truman."[18] Byrnes, once again in Paris occupied with the rigors of writing peace treaties, originally endorsed the Morrison Plan but quickly retreated after seeing the fury which it had aroused in the United States. On July 30 he wired the President: "I hope you will consider proposal entirely independent of any view I may have expressed because I do not know views people at home."[19]

At a Cabinet luncheon on July 30, Truman finally decided not to go along with the British in their advocacy of the proposals. He was forthright in giving the reasons for his actions. "In view of the extreme intensity of feeling in centers of Jewish population in this country neither political party would support this program," he had Acheson tell the British Ambassador. Since he would be unable to win the backing necessary to fulfill the recommendations of the Morrison Plan, he was left with no alternative but to reject it. To Attlee he wrote, "The opposition in this country to the plan has become so intense that it is now clear it would be impossible to rally in favor of it sufficient public opinion [to] enable this Government to give it effective support."[20] What he neglected to add was that his own actions over the previous twelve months had contributed significantly in the development of the expectations which produced this negative public reaction. Instead, the President issued a statement saying he had decided to recall Grady for consultations. The wisdom of this course of action seemed justified when he received a letter from the chairman of the New York Democratic State Committee a few days later. "Looking only at the political side of the question," the party leader informed Truman, "if this plan goes into effect, it would be useless for the Democrats to nominate a state ticket for the election this fall. I say this without reservation and am certain that my statement can be substantiated."[21]

A last desperate attempt to obtain some sort of agreement fared no better. Deeply frustrated, Truman directed Grady to meet with the American members of the Inquiry for the purpose of reconciling the differences in their recommendations. Two days of talks, however, made it plain that no compromise between the plans was possible. The six Inquiry members angrily labeled the Morrison Plan a "sellout" and unanimously urged its rejection.[22] Truman despondently concluded that the problem was "insoluble" and seriously considered having nothing further to do with it. "[N]ot only are the British highly successful in muddling the situation as completely as it could possibly be muddled," he complained, "but the Jews themselves are making it almost impossible to do anything for them."[23] Wallace has recorded that during the luncheon at which he decided to turn down the Morrison Plan, Truman was quite "put out" with the Zionist groups who seemed at times so intractable. According to the Commerce Secretary, the

President bitterly declared he had no use for any of them and did not care what happened to the Jews, adding, "Jesus Christ couldn't please them when he was here on earth, so how could anyone expect that I would have any luck?"[24]

But political exigencies refused to allow Truman to turn his back on the issue. Having once committed himself to support of the demand for the immediate entry of 100,000 Jews into Palestine, he found that Zionist and other organizations sympathetic to the plight of the Jews insisted on further action. Unfortunately, his foreign policy advisers counseled otherwise. Shortly after the President decided to reject the Morrison Plan, Byrnes cautioned him that it would be unwise to make any more public demands about the 100,000 immigration permits, in order to avoid conflict with the British.[25] Such a consideration, events were to point out, was not a priority concern in Washington in the autumn of 1946. Of more immediate interest were the impending November elections and the increasingly likely prospect of a crushing Democratic defeat.

Political strategists in the White House were particularly worried by the staggering manner in which Truman's public rating had plummeted in the months since his unassuming demeanor had won him such popular approval in the first weeks after Roosevelt's death. Polls which had shown that 63 percent of the public approved of his handling of the immense responsibilities of his office at the first of the year indicated that by mid-September his standing had fallen to a mere 32 percent, a decline virtually unprecedented in its swiftness and extent.[26] For millions of voters that autumn the Republican campaign slogan "Had Enough?" symbolized their dissatisfaction with the rewards of four years of wartime scarcity and restrictions: ugly and protracted labor disputes; shortages in meat, housing, clothing, and countless other consumer items; raging inflation; and an international scene which bore little resemblance to that which they had been promised. Truman himself more and more came to look like an impostor, a rank amateur awash in problems over his head. The quality of many of his appointments, his tendency to turn to cronies with even less experience and fewer qualifications than himself, led many to question whether the business of governing the country was entrusted to the right party. From all directions came dire predictions of a G.O.P. sweep in November.

Indications that the Republicans intended to make the Palestine issue one of the focal points of their attack on the administration particularly irritated the President, who not unjustifiably felt he had taken a more active interest in questions important to American Jews than had any of his predecessors. Word reached the White House that Thomas Dewey, governor of the nation's largest state, intended to release a statement favoring the Zionist position on Palestine, a development which was likely to draw thousands of votes into the Republican column, including vast numbers in New York. Unless Truman beat Dewey to this, the President's political advisers insisted, New York would be lost. In the four weeks prior to October 4, Truman saw Democratic officials from New York at least seven times. Most if not all of these meetings were for the express purpose of discussing the upcoming election. Though it is virtually impossible to determine exactly what was said in these sessions, it is likely that the critical Jewish vote was one of the topics discussed.[27] At least one journalist was later to report unequivocally that two New York Democratic officials made a special trip to Washington during these weeks specifically to demand a new statement from Truman to counter Dewey's anticipated announcement.[28]

Few voices counseling restraint reached the President's ears. According to Forrestal, Truman's rejection of the Morrison Plan led to Byrnes' "washing his hands of the whole Palestine matter."[29] Instead, the President increasingly relied on the advice of one of the White House aides he had inherited from Roosevelt, David K. Niles. An intensely private man who shunned public exposure, Niles was Truman's liaison with labor and minority racial groups. Later credited with being instrumental in the creation of Israel, Niles worked particularly hard throughout 1946 to insure that American policy followed a generally pro-Zionist course, arranging for Truman to see various Jewish leaders and even lending his White House office to Zionist activists. It was Niles perhaps as much as any other single individual who persuaded the President that he must issue a statement which would reiterate his sympathy for the plight of the Jewish DPs and defuse the Palestine issue in the ensuing election.[30]

When officials in London learned that Truman intended to make some further pronouncement on Palestine, Attlee cabled the President asking him to delay any action at least until the Prime Minister could confer with Bevin, and warning him that any inflammatory words at just that moment might destroy all remaining chances for the success of a conference between Jewish and Arab leaders which the British were then sponsoring in London.[31] Bevin hurriedly arranged to confer with Byrnes (both were again in Paris) to enlist his aid in obtaining postponement of Truman's statement. If the President's words provoked further disorders in Palestine, the Foreign Secretary told his American colleague, there would be "a real risk of His Majesty's Government throwing their hand in" in that troubled region. An alarmed Byrnes promised to urge the President to move cautiously on this matter.[32]

Truman arbitrarily turned them all down. Instead, the White House released a statement to the press on Yom Kippur, October 4, 1946. In it the President repeated his call for the immediate immigration of 100,000 Jews and came very close to supporting the Zionist demand for a separate state in Palestine, a position no administration in Washington had ever before taken.[33]

This overtly political action thoroughly appalled the British. Meeting with Eisenhower in London, the Chiefs of Staff stiffly remarked that comments of this sort could not help but aggravate an already complicated situation. Attlee bitterly wrote Truman of his dismay that the President could not give "even a few hours grace to the Prime Minister of the country which has the actual responsibility for the government of Palestine in order that he might acquaint you with the actual situation and the probable results of your action." The White House statement, he declared, might well result in the total frustration of patient efforts to achieve a settlement and the loss of still more lives in Palestine. The British leader confessed he was "astonished" that Truman could not even delay until receiving word of the latest developments in the conference then in progress between the Arabs and the Jews. "I shall await with interest," he concluded, "to learn what were the imperative reasons which compelled this precipitancy."[34]

In the United States, the President's statement provoked a mixed reaction. Zionists and their supporters hailed it with enthusiasm. Representative Emanuel Celler, one of Congress's most vocal Jewish sympathizers, wrote to congratulate Truman. Not incidentally, he noted that the statement should also have a "very desirable political effect upon our chances in New York."[35] Other observers were less laudatory. The *New York Herald Tribune* questioned the wisdom and helpfulness of Truman's action, pointing out that the President had totally ignored the background of world politics against which the Palestine issue was inevitably framed. James Reston wrote that the statement demonstrated the limitations of the theory that politics stops at the water's edge, while the *Washington Post* argued that the whole sorry affair provided an excellent reason for Palestinian policy to be taken out of the White House and returned to the direction of the State Department.[36]

Truman, obviously stung by these accusations of political expediency, heatedly denied that electoral considerations had influenced his decision to issue a further pronouncement at that particular time. "Presidents have often made statements on this holiday," he was later to write, "so the timing was nothing unusual, and what I had said was simply a restatement of my position." When announcement of the temporary adjournment of the Arab-Jewish conference reached Washington on October 2, he explained to Attlee, "I considered that it was incumbent on me to express regret at this outcome and again to call attention to the urgency of this matter." News of the adjournment had so depressed the DPs in Europe as well as millions of American citizens that "I could not even for a single day postpone making clear the continued interest of this Government in their welfare."[37] Later in the year, however, the President implied that a different set of motives had prompted his statement. Meeting alone with Bevin in December, Truman apologized for his public remarks on Palestine and said that now that the election was over, he hoped to be of greater assistance to the British.[38]

Actually, the dissension over Palestine which marred relations between Britain and the United States throughout 1946 hid a fundamental assessment which the foreign affairs experts in both nations increasingly shared as the year progressed. Growing apprehensions about the Soviet Union gradually convinced diplomats in the two capitals that Great Britain and America had much more reason to collaborate in the Middle East than to bicker. Officials in London came to believe that Moscow was encouraging illegal immigration into Palestine in order to add to British problems. By midyear the Chiefs of Staff were urging Whitehall to involve the United States much more closely in discussions concerning the defense of the Middle East.[39] At precisely this same moment, American military officers, disturbed by Soviet pressure on Turkey and Iran, were writing that "assurance that the peoples of [the Middle East] will not turn to Russia against the United States" was a "vital element" of American security.[40] Earlier in the year, representatives from both the State Department and the Foreign Office had warned members of the Inquiry that the question of Palestine had to be viewed in the context of Russian expansionism.[41] By the first of the following year, the State Department's desk officer in charge of Palestinian affairs was cautioning that continued "agitation and uncertainty regarding the Palestine question, by weakening the Anglo-American position in the Near East, permits a more rapid extension of Soviet Russian objectives."[42]

But disgust with Washington's behavior and frustration with what they saw as Jewish intransigence made it difficult for the British to act on the perception of a similarity of interests. The growing Jewish campaign of terrorism in Palestine gradually succeeded in nullifying the compassion found in London policy making circles for the terrible sufferings inflicted upon the Jews. Increasingly, this sympathy was replaced by the conviction that to yield to Zionist violence would only stir up the Irish and the Indians as well as the Arabs. The War Office and the Army continued to chafe at the restrictions placed upon the authorities in Palestine by the Cabinet in its desperate attempt to prevent the outbreak of full-scale warfare. Casualties were rising, Montgomery protested; London's "policy of appeasement" had failed. British military commanders must now be given permission to use all forces at their disposal to maintain strict law and order.[43]

The Americans, however, who seemed too often to criticize from the sidelines without offering any positive contribution themselves, drew the bulk of Whitehall's bitterness. To growing numbers of British diplomats, much of the violence in Palestine seemed possible only because of the moral and financial support extended to the underground Jewish groups by American Zionists. Officials of the British embassy in Washington pointedly asked why the American government persisted in granting tax exempt status to organizations whose purpose was to assist illegal immigration into Palestine or to support the Jewish underground. Foreign Office representatives noted the anti-British advertisements of American Zionist groups in the American press and complained of American laws which permitted the advertisers to deduct the cost of these offensive and slanderous broadsides from their income taxes.[44]

Increasingly, senior statesmen in London concluded that no way out of the Palestinian imbroglio existed for Britain other than total withdrawal. Initially, the War Office vigorously resisted this suggestion. With its position in Egypt becoming more and more untenable, Ismay explained, Palestine might well represent Great Britain's last foothold in the eastern Mediterranean. Even as late as December 1946, the consensus in the Foreign Office was that withdrawal would have "disastrous consequences."[45] But the absence of any viable alternative proved decisive. On January 21, 1947, Lord Inverchapel, Halifax's replacement as British Ambassador to the United States, approached Acheson to determine what the American reaction might be to Britain turning the mandate over to the United Nations. Acheson attempted to discourage the idea, saying that such a proposal was not so much a solution as an invitation to civil war.[46] London officials, of course, recognized this danger. In the face of renewed American insistence that the United States would not participate in carrying out any solution by armed force, however,[47] they could discover no other course of action which would extract their nation from what had become a thankless, unsolvable situation which demanded an ever larger commitment of the men and money which they could ill afford. In early February, both Arabs and Jews rejected the final British attempt at compromise. Bevin forthwith announced that London was submitting the whole problem to the United Nations. The United Kingdom refused to be plagued with the dilemma any longer.

Even this drastic measure failed to free relations between the British and the Americans of the irritant which Palestine had represented. On February 21, George Marshall, the new American Secretary of State, asked Bevin once again whether immigration into Palestine could not be appreciably increased. Three days later Truman publicly pledged his continuing efforts toward the entry of 100,000 Jews.[48] An exasperated Bevin angrily lashed back on the floor of the House of Commons. Britain might have been able to increase the immigration quotas, he asserted, had not American pressure for immediate entry of 100,000 refugees engendered an acute feeling of bitterness in both Arab and Jew. Washington's intervention in the problem had "set the whole thing back."[49]

The irate Foreign Secretary then directed his listeners to Truman's Yom Kippur statement of the previous October. "I think the country and the world ought to know about this," he declared. Bevin reported that he had "begged" Byrnes to dissuade Truman from issuing the statement, "but I was told that if it was not issued by Mr. Truman, a competitive statement would be issued by Mr. Dewey." The subsequent White House release, he continued, had spoiled the talks then in progress. "In international affairs I cannot settle things if my problem is made the subject of local elections," Bevin acidly remarked.[50]

In the United States anger and incredulity met this unexpected attack. The White House issued what the *New York Times* termed an "unprecedented" statement denying that partisan considerations had motivated Truman's October 4 pronouncement. Sol Bloom, who had been chairman of the House Foreign Affairs

Committee the preceding October, curtly stated that Bevin did not know what he was talking about, while Emanuel Celler termed the Foreign Secretary's accusation "a damnable lie." Republicans as well as Democrats defended the President against the charge of "playing politics." "The conclusion is inescapable," editorialized the *Washington Post*, "that Mr. Bevin is trying to disguise his failure by making himself a martyr."[51]

British newspapers rushed to Bevin's defense. The *Economist* wrote that the Foreign Secretary's charges were "fully justified and no blunter than fairness required." The *Manchester Guardian* complained of American "carping and sniping and needling."[52] For a brief but disconcerting time, Americans and Englishmen engaged in an orgy of angry accusations and recriminations reminiscent of the one which had so disturbed Anglo-American ties two years earlier. Near the end of March, the State Department's John Hickerson, himself a central figure in that earlier dispute, disgustedly wrote that the British in recent weeks "have blamed on us practically everything except the blizzard and the declining British birth rate."[53] Once again, it proved impossible to suppress the thought that the "special relationship" binding Great Britain and the United States expressed itself in most peculiar ways.

Unhappily, the bickering and bruised feelings which colored British-American exchanges over these issues throughout these months obscured a more important reality: the tortured problems involving Palestine remained unresolved. The DPs in Europe, moreover, continued to suffer, having become pawns both in Big Power rivalries on the international scene and in domestic political maneuvering within Great Britain and the United States. Directors of the world's mightiest democracies, diplomats in Washington and London proved singularly ineffectual in their policies toward either of these tragedies.

Judging from the perspective of four additional wars in a quarter century, perhaps it is not too pessimistic to suggest that a felicitous resolution of these problems, particularly of the Palestine puzzle, lay beyond the grasp of the statesmen of the era. Passions were too high, enmities too ancient, the willingness to compromise too infrequent. If this in fact is the case, then one must not castigate British and American policy too severely. Basic fairness requires this. And yet, one might have wished for greater wisdom on the part of both nations in the years immediately following the Second World War. Certainly neither Truman nor Attlee can be held responsible for those four subsequent conflicts. But neither can they be applauded for a vision or a discernment which might have made this bloodshed less likely.

In the United States, administration policy undoubtedly exhibited little of that responsibility and restraint one would like to associate with Great Power status. Truman's Yom Kippur statement provides a good illustration. Although it appeared to offer the prospect of immediate political benefits, it hardly served to induce either Jewish moderation or Arab trust. But the President's perceived political needs—"I have to answer to hundreds of thousands who are anxious for the success of Zionism; I do not have hundreds of thousands of Arabs among my constituents," he explained at one point—won out.[54] American policy, one disgruntled State Department officer complained, consisted of going "as far as we can to please the Zionists and other Jews without making the Arabs and the British too angry." This course, he observed, was of no real assistance to the Jews and kept the United States constantly "on the edge of embroilment" with both the British and the Arabs. Washington's policy, he ruefully concluded, "is one of expediency, not one of principle."[55]

Even American expressions of concern for the DPs in Europe took on a hollow ring, given the intense opposition in the United States to any liberalization of America's own restrictive immigration laws. While Truman's public utterances continually referred to the unfortunate Jewish victims of Nazi atrocities, Niles advised him that "there would be terrific resistance if we attempted at this time to bring *even a small portion* into our own country beyond the present quota limitations."[56] But if the President was able to find legitimate reasons why Americans should not be asked to accept a large influx of poverty-stricken, physically and mentally tormented immigrants, a certain provincialism prevented him from admitting that the Arabs might have equally valid objections.

Moreover, Truman's persistent demand that Great Britain permit the immediate entry of 100,000 refugees into Palestine soon lost any concrete meaning except as a symbol of his commitment to helping the Jews. Though this was the approximate number of Jews in DP camps in the American and British zones of Germany and Austria in August of 1945, the number had swelled by the end of the following year to a figure closer to 250,000. Nor, since there were well over 1 million DPs in Germany and Austria alone (perhaps as many as 2 million), would the removal of 100,000 to Palestine really go very far in alleviating the problem of European refugees.[57] So the British were not simply overly cynical in questioning Truman's alleged exclusively humanitarian concern.

The President's obstinate retention of the number 100,000 illustrates another facet of the American foreign policy process in addition to its itimacy with domestic partisan battles. At no time after Truman's first public statement in August 1945 does there appear to have been any thorough reevaluation of United States policy. Early in his presidency, Truman described the manner in which he decided policy in a letter to his family. "I have to take things as they come and make every decision on the basis of the facts as I have them and then go on from there; then forget that one and take the next."[58] Sometime later he wrote of his irritation upon receiving reports and intelligence estimates "on the same subject at different times from the various departments, and these reports often conflicted."[59] What he was saying in both instances is that reassessment was foreign to his nature. Partly because of the heavy demands of the job, partly because of his own personal make-up, the President spent little time reflecting upon the wisdom of previous decisions or their continued applicability under altered circumstances. And because his chief aides recognized this characteristic in their boss, they also insured, both deliberately and unconsciously, that information casting doubt on past actions seldom reached Truman's desk. Reassessment, of course, may not have generated other policies any more likely to unravel the tangled problems confronting American diplomats, but in the absence of any real accomplishment by current policies, it could not have hurt.

Beyond the domestic political considerations involved, Truman as late as his Yom Kippur statement continued to be concerned "almost exclusively," as Acheson has remembered, with the matter of securing the 100,000 immigration permits. This was in his mind completely separate from the question of the ultimate fate of Palestine, which he saw as an entirely different matter which could be decided at a later date by the United Nations. But as Acheson has again observed, the President failed to understand the inescapable connection between the two issues, or that the United Nations was unlikely to be capable of finding any peaceful solution for either problem if the United States and the United Kingdom could not reach a common position.[60] Unfortunately, this incomprehension served to nullify any beneficial effects which the worthy humanitarianism that propelled Truman might have had.

Nor can it be said that British policy demonstrated that skill or perception which Whitehall casually assumed it did. The British obsession with the dangers of alienating the Arab world, for instance, rested upon an exaggerated view of the unity and the fighting power of these peoples. Indeed, based on the record of the previous thirty years, every reason existed for United States officials to discount any proposals Whitehall offered for that troubled region. It appeared patently obvious to American observers that the Attlee government, which prided itself on its sensitivity toward aspiring nations and peoples desirous of escaping the constraints of foreign domination, possessed little more comprehension of the pervasive anti-British sentiment in the Arab world than its Tory predecessor had. London's policies in 1945 and 1946 looked all too often to be nothing more than warmed-over versions of the same assumptions and the same misguided notions which had so heavily contributed to the current problems.

Not even in their understanding of American policy did Whitehall officials display much acumen. The British conviction that calculations of partisan political advantage largely guided Truman's actions—however easy it was to come to this conclusion—led

London to discount the very real concern for the Jewish DPs which figured even more prominently in the President's thinking. Nor did the comforting explanation that pro-Zionist opinion in the United States could be attributed to American anti-Semitism induce British decision makers to reexamine their own assumptions for dealing with these anguishing questions.[61] "The essence of our policy," Bevin told the Cabinet in April 1946, "should be to retain the interest and the participation of the United States Government in this problem."[62] But without any real effort to comprehend the American position, the pursuit of this goal was not likely to result in a common approach to the issues of Palestine and the DPs. British policy in the final analysis was dependent upon American backing, a backing which for reasons justifiable and otherwise was not forthcoming. London as much as Washington bears the responsibility for this failure to obtain British-American accord.

And so the Palestine question and the related issue of the future of the Jewish DPs continued to fester, breeding hatred and violence yet with us a generation later. Undoubtedly, the prospects for a happy resolution to these twin problems had never been very promising. If Washington and London—so close in so many ways—could not work in tandem on these issues, what hope was there that two people as diverse as the Arabs and the Jews would be able to surmount the wide gap of misunderstanding dividing them? Anglo-American diplomacy had failed—perhaps had never had a chance of succeeding—and the world still reaps the harvest.

15

Independence and Interdependence

London officials spent most of 1946 waging a delaying action, seeking against increasingly imposing odds to forestall a renunciation of Britain's position in the select circle of the world's Great Powers. Throughout 1946, they succeeded—barely. But the first sixty days of the new year unceremoniously exposed the hollowness of this pretense. By the end of February 1947, the United Kingdom lay naked before the world, stripped of its status, its aspirations, and much of its pride. Like Greece and Rome before it, Great Britain was forced to step aside before younger, more virile nation-states.

Unlike the imperial powers of the ancient world, however, Britain was not overcome by force of arms. Instead, money, or rather a lack of it, proved the downfall of the United Kingdom. Perhaps, after centuries of what men euphemistically chose to call "progress," this was the essential difference between international relations in the twentieth century and in previous eras. Exhausted by war and buffeted by less dramatic but ultimately more devastating longer-range trends, Great Britain finally found its strength insufficient for its obligations. As Halifax told the House of Lords, the British government was in the "most distasteful position . . . in which its responsibility is greater than its power."[1]

Superficially, the nation's economic condition improved considerably during 1946. Imports were neither as high, nor exports as low as had been earlier estimated. Britain's balance of payments deficit for the year was less than half that which had been predicted during the negotiations for the American credit. In reality, however, the low level of imports simply indicated that manufacturers had been unable to purchase the machinery and raw materials which were essential if British exports were to compete in world markets. Moreover, a critical shortage of manpower still plagued basic export industries such as textiles, coal, and potteries. Partial demobilization of the armed forces did not even begin to fill the vacancies created by the withdrawal from the labor force of huge numbers of women and the reduction of the normal working week to forty-four hours. Industrial production in 1946 failed to reach the level of 1938, which had been in itself a poor year.[2]

In October, only three months after the United States credit had first become available, Hugh Dalton warned his Cabinet colleagues that London was in serious danger of drawing upon the American dollars too quickly. Roaring inflation in the United States, by raising American prices and thereby reducing the amount of goods the credit could purchase, aggravated matters still further. Following the continued decline of Britain's gold and dollar reserves, the Chancellor of the Exchequer told a friend, was "like watching a child bleed to death."[3] Officials from the British Treasury started talking to their American counterparts as early as November about the possibility of postponing some of the obligations which London had assumed at the time the line of credit was negotiated.[4] By the end of the year, the Conservatives felt it politic to attack the government's apparent inability to alleviate any of the problems threatening the economic stability of the United Kingdom, while London newspapers increasingly voiced anxiety about mounting competition in British markets abroad.[5]

Military expenditures continued to constitute a major drain on British resources. The election of a Labour government in 1945 had brought no more radical changes in Great Britain's basic defense policies that it had in London's foreign policy. Due to the unsettled political situation throughout much of the world and Britain's desire to bear its traditional responsibilities as a major power, defense expenditures remained at a much higher level than had originally been anticipated. The £300 million spent on maintaining British overseas defense commitments in 1946, primarily in Germany and the Middle East, accounted for the entire budget deficit for the year. Demobilization of the armed forces took place far less rapidly in Britain than in the United States, despite the fact that British troops had been fighting considerably longer than their American comrades. For fiscal year 1946, 18.7 percent of all British men between the ages of eighteen and forty-four remained under arms, compared to a figure of 10 percent in the United States. Similarly, Britain's defense expenditures in 1946 devoured 18.8 percent of the national income, against 10.6 percent for the Americans.[6] Yet, in November 1946, Attlee announced that the rate of demobilization would be slowed still further.

Quite clearly, spending on this scale could not continue. Financial pressures had been the chief factor in the adoption of Britain's ten year no-war planning assumption. This had been a political rather than a military decision, made by the Attlee government and not the Chiefs of Staff. Financial constraints also prevented the United Kingdom from following through on many of the military discoveries made during the war. The RAF, for instance, had to continue to rely on the Lancaster bomber, even though its limited range and lack of speed severely restricted its usefulness.[7] As early as September 1945, Attlee was considering a total withdrawal from the Middle East, leaving the United Nations responsible for maintaining order in that region of the world. As relations with the Soviets increasingly soured, Dalton resuscitated this idea, arguing for the creation of a new line of defense across Africa from Lagos to Kenya, thereby putting, as he recorded, "a wide glacis of desert and Arabs between ourselves and the Russians."[8] Bevin, more attuned to diplomatic than financial considerations, stoutly resisted any such proposal, but to a growing number of individuals in the Whitehall bureaucracy, the suggestion appeared increasingly attractive. Eventually the Chiefs of Staff let it be known they would resign before agreeing to abandon the Middle East.[9] For the moment the idea was dropped.

A White Paper on Defense issued in February 1947 explicitly spelled out the order of priorities in a Britain no longer able to provide both guns and butter. It was inevitable, this statement read, "that the rehabilitation of the civil economy should increasingly absorb the country's efforts and resources, to the diminution of activities in the defence field."[10] Translated into concrete terms, this declaration contained implications of the most serious nature for British diplomats. On more than one occasion, Attlee has remembered, Bevin ruefully remarked that a few million tons of coal at his disposal would have made all the difference in the outcome of some of his negotiations.[11]

Incredibly, it was coal—dirty, ordinary coal—which finally halted the charade that Britain remained one of the world's three Great Powers. British miners proved unable to produce enough of the fossil fuel. By January of 1947, the gap between production and consumption was 300,000 tons a week. On January 13, the government reduced coal allocations to all industry by one-half, and many plants converted to the four-day week or shut down completely. Twelve days later, the first of a succession of blizzards hit Great Britain, accompanied by temperatures of unprecedented bitterness. Before long, British transportation systems were paralyzed, as ice and snow clogged rail lines, canals, and highways. On February 7, the Minister of Fuel and Power stunned the House of Commons with the announcement that gas and electricity would have to be strictly rationed. Industries all over the country closed their doors. Unemployment, which just before the crisis had been 397,000 or 2.5 percent of the insured work force, quickly rose to a peak of 2.3 million, or 15.5 percent. As the world watched in awed wonder, winter's gales humbled the once-proud Britons in a way Hitler's legions never could.[12]

In the midst of Britain's distress, the government released another White Paper entitled "Economic Survey for 1947." Its contents underscored the perilous nature of the British position, leading the *Times* to call it "the most disturbing statement ever made by a British Government." "The central fact of 1947," Britishers were told, "is that we have not enough resources to do all that we want to do. We have barely enough to do all that we *must* do."[13] In sending a copy of the survey to Secretary Snyder, Dalton candidly admitted, "The plain truth . . . is that we are trying to do more . . . than our physical and financial resources allow."[14] American officials were to learn the very day that the Attlee government published its bleak analysis exactly what this implied for the United States.

Late in the afternoon of February 21, an official of the British embassy in Washington telephoned the State Department to request an immediate appointment for Inverchapel with the Secretary. Told that Marshall was on his way out of town, the British diplomat decided to send the Department two notes from London anyway in order that the Americans might have an opportunity to study them over the weekend. As Dean Acheson later wrote Marshall, these communications raised issues requiring "the most major decision with which we have been faced since the war."[15] The fuel crisis and the subsequent disruption of Great Britain's economic life had vividly illustrated the extent to which the United Kingdom had slipped from the ranks of the world's leading powers. Now as a result of these two messages, the United States moved to fill the void.

The two notes unveiled their significance in straightforward, restrained language. After reminding the United States of Greece's strategic and political importance and past commitments to that nation by both the British and the Americans, the first observed that Greece was on the point of collapse. Its government was unable to inspire confidence among the people, its economy was in shambles, and bands of guerrillas roamed much of the country at will. The note then went on to say that Great Britain would be unable to furnish any further financial assistance to the Greeks after March 31; officials in London hoped that the United States would make up this deficit by increasing its own aid. The second note concerned Turkey and repeated much the same information. Though the situation in Turkey was not then as critical as that in

Greece, the Turks still needed extensive assistance which White-hall was no longer able to provide.[16]

These two messages did not represent any precipitous action on the part of the British. Officials in the Foreign Office and the Treasury had debated the move for months, the former insisting that British prestige and security dictated a continuing presence in Greece, the latter claiming that financial constraints made this impossible. As early as July 1946, Dalton had informed the Greek Premier that Britain could no longer support Athens by itself; the Americans would have to be brought in. Shortly afterwards, London had withdrawn more than 15,000 troops, half the British total, from Greece, but this seemed to have virtually no effect in slowing the decline in the nation's financial situation. Soon Dalton was again complaining of "our endless dribble of British taxpayers' money to the Greeks."[17] Following the Cabinet's refusal in mid-January to accept his recommendation for further cuts in military manpower, the Chancellor threatened to resign. The government, he lectured Attlee, "must think of our national defence, in these hard and heavy years of transition, not only against the more distant possibility of armed aggression, but also against the far more immediate risk of economic and financial overstrain and collapse."[18] The economic dislocations which followed on the heels of his warning underscored the cogency of this argument in a way which mere eloquence could never do and in fact provided the final push which led to the decision to terminate all further aid to Greece and Turkey at the end of the fiscal year.

British officials had kept their American colleagues informed of this debate, so the contents of the British notes on February 21 came as no surprise, even though the timing did.[19] Considering the break with tradition which subsequent American actions represented, it is remarkable to see the ease with which the American response to these notes was decided, to see how little opposition actually existed within the complex Washington bureaucracy to the assumption of commitments and responsibilities which had heretofore been shunned. A consensus of opinion about the proper course of action formed almost by itself throughout the State Department, the War and Navy Departments, the Cabinet, and among the President's closest advisers. Washington official-dom had decided months earlier that that strategic region, and particularly Greece and Turkey, had to be defended, by force of arms if necessary, from further encroachment. By February of 1947, the fundamental decisions had already been made. The British notes merely presented the administration with an opportunity for public acknowledgment of its newly discovered interests in the eastern Mediterranean.

Even as early as the autumn of 1945, the United States had considered assuming some of the British responsibilities in aiding Greece. In August of the following year, Truman decided that Washington should resist Russian efforts to gain control of the strategic Dardanelles, a decision which unavoidably implied support for Turkey against Soviet pressures.[20] American interest in and concern for Greece and Turkey had appreciably quickened thereafter. On September 24, Byrnes recommended additional aid for both nations, a suggestion strongly endorsed by Secretaries Forrestal and Patterson. "The world is watching the support or lack thereof which we furnish our friends at this critical time," the Secretary of State wrote. "[T]he future policies of many countries will be determined by their estimate of the seriousness or lack thereof with which the US upholds its principles and supports those of like mind."[21] A month later Byrnes agreed to provide the United Kingdom with arms, which London would then give to Greece and Turkey.[22] In December the State Department dispatched an economic mission to Greece to study possible ways to make American assistance more effective. By the following February American representatives in Athens were warning that Greece was on the verge of collapse and predicted an impending move by native communists, assisted by Yugoslavia and Albania, to seize control of the country.[23] On the very morning that the British embassy presented the Americans with its twin notes, Marshall sent Acheson a memorandum recommending a direct loan and additional military equipment for Greece.[24]

With these developments as a background, the decision to fill the void created by the abrupt British withdrawal came naturally. And out of this decision came what was to be known as the Truman

Doctrine. The United States accepted the responsibility for maintaining the European balance of power, a role which barely two years earlier it had roundly condemned the British for playing. The reins of leadership were slipping from London's hands, Clayton warned his State Department colleagues; either the United States or Soviet Russia must pick them up. Truman's March 12 speech announcing a new program of aid to Greece and Turkey left no doubt about American's decision. Great Britain was fading rapidly, Congressman Carl Durham explained to a constituent following the President's historic address. London was no longer able to fulfill its traditional function in maintaining the balance. "It looks as if we are going to have to step into that role whether we like it or not," Durham concluded.[25]

From the moment the State Department received the two British notes on February 21, a participant in the subsequent deliberations has remembered, "the consciousness that a chapter in world history had come to an end was so real and ever-present as to seem almost tangible."[26] Great Britain's twin notes were "an irrevocable admission of impotence," tantamount to final British abdication of its leading role on the world stage. The director of the State Department's Office of Public Affairs told representatives of the War and Navy Departments that Secretary Marshall "takes the position that the world has arrived at a point in its history that has not been paralleled since ancient history."[27] Another State Department official has written that during the weeks following February 21, "emotion—proceeding from a realization that world power was at that moment changing hands—was not far from the surface" of the minds of diplomats in Washington.[28] The significance of the occasion even permeated the customary sluggishness of bureaucratic procedure. Following the March 7 Cabinet meeting in which it was decided to ask Congress for funds with which to aid Greece and Turkey, Leahy marveled that this was the first Cabinet meeting he had ever attended "where a definite decision was reached and clearly announced."[29] With typical British understatement, Dalton was later to write that his "little push for a small economy in Whitehall had released world forces far more powerful than I ever guessed."[30]

At the same time, senior officials in Washington emphasized again and again the need to avoid the appearance of standing in for London in the Middle East, of simply taking over traditional British responsibilities. The administration's new policy was to be presented as a positive American action. "Insofar as possible," policy makers were cautioned, "mention of the British should be avoided."[31] Leaders from the Congress, when the proposed American action was first explained to them, suspiciously asked whether this was not little more than simply pulling British chestnuts out of the fire once again. During the Senate hearings on appropriating funds for aid to Greece and Turkey, various legislators indicated that this same question bothered them and directed some of their sharpest queries at this point. Arthur Vandenberg, who supported the administration in its determination to assist the Greeks and the Turks, emphatically insisted that while British behavior in Greece could be seen as a continuation of a centuries-old tradition, the proposed American action was something entirely different. The United States was not in any way assuming the obligations of the United Kingdom or underwriting the British position in Greece or Turkey.[32]

In fact, the sweeping globalism of the Truman Doctrine, the target of much later criticism, was to some extent a response to and a rejection of these suspicions that the United States was merely standing in for Great Britain. If the aid could be presented as a maneuver in a broad ideological battle, pitting giant impersonal forces of good and evil against one another, this would easily dispose of the bothersome accusations leveled by those leery of too close an identification with Great Britain. Ultimately, the shrill moralizing and uncompromising tone of much of America's foreign policy in the succeeding quarter-century must be attributed in part to the administration's determination to avoid any suggestion that the United States had simply stepped into Britain's shoes in the unsavory world of European power politics.

Officials in Whitehall, as they prepared to turn over traditional British responsibilities in Greece and Turkey to the Americans, experienced no sense of history comparable to that felt by their counterparts in Washington.[33] For them the pullback represented little more than a routine adjustment in the load of Britain's postwar commitments dictated by the altered balance of power arising out of the war. As such, it was only one more withdrawal, little different from any number of others concurrently taking place. In January London had pledged to grant Burma independence within the near future. A week before its two notes to Washington on Greece and Turkey, the Cabinet had decided to turn the Palestine question over to the United Nations, a frank acknowledgment that Whitehall could find no solution to a problem squarely in the middle of an area traditionally considered a British preserve. Only the day before London's notes to the State Department, Attlee had announced that Britain would withdraw completely from India not later than June of the following year, ending four centuries of British domination. The Egyptians, another people over whom London had traditionally held suzerainty, were agitating for the dissolution of all ties with the United Kingdom and threatened to carry their case before the United Nations. Cyprus was in such a seething state that the British official nominally in charge there hesitated to assume his duties on the island. And in the midst of all this, a cruel winter had shown the world just how crippled Britain had become, a condition reiterated by the government's gloomy White Paper. As Bevin plaintively remarked, "All the world is in trouble at once; the troubles do not come one at a time."[34] It is small wonder that the notes on Greece and Turkey appeared no more significant than any of a number of other problems pressing in upon the harried British.

Besieged on all fronts, the proud Britons resolutely denied that their nation's glorious history was coming to an end, but still the whispers continued. The *New York Times* reported that responsible people could be heard talking about the possibility of "the biggest crash since the fall of Constantinople." On the first of March, Richard Russell, one of the Senate's most respected members, proposed that England, Scotland, Wales, and Northern Ireland be admitted as new states in the American Union. King George, he suggested, could resign his throne and run for a Senate seat. Freely admitting the apparently far-fetched nature of this idea, Russell nonetheless predicted that it would one day come to pass.[35] The Senator's comments, besides displaying incredible insensitivity from one in such a high office, were symbolic of the sad fate which seemed in store for the British Empire.

Appearances, of course, were deceptive. Great Britain was battered and bent, but in no way prepared to concede defeat. If the United Kingdom was no longer the world's paramount nation, its leaders fought stoutly to retain its status as a Great Power, an equal of the giants to its east and west. Great Britain would be no mere satellite, to the United States or any other nation. In fact, despite Britain's restricted power and the reduced range of options available to its leaders, officials in London had reason to believe that many traditional British policies would be continued with determination and vigor. In a fine twist of irony, prostrate England had in some important ways captured mighty America and converted Washington to London's way of thinking.

One had only to compare the experiences of 1939–40 to the situation in 1947 to see the extent to which American ideas had shifted. By the latter date, American neutrality, if Britain should ever become involved in a world conflict, was no longer conceivable. The security of the United States had become too closely entwined with that of the United Kingdom for America to watch from the sidelines, as it had done before 1941, while Great Britain struggled for its life. This was the change which half a dozen years had wrought. In some ways, it was the most important development for British security in over a century, the realization of London's hopes for at least a generation.

In a more immediate sense, Washington's assumption of an active role in the worldwide balance of power represented the fulfillment of another long-time British desire. "The epoch of isolation . . . is ended," the *New York Times* grandly announced on the morning of Truman's historic March 12 address. "It is being replaced by an epoch of American responsibility."[36] Nor was America's new interest in affairs outside its own borders exemplified merely by a passive commitment to an international peacekeeping body. After years of condemning Britain for the same thing, the United States had itself embraced an interventionist policy in many countries around the globe. The acceptance of a leading role in the occupation of Germany and Japan was a clear manifestation of this. Even more significant, since it did not flow directly from victory in the war, was Washington's participation in observing the 1946 Greek elections. Prior to this time the United States had voiced grave suspicions about British "interference" in that country, doubts which had in late 1944 very nearly exploded the wartime partnership. By mid-1946, however, Washington had itself assumed a far more dominant role in Greece than would have been conceivable only a few years earlier. United States actions did not entail a straightforward American assumption of British responsibilities, of course. But to London officials, the mere American presence there seemed a signal triumph for British diplomacy.

American policy also moved closer to Britain's in other ways during 1946. By the second half of the year, the United States had become Iran's chief supporter in resisting Soviet pressure, even though Iran was traditionally part of the British sphere of influence. In September an American naval squadron steamed toward the Mediterranean to reinforce the British position in the region. But this new parallelism of action was nowhere better illustrated than in the Truman Doctrine. Following their decision to aid the Greeks and Turks, Washington officials quite consciously saw themselves as inheritors of Britain's imperial responsibilities. They assumed that they would exercise these obligations more wisely and humanely than Britain, of course, but the significant fact was that they had deliberately accepted them. That an official position paper of the United States government could say: "It is the US view that the presence of British troops has been a stabilizing influence in Greece" indicates just how much the Truman administration had come to embrace London's perspective in international relations.[37]

The years 1944–47 also saw a striking change in the official American attitude, and to a lesser extent in United States public opinion, toward the British empire. In part this represented the different priorities and inclinations of Roosevelt and Truman, but since FDR himself vacillated in his actual policies, as opposed to rhetoric, with respect to the empire, not too much emphasis should be attributed to his untimely death. More important were events themselves in China, India, and the Middle East, where bloodshed and violence tragically demonstrated that independence and peace were not simply accomplished at will or by a simple act of abdication. Equally instrumental in stimulating the gradual shift in American attitudes were the obviously sincere efforts by the Labourites to lead many of the peoples of the empire to self-government.[38]

Finally, mounting fears of communism and the Soviet Union worked to mute American criticism of British imperialism. One Washington diplomat in mid-1945 asked: "When perhaps the inevitable struggle came between Russia and ourselves, the question would be, who are our friends[?] . . . Would we have the support of Great Britain if we had undermined her [colonial] position?" In March 1946, Leahy cautioned Byrnes that the "defeat or disintegration of the British Empire would eliminate from Eurasia the last bulwark of resistance between the United States and Soviet expansion."[39] Even a year earlier, when fighting broke out in the Levant and Britain intervened to forestall further hostilities, there had been little public distrust of Whitehall's intentions or actions. The administration had issued a public statement supporting British policy, and commentators who had not been slow to condemn London's behavior in eastern Europe and Italy only a few months before had endorsed Britain in its policeman's role.[40] Diplomats in the Foreign Office gradually came to feel that American opinion about the empire depended more on Anglo-American relations in general than on specific concern about imperialism per se. Though there were groups in the United States who were genuinely interested in colonial peoples, most comment on the empire, it was believed, measured rather than determined the vitality and cordiality of relations between London and Washington.[41]

Obstinately determined to maintain their position vis-à-vis Washington and Moscow, British statesmen gloated. That America's foreign policies in both Europe and Asia increasingly mirrored those which Great Britain had long pursued seemed conclusive refutation to the insulting remarks about a decrepit, worn-out, third-rate nation. Retaining their Great Power status had been, of course, a primary consideration in the British decision to develop their own atomic capabilities rather than rely on the Americans. It also explained their indignation when Washington officials failed to consult with them before approaching the Soviets. A recurring theme within the Foreign Office was that Great Britain must not let itself be forced into the role of Lepidus, caught between the powerful Octavius and the equally mighty Marc Antony.[42] The United Kingdom "cannot and will not be dismissed," Bevin insisted. When reminded of London's meager resources, the Foreign Secretary fell back into talking of Britain's "moral example, her steadiness." Evidently, the Labour government believed just as fervently as had its predecessor that Great Britain's "prestige and moral leadership," other phrases Bevin invoked, should give it equal voice with Russia and America in international affairs.[43]

In their less sanguine moments, however, London officials recognized that the world was not likely to acknowledge British superiority in these areas. As a consequence, they did not rest their diplomacy simply on hopes that others would utilize Britain's experience and leadership abilities. Rather, they boldly sought to play an active role in the American decision-making process. The unavoidable corollary was that the diplomats in Whitehall worried about the method by which American policy was made in a way and to an extent which never even occurred to their counterparts in other world capitals. If this indicated Britain's relative impotence in comparison with its two chief rivals, as well as Whitehall's dependence upon the United States, it also represented something truly unique, a manifestation of the peculiar ties linking London and Washington.

And precisely because they did rely so heavily upon the United States, diplomats in London repeatedly expressed horror at what they perceived to be the undisciplined, haphazard manner in which American policy was often contrived. At times they wondered whether such mismanagement could really be unintentional, or whether it was in fact part of a sophisticated ploy to gain some advantage over the British.[44] There seemed all too little conscious, rational choosing among carefully considered alternatives. Instead, American policy appeared to come, as one frustrated Whitehall official wrote in exasperation, from "a sort of cauldron in which all the special interests, the various schools of political and moral thought, the extremely powerful and completely individualistic organs of information and publicity and the governmental structure are all cooking together, all more or less as ingredients of equal value and importance." United States policy, according to this assessment, was simply the vapor which rose from this concoction, of which administration desires formed only one part.[45] Given this perspective, it is little wonder that London statesmen were contemptuous of the American decision-making process and repeatedly referred to Washington's need for Britain's greater experience and highly developed leadership talents.

A 1944 analysis by the Foreign Office's R.A. Gallop illustrated some of these concerns. Following a frustrating stay in Washington, Gallop attempted to explain why Britain and America, even when they had similar goals, seemed so often to end up working at cross purposes. Part of the answer, he decided, lay in the fact that the thinking of Washington officials lacked precision or depth. This he attributed to the vast resources available to Americans in both personnel and material. "It was as though the United States methods were those of area bombing (some shots hitting the target while the majority missed it)," he wrote, "while ours are perforce those of precision bombing." This observation then led him to conclude that "our more academic and intellectual approach with its precise statement of data and its tendency to work out each problem as an algebraical equation" might be no more comprehensible to the Americans than "their more superficial and facile approach is to us."

Inconsistency and lack of coordination appeared the chief defects of American policy making. The inconsistency, he judged, came at least partially from the American system where policy was initiated not at the expert level, to be endorsed or modified at the top, but where the State Department was called upon to apply directives or implement decisions from the White House or Cabinet which had been drawn up without any input by those most knowledgeable about the issues involved. The lack of coordination resulted primarily from the habit of each department within the Washington bureaucracy making its own policy without consultation with other interested agencies or departments, and then trying to "sell" it to the President. The principle of "competitive business rather than that of responsible, collective administration" prevailed in Washington, he wrote.

Gallop's conclusions were sobering. "The United States and British mechanics of thinking and administrative methods are so different as to make it extremely difficult for both countries to work in any sort of double harness." It was entirely understandable that officials in the State Department found it "difficult, irksome and in the long run impossible to commit themselves to any consistent policy, and, since they do not easily understand our totally different approach, dislike and possibly suspect attempts on our part to get them to do so." This would explain why British and American policies often clashed even when they were directed toward the same ends. These disputes were "due less to any disinclination to cooperate with us . . . than to an inherent inability to work to any long-term policy or commit themselves in advance."[46]

This assessment attributed a greater consistency and more coherence to British policy than it always exhibited. It also failed to take into consideration the infinitely larger and more complex governmental structure in Washington, or the less disciplined system which governed both Congressmen and bureaucrats in the executive branch, or the traditionally more open nature of the American decision-making process. Because public opinion in foreign affairs was not nearly as important in Britain as in the United States, this study, like many other British analyses, did not sufficiently deal with the problem of reconciling a democratic form of government with an efficient, skillfully devised foreign policy.[47] Finally, and perhaps most significantly, it discreetly refrained from any personal characterizations, although the idiosyncrasies of American foreign policy during the wartime and early postwar years cannot be explained without extensive reference to the domineering personality of Roosevelt, the ineffectualness of Hull, the caution of Crowley, the occasional provincialism of Truman. How else does one explain a President of the United States referring to atomic energy as a "trade secret"?

In some respects the decision-making processes in the two countries did not even lend themselves to comparison, a condition to which Gallop's analysis indicates no sensitivity. Many Britishers were simply unable to comprehend a procedure for devising policy which seemed as if it should be similar to their own, but which in fact was quite dissimilar in a number of essential aspects. Because political parties in the United Kingdom were relatively disciplined, British observers failed to appreciate the broad latitude for independent judgment, obstructionism, or even sheer cussedness which American senators and representatives enjoyed. Because the Prime Minister and the Cabinet, particularly in a Labour government, possessed substantial power over individual M.P.s, Whitehall officials found it difficult to comprehend the considerably fewer levers at the disposal of the American executive in its efforts to line up congressional support for its policies. Because British political life still functioned to an important degree within a deferential society which limited the demands it placed on its diplomats, statesmen in London very often underestimated the degree to which Washington decision makers were subjected to pressures of this sort. To a surprising extent, London officialdom was plagued, even after six years of the most intimate wartime collaboration with the United States, by an inflexibility and an incomprehension in its thinking about the Americans and the Washington policy-making process. In a fundamental sense, Whitehall stubbornly persisted in viewing the United States almost as if it were but another dominion—one which through an accident of history had become completely sovereign but one still in need of Britain's tutelage and guidance.

This basic failure in understanding led, as might be expected, to a number of miscalculations and false expectations on the part of the British, and consequently, to extensive disappointment and bitterness. London's hope for an unprecedented degree of postwar financial assistance unaccompanied by any corresponding concessions for the United States was a case in point. The belief that the Palestine policy of the Truman administration should be drawn up without reference to domestic political considerations was another. The resentment felt by the Attlee government over what it considered shabby treatment at the hands of the Americans in matters relating to atomic energy was a third instance. In all these cases, and a number of others as well, it was British ignorance of the true nature of the Washington decision-making process, and British parochialism in assuming that the American system should and would mirror their own, which led to these disappointments.

Although Gallop reflected many of these typically British misconceptions, he still offered useful judgments. In certain respects his analysis of the manner in which Americans made policy did point up some of the deficiencies which characterized attempts in Washington to devise a sophisticated stance in international affairs. American diplomats themselves often compared British methods favorably with those which prevailed within their own government. Because British policy was so ably directed, one middle level bureaucrat noted, it was inevitable that Whitehall would look for some deliberate motive on the part of the Americans for failures and vacillations in United States policy which had their origin not in disreputable intentions but in faulty planning and organization.[48] Forrestal on one occasion told Stettinius he had become rather "finatical [*sic*] on the way the British have run their show. Everybody finds out what their policy is and shoves the ball in that direction."[49]

Even so—and more to the point—orderly procedure does not ensure wise policy, as Britons who remembered the 1930s should have been the first to admit. In focusing so intently upon the methods by which American policy was devised, Gallop totally ignored the larger question of the substance of that policy. Nowhere did he stop to ask whether Washington had a conception of its national interest different from that held by the Foreign Office. At no point did he consider that the American interest might consist of something other than simply getting along with Great Britain. In no measure did he acknowledge that in some areas the interests of the two countries might—in fact, did—clash rather than coincide. Here, too, Gallop's analysis showed itself, in spite of its astute observations, mired in uncomprehension.

What most disturbed Gallop and other British observers about American methods was the reluctance or inability of senior diplomats to formulate any broad, coherent policy which would then guide their subordinates in the field in dealing with their British colleagues. Lord Moran's assessment of Roosevelt—"he doesn't like thinking things out, but waits for situations to develop and then adapts himself to them"[50]—seemed to describe Washington policy makers in general. That this should have been so is not surprising—but it was clearly disturbing to the British, for they suffered most often from this lack of design or consistency.

It was easy enough to say that cooperation with Great Britain should be a primary goal of American foreign policy, but when it came time to translate this generalization into specific policy decisions—relations with the Argentines, for instance, or the terms of an atomic partnership—diplomats in Washington and London and around the world discovered time and again that the needs of the moment usually outweighed any theoretical commitment to broad-scale collaboration. As a consequence, ties between Great Britain and the United States were often buffeted by gales of public suspicion and official indignation, by injured sensibilities and angry recriminations.

These unfortunate episodes did not, of course, derive from deficiencies in American policy alone. The unrealistic expectations which plagued the British from time to time about what was both possible and probable in Washington have already been mentioned. Nor were London officials immune from resenting American behavior which they had found perfectly acceptable for themselves when Great Britain had been the world's paramount power. On the whole, however, London's policy did not exhibit the fluctuations and the inconsistencies which characterized American behavior in international affairs.

But then, the British could scarcely afford such imprecision. The essential fact of the Anglo-American relationship was that it was not a symmetrical one. Great Britain needed and relied upon the Americans much more than the United States depended on

Britain. The natural result was that the statesmen in Whitehall devoted considerably more energy and thought to insuring that ties between the two nations were as smooth as possible. Policy makers in London could never be as cavalier toward Anglo-American relations as their counterparts in Washington could be, and were. Not surprisingly, the British were much more conscious than were the Americans of the "special relationship" which linked the two nations together.

That a special relationship existed is difficult to deny. The British and the Americans were bound by an international bond unlike that which had ever connected any two sovereign, fully independent states. The war years had seen an effort to coordinate their policies toward all other countries never duplicated before or since, so much so that Cordell Hull could write (in admittedly overstated fashion) of a "virtual unification of our foreign policies."[51] Later, after what Joseph Davies called the "compulsion of unity" became less acute, the basis of this special relationship was less obvious.[52] Nonetheless, the British expectation of unprecedented largesse from the United States during the financial negotiations in late 1945 said much about London's conception of the relationship. So, too, despite the British disappointment, did the ultimate terms agreed upon between the delegations of the two countries. "The United Kingdom is the best friend of the United States and no one in his right mind can visualize our two countries lining up on opposite sides in armed conflict," John Hickerson had written in 1944.[53] This fundamental assessment continued to guide American policy during the loan talks and on into the postwar years, despite the momentary squabbles and the superficial irritants.

Still, though conscious that the basis for a special partnership existed, American officials often proved reluctant to act on that knowledge, as if to admit publicly that the United States shared unusually close ties with the British might somehow threaten that relationship. "We desire a common agreement with the U.K. but on the other hand do not want to form a U.K.-U.S. bloc," observed one State Department bureaucrat in mid-1945.[54] His comment describes much of American thinking about relations with Great

Britain in these years. A remark made by Truman about this same time is equally revealing. "I did not want to give [the] impression I was acting for Great Britain in any capacity, although I wanted [the] support of Great Britain in anything we do. . . ."[55] Neither the President nor his chief advisers ever comprehended the inconsistency in this statement. The British "find it difficult to understand 'cooperation' on our terms rather than on theirs," complained planners in the War Department the following year.[56] It seldom occurred to Washington officials that cooperation by definition meant neither "our" nor "their" but an amalgamation of the wishes and desires of the two. Lacking this awareness, American policy often displayed a blustering insensitivity toward the feelings of a British nation no longer entirely sure of its power or its place in the world. Perhaps because they had so seldom been losers, Americans were not the most gracious of winners.

This luxury of defining cooperation on their own terms rather than working for a true compromise, of seeking partnership while still retaining the freedom to go their own way when this better suited their purposes, was not an option open to British officials by 1944. Technological advances, shifting patterns of international trade and finance, and the ravages of war had all placed the United Kingdom in a position of dependence upon the United States. British journalists bravely wrote that it was pointless to quibble about the relative degrees of dependence and independence in relations between the two. The "whole Atlantic Commonwealth is strategically interdependent," the *Economist* noted, "and the position of either of its two major partners would be immeasurably weaker if it could not rely, in a crisis, on the other."[57] This was true, but it was not enough. Britain still relied on the United States in a way and to a degree in which the Americans would never depend upon the United Kingdom.

Thus, Churchill could tell Truman at Potsdam that he wanted the United States to be a wife to Great Britain, not merely a sister (and certainly no longer a daughter). The metaphor was deliberately chosen; there is no closer, more intimate relationship than marriage. The election of a Labour government brought no change in this fundamental tenet of British thinking. London wanted nothing more than a common policy with the United States, Bevin assured Clayton shortly after taking office. "If we choose to pull together, we can give leadership to the world in the very best sense," another British official told a gathering of American businessmen some months later. But "if we don't, the world will have no leadership at all."[58] In early 1947, when domestic pressures forced the Foreign Secretary into negotiations with the Russians looking toward a revision of the Anglo-Soviet treaty of alliance, he quickly sent word to Washington that the exchange of messages with Moscow did not indicate in any way a weakening in London's desire for the closest Anglo-American cooperation.[59] Britain would not allow any wedge to be driven between the United States and the United Kingdom, he promised in a speech to the House of Commons on February 27, 1947.[60]

And yet the Americans held back. Much more conscious than were the British of the points where the interests of their two nations clashed, Washington authorities retained a reluctance to form a united front with Whitehall except on terms unacceptable to a Great Britain preoccupied with maintaining a show of independence. The British were not, in 1947 or afterwards, to attain the intimate bilateral ties with America which they desired. As relations with the Soviet Union deteriorated still further, the United States offered western Europe first economic aid with the Marshall Plan, and then a military alliance under the auspices of the North Atlantic Treaty Organization. In both cases statesmen in Washington opted for a more encompassing, less exclusive, multilateral arrangement. The pattern of the immediate postwar years was preserved: American diplomats still resisted acknowledging any special relationship with Great Britain.

In 1944, well before the war was won, a junior bureaucrat in the Foreign Economic Administration recalled that the great Marlborough had once remarked that in every alliance one party wears boots and spurs while the other wears a saddle. "Even though neither Winston Churchill nor Col. McCormick might be willing to admit it," he observed, "we obviously are wearing the boots."

This fundamental condition was the decisive factor in the turbulent, often paradoxical relationship between Great Britain and the United States. This same official, however, then went on to add, "If we want to stay in this fortunate position, we have to find some way to feed the horse."[61] Self-assurance, yet interdependence; unbalanced, but symbiotic: here again was that unique blend which tied the two Atlantic democracies together in a partnership of intimacy and strife. Born of war, nurtured by victory, threatened by peace, Anglo-American cooperation remained in 1947 as it had been three years earlier, a substantial and yet ambiguous feature of the global order.

Abbreviations Used
in the Notes

CAB	Cabinet Office Records, Public Record Office, London.
D.O.	Dominions Office Records, Public Record Office, London.
FDRL	Franklin D. Roosevelt Library, Hyde Park, New York.
F.O. 371	Foreign Office Records, Class 371: General Correspondence, Political, Public Record Office, London.
FRUS	U.S. Department of State, *Foreign Relations of the United States.* Annual volumes.
FRUS, Malta and Yalta	U.S. Department of State, *Foreign Relations of the United States: The Conferences at Malta and Yalta, 1945* (Washington: Government Printing Office, 1955).
FRUS, Potsdam	U.S. Department of State, *Foreign Relations of the United States: The Conference of Berlin (The Potsdam Conference), 1945.* 2 vols. (Washington: Government Printing Office, 1960).
FRUS, Quebec	U.S. Department of State, *Foreign Relations of the United States: The Conference at Quebec,*

	1944 (Washington: Government Printing Office, 1972).
HSTL	Harry S. Truman Library, Independence, Missouri.
MMRD	Modern Military Records Division, National Archives, Washington, D.C.
PREM	Prime Minister's Office Records, Public Record Office, London.
SDR	RG 59, General Records of the Department of State, National Archives, Washington, D.C.
TDR	RG 56, General Records of the Department of the Treasury, National Archives, Washington, D.C.
Trea.	Treasury Records, Public Record Office, London.
W.O.	War Office Records, Public Record Office, London.

Notes

◇

INTRODUCTION

1. Only in the past three or four years have historians finally begun to publish full-length studies examining British-American as well as Soviet-American relations during the war period. Most notable of these are Christopher Thorne, *Allies of A Kind: The United States, Britain, and the War Against Japan, 1941–1945*, and William Roger Louis, *Imperialism At Bay: The United States and the Decolonization of the British Empire, 1941–1945*. But to date the literature dealing with American policy after the Japanese surrender is still characterized, with perhaps one or two exceptions, by this confining bipolarity. Yet as Joyce and Gabriel Kolko have rightly pointed out, Soviet-American rivalry may not even have been the most significant aspect of postwar international politics. See Joyce Kolko and Gabriel Kolko, *The Limits of Power: The World and United States Foreign Policy, 1945–1954*, p. 6.

2. This is nowhere better illustrated than in Leon D. Epstein, *Britain—Uneasy Ally*. Epstein's avowed intention, stated on his first page, is "to analyze British responses to American foreign policy in the postwar years 1945 through 1952."

3. This point is ably brought out in Henry Pachter, "Revisionist Historians & the Cold War," p. 507.

4. Paul Mason to Michael Wright, Dec. 22, 1945, AN 2851/763/45, F.O. 371.

1. THE EQUIVOCAL BACKDROP

1. The most exhaustive study of American policy toward the belligerents in the two years preceding Pearl Harbor remains the two volumes by William L. Langer and S. Everett Gleason: *The Challenge to Isolation, 1937–1940* and *The*

Undeclared War, 1940–41. A well-publicized account of the 1939–41 collaboration between Great Britain and the United States, but one which must be used with circumspection, is William Stevenson's A Man Called Intrepid: The Secret War. The fullest treatment of the Argentia conference may be found in Theodore A. Wilson's The First Summit: Roosevelt and Churchill at Placentia Bay 1941.

2. Stevenson, A Man Called Intrepid, p. 364. For the latest work on one of the major strategic disputes dividing the two western allies, see Mark A. Stoler, The Politics of the Second Front: American Military Planning and Diplomacy in Coalition Warfare, 1941–1943. Combined staff discussions, Stoler writes (p. 162), often "resembled battles rather than conferences between allies." Also see Robert Dallek's prize-winning Franklin D. Roosevelt and American Foreign Policy, 1932–1945, p. 322.

3. In connection with this it is instructive to repeat the observation of a Foreign Office official more than three decades ago: "It is one of the tragedies of Anglo-American relations that, in the U.S.A., disagreement is news but agreement is not." Unidentified minute, July 1946, AN 2016/5/45, F.O. 371.

4. Though in practice this worked considerably better in Europe than in Asia. On this see Thorne, Allies of a Kind; Gabriel Kolko, The Politics of War: The World and United States Foreign Policy, 1943–1945, pp. 198–200. For postwar assessments of this exceptional military collaboration, see "Report on the British Army Staff (Washington) by Lieutenant-General Sir Gordon N. Macready . . . for the Period June 1942 to December 1945," Jan. 17, 1946, W.O. 32/12178; comments of General George Lincoln, Aug. 13, 1946, ABC 350.001 Speeches, RG 165, MMRD. Also Warren F. Kimball, "Churchill and Roosevelt: The Personal Equation," p. 179.

5. Stephen E. Ambrose, The Supreme Commander: The War Years of General Dwight D. Eisenhower, p. 23; Forrest C. Pogue, "SHAEF—A Retrospect on Coalition Command," p. 331.

6. Quoted in Arthur Campbell Turner, The Unique Partnership: Britain and the United States, p. 65.

7. As surprising as it sounds three decades later, for a great many Americans in the mid-1940s, China, not Great Britain, was the ally with whom they felt the most kinship. "Untainted by Communism or imperialism, a victim rather than a practitioner of power politics," Robert Dallek has recently written, "China above all was seen as America's natural democratic ally." Dallek, Franklin D. Roosevelt, p. 329. Much of the discussion in this and the following paragraphs depends heavily on the comprehensive analysis of the underlying factors conditioning the Anglo-American relationship found in the first 200 pages of Harry C. Allen, Great Britain and the United States. I have attempted only to mention some of the more obvious of the numerous points which Professor Allen explores in detail. There are also several helpful surveys examining public attitudes toward Great Britain scattered throughout the 711.41 file, SDR.

8. Quoted in William Clark, Less than Kin: A Study of Anglo-American Relations, p. 41.

9. Establishing the racial make-up of the American people is a notoriously treacherous business. For some of the problems inherent in this task, see the discussion in Allen, *Great Britain and the United States*, pp. 98–106. Allen cautiously avoids assigning a specific percentage of the American population with British origins, observing only that "the English-speaking contribution to the American population was by far the biggest of all the national and racial groups" (p. 104). Arthur Turner accepts 61 percent as a realistic estimate but notes that a 1935 study concluded that 53.6 percent was a more accurate figure. See Turner, *The Unique Partnership*, pp. 22–23. In any event, specific numbers are not nearly as important as the fact that Great Britain and the United States shared this common demographic bond.

10. Honora Bruere McIver, "American Invasion," p. 165.

11. Minute by J. C. Donnelly, Nov. 7, 1944, AN 4213/20/45, F.O. 371. More detached observers have also noted this American tendency to judge the British by loftier standards than those applied to other countries. On this see Henry Steele Commager, ed., *Britain Through American Eyes*, p. xxix. The James quote is from Commager, p. xxvii.

12. Roosevelt to Churchill, No. 106, Feb. 18, 1942, in Francis L. Loewenheim, Harold D. Langley, and Manfred Jonas, eds., *Roosevelt and Churchill: Their Secret Wartime Correspondence*, pp. 179–80; Lord Moran, *Churchill: Taken from the Diaries of Lord Moran*, p. 243. Alastair Buchan, one of the shrewdest observers of the Anglo-American relationship, has termed the Roosevelt-Churchill friendship "the most significant intimacy since the end of the dynastic era." "Mothers and Daughters (or Greeks and Romans)," p. 654. For the evolution of this unique relationship, Joseph P. Lash's *Roosevelt and Churchill, 1939–1941: The Partnership That Saved the West* is particularly good.

13. Kimball, "Churchill and Roosevelt," pp. 178–80; Pogue, "SHAEF—A Retrospect," p. 329; Churchill quoted in Moran, *Churchill*, p. 614.

14. Clark, *Less than Kin*, p. 104.

2. THE ECONOMICS OF PARTNERSHIP

1. Kolko, *Politics of War*, p. 280.

2. Alfred E. Eckes, Jr., *A Search for Solvency: Bretton Woods and the International Monetary System, 1941–1971*, p. 37; Hull letter quoted in Richard N. Gardner, *Sterling-Dollar Diplomacy*, p. 9.

3. Cordell Hull, *The Memoirs of Cordell Hull*, 1:81, 525; Clayton quote in U.S., Dept. of State, *Bulletin*, 12:979. Also helpful on this point is Arthur W. Schatz, "The Anglo-American Trade Agreement and Cordell Hull's Search for Peace, 1936–1938," pp. 85–87.

4. Statement by Secretary Fred M. Vinson before the Senate Committee on Banking and Currency, March 5, 1946, General Correspondence, 1933–56, Office of the Secretary, TDR.

5. *New York Times*, April 26, 1945, p. 6.

6. Frederick S. Northedge, *British Foreign Policy: The Process of Readjustment, 1945–1961*, p. 182. Hull in particular worried that the organization and regimentation which he saw as the alternative to a multilateral, nondiscriminatory world would threaten private enterprise and ultimately undermine American democracy.

7. Thomas G. Paterson, *Soviet-American Confrontation: Postwar Reconstruction and the Origins of the Cold War*, p. 151; Clayton quote in *New York Times*, March 21, 1945, p. 12.

8. J. A. Maxwell to Charles Taft, Jan. 18, 1945, 611.0031/1-1945, SDR.

9. *New York Times*, Jan. 19, 1945, p. 14. For other statements of this idea by State Department officials, see Herbert Feis, "On Our Economic Relations With Britain," pp. 462, 465; William L. Batt, "British and American Opinion," *Vital Speeches*, p. 288.

10. Gardner, *Sterling-Dollar Diplomacy*, p. 19; Hull, *Memoirs*, 1:519. The Master Lend-Lease Agreement may be found in U.S. Senate, Committee on Foreign Relations, *A Decade of American Foreign Policy: Basic Documents, 1941–49*, S. Doc. 123, 81st Cong., 1st sess., 1950, pp. 3–5.

11. These reports were especially prevalent in Latin America, which had long been considered a special American preserve. Random examples may be found in American Embassy, Mexico City, to Secretary of State, Dec. 22, 1944, 812.9111/12-2244, SDR; American Embassy, Mexico City, to Secretary of State, Dec. 26, 1944, 841.20212/12-2644, *ibid.*; Commanding General, Caribbean Defense Command, to Chief of Staff, U.S. Army, April 29, 1945, OPD dec. file, 1942–45: OPD 350.05, RG 165, MMRD; "British Activities in the Other American Republics," n.d., "Yalta Notes," box 170, Harry L. Hopkins Papers, FDRL.

12. Memorandum of a meeting in the office of the Chancellor of the Exchequer, Aug. 11, 1944, folder 22d, box 7, Harry Dexter White Papers, Princeton University.

13. U.S. Dept. of Commerce, Bureau of the Census, *Historical Statistics of the United States, Colonial Times to 1970*, part 1, p. 224; U.S. War Production Board, *Wartime Production Achievements and the Reconversion Outlook: Report of the Chairman*, p. 1; Vinson quote in the *Times*, July 2, 1945, p. 3. For a convenient summation, see Alan S. Milward, *War, Economy and Society, 1939–1945*, pp. 63–67.

14. Northedge, *British Foreign Policy*, p. 33; James F. Byrnes, *Speaking Frankly*, p. 93; U.K., *Statistics Relating to the War Effort of the United Kingdom*, p. 26. Senator Joseph H. Ball repeats the Englishman's story in his "There is No Ivory Tower for Us," *New York Times Magazine*, Jan. 14, 1945, p. 37.

15. "Meeting with Mr. Morgenthau, Mr. Stettinius and Other Officers of the Departments of Treasury and State," Jan. 17, 1945, 740.00119 Control (Germany)/1-445, SDR.

16. Statement by Secretary Fred M. Vinson before the Senate Committee

on Banking and Currency, March 5, 1946, General Correspondence, 1933–56, Office of the Secretary, TDR. Economic historians have recently begun to challenge this picture of stagnation and decline in the British economy during the interwar years. Generally speaking, however, this revisionist argument focuses most intently on internal growth and development, while down-playing the heavy unemployment and continuing deterioration in Britain's external position which characterized this period. See Derek H. Aldcroft and Harry W. Richardson, *The British Economy, 1870–1939*, pp. 219–26.

17. Statement by Secretary Fred M. Vinson before the Senate Committee on Banking and Currency, March 5, 1946, General Correspondence, 1933–56, Office of the Secretary, TDR; Gardner, *Sterling-Dollar Diplomacy*, p. 178; "The Effect of our External Financial Position on our Foreign Policy," Sept. 1944, UE 615/169/53, F.O. 371.

18. As measured in actual dollar value. Wartime inflation meant, of course, that the volume increase would not be this great. "Foreign Trade Requirements of the United Kingdom in the First Three Years Post-Hostility Period," April 25, 1945, folder "Correspondence, 1945," James S. Earley Papers, HSTL.

19. "Estimate of British Post-War Capabilities and Intentions," Feb. 13, 1946, CCS geog. files, 1942–45: CCS 000.1 Gr. Britain, RG 218, MMRD.

20. Gardner, *Sterling-Dollar Diplomacy*, p. 174; John S. Fischer to Lauchlin Currie, July 20, 1944, folder "Phase Two," box 5, Clayton-Thorp Files, HSTL; William Hardy McNeill, *America, Britain, and Russia: Their Co-Operation and Conflict, 1941–1946*, p. 440.

21. "Brief Analysis of British Post-War Export Requirements," August 1945, folder "Correspondence, 1945," Early Papers; "Foreign Trade Requirements of the United Kingdom in the First Three Years Post-Hostility Period," April 25, 1945, *ibid.*; *Barron's*, June 4, 1945, p. 3.

22. William Stix Wasserman, "America and Britain: Rivals or Partners?" *New York Times Magazine*, Feb. 4, 1945, p. 53.

23. Statement by Secretary Fred M. Vinson before the Senate Committee on Banking and Currency, March 5, 1946, General Correspondence, 1933–56, Office of the Secretary, TDR.

24. Gardner, *Sterling-Dollar Diplomacy*, pp. 37, 122–23; Eckes, *Search for Solvency*, p. 39; A.J.P. Taylor, *Beaverbrook*, pp. 562–63; Milward, *War, Economy and Society*, p. 337.

25. Gardner, *Sterling-Dollar Diplomacy*, p. 123.

26. Kolko, *Politics of War*, p. 488; Paterson, *Soviet-American Confrontation*, pp. 14–15.

27. McNaughton Reports, June 9, 1945, Frank McNaughton Papers, HSTL; E. F. Penrose, *Economic Planning for the Peace*, p. 92; Gardner, *Sterling-Dollar Diplomacy*, p. 108; A. J. Youngson, *The British Economy, 1920–1957*, p. 155; Francis B. Sayre, *The Way Forward: The American Trade Agreements Program*, pp. 99–100.

28. *New York Times*, March 14, 1945, p. 18.

29. Report #109757, Jan. 2, 1945, Office of Strategic Services, RG 226, MMRD.

30. *New York Times*, Jan. 26, 1945, p. 8.

31. *Ibid.*, Oct. 1, 1944, p. E4; Thorne, *Allies of a Kind*, p. 553. For one indication that British fears were not entirely far-fetched, see Clayton R. Koppes and Gregory D. Black, "What to Show the World: The Office of War Information and Hollywood, 1942–1945," p. 104.

32. *New York Times*, March 6, 1945, p. 7.

33. Clayton to Ambassador Winant, Feb. 7, 1945, 841.4061/9-1444, SDR; *New York Times*, July 3, 1945, p. 5. State Department archives are filled with complaints against British restrictions, most of which were eventually channeled to Assistant Secretary Clayton. The 611.4131 file is a good place to get many of these. Also see "British Post-War Activity," #L49185, Nov. 14, 1944, Office of Strategic Services, RG 226, MMRD.

34. *New York Times*, March 23, 1945, p. 4; Oct. 20, 1944, p. 5.

35. *Ibid.*, Nov. 29, 1944, p. 14.

36. Gardner, *Sterling-Dollar Diplomacy*, pp. 25–26; *The Economist*, July 21, 1945, p. 75.

37. "The Washington Negotiations for Lend-Lease in Stage II," Dec. 12, 1944, PREM 4, 18/6.

38. "The Effect of our External Financial Position on our Foreign Policy," Sept. 1944, UE 615/169/53, F.O. 371.

39. Quoted in William C. Mallalieu, *British Reconstruction and American Policy, 1945–1955*, p. 34.

3. BRICKS WITHOUT STRAW

1. Taylor, *Beaverbrook*, p. 561.

2. For amplification of these points, two studies initiated by the American Joint Chiefs of Staff are particularly helpful: "Estimate of British Post-War Capabilities and Intentions," Feb. 13, 1946, CCS geog. files, 1942–45: CCS 000.1 Gr. Britain, RG 218, MMRD; and "British Capabilities versus the USSR," March 27, 1946, *ibid.*

3. *The Times*, Nov. 6, 1944, p. 5.

4. American planners realized that this altered strategic situation and the relative decline in British power contained implications for the safety of their own country. In early 1945 a Joint Chiefs of Staff committee warned that "the day when the United States can take 'a free ride' in security is over." Henceforth, the United States "must expect to pay its own way." Michael S. Sherry, *Preparing for the Next War: American Plans for Postwar Defense, 1941–45*, p. 163.

5. "Soviet Policy in Europe," Aug. 9, 1944, W.P. (44) 436, F.O. 371.

6. Minutes of meeting between Eden and Chiefs of Staff, Oct. 4, 1944, N 6144/183/38, *ibid.*

7. Clark Kerr to Eden, Aug. 31, 1944, N 5598/183/38, *ibid.*; Winston S. Churchill, *The Second World War*, vol. 6, *Triumph and Tragedy*, pp. 228, 712.

8. Anthony Eden, *The Reckoning: The Memoirs of Anthony Eden*, p. 632; David Dilks, ed., *The Diaries of Sir Alexander Cadogan, 1938–1945*, p. 716; Moran, *Churchill*, pp. 295–96.

9. Churchill, *Triumph and Tragedy*, p. 401; *The Times*, Nov. 6, 1944, p. 5.

10. U.S. Congress, *Congressional Record*, 78th Cong., 1st sess., 1943, vol. 89, pt. 7, p. 9679.

11. Memorandum of Conversation, July 24, 1944, 711.41/7-2444, SDR.

12. Dilks, *Cadogan Diaries*, pp. 653, 670, 688, 705.

13. Eden memorandum, Nov. 29, 1944, PREM 4, 30/8; U.K. Parliament, *Parliamentary Debates* (Commons), 5th series, 403 (1944):706. Eden has described his ideas for a western European bloc in *The Reckoning*, pp. 572–73.

14. "British Plan for a Western European Bloc," Jan. 16, 1945, 840.00/1-1645, SDR.

15. War Cabinet minutes, Nov. 27, 1944, CAB 65/48; Churchill, *Triumph and Tragedy*, p. 261.

16. Leahy Diary, Sept. 19, 1944, William D. Leahy Papers, Library of Congress; Lord Normanbrook et al., *Action This Day: Working With Churchill*, p. 82. The letter to Roosevelt is in Churchill, *Triumph and Tragedy*, p. 429.

17. Perry McCoy Smith, *The Air Force Plans for Peace, 1943–1945*, pp. 39–53 *passim*; Vincent Davis, *Postwar Defense Policy and the U.S. Navy, 1943–1946*, p. 95.

18. "Memorandum of Joint United States-United Kingdom Relations in Connection with Approach to Third Countries," Nov. 10, 1944, folder "Procedures," box 5, Clayton-Thorp Files. For an unofficial but thorough discussion of the benefits and liabilities of an Anglo-American alliance, see John D. Hickerson memorandum, March 31, 1944, 711.41/3-3144, SDR.

19. In 1946 the United States and Australia, at the latter's initiative, elevated their legations in Washington and Canberra to embassies, with a comparable promotion of their respective representatives from minister to ambassador. This step underscored the new importance which the United States had acquired in Australian, and more generally, in heretofore primarily British affairs. From here it was just a short step to the ANZUS pact, an alliance which reportedly greatly angered Churchill because of Britain's obvious exclusion. In this respect, the fall of Singapore in early 1942 should be emphasized. In the long run, the symbolic importance of this crushing British defeat was more significant than its military importance, in that to both the Commonwealth nations and the colonial peoples of the East, this was seen as a clear indication that British suzerainty in the region should no longer be unquestionably assumed.

20. Herbert Morrison, Speech to the Anglo-American Press Association, Oct. 6, 1943, Reference File, box 146, Raymond Clapper Papers, Library of Congress.

21. For an illustration of this attitude in the popular media, see "An Open

Letter from the Editors of *Life* to the People of England," *Life*, Oct. 12, 1942, p. 34.

22. Winston S. Churchill, *The End of the Beginning: War Speeches*, p. 268.

23. U.K. Parliament, *Parliamentary Debates* (Commons), 5th series, 374 (1941):69. On this matter see Louis, *Imperialism at Bay*, pp. 121–30.

24. U.S. Dept. of State, *Bulletin* (February 28, 1942), 6:188.

25. Luther Huston, "Englishman Who Talks American," *New York Times Magazine*, Aug. 20, 1944, p. 24; Herbert Morrison, Speech to the Anglo-American Press Association, Oct. 6, 1943, Reference File, box 146, Clapper Papers; H. Freeman Matthews memorandum, Nov. 2, 1944, 851G.01/11-244, SDR.

26. Minute by Sir Ronald I. Campbell, Aug. 12, 1944, AN 3333/20/45, F.O. 371. "Wallace up-lift" referred to Vice President Henry A. Wallace and his moralizing, frequently abrasive assertions that the true interests of the peoples of the British Empire could be easily achieved if only London would grant them immediate, unconditional independence.

27. Eden, *The Reckoning*, p. 593; minute by J. C. Connelly, May 17, 1946, AN 1515/1/45, F.O. 371.

28. Churchill to Halifax, Sept. 15, 1944, F.O. 800/413.

29. Memorandum of conversation, July 24, 1944, 711.41/7-2444, SDR.

30. "Problems and Objectives of United States Policy," April 2, 1945, folder "Chronological File," Harry S. Truman Papers, HSTL. Louis's *Imperialism At Bay* is a detailed account of the colonial question as it impinged upon wartime relations between Great Britain and the United States.

31. Thorne, *Allies of a Kind*, especially pp. 547–48, ch. 27; Elmer Belmont Potter, *Nimitz*, pp. 312, 319.

32. Walter LaFeber, "Roosevelt, Churchill, and Indochina: 1942–45," p. 1282.

33. General Patrick J. Hurley to the President, May 21, 1945, OPD Exec. files, 1940–45, RG 165, MMRD. See also Hull memorandum to the President, Sept. 8, 1944, *FRUS, Quebec*, 264; Halifax to Eden, Aug. 25, 1944, Papers of Edward Frederick Lindley Wood, 1st Earl of Halifax, Churchill College, Cambridge, England; Akira Iriye, *The Cold War in Asia: A Historical Introduction*, p. 87.

34. Quoted in Christopher Thorne, "Indochina and Anglo-American Relations, 1942–1945," p. 83.

35. Memorandum of conversation, July 24, 1944, 711.41/7-2444, SDR; Wedemeyer to General George C. Marshall, Dec. 29, 1944, OPD Exec. files, 1940–45, RG 165, MMRD; and of greatest help, Thorne, *Allies of a Kind*.

36. Minutes, State-War-Navy Coordinating Committee, March 3, 1945, RG 353, National Archives; Hickerson memorandum, Dec. 2, 1944, Records of the Office of European Affairs, SDR.

37. Hull to Ambassador John G. Winant, Oct. 17, 1944, *FRUS*, 1944, 5:667. For two recent examinations of this topic, see Phillip J. Baram, *The Department*

of State in the Middle East, 1919–1945, and Michael B. Stoff, *Oil, War, and American Security: The Search for a National Policy on Foreign Oil, 1941–1947.*

38. Halifax to Beaverbrook, Sept. 6, 1944, Halifax Papers.

39. Halifax to Churchill, April 22, 1946, *ibid.*

40. Eckes, *Search for Solvency*, p. 146; Clark, *Less than Kin*, p. 145.

41. Roosevelt to Ambassador Averell Harriman, Oct. 4, 1944, *FRUS, Malta and Yalta*, 6.

42. Halifax to Eden, Feb. 19, 1945, AN 763/763/45, F.O. 371.

43. "The Effect of our External Financial Position on our Foreign Policy," Sept. 1944, UE 615/169/53, *ibid.*

44. War Cabinet minutes, April 3, 1945, CAB 65/52.

45. "The Essentials of an American Policy," March 21, 1944, AN 1538/16/45, F.O. 371.

4. THE HOLLOW SUCCESSES OF OCTAGON

1. Robert E. Sherwood, *Roosevelt and Hopkins: An Intimate History*, p. 818.

2. Edward R. Stettinius memorandum, Sept. 6, 1944, *FRUS, Quebec*, 38.

3. Shortly after leaving his position in the Treasury Department the following summer, Morgenthau published a slim volume outlining his ideas on the need for strict controls to prevent a recurrence of German militarism. See his *Germany Is Our Problem*. Also helpful for the Secretary's thinking on this issue is John Morton Blum, *From the Morgenthau Diaries: Years of War, 1941–1945*, pp. 339 ff.

4. Department of State Briefing Paper, n.d., *FRUS, Quebec*, 207; Hopkins memorandum to the President, Sept. 13, 1944, *ibid.*, p. 412.

5. See George M. Elsey memorandum, n.d., *ibid.*, pp. 145–58 *passim*, for a general summary of this controversy. Roosevelt fully expected France to be racked by civil strife once the Germans had been driven from the country, and feared that the United States would inevitably become embroiled in the internal affairs of France and the other nations of southern Europe if American lines of communication and supply to southwest Germany ran through France. The American electorate would not stand for this, the President had Leahy tell the British Chiefs of Staff. Furthermore, American troops, resources, and attention would be devoted entirely to the war against Japan for many months after Hitler's defeat. The reconstruction burdens of these European countries were more justifiably a British responsibility. "I denounce and protest the paternity of Belgium, France and Italy," the President wired Churchill at one point. "You really ought to bring up and discipline your own children. In view of the fact that they may be your bulwark in future days, you should at least pay for their schooling now!" For FDR's apprehensions about civil war in France, see Henry L. Stimson and McGeorge Bundy, *On Active Service in Peace and War*, pp. 575–76; memorandum by Richard Law, Dec. 22, 1944, AN 154/82/45, F.O. 371. Leahy's

argument about the political constraints on the administration is found in minutes, CCS meeting, Sept. 12, 1944, *FRUS, Quebec*, 308. Roosevelt's letter to Churchill is dated Feb. 29, 1944, and is in *FRUS*, 1944, 1:189. Also helpful are Forrest C. Pogue, *The Supreme Command*, United States Army in World War II: The European Theater of Operations, p. 349; Maurice Matloff, *Strategic Planning for Coalition Warfare, 1943–1944*, United States Army in World War II: The War Department, p. 491; and Earl F. Ziemke, *The U.S. Army in the Occupation of Germany, 1944–1946*, Army Historical Series, pp. 115–24.

6. Stimson and Bundy, *On Active Service*, p. 575. This statement is in itself a fine illustration of the fundamental nature of the relationship—cooperative rather than competitive—which tied the two nations together.

7. Arthur Bryant, *Triumph in the West, 1943–1946*, p. 214.

8. Winant to Hopkins, Sept. 1, 1944, *FRUS, Quebec*, 255–56; Lord Halifax, *Fullness of Days*, p. 267; Churchill, *Triumph and Tragedy*, p. 155.

9. Bryant, *Triumph in the West*, pp. 214–17. Ismay in his memoirs makes no reference to his attempted resignation, although he does recall that Churchill's ill humor made the journey to Quebec aboard the *Queen Mary* trying. Hastings Ismay, *The Memoirs of General Lord Ismay*, p. 373.

10. John Lewis Gaddis, *The United States and the Origins of the Cold War, 1941–1947*, p. 70. For illustrations of this conviction on the part of American military personnel that Churchill was determined to prove in the current war that he had not been wrong about the disastrous Gallipoli operation in 1915, see Dwight D. Eisenhower, *Crusade in Europe*, p. 195; Oral History Interview, Thomas T. Handy, interview IV, p. 5, U.S. Army Military History Institute, Carlisle Barracks, Pa.

11. Churchill, *Triumph and Tragedy*, p. 151; Churchill to Roosevelt, Aug. 29, 1944, *FRUS, Quebec*, 222. Also Bryant, *Triumph in the West*, p. 214; Plenary meeting, Sept. 13, 1944, *FRUS, Quebec*, 314.

12. British Treasury memorandum, Sept. 4, 1944, *FRUS, Quebec*, 169–72; Churchill to Roosevelt, Sept. 12, 1944, *ibid.*, p. 43.

13. On Roosevelt's change of thinking about the occupation zones, see Stimson and Bundy, *On Active Service*, p. 569; Dallek, *Franklin D. Roosevelt*, pp. 476–77; William M. Franklin, "Zonal Boundaries and Access to Berlin," p. 21; Warren F. Kimball, *Swords or Ploughshares?: The Morgenthau Plan for Defeated Nazi Germany, 1943–1946*, p. 41; and Ziemke, *The U.S. Army in the Occupation of Germany*, p. 124.

14. Exchanges between Eisenhower and Montgomery on this matter may be found in box 277, Carl Spaatz Papers, Library of Congress. The principals recall the controversy in Eisenhower, *Crusade in Europe*, pp. 305–7; and Bernard Law Montgomery, *Memoirs*, ch. 15.

15. American sea and air power in the central Pacific was already deemed sufficient for the drive against Japan, and the introduction of British forces into the area would necessitate, for logistical reasons, the withdrawal of American units. To King in particular, who never for a moment forgot that the Navy had

played a clearly secondary role in the war against Germany, the British desire for an expanded presence seemed an effort to seize some of the glory which rightfully belonged to the United States Navy. In addition, the more the British were brought into the region, the more likely it was that political considerations concerning postwar dominance in many of the former colonial areas would intrude to complicate affairs. King was supported in many of these arguments by General Henry H. Arnold, the head of the Army Air Force. See Ernest J. King and Walter Muir Whitehill, *Fleet Admiral King: A Naval Record*, pp. 569–70; Krock memorandum, Oct. 16, 1944, box 1, Arthur Krock Papers, Princeton University; Henry H. Arnold, *Global Mission*, p. 526; Sir Andrew Cunningham, *A Sailor's Odyssey*, pp. 611–12; Matloff, *Strategic Planning for Coalition Warfare*, pp. 496, 513, 514, 528; John Ehrman, *Grand Strategy, October 1944-August 1945*, vol. 6 of *History of the Second World War*, p. 220. These matters are also discussed at some length in John Ehrman, *Grand Strategy, August 1943–September 1944*, vol. 5 of *History of the Second World War*, pp. 517–24.

16. Bryant, *Triumph in the West*, pp. 218, 220; Churchill, *Triumph and Tragedy*, p. 156.

17. Moran, *Churchill*, p. 193.

18. *FRUS, Quebec*, 128–40; Dallek, *Franklin D. Roosevelt*, pp. 472–74.

19. John W. Wheeler-Bennett and Anthony Nicholls, *The Semblance of Peace: The Political Settlement after the Second World War*, p. 179; Churchill quote in *FRUS, Quebec*, 326.

20. Moran, *Churchill*, pp. 190–91.

21. Prime Minister to War Cabinet, Sept. 15, 1944, F.O. 800/413. A number of scholars have seen Churchill's acceptance of the Morgenthau Plan as part of an at least implicit bargain in which he obtained Roosevelt's promise for extensive Phase II aid or a postwar loan. Undoubtedly, the necessity of gaining Morgenthau's support for generous Phase II assistance must have been obvious to the Prime Minister. Still, it appears that Phase II and lend-lease had not even been mentioned at the conference when Churchill reversed his original position and committed himself to Morgenthau's program. The American Treasury Secretary was later to tell his staff that "the thing that attracted Churchill the most [about the Morgenthau Plan] was a suggestion that they would get the German export business [;] that is the bait that he bit and swallowed and got hooked so deep that he couldn't . . . cough it up." Immediately after this, he added, "Of course, the parallel all through this was . . . Phase II," but Morgenthau later denied there was a connection between Churchill's acceptance of his plan for Germany and Roosevelt's approval of generous Phase II assistance. Morgenthau himself, in fact, continued to work for extensive financial aid to Britain even after Churchill backed away from the Morgenthau Plan. See Blum, *Years of War*, pp. 373–74. Stimson has noted that Morgenthau convinced the President of the merits of his program with the argument that by closing down the Ruhr industries, the British would be enabled to take Germany's place in supplying the needs of much of Europe. Stimson and Bundy, *On Active Service*, pp. 574, 579. Important

members of the American embassy staff in London also accepted this reasoning as the explanation of Churchill's behavior. Penrose, *Economic Planning for the Peace*, pp. 256–57. And officials in the Foreign Office recognized the relationship between the Morgenthau Plan's deindustrialization of Germany and England's economic woes. One diplomat wrote that the program provided for "supporting our economy at the expense of Germany's." Others suspected Washington saw the plan as a *substitute* for Phase II aid, not in exchange for it. See Kimball, *Swords or Ploughshares?* pp. 35–36. So in the absence of any other records tying Phase II lend-lease to the Morgenthau Plan, one must accept the explanations offered by the participants at the time that it was primarily a desire to take over the German export trade that led Churchill to agree to the Treasury Secretary's proposals. But for the contrary view, see Paterson, *Soviet-American Confrontation*, p. 237; Dallek, *Franklin D. Roosevelt*, p. 475; Bruce Kuklick, *American Policy and the Division of Germany: The Clash with Russia over Reparations*, p. 54; and Gaddis Smith, *American Diplomacy During the Second World War*, pp. 124–25.

22. *FRUS, Quebec*, p. 361. The final text of the Morgenthau Plan may be found *ibid.*, pp. 466–67.

23. Eden quote *ibid.*, p. 362; Eden, *The Reckoning*, p. 552.

24. Roosevelt to Hull, Sept. 29, 1944, *FRUS, Malta and Yalta*, 155. Also see Stimson and Bundy, *On Active Service*, p. 580.

25. Dilks, *Cadogan Diaries*, p. 665; Hull is quoted *ibid.*, p. 666.

26. Hull memorandum to the President, Sept. 8, 1944, *FRUS, 1944*, 3:53–56. Other illustrations of this restrictive approach may be found in Hopkins's memorandum to the President, Sept. 8, 1944, *ibid.*, pp. 56–57; and Matthews memorandum, Sept. 6, 1944, Records of the Office of European Affairs, SDR. An example of the more liberal view may be seen in "Phase Two: Cutback of Military Production in the United Kingdom," Aug. 11, 1944, folder "Phase Two," box 5, Clayton-Thorp Files.

27. Blum, *Years of War*, p. 310. For a record of Morgenthau's London talks with British Treasury officials, see folder 22d, box 7, White Papers.

28. Cherwell memorandum, Sept. 14, 1944, *FRUS, Quebec*, 344–46; Harry D. White memorandum, n.d., *ibid.*, p. 330.

29. Blum, *Years of War*, pp. 313–14.

30. Deputy Prime Minister to Prime Minister, Sept. 18, 1944, F.O. 800/412; Hull, *Memoirs*, 2:1614.

31. Alexander C. Kirk to the Secretary, Aug. 24, 1944, 865.01/8-2444, SDR.

32. These negotiations can be found in *FRUS, Quebec*, 493–97. For the White House statement see *ibid.*, pp. 497–98. Two weeks after the election, Roosevelt candidly wired Churchill that "the great number of Italians in this country" had forced him to "jump some fences" in the past and would require him to follow the same practice in the future. "I know you will understand," he hopefully added. Roosevelt to Churchill, Nov. 21, 1944, Map Room File, Franklin D. Roosevelt Papers, FDRL.

33. Churchill to Eden, Sept. 18, 1944, *FRUS, Quebec*, 490–91. Upon further reflection, Churchill and Roosevelt decided not to send Stalin this message.

34. Churchill to Roosevelt, Sept. 4, 1944, *ibid.*, pp. 188–89.

35. *Ibid.*, pp. 316–17, 327; J. W. Pickersgill and D. F. Forster, *The Mackenzie King Record*, 2:71.

36. Franklin D. Roosevelt, *The Public Papers and Addresses of Franklin D. Roosevelt*, 13:260, 267.

37. On this point see Ehrman, *Grand Strategy, October 1944–August 1945*, p. 220.

5. COERCIVE LIBERALITY

1. Hardingism quote in Eckes, *Search for Solvency*, p. 74. While these fears of a Republican victory appear overblown in light of actual postwar events, the contemporary observer should not underestimate the degree to which many informed people in the mid-1940s associated the Republican Party with narrow nationalism and a refusal to accept international responsibility.

2. Churchill to Hopkins, Nov. 8, 1944, PREM 4, 27/7; *The Times*, Nov. 9, 1944, p. 5; *Daily Express* quoted in *New York Times*, Nov. 12, 1944, p. E1.

3. Robert A. Divine, *Second Chance: The Triumph of Internationalism in America During World War II*, p. 260.

4. Minute by Nevile Butler, Nov. 11, 1944, AN 4252/20/45, F.O. 371; *News Chronicle* quoted in *New York Times*, Nov. 12, 1944, p. E1.

5. Halifax to Foreign Office, Nov. 11, 1944, AN 4294/20/45, F.O. 371; Halifax to Eden, Nov. 27, 1944, AN 4614/34/45, *ibid.*

6. *The Economist*, Nov. 11, 1944, p. 626.

7. John E. Orchard memorandum, Oct. 17, 1944, Reading File, Clayton-Thorp Files.

8. British Embassy to Exchequer, Oct. 4, 1944, T 160/1244/F17660/074, Trea.; Orchard memorandum, Sept. 30, 1944, folder "Phase Two," box 5, Clayton-Thorp Files.

9. Transcript of telephone conversation, Oct. 5, 1944, box 242, Edward R. Stettinius, Jr. Papers, Charlottesville, Virginia; "Statement Made by Leo T. Crowley to James F. Byrnes," July 7, 1947, folder 637, James F. Byrnes Papers, Clemson, South Carolina; diary, Nov. 18, 1944, Leahy Papers.

10. William D. Leahy, *I Was There*, p. 273; George C. Herring, Jr., "The United States and British Bankruptcy, 1944–1945: Responsibilities Deferred," pp. 267–68.

11. Cornelius de Witt to Stettinius, Aug. 8, 1944, 841.24/8-844, SDR. The 841.24 file is filled with letters of this nature.

12. U.S. Office of the President, *Seventeenth Report to Congress on Lend-Lease Operations: Reverse Lend-Lease Aid from the British Commonwealth of Nations*. The survey of American newspapers may be found in Halifax to Foreign Office, Nov. 27, 1944, UE 2422/5/71, F.O. 371.

13. Memorandum for the President, "Latest Opinion Trends in the U.S.A.," Jan. 12, 1945, box 91, President's Secretary's File, Roosevelt Papers.

14. British Supply Council, Dec. 5, 1944, folder "British," box 1, Clayton-Thorp Files; "Report of alleged British export sales of Lend-Lease farm machinery," Sept. 30, 1944, 841.24/10-1244, SDR.

15. Hull to Winant, Oct. 23, 1944, 841.24/10-2344, SDR; Acheson to Philip Reed, Oct. 27, 1944, 841.24/9-3044, *ibid.*

16. Stettinius, *Diaries*, pp. 172–73; Samuel M. Duffie to Congressman Milton West, Aug. 16, 1944, 841.24/8-2144, SDR.

17. *Business Week*, Oct. 28, 1944, p. 116.

18. Stimson and Bundy, *On Active Service*, pp. 592–93; Orchard memorandum, Oct. 17, 1944, Reading File, Clayton-Thorp Files; Blum, *Years of War*, pp. 317–18.

19. *Washington Post*, Nov. 12, 1944, p. 4B; Leahy, *I Was There*, p. 280. For additional warnings of this nature, cf. diary, Oct. 9 and 18, 1944, Henry L. Stimson Papers, Yale University; *Kansas City Star*, Nov. 27, 1944, p. 16; *Detroit Free Press*, Dec. 5, 1944, p. 4.

20. Hull memorandum, Sept. 30, 1944, *FRUS*, 1944, 3:61–65. Also Hull memorandum, Sept. 17, 1944, box 335, Hopkins Papers.

21. Hickerson memorandum, Nov. 2, 1944, *FRUS*, 1944, 3:70–74; "Commercial Phases of Lend-Lease Phase II Discussions," Oct. 7, 1944, folder "Phase Two," box 5, Clayton-Thorp Files.

22. Hull memorandum, Oct. 2, 1944, *FRUS*, 1944, 3:65; Hickerson memorandum, Nov. 2, 1944, *ibid.*, p. 72.

23. Blum, *Years of War*, p. 320; Edward R. Stettinius, Jr., *The Diaries of Edward R. Stettinius, Jr., 1943–1946*, pp. 175–76; transcript of telephone conversation with Leahy, Oct. 18, 1944, Morgenthau Diary, vol. 783, Henry M. Morgenthau, Jr. Papers, FRDL.

24. Chancellor of the Exchequer to Keynes, Nov. 16, 1944, T 160/1245/F17660/075/2, Trea.

25. For indications that each of these considerations was a factor in shaping American policy, see enclosure, J. Edgar Hoover to Adolf A. Berle, [Sept. 12, 1944], reel 26, Cordell Hull Papers, Library of Congress; *aide mémoire*, Sept. 26, 1944, 841.244/9-2644, SDR; Norman Armour memorandum, Sept. 30, 1944, 841.244/9-3044, *ibid.*; Hull to Sen. Richard B. Russell, Sept. 29, 1944, 841.244/9-244, *ibid.*; memorandum of conversation, Sept. 16, 1944, *FRUS*, 1944, 7:351–52; and Secretary of Agriculture Claude R. Wickard to the President, Aug. 23, 1944, *FRUS, Quebec*, 162–63. Personal animosities may also have played a role in Hull's unyielding attitude toward the Farrell government, for his former Under Secretary and bitter rival for the ear of the President, Sumner Welles, was openly critical of the Department's position on Argentina. See Welles's column in *New York Herald Tribune*, Aug. 9, 1944; Hull memorandum to the President, Sept. 26, 1944, reel 26, Hull Papers; diary, Sept. 20,

1944, Stimson Papers; David Green, *The Containment of Latin America: A History of the Myths and Realities of the Good Neighbor Policy*, p. 161. Professor Ernest May suggests that rivalry between Hull and Morgenthau may also have been at work here, but conclusive evidence of this sort is difficult to come by. "The 'Bureaucratic Politics' Approach: U.S.–Argentine Relations, 1942–47," p. 150.

26. Hickerson memorandum, Nov. 2, 1944, *FRUS*, 1944, 3:73.

27. Foreign Office to Eden, Sept. 17, 1944, F.O. 800/412.

28. Sir David Kelly to Foreign Office, July 7, 1944, PREM 3, 50A. Some months later the FBI arrived at a similar conclusion regarding the absence of any significant Argentine aid to the Axis. Stettinius to the President, Feb. 23, 1945, folder "Argonaut Sec. 3A," box 22, Map Room File, Roosevelt Papers.

29. Halifax to Foreign Office, Nov. 27, 1944, CAB 122/1035; May, "The 'Bureaucratic Politics' Approach," p. 145.

30. War Cabinet minutes, Oct. 4, 1944, CAB 65/44; Randall B. Woods, "Hull and Argentina: Wilsonian Diplomacy in the Age of Roosevelt," p. 369. Great Britain imported from Argentina somewhere between one-quarter and two-fifths of its total meat supply. Roosevelt, upon learning of this, had in July 1944 promised that he would do nothing to cut the British supply or to prevent the conclusion of a new contract. Sir Llewellyn Woodward, *British Foreign Policy in the Second World War*, p. 416; E. Louise Peffer, "Cordell Hull's Argentine Policy and Britain's Meat Supply," p. 12; Roosevelt to Churchill, July 22, 1944, *FRUS*, 1944, 7:333.

31. The head of the United States delegation at this conference has described the American position in Adolf A. Berle, *Navigating the Rapids, 1918–1971: From the Papers of Adolf A. Berle*, pp. 497–511. Also see "International Aviation Conference," Sept. 16, 1944, box 216, Adolf A. Berle Papers, FDRL; Clayton to Sen. Josiah W. Bailey, March 22, 1945, "State Dept., 1943–1945," Josiah W. Bailey Papers, Duke University; "Civil Aviation Matters—Great Britain," n.d., Records of the Office of European Affairs, SDR. A British participant recalls the conference in Paul Gore-Booth, *With Great Truth and Respect*, pp. 130–32. Also helpful are "Long Term Civil Aviation Negotiations with the United States," Nov. 8, 1945, PREM 8/16; C. R. Smith to Baruch, Oct. 18, 1944, Washington File, box 48, Bernard M. Baruch Papers, Princeton University; McNeill, *America, Britain, and Russia*, p. 514; Lloyd C. Gardner, *Economic Aspects of New Deal Diplomacy*, pp. 273–74; John Andrew Miller, "Air Diplomacy: The Chicago Civil Aviation Conference of 1944 in Anglo-American Wartime Relations and Post-War Planning."

32. Hull to Winant, Oct. 10, 1944, *FRUS*, 1944, 7:363; Matthews memorandum, Nov. 16, 1944, 841.244/11-1644, SDR.

33. Roosevelt to Churchill, Nov. 18, 1944, *FRUS*, 1944, 7:365; Matthews memorandum, Nov. 20, 1944, 841.244/11-2044, SDR; Gallman to Perowne, Nov. 20, 1944, 841.244/11-2044, *ibid.*

34. Churchill to Roosevelt, Nov. 22, 1944, *FRUS*, 1944, 2:585–86.

35. Roosevelt to Winant, Nov. 24, 1944, *ibid.*, p. 589; Morgenthau Diary, Nov. 24, 1944, vol. 798, Morgenthau Papers; James V. Forrestal, *The Forrestal Diaries*, p. 19.

36. Kimball, "Churchill and Roosevelt," p. 181.

37. Normanbrook, *Action This Day*, p. 96.

38. Churchill to Roosevelt, Nov. 28, 1944, *FRUS*, 1944, 2:590–92; Roosevelt to Churchill, Nov. 30, 1944, *ibid.*, pp. 594–95.

39. Keynes to Chancellor of the Exchequer, Nov. 23, 1944, UE 2315/5/71, F.O. 371. The final recommendations to the President by the Morgenthau Committee come closer than anything else to providing a formal record of these unofficial agreements and may be found in *FRUS*, 1944, 3:77–78. Roosevelt's reluctance to formalize these arrangements may be seen in "American Steering Committee—British L-L," Nov. 21, 1944, Morgenthau Diary, vol. 797, Morgenthau Papers. McNeill, *America, Britain, and Russia*, pp. 512–13, is also helpful.

40. "The Washington Negotiations for Lend-Lease in Stage II," Report by Lord Keynes, Dec. 12, 1944, PREM 4, 18/6. Also see Stettinius, *Diaries*, pp. 179–80.

41. Minute by John E. Coulson, Nov. 28, 1944, UE 2390/5/71, F.O. 371.

42. Herring, "The United States and British Bankruptcy," p. 270.

43. Press release, Nov. 30, 1944, *FRUS*, 1944, 3:81–82.

44. Keynes to Chancellor of the Exchequer, Nov. 26, 1944, UE 2390/5/71, F.O. 371.

45. For FEA thinking see Cox diary, Nov. 11, 1944, Oscar Cox Papers, FDRL; Cox to Crowley, Nov. 21, 1944, box 150, *ibid.*

46. "The Washington Negotiations for Lend-Lease in Stage II," Report by Lord Keynes, Dec. 12, 1944, PREM 4, 18/6.

47. *Ibid.*; McNeill, *America, Britain, and Russia*, p. 514; Herbert Nicholas, *Britain and the U.S.A.*, p. 24.

6. TRANSATLANTIC CACOPHONY

1. Halifax to Foreign Office, Nov. 27, 1944, PREM 4, 27/10.

2. Churchill to Halifax, Dec. 4, 1944, *FRUS, Malta and Yalta*, 267–69; Sir Noel Charles to Foreign Office, Nov. 24, 1944, R 19289/15/22, F.O. 371; Eden to Halifax, Dec. 1, 1944, R 19685/15/22, *ibid.*

3. Myron Taylor to Secretary, Nov. 25, 1944, 865.01/11-2544, SDR. Earlier in the war Sforza had spent several years of exile in the United States, carefully cultivating the image of a fierce opponent of Mussolini and the prevailing order in Italy. See *Kansas City Star*, Dec. 9, 1944, p. 10, for the laudatory portrait of Sforza prevalent in America.

4. Stettinius to Winant, Nov. 30, 1944, *FRUS*, 1944, 3:1160.

5. Broadcast of Dec. 4, 1944, box 25, Raymond Gram Swing Papers, Library of Congress.

6. *St. Louis Post-Dispatch*, Nov. 30, 1944, p. 2B; Dec. 4, 1944, p. 2B. Also *Chicago Tribune*, Nov. 30, 1944, p. 14.

7. Stettinius "Record," *FRUS, Malta and Yalta*, 430; Matthews memorandum, Dec. 1, 1944, box 222, Stettinius Papers.

8. Stettinius "Record," *FRUS, Malta and Yalta*, 430. Perhaps it is instructive that during these same days, Stettinius was also assuring Archibald MacLeish, his recently designated assistant secretary in charge of public information, that MacLeish's new position would not simply be that of a "public relations expert," but would afford him an active role in the policy-making process itself. See Michael Leigh, *Mobilizing Consent: Public Opinion and American Foreign Policy, 1937–1947*, pp. 106, 109. For the characterization of Stettinius, see Stettinius, *Diaries*, p. xxvii.

9. U.S. Dept. of State, *Bulletin*, 11:722.

10. Stettinius to Kirk, Dec. 6, 1944, 800.0146/12-644, SDR; *Manchester Guardian* quoted in Winant to Secretary, Dec. 6, 1944, *ibid*.

11. Sherwood, *Roosevelt and Hopkins*, p. 839; Churchill to Roosevelt, Dec. 6, 1944, in Loewenheim, Langley, and Jonas, *Roosevelt and Churchill*, pp. 619–21. Churchill was not soon to forget this episode or the accompanying denunciations of British "power politics" in the American press. More than a month later, he was still seething at Stettinius and directed Halifax to obtain a definition of the term "power politics" from the American Secretary. "Is having a Navy twice as strong as any other 'power politics'?" Churchill asked.

"Is having an overwhelming Air Force, with bases all over the world 'power politics'? Is having all the gold in the world buried in a cavern 'power politics'? If not, what is 'power politics'? Is it giving all the bases in the West Indies which are necessary to American safety to the United States—is that 'power politics'? Was it bleeding ourselves white financially, while the Americans were preparing and arming 'power politics'? Is holding the ring in Greece to enable the people to have a fair election 'power politics'?" Churchill to Halifax, Jan. 8, 1945, PREM 4, 27/10.

12. Churchill, *Triumph and Tragedy*, p. 297; Eden to Halifax, Dec. 6, 1944, R 20027/15/22, F.O. 371; Winant to Hopkins, Dec. 17, 1944, box 13, Map Room File, Roosevelt Papers.

13. Churchill, *Triumph and Tragedy*, p. 297.

14. Halifax to Foreign Office, Dec. 7, 1944, R 20235/15/22, F.O. 371.

15. Eden to Halifax, Dec. 6, 1944, R 20027/15/22, *ibid*.

16. *Washington Post*, Dec. 5, 1944, p. 12; Dec. 4, 1944, p. 4.

17. Stettinius to Matthews, Dec. 5, 1944, box 220, Stettinius Papers.

18. Stettinius to Winant, Nov. 30, 1944, *FRUS, 1944*, 3:1159.

19. Summaries of Telephone Conversations, Dec. 5, 1944, box 236, Stettinius Papers; Stettinius to McKellar, Jan. 3, 1945, F.W. 800.0146/12-2044, SDR.

20. Stettinius "Record," *FRUS, Malta and Yalta*, 432. Also see Secretary of

State to Winant, Dec. 14, 1944, *ibid.*, pp. 274–75; Lawrence S. Wittner, "American Policy Toward Greece During World War II," pp. 144–45.

21. Stettinius to the President, Dec. 6, 1944, box 20, Map Room File, Roosevelt Papers. A copy of this memorandum may also be found in Records of the JCS, Leahy Files, RG 218, MMRD. The President evidently agreed with his Secretary of State's assessment regarding the objectionable aspects of British policy. London's efforts to control developments in the eastern Mediterranean, FDR's latest biographer has written, "in themselves concerned Roosevelt less than the demoralizing effect they would have on internationalist opinion in the United States." The American ambassador in Moscow concurred in this judgment. The President exhibited very little interest in the small liberated European nations, Averell Harriman reported following a White House meeting in late October, "except as they affect sentiment in America." Cf. Dallek, *Franklin D. Roosevelt*, pp. 503–4.

22. Stettinius "Record," 1:13, SDR; Stettinius to Kirk, Dec. 6, 1944, 800.0146/12-644, *ibid.; Detroit Free Press*, Dec. 7, 1944, p. 6; *St. Louis Post-Dispatch*, Dec. 6, 1944, p. 2B. Fragments of the Stettinius "Record," a sketchy summary of the Secretary's activities compiled by his assistants, have been published in *FRUS, Malta and Yalta*, but a substantial portion of it, including the citation in this note, still remains unpublished.

23. Shotwell to Stettinius, Dec. 6, 1944, 865.01/12-644, SDR.

24. McNaughton Reports, Dec. 7, 1944, McNaughton Papers; *New York Times*, Dec. 9, 1944, p. 3; Dec. 14, 1944, p. 10; Dec. 19, 1944, p. 9.

25. *New York Times*, Dec. 7, 1944, p. 24; *Time*, Dec. 18, 1944, p. 17. Also *Los Angeles Times*, Dec. 7, 1944, p. 4; "Inside Your Congress," Dec. 21, 1944, Samuel Pettengill Papers, University of Vermont.

26. *Houston Post*, Dec. 7, 1944, p. 8; Dec. 8, 1944, p. 4-II; *Detroit Free Press*, Dec. 8, 1944, p. 6; *St. Louis Post-Dispatch*, Dec. 6, 1944, p. 2B.

27. Memorandum for the President, Dec. 30, 1944, box 231, Stettinius Papers; Stettinius, *Diaries*, p. 208.

28. Halifax to Foreign Office, Dec. 12, 1944, AN 4617/34/45, F.O. 371; *Detroit Free Press*, Dec. 8, 1944, p. 6; *Miami Herald*, Dec. 11, 1944, copy in box 240, John G. Winant Papers, FDRL.

29. Memorandum to Dunn, Dec. 12, 1944, box 220, Stettinius Papers; Herring, "The United States and British Bankruptcy," p. 271.

30. U.S. Senate, *Congressional Record*, 78th Cong., 2d sess., 1944, vol. 90, pt. 7, p. 8976.

31. Minute by Sir Gerald Campbell, Dec. 18, 1944, AN 227/22/45, F.O. 371.

32. Hadley Cantril and Mildred Strunk, *Public Opinion, 1935–1946*, p. 1111; Churchill, *Triumph and Tragedy*, p. 293.

33. Memorandum, British Supply Council, Dec. 18, 1944, folder "British," box 1, Clayton-Thorp Files; Stettinius "Record," 2:24, SDR.

34. Memorandum of conversation, Dec. 9, 1944, 868.00/12-944, SDR; Sherwood, *Roosevelt and Hopkins*, pp. 840–41. Here again, one gets the impression that British policy was not deplored nearly as much as was the unfortunate effect which that policy was having on American opinion. Withdrawing the landing craft, Hopkins told Leahy, "was like walking out on a member of your family who is in trouble." Sherwood, *Roosevelt and Hopkins*, p. 841.

35. On this point see Diary, Dec. 6, 1944, Leahy Papers.

36. Kirk to Secretary of State, Dec. 5, 1944, *FRUS*, 1944, 5:143–44; Kirk to Secretary of State, Dec. 18, 1944, 868.00/12-1844, SDR; Roosevelt, *Public Papers*, 13:438–41; *Christian Century* quote in Divine, *Second Chance*, p. 259.

37. "Memorandum by the Department of State," Dec. 26, 1944, 800.0146/1-345, SDR.

38. Memorandum for the President, Dec. 21, 1944, box 231, Stettinius Papers; undated minute by Richard Law, U 242/5/70, F.O. 371; extract from *PM*, Dec. 22, 1944, *ibid.*

39. Blum, *Years of War*, p. 324.

40. U.S. Dept. of State, *Bulletin*, 11:713; *Roosevelt and Churchill*, pp. 628–29.

41. *New York Times*, Dec. 9, 1944, p. 3; Dec. 24, 1944, p. 1; Halifax to Foreign Office, Dec. 7, 1944, R 20235/15/22, F.O. 371.

42. Halifax to Foreign Office, Dec. 7, 1944, R 20235/15/22, F.O. 371.

43. Louis Fischer to Sumner Welles, Sept. 2, 1944, Louis Fischer Papers, FDRL.

44. Blum, *Years of War*, p. 325.

45. "Noble Negatives," *The Economist*, Dec. 30, 1944, pp. 857–58.

46. *Yorkshire Post* quoted in *New York Times*, Jan. 3, 1945, p. 8; *The Times*, Jan. 3, 1945, p. 5.

47. *Washington Post*, Jan. 2, 1945, p. 8.

48. American News Summary, British Information Services, Jan. 2, 1945, AN 121/23/45, F.O. 371.

49. *Ibid.; Wall Street Journal*, Jan. 5, 1945, p. 6; *New York Times*, Jan. 17, 1945, p. 12; Jan. 18, 1945, p. 1.

50. Roosevelt, *Public Papers*, 13:497–98.

51. Eisenhower, *Crusade in Europe*, p. 356; Montgomery, *Memoirs*, pp. 311–14.

52. Nazi attempts to create Anglo-American discord sometimes went to ridiculous lengths. One V-bomb, for instance, dropped crossword puzzles over the southern English countryside instead of its normal deadly load. One of the clues was: "He wants all you've got." The answer, of course: "Roosevelt." *New York Times*, Jan. 14, 1945, p. 16.

53. Minute by John C. Connelly, Jan. 11, 1945, AN 71/23/45, F.O. 371.

54. *New York Times*, Jan. 11, 1945, p. 11. For an example of the opposition to this agreement, see *ibid.*, Aug. 22, 1944, p. 16. Herbert Feis, who as the State Department's Adviser on International Economic Affairs was integrally involved

in the negotiation and subsequent withdrawal of the treaty, has recorded his recollections of this episode in *Seen from E.A.: Three International Episodes*, pp. 156–69. Also see Stoff, *Oil, War, and American Security*, pp. 180–82.

55. *New York Times Magazine*, Jan. 14, 1945, pp. 5, 36. For another example of this turning inward, see John Foster Dulles, "America's Role in the Peace," *Christianity and Crisis* (January 22, 1945), in box 283, John Foster Dulles Papers, Princeton University.

56. Stettinius, *Diaries*, p. 208; Memorandum for the President, Jan. 6, 1945, box 91, President's Secretary's File, Roosevelt Papers. According to the United Press reporter covering the Senate, FDR's message "soured the idealists, confirmed the isolationists, and disturbed the middle-of-the-roaders." For this see Allen Drury, *A Senate Journal, 1943–1945*, p. 332.

57. U.S. Senate, *Congressional Record*, 79th Cong., 1st sess., 1945, vol. 91, pt. 1, pp. 164–67. For the background to this speech, cf. C. David Tompkins, *Senator Arthur H. Vandenberg: The Evolution of a Modern Republican, 1884–1945*, pp. 237–38.

58. "Cooperation between the Foreign Office and the Department of State," Jan. 2, 1945, 711.41/1-245, SDR; Cox to Hopkins, Dec. 19, 1944, folder "Post Election Problems," box 338, Hopkins Papers; *New York Times*, Dec. 17, 1944, p. E3.

59. Quoted in *New York Times*, Jan. 6, 1945, p. 3; Jan. 8, 1945, p. 10.

60. Lippmann in *Kansas City Star*, Jan. 4, 1945, p. 14; Wiley in *Denver Post*, Jan. 2, 1945, p. 2.

61. Minute by Richard Law, Jan. 26, 1945, U 242/5/70, F.O. 371.

62. Undated minute by Richard Law, *ibid.*

63. This, at any rate, was Halifax's assessment. See Halifax to Eden, Jan. 8, 1945, Halifax Papers.

64. Memorandum for the President, Jan. 6, 1945, box 232, Stettinius Papers; British consulate to Harold Butler, Dec. 30, 1944, AN 294/22/45, F.O. 371.

65. Report from Military Attaché, London, Jan. 26, 1945, OPD dec. files, 1942–45; OPD 384 ETO, Case 46, RG 165, MMRD.

66. War Cabinet minutes, Jan. 2, 1945, CAB 65/51; Churchill to Eden, Jan. 3, 1945, PREM 4, 27/9.

67. Churchill, *Triumph and Tragedy*, p. 341.

68. Herbert Agar, "Our Last Great Chance," p. 153.

7. THE FINAL JOURNEY

1. Athan G. Theoharis has documented the progressive distortion which the Yalta conference suffered in the years after 1945 in his *The Yalta Myths: An Issue in U.S. Politics, 1945–1955*. Theoharis demonstrates how politicians and other partisans adopted the issue of Soviet-American confrontation during and after the Yalta meeting for purposes of their own, purposes which had little or

nothing to do with the cold war pattern of international relations. This emphasis on competition and hostility between the United States and the Soviet Union characterized virtually everything that was written on the conference prior to the publication of Diane Shaver Clemens' *Yalta* in 1970. Though overstated in places and somewhat uncritical in its acceptance of source materials, Clemens' study is far and away the best monograph on Yalta that has yet appeared. The conceptual framework for this chapter, as will soon be obvious, draws heavily from the Clemens book.

2. Clemens has pointed out the quotation on Anglo-American solidarity, which may be found in John Snell, ed., *The Meaning of Yalta*, p. 72. See Clemens, *Yalta*, p. 275. Examples of British complaints about Roosevelt's aloofness will be brought out later in this chapter.

3. Sherwood, *Roosevelt and Hopkins*, p. 847; Hopkins to the President, Jan. 24, 1945, *FRUS. Malta and Yalta*, 39–40.

4. Minute by Cadogan, Jan. 22, 1945, AN 154/82/45, F.O. 371; Edward R. Stettinius, Jr., *Roosevelt and the Russians: The Yalta Conference*, p. 139.

5. Smith, *American Diplomacy*, p. 133; Roosevelt wire in Churchill, *Triumph and Tragedy*, p. 259.

6. Law and Sargent to Eden, Feb. 9, 1945, PREM 4, 78/1.

7. Eden, *The Reckoning*, pp. 583–84; Calendar Notes, Jan. 18, 1945, Stettinius Papers; Churchill to Roosevelt, Jan. 8, 1945, *FRUS. Malta and Yalta*, 31; Churchill to Roosevelt, Jan. 10, 1945, *ibid.*, p. 33. Chip Bohlen, the State Department's liaison with the White House and Roosevelt's interpreter at Yalta, has also remarked on the British concern at FDR's refusal to coordinate British and American plans prior to Yalta. See Charles E. Bohlen, *Witness to History, 1929–1969*, p. 172.

8. Briefing Book Paper, *FRUS, Malta and Yalta*, 102–3; W. Averell Harriman and Elie Abel, *Special Envoy*, pp. 390–91; British Plan for a Western European Bloc, n.d., "Yalta Notes," box 170, Hopkins Papers; McNaughton Reports, Jan. 12, 1945, McNaughton Papers.

9. Stettinius, *Diaries*, p. 210; Briefing Book Papers, *FRUS. Malta and Yalta*, 352; "Imperialism Versus an Enlightened Colonial Policy in the Area of the South East Asia Command," Jan. 6, 1945, "Yalta Notes," box 170, Hopkins Papers.

10. Briefing Book Papers, *FRUS. Malta and Yalta*, 325–27; Bohlen memorandum, Jan. 2, 1945, box 224, Stettinius Papers; minutes, Secretary's Staff Committee, Jan. 19, 1945, box 235, ibid.

11. Gaddis, *The United States and the Origins of the Cold War*, p. 159; McNaughton Reports Jan. 12, 1945, McNaughton Papers; Roosevelt to Laski, Jan. 16, 1945, copy in General Correspondence, box 98, Felix Frankfurter Papers, Library of Congress.

12. Hickerson to the Secretary of State, Jan. 8, 1945, *FRUS. Malta and Yalta*, 93–96.

13. Most scholars have failed to see this point. Even Clemens, who goes to

great pains to point out Anglo-American differences at Yalta, calls it "a declaration on eastern Europe" and treats it as directed solely against the Soviet Union. Clemens, *Yalta*, pp. 205, 247. But see Sherwood, *Roosevelt and Hopkins*, p. 864; and Memorandum for Judge Rosenman, Feb. 18, 1945, folder "Address to Congress on Yalta Conference, March 1, 1945," box 27, Samuel I. Rosenman Papers, FDRL. James F. Byrnes, at a press conference upon his return from Yalta, also made it clear that the Declaration was formulated with Britain as much as Russia in mind. See *Washington Post*, Feb. 14, 1945, p. 1.

14. Sherwood, *Roosevelt and Hopkins*, p. 847; Stettinius, *Roosevelt and the Russians*, p. 54. Bohlen, who accompanied Hopkins to London, and Churchill also mention this mission of reconciliation, though without adding much to our knowledge of the proceedings. Bohlen, *Witness to History*, pp. 167–70; Churchill, *Triumph and Tragedy*, p. 342.

16. The official minutes may be found in *FRUS. Malta and Yalta*, but more helpful are Sherwood, *Roosevelt and Hopkins*, p. 848; Bryant, *Triumph in the West*, p. 312; Ismay, *Memoirs*, p. 385; Eisenhower, *Crusade in Europe*, pp. 370–72; and Ambrose, *The Supreme Commander*, pp. 585–86.

16. Agreed minutes, Feb. 1, 1945, *FRUS. Malta and Yalta*, 498–507; minutes, Feb. 1, 1945, U 888/888/70, F.O. 371; Bohlen, *Witness to History*, p. 171; Eden, *The Reckoning*, pp. 590–591.

17. Stettinius, *Roosevelt and the Russians*, p. 61.

18. Moran, *Churchill*, p. 236; Stettinius, *Diaries*, p. 233.

19. Churchill, *Triumph and Tragedy*, pp. 343–44. Churchill was not in a very strong position to argue this particular point, for it had been the British who had originally insisted that the Soviet zone of occupation in Germany extend as far westward as it eventually was to do. Roosevelt had maintained that the northwest zone (which he had anticipated the United States would occupy) should reach all the way to Berlin and had accepted the more westerly boundary only because of London's insistence. Now Churchill was asking him to reverse his position once again, at a time when such a move was certain to antagonize the Russians. It seems likely that Roosevelt's irritation with Churchill's belated admission that the President's own position had been correct all along served to reinforce his original disposition not to consider the Prime Minister's pleas seriously. On the British plan and Roosevelt's ultimate acceptance, see Franklin, "Zonal Boundaries," pp. 8–11, 18.

20. Eden, *The Reckoning*, p. 592.

21. Cadogan to Halifax, Feb. 20, 1945, Halifax Papers. A portion of this letter may be found in Dilks, *Cadogan Diaries*, p. 717.

22. Bridges to Radcliffe, Feb. 12, 1945, Jason 355, F.O. 800/416.

23. Churchill, *Triumph and Tragedy*, p. 401; Eden, *The Reckoning*, p. 604. For the American side see Stettinius, *Roosevelt and the Russians*, pp. 295, 306–7; Sherwood, *Roosevelt and Hopkins*, pp. 869–70; Byrnes, *Speaking Frankly*, p. 45; Bohlen, *Witness to History*, p. 200; minutes, Secretary's Staff Committee, Feb. 23, 1945, box 235, Stettinius Papers; Memorandum for Judge Rosenman, Feb.

18, 1945, folder "Address to Congress on Yalta Conference, March 1, 1945," box 27, Rosenman Papers; diary, March 13, 1945, Stimson Papers.

24. Moran, *Churchill*, pp. 242, 243, 250; Eden, *The Reckoning*, p. 592, 593; Cadogan to Halifax, Feb. 20, 1945, Halifax Papers.

25. Moran, *Churchill*, p. 247; diary, March 13, 1945, Stimson Papers; Forrestal, *Diaries*, p. 35.

26. Sherwood, *Roosevelt and Hopkins*, pp. 861–62; Bohlen, *Witness to History*, p. 186; Stettinius, *Roosevelt and the Russians*, p. 265. The protocol of the Yalta conference, from which the quoted phrase comes, may be found in *FRUS, Malta and Yalta*, 975–82.

27. Francis Williams, *Twilight of Empire: Memoirs of Prime Minister Clement Attlee*, p. 52.

28. Stettinius, *Roosevelt and the Russians*, pp. 104–5; Normanbrook, *Action This Day*, p. 210; Eden, *The Reckoning*, p. 599.

29. Eden, *The Reckoning*, pp. 375, 593.

30. Moran, *Churchill*, p. 249; *FRUS, Malta and Yalta*, 572, 770.

31. Stettinius, *Roosevelt and the Russians*, pp. 236, 238.

32. Sherwood, *Roosevelt and Hopkins*, p. 871.

33. Eden, *The Reckoning*, p. 594.

34. Bryant, *Triumph in the West*, p. 320; Stettinius, *Roosevelt and the Russians*, p. 278.

35. For Roosevelt's concern about domestic opinion, see Dallek, *Franklin D. Roosevelt*, pp. 516, 524.

36. Minute by Cadogan, Feb. 20, 1945, U 1155/12/70, F.O. 371.

37. *New York Times*, Feb. 13, 1945, p. 22; Grew to the Secretary, Feb. 13, 1945, 740.0011 E.W./1-2745, SDR; Winant to Secretary of State, Feb. 20, 1945, 740.0011 E.W./2-2045, *ibid.*; R&A No. 3037, April 13, 1945, Office of Strategic Services, *ibid.*; *Time*, Feb. 19, 1945, p. 15; "Latest Opinion Trends in the U.S.A.," March 10, 1945, box 232, Stettinius Papers.

38. The Colonial Office alone dissented from this general satisfaction, due to concern that the American trusteeship proposals accepted at Yalta undermined British colonial rule. On this see Louis, *Imperialism At Bay*, p. 463.

39. Eden, *The Reckoning*, p. 607.

40. Churchill, *Triumph and Tragedy*, p. 512. For another instance of this, see Churchill to Roosevelt, April 1, 1945, in Loewenheim, Langley, and Jonas, *Roosevelt and Churchill*, p. 699.

41. Churchill to Roosevelt, March 8, 13, 27, 1945, in Loewenheim, Langley, and Jonas, *Roosevelt and Churchill*, pp. 662, 670, 685 respectively. Particularly helpful on Anglo-American differences over Poland is Lynn Etheridge Davis, *The Cold War Begins: Soviet-American Conflict over Eastern Europe*, pp. 204–10.

42. Forrestal, *Diaries*, pp. 36–37.

43. Churchill to Roosevelt, March 6, 1945, and Roosevelt to Churchill, March 15, 1945, folder "Air Conference (1), Chicago Air Conference," box 32, Map Room File, Roosevelt Papers.

44. Samuel I. Rosenman, *Working with Roosevelt*, pp. 525–27.

45. Untitled report, Feb. 20, 1945, Office of Strategic Services, RG 226, MMRD; Grew to the President, Feb. 19, 1945, folder "Argonaut Sec. 3A," box 22, Map Room File, Roosevelt Papers.

46. Memorandum of conversation, Feb. 13, 1945, OPD Exec. files, 1940–45, RG 165, MMRD.

47. Memorandum to Hickerson, Feb. 26, 1945, FW 841.50/2-2045, SDR.

48. Bernard M. Baruch, *Baruch: The Public Years*, pp. 343–44. Examples of Baruch's strong opinions on the need for Britain to shoulder more of its own burdens can be seen in Baruch to Stettinius, Dec. 13, 1944, box 719, Stettinius Papers; Baruch memorandum, Dec. 1, 1944, Washington File, box 37, Baruch Papers.

49. Diary, April 12, 1945, Leahy Papers.

50. Churchill, *Triumph and Tragedy*, p. 471.

51. *Ibid.*, p. 478. The *New York Times* in the days after April 12, 1945, has extensive coverage of the reaction in Great Britain to Roosevelt's death. The *Daily Telegraph* quotation may be found in the *New York Times*, April 13, 1945, p. 4.

52. Dalton Diary, April 13, 1945, Hugh Dalton Papers, British Library of Political and Economic Science, London; *New York Times*, April 15, 1945, p. E4; *The Economist*, April 21, 1945, p. 501.

8. CHANGE IN COMMAND

1. *Time*, April 23, 1945, p. 22.

2. Sir R. I. Campbell to Foreign Office, July 23, 1944, AN 2874/20/45, F.O. 371; minute by J. C. Donnelly, Nov. 1, 1944, AN 4109/20/45, *ibid.*

3. Hopkins quoted in Churchill, *Triumph and Tragedy*, p. 481; minute by Isaiah Berlin, April 16, 1945, AN 1332/22/45, F.O. 371; *The Economist*, April 21, 1945, pp. 502, 512.

4. McNaughton Reports, April 12, 1945, April 14, 1945, McNaughton Papers.

5. Berlin memorandum, May 7, 1945, PREM 4, 27/10.

6. Unsigned, undated minute, AN 1194/82/45, F.O. 371.

7. Halifax to Foreign Office, April 13, 1945, *ibid.*

8. Churchill, *Triumph and Tragedy*, pp. 483–84.

9. Balfour to Halifax, May 21, 1945, AN 1641/4/45, F.O. 371; Halifax to Viscount Simon, April 19, 1945, Halifax Papers. Cadogan reacted to Truman in much the same way. See Dilks, *Cadogan Diaries*, p. 746.

10. Harry S. Truman, *Memoirs*, vol. 1: *Year of Decisions*, p. 14.

11. Forrestal, *Diaries*, p. 58; diary, April 30, 1945, Stimson Papers.

12. Journal, April 30, 1945, Joseph E. Davies Papers, Library of Congress; Baruch to Truman, April 20, 1945, folder 632, Byrnes Papers. Also consult Baruch, *The Public Years*, pp. 349–51. For warnings from Budget Director Har-

old Smith that British and American policy differed sharply in other areas of the globe, see "Conference with the President," April 26, 1945, box 15, Harold D. Smith Papers, FDRL; from Patrick Hurley, see Hurley to Stettinius, April 14, 1945, *FRUS*, 1945, 7:331.

13. Truman, *Year of Decisions*, p. 246.

14. This Churchill-Truman correspondence may be found in Records of the JCS, Leahy Files, RG 218, MMRD; and in Truman Papers, White House Map Room file. Churchill's memoirs contain selected wires, especially in chapters 10 and 11. Also see Truman, *Year of Decisions*, pp. 25, 298–302.

15. Churchill, *Triumph and Tragedy*, pp. 491–92.

16. Halifax to Churchill, April 22, 1945, PREM 4, 27/10.

17. Truman, *Year of Decisions*, pp. 212.

18. *Ibid.*, p. 248; Leahy's argument repeated in Diary, June 4, 1945, Davies Papers.

19. Churchill to Truman, June 14, 1945, Records of the JCS, Leahy Files, RG 218, MMRD. Churchill's relatively restrained acceptance of this decision worried Leahy, who wondered whether the Prime Minister's health was failing. "It is not in accordance with his past performance to give up so easily, even when he is plainly in the wrong as he was in this matter," Leahy recorded in his diary. Diary, June 13, 1945, Leahy Papers.

20. For specific illustrations of this, see Truman, *Year of Decisions*, pp. 37–38; memorandum of conversation, April 21, 1945, box 224, Stettinius Papers; memorandum of conversation, May 4, 1945, *FRUS*, 1945, 5:281–84.

21. Harriman's advice is in Minutes, Secretary's Staff Committee, April 20, 1945, *FRUS*, 1945, 5:840; "Problems and Objectives of United States Policy," OSS memorandum, April 2, 1945, folder "Chronological File," Truman Papers.

22. Calendar Notes, April 16, 1945, Stettinius Papers.

23. Press release, May 8, 1945, OF 48, Truman Papers.

24. Churchill, *Triumph and Tragedy*, p. 551; Churchill to Alexander, May 1, 1945, and May 7, 1945, PREM 3/495/6; Churchill to Alexander, May 15, 1945, PREM 3/495/9.

25. Joseph C. Grew, *Turbulent Era: A Diplomatic Record of Forty Years, 1904–1945*, 2:1479; Churchill, *Triumph and Tragedy*, pp. 555–56; Truman, *Year of Decisions*, pp. 247–48; James F. Schnabel, *The Joint Chiefs of Staff and National Policy*, 1:45–47; Halifax to Foreign Office, May 14, 1945, PREM 3/495/9.

26. Grew, *Turbulent Era*, 2:1479–80; Churchill, *Triumph and Tragedy*, p. 557; Truman, *Year of Decisions*, pp. 248–49; Sherry, *Preparing for the Next War*, p. 183.

27. Truman, *Year of Decisions*, pp. 250–52; Truman to Churchill, May 21, 1945, R 8952/6/92, F.O. 371; Schnabel, *Joint Chiefs of Staff*, 1:48–52; Harold Macmillan, *Tides of Fortune, 1945–1955*, pp. 19–20. For a convenient summary of these events, see Lisle A. Rose, *Dubious Victory: The United States and the End of World War II*, The Coming of the American Age, 1945–1946, pp. 120–26.

28. Churchill to Eden, May 22, 1945, R 8852/6/92, F.O. 371; Eden to British Embassy, Washington, May 23, 1945, R 8853/6/92, *ibid.*
29. "Conference with the President," April 26, 1945, box 15, Harold Smith Papers; Baruch memorandum, Dec. 1, 1944, folder 92, Byrnes Papers; Baruch to Truman, April 20, 1945, folder 632, *ibid.*
30. Crowley memorandum, Jan. 20, 1945, folder 88, Byrnes Papers.
31. George C. Herring, Jr., *Aid to Russia, 1941–1946: Strategy, Diplomacy, the Origins of the Cold War,* pp. 190–91.
32. "Conference with the President," April 26, 1945, box 15, Harold Smith Papers; Briefing Book Paper, *FRUS, Potsdam,* 1:808.
33. Grew to Winant, May 4, 1945, folder "London, England (Radios to and from)," box 156, Hopkins Papers; Herring, "The United States and British Bankruptcy," p. 274; *Year of Decisions,* p. 228. For Truman to claim that he was unaware of what he was signing, as he was later to do, is simply unbelievable. But so too is the accusation made by some more suspicious scholars that the purpose behind this abrupt cutback was coercion. Insofar as this action related to Great Britain at any rate—and the greatest part of lend-lease aid was going to the British—this view credits the administration's thinking on foreign affairs with a coherent design and a degree of sophistication which it did not possess.
34. Herring, "The United States and British Bankruptcy," p. 274; Morgenthau quote in Blum, *Years of War,* p. 450.
35. Stimson to Fred Vinson, May 15, 1945, OPD dec. files, 1942–45: OPD 400.3295, RG 165, MMRD; Matthew J. Connelly to Crowley, May 26, 1945, Confidential File, Truman Papers. In fairness to those who argued that the Phase II figures did not represent a binding commitment, it should be pointed out that Roosevelt's secrecy the previous autumn fostered this very impression, except among that small circle of advisers who realized the President's caution was largely inspired by fear of adverse public and congressional reaction to what would undoubtedly be interpreted as undue generosity to the British. Representative of the War Department's attitude was the remark by one of Stimson's top civilian aides, who warned that the British "are trying to pull our leg" concerning their requirements for lend-lease after V-E Day. Diary, April 30, 1945, Stimson Papers. Grew's press statement may be found in U.S. Dept. of State, *Bulletin,* 12:940.
36. Grew to Winant, June 4, 1945, *FRUS,* 1945, 6:52; Truman, *Year of Decisions,* p. 230; Churchill to Truman, May 28, 1945, *FRUS, Potsdam,* 1:807, n. 5.
37. "Lend-Lease to Britain," n.d., OPD Exec. files, 1940–45, RG 165, MMRD; Stimson to the Secretary of State, June 19, 1945, *FRUS, Potsdam,* 1:815.
38. Diary, July 2, 1945, Leahy Papers.
39. *Ibid.,* June 19, 1945. A copy of the White House directive is in *FRUS, Potsdam,* 1:818.
40. Stimson to the Secretary of State, July 11, 1945, *FRUS, Potsdam,* 1:819.

41. McNaughton Reports, May 11, 1945, McNaughton Papers.

42. *Ibid.*, Sept. 4, 1945; Graham H. Stuart repeats the senator's quip in *The Department of State: A History of Its Organization, Procedure, and Personnel*, p. 425.

43. The *Times*, July 2, 1945, p. 5; Halifax to Eden, July 3, 1945, AN 2136/245/45, F.O. 371.

44. Minute by Nevile Butler, July 13, 1945, AN 2136/245/45, F.O. 371.

45. Diary, July 10, 1945, Davies Papers; Bernard Bellush, *He Walked Alone: A Biography of John Gilbert Winant*, p. 176.

46. Minute by Nevile Butler, Jan. 10, 1946, AN 3853/35/45, F.O. 371. Also see John Hickerson's quote in Thomas G. Paterson, *On Every Front: The Making of the Cold War*, p. 112.

47. Kolko, *Politics of War*, p. 381; Bohlen, *Witness to History*, p. 228.

48. A. H. Birse, *Memoirs of an Interpreter*, p. 207.

9. THE BIG TWO AND A HALF

1. See *New York Times*, May 27, 1945, p. E4; May 28, 1945, p. 5; July 26, 1945, p. 18. Halifax's statement is *ibid.*, June 23, 1945, p. 8.

2. *New York Times*, May 24, 1945, p. 18; George H. Gallup, *The Gallup Poll: Public Opinion, 1935–1971*, 1:511. For American predictions of a Conservative victory, see *New York Times*, May 24, 1945, p. 1; May 27, 1945, p. E2; July 26, 1945, p. 18; "Press Comment on National and International Affairs," Office of War Information, Truman Papers; Diary, June 4, 1945, Leahy Papers. Information on feeling in the London embassy comes from an interview with Ambassador Waldemar John Gallman, Washington, D.C., June 16, 1978. Halifax also predicted Churchill's reelection in private conversations with American friends. See Forrestal, *Diaries*, p. 72.

3. Churchill, of course, was in a most tenuous position in deploring Soviet actions in eastern Europe, for not twelve months previously he had journeyed to Moscow and callously proceeded to carve up the five Balkan states into areas of British and Russian preponderance. Although he claimed at times that these arrangements were only for the duration of the war, on two separate occasions in June and July of 1945 he referred to them as though they were still in effect. Yet his indignation over Russian behavior made it seem that he was trying, as in the case of the German occupation zones, to renege on an agreement originally made despite strong American objections, and now shown to be less advantageous to Great Britain than he had at first anticipated. On the October 1944 agreement, see Churchill, *Triumph and Tragedy*, pp. 227–28; and Woodward, *British Foreign Policy*, pp. 307–8. For the post V-E Day references to this agreement, see Churchill, *Triumph and Tragedy*, pp. 560, 636.

4. Churchill to Truman, May 6, 1945, *FRUS, Potsdam*, 1:3; Truman to Churchill, May 9, 1945, *ibid.*, p. 4.

5. Churchill, *Triumph and Tragedy*, p. 572. Also see Churchill to Truman, May 21, 1945; June 1, 1945; June 4, 1945, in *FRUS, Potsdam*, 1:19, 91, 92.

6. Grew memorandum, May 15, 1945, *FRUS, Potsdam*, 1:12–13; Harriman and Abel, *Special Envoy*, pp. 460–61.

7. Memorandum of conversation, April 16, 1945, 711.41/4-1645, SDR.

8. Herbert Feis, *Between War and Peace: The Potsdam Conference*, p. 82; Diary, June 4, 1945, Leahy Papers.

9. Churchill to Truman, May 11, 1945, *FRUS, Potsdam*, 1:5; Truman, *Year of Decisions*, p. 256. Churchill had already sent separate messages via Baruch and White House aide Samuel Rosenman that a presidential visit before the July 5 poll would not be unappreciated. Baruch, *The Public Years*, p. 351; Rosenman, *Working with Roosevelt*, p. 547.

10. Truman to Churchill, May 11, 1945, *FRUS, Potsdam*, 1:8. A few days later the President evidently reconsidered the merits of conferring alone with Churchill prior to the tripartite conference. But although Bohlen advised him that the Soviets considered it logical that London and Washington should be close, and that such a meeting, demonstrating Anglo-American unity, might make Stalin more reasonable, Truman stuck by his initial resolve. For this see Grew, *Turbulent Era*, 2:1463; Bohlen, *Witness to History*, p. 217.

11. Draft letter, Davies to Churchill, May 20, 1945, Chronological File, Davies Papers. Also see Diary, May 13, 1945, *ibid.*

12. Quoted in Margaret Truman, *Harry S. Truman*, p. 253. Notice the clichés, suggesting that Truman thought of Britain in much the same hackneyed, suspicious manner as did the typical small-town merchant or Midwestern farmer.

13. Truman, *Year of Decisions*, pp. 260–62; Churchill to Truman, May 31, 1945, *FRUS, Potsdam*, 1:89; Churchill, *Triumph and Tragedy*, p. 577; Eden, *The Reckoning*, p. 623. Hopkins' May 30 cable to Truman from Moscow indicated that he had talked with Stalin of the forthcoming summit along the lines of the three statesmen meeting at the same time. So this is probably what Truman had in mind, regardless of how Davies presented it to Churchill. Hopkins to the President, May 30, 1945, *FRUS, Potsdam*, 1:88. But also see Davies' diary entries for May 21 and June 4, 1945, in the Davies Papers; and Davies' Supplemental Report, June 12, 1945, *FRUS, Potsdam*, 1:78. The incident with the Mae West belts is in Diary, May 24, 1945, Davies Papers. This entire mission has been most thoroughly discussed in Keith M. Heim, "Hope Without Power: Truman and the Russians, 1945," esp. pp. 133–52.

14. Davies' report to Truman, from which much of the above is taken, may be found in *FRUS, Potsdam*, 1:64–81.

15. *Ibid.*, pp. 69–77.

16. Eden, *The Reckoning*, p. 624.

17. Churchill, *Triumph and Tragedy*, p. 579.

18. Foreign Office to Eden, July 15, 1945, PREM 4, 80/1. Stimson, Marshall, and Eisenhower all worried about fostering the appearance of an Anglo-American bloc directed against the Soviet Union. On this see Sherry, *Preparing for the Next War*, pp. 182–83.

19. Memorandum to Prime Minister, July 13, 1945, PREM 4, 17/15.

20. Sherwood, *Roosevelt and Hopkins*, p. 913.

21. Churchill to Truman, July 3, 1945, *FRUS. Potsdam*, 1:733–34; Eden, *The Reckoning*, p. 630.

22. Grew memorandum, July 7, 1945, *FRUS. Potsdam*, 1:150–51; H. Maitland Wilson, Head of the British Joint Staff Mission, to Leahy, June 12, 1945, *ibid.*, pp. 95–96.

23. Cadogan to Churchill, July 2, 1945, F.O. 800/416. One of the few exceptions to this general pattern of uncooperativeness was American support of British intervention in the fighting between French troops and Arabs in the Levant. For this see Truman, *Year of Decisions*, pp. 242–43.

24. "Stocktaking after VE-Day," memorandum by Sir Orme Sargent, July 11, 1945, PREM 4, 31/5.

25. *The Economist*, July 21, 1945, p. 74.

26. This had been Churchill's assessment at the time of his talks with Davies at the end of May. Supplemental Report, June 12, 1945, *FRUS. Potsdam*, 1:73.

27. Moran, *Churchill*, pp. 276, 297.

28. *Ibid.*, pp. 285, 300. Also see Leahy, *I Was There*, p. 398.

29. Eden, *The Reckoning*, p. 632. For an illustration of Eden's despair even before learning for certain of his son's death, see Eden to Churchill, July 12, 1945, U 6125/3628/70, F.O. 371.

30. Cadogan to Churchill, July 2, 1945, F.O. 800/416.

31. "Stocktaking after VE-Day," memorandum by Sir Orme Sargent, July 11, 1945, PREM 4, 31/5.

32. Balfour quote in Terry H. Anderson, "Britain, the United States, and the Cold War, 1944–1947," p. 120; Halifax cable in Churchill, *Triumph and Tragedy*, pp. 611–12 (Churchill's italics).

33. Eden, *The Reckoning*, pp. 629–30.

34. Briefing Book Paper, June 28, 1945, *FRUS. Potsdam*, 1:257; Paterson, *Soviet-American Confrontation*, p. 79; Record of Conversation with John Hickerson, July 20, 1945, AN 2438/35/45, F.O. 371.

35. Random examples include Hurley to the President, May 21, 1945, OPD Exec. files, 1940–45, RG 165, MMRD; COMNAVGRP CHINA to the President, May 29, 1945, White House Map Room file, Truman Papers; "Civil Aviation Matters—Great Britain," n.d., Records of the Office of European Affairs, SDR.

36. Memorandum for the President, June 14, 1945, *FRUS. Potsdam*, 1:164.

37. Kirk to Grew, July 12, 1945, *ibid.*, p. 266; Davies to the President, July 3, 1945, *ibid.*, p. 219.

38. Truman to Eleanor Roosevelt, May 10, 1945, Eleanor Roosevelt Papers, FDRL; Samuel and Dorothy Rosenman, *Presidential Style: Some Giants and a Pygmy in the White House*, pp. 441–42.

39. Remarks by Senator Homer E. Capehart, in U.S. Senate, *Congressional Record*, 82d Cong., 2d sess., 1952, vol. 98, pt. 2, p. 2467.

40. Briefing Book Paper, June 28, 1945, *FRUS. Potsdam*, 1:256–66. This

advice was also good politics. In a public letter to Stettinius at the end of May, a dozen congressmen had expressed the fear that the United States "has begun to lose the position which President Roosevelt struggled to win and maintain for our country, as an independent mediator among the great powers, friendly to all and a partisan to none." Had America, they demanded to know, "through some tacit understanding or through day to day working relations, become *de facto*, part of an Anglo-American 'front' against the Soviet Union?" Rose, *Dubious Victory*, pp. 274–75.

41. Harriman and Abel, *Special Envoy*, p. 488. Also see Cadogan minute, Aug. 4, 1945, AN 2438/35/45, F.O. 371. In the weeks before the conference the State Department's Middle East experts dealt with the problem created by Soviet troops in northern Iran as part of a pattern of Anglo-Soviet rivalry rather than as a unilateral Russian power play. On this, see Briefing Book Paper, n.d., *FRUS. Potsdam*, 1:951–52; memorandum of conversation, June 18, 1945, *ibid.*, p. 953.

42. Diary, June 15, 1945, Leahy Papers.

43. Memorandum for Gen. Hull, June 16, 1945, OPD Exec. files, 1940–45, RG 165, MMRD.

44. Memorandum for the President from John Snyder, Samuel Rosenman, and George Allen, July 6, 1945, *FRUS. Potsdam*, 1:228. "I [am] giving nothing away except to save starving people and even then I hope we can only help them to help themselves," wrote the President as he sailed toward Europe, unconsciously reflecting this advice. Robert H. Ferrell, ed., "Truman at Potsdam," p. 39.

45. Leahy, *I Was There*, p. 381; Roosevelt to Truman, May 14, 1945, Eleanor Roosevelt Papers. Churchill's pleasure is in T. L. Rowan to Anthony Bevir, July 17, 1945, PREM 4, 79/2; Moran, *Churchill*, p. 292; Dilks, *Cadogan Diaries*, p. 763.

46. Moran, *Churchill*, p. 299.

47. Ferrell, "Truman at Potsdam," p. 41. Also see Truman, *Year of Decisions*, p. 340.

48. Truman, *Year of Decisions*, pp. 341–42; Byrnes, *Speaking Frankly*, p. 68; Leahy, *I Was There*, p. 397; Ferrell, "Truman at Potsdam," p. 41.

49. Secretary of War Stimson recorded Churchill's comment in his diary entry of July 22, 1945, Stimson Papers.

50. Clement R. Attlee, *As It Happened*, p. 209; Eden, *The Reckoning*, p. 631; Churchill, *Triumph and Tragedy*, pp. 656, 659; Moran, *Churchill*, p. 297.

51. Byrnes, *Speaking Frankly*, p. 207.

52. Moran, *Churchill*, p. 306.

53. Aide-mémoire, July 16, 1945, *FRUS. Potsdam*, 2:621–22.

54. Ferrell, "Truman at Potsdam," p. 42; Truman, *Year of Decisions*, pp. 359–60; Truman, *Harry S. Truman*, p. 269.

55. Rowan to Private Office, July 23, 1945, PREM 4, 80/1. Truman later changed his mind again and did stop briefly in Britain, but only after it was

explained to him that by having his ship meet him in Plymouth, he could actually get home sooner. Truman, *Year of Decisions*, p. 414.

56. Leahy, *I Was There*, pp. 409, 410.

57. Memorandum by Chiefs of Staff, July 15, 1945, CCS 891, AN 2627/38/45, F.O. 371. Also Ismay to Churchill, June 21, 1945, PREM 3, 465/4.

58. Memorandum by the United States Chiefs of Staff, July 19, 1945, *FRUS. Potsdam*, 2:1202; Memorandum for the President, July 21, 1945, *ibid.*, p. 1203.

59. Churchill, *Triumph and Tragedy*, pp. 632–33. Also see Churchill memorandum, July 18, 1945, F.O. 800/417.

60. Stimson to Secretary of State, July 11, 1945, *FRUS. Potsdam*, 1:818–19; Vinson to Secretary of State, July 13, 1945, *ibid.*, p. 820.

61. Churchill, *Triumph and Tragedy*, pp. 631–32. Churchill memorandum, July 18, 1945, F.O. 800/417 repeats much of this.

62. Minutes, CCS, July 24, 1945, *FRUS. Potsdam*, 2:341. Also Leahy, *I Was There*, p. 414.

63. Diary, July 27, 1945, July 28, 1945, Leahy Papers; Sinclair memorandum, July 27, 1945, PREM 4, 17/15.

64. Memorandum Directive to the Joint Chiefs of Staff, July 29, 1945, *FRUS. Potsdam*, 2:1184–85; Grew to Winant, Aug. 1, 1945, *ibid.*, 1945, 6:78.

65. Diary, July 26, 1945, July 27, 1945, Leahy Papers.

66. *New York Times*, July 27, 1945, p. 1; *Wall Street Journal*, July 27, 1945, p. 6. Other press comment, including that quoted here, is conveniently reprinted in the *New York Herald Tribune*, July 27, 1945, p. 3. When Truman stopped in Plymouth on his way home from Potsdam for a brief luncheon with George VI, he referred to the surprising election results as a "revolution." "Oh, no!" the King hastily replied. "We don't have those here." Diary, July 28, 1945, Dalton Papers. Although this incident occurred several days later, Dalton's diary entry is dated July 28.

67. Rep. John E. Rankin, in *New York Times*, July 27, 1945, p. 2.

68. Balfour to Foreign Office, July 27, 1945, AN 2301/22/45, F.O. 371; British Information Service memorandum, n.d., AN 2522/22/45, *ibid.; Business Week*, Aug. 4, 1945, p. 15. The *Christian Science Monitor* quote is found in an article dated July 27, 1945, and located in Subject File, Davies Papers.

69. Attlee, *As It Happened*, p. 208; James F. Byrnes, *All in One Lifetime*, p. 298; Calendar Notes, Sept. 7, 1945, Stettinius Papers. Halifax had planned on retiring with the end of the war, but agreed to stay on into 1946 in order to demonstrate the continuity of British policy. Both the State Department and the OSS concluded that there would be few important differences in a Labour foreign policy insofar as relations with the United States were concerned. Britain's strategic demands, after all, would remain unchanged. "Implications of the Labor Landslide in Great Britain," Hickerson memorandum, Aug. 1, 1945, folder "Great Britain," Clayton-Thorp Files; R&A No. 3316, July 26, 1945, Office of Strategic Services, SDR; Report XL 16403, Aug. 25, 1945, Office of Strategic Services, RG 226, MMRD.

70. Truman, *Harry S. Truman*, p. 278; Saltonstall quoted in *New York Times*, July 27, 1945, p. 2.

71. *New York Herald Tribune*, July 27, 1945, p. 12.

72. Dilks, *Cadogan Diaries*, p. 776.

73. See, for instance, *New York Herald Tribune*, July 27, 1945, p. 4; Rep. Louis Ludlow to "Atlee," March 18, 1946, AN 920/4/45, F.O. 371; Henry H. Arnold, *Global Mission*, p. 593; Mallalieu, *British Reconstruction*, pp. 36, 46; Baram, *Department of State*, p. 166.

74. Ismay, *Memoirs*, p. 403.

75. Byrnes, *Speaking Frankly*, p. 79. For other indications of American doubts about Bevin, see Leahy, *I Was There*, p. 420; Halifax to Churchill, Aug. 3, 1945, Halifax Papers.

76. Bohlen, *Witness to History*, p. 240.

77. Cadogan to Bridges, July 27, 1945, PREM 4, 80/1; minutes, Third Staff Conference, July 31, 1945, PREM 4, 79/1.

78. Attlee, *As It Happened*, p. 205; Dilks, *Cadogan Diaries*, p. 778. In her biography of her father, Margaret Truman has written, "Dad thought he would have a better chance of reaching an agreement with Stalin without Mr. Churchill in the way." Truman, *Harry S. Truman*, p. 278.

79. Williams, *Twilight of Empire*, p. 75.

80. Aide-mémoire, July 16, 1945, *FRUS. Potsdam*, 2:621; the Leahy quote came from Diary, July 24, 1945, Leahy Papers.

81. Cadogan minute, Aug. 4, 1945, AN 2438/35/45, F.O. 371. For a similar assessment of Byrnes, see Dilks, *Cadogan Diaries*, p. 777.

82. Minute by Berkeley Gage, Aug. 21, 1945, AN 2505/4/45, F.O. 371; "Stocktaking after VE-Day," memorandum by Sir Orme Sargent, July 11, 1945, PREM 4, 31/5.

83. Halifax to Bevin, Aug. 9, 1945, AN 2560/22/45, F.O. 371.

84. Stimson memorandum, July 19, 1945, *FRUS. Potsdam*, 2:1155. For Truman's own feelings about the Soviets, see Truman, *Year of Decisions*, p. 412.

85. Minutes, Secretary's Staff Committee, July 17, 1945, folder 589, Byrnes Papers; Robert L. Messer, "The Making of a Cold Warrior: James F. Byrnes and American-Soviet Relations, 1945–1946," p. 303.

86. The first and third quotations come from a minute by Berkeley Gage, Aug. 21, 1945, AN 2505/4/45, F.O. 371; the second from a minute by H. A. Clarke, Aug. 20, 1945, *ibid.*

10. THE POLITICS OF MONEY

1. Byrnes to Winant, Aug. 18, 1945, *FRUS*, 1945, 6:102.

2. Churchill to Truman, July 24, 1945, *ibid., Potsdam*, 2:1181.

3. Hugh Dalton, *High Tide and After: Memoirs, 1945–1960*, p. 68. Also see Williams, *Twilight of Empire*, p. 128.

4. Winant to the Secretary, Aug. 12, 1945, 800.24/8-1245, SDR; Dean Acheson, *Present at the Creation: My Years in the State Department*, p. 122.

5. J. A. Maxwell memorandum, Aug. 17, 1945, 800.24/8-1745, SDR; Maxwell memorandum, Aug. 21, 1945, FW 611.4131/8-1845, *ibid.*; Cantril and Strunk, *Public Opinion*, p. 415; *Public Opinion Quarterly* (Fall 1945), 9:383.

6. Balfour to Foreign Office, Sept. 8, 1945, AN 2767/4/45, F.O. 371.

7. "Termination of FEA Lend-Lease to the British Commonwealth," Aug. 13, 1945, Subject File, Lend-Lease and International Finance Files of Hubert Havlik, SDR; F. W. Fetter memorandum, Aug. 27, 1945, 800.24/8-2745, *ibid.*; diary, Aug. 17, 1945, Leahy Papers.

8. U.S., Dept. of State, *Bulletin*, 13:284. Truman's press secretary was later to admit that although lend-lease deliveries had to be terminated, this should have been done "with better manners." On the other hand, Italy continued to receive lend-lease supplies for civilian relief until the end of the year, and China was the recipient of huge amounts of lend-lease aid well into 1946. Charles Ross is quoted in Herring, *Aid to Russia*, p. 236.

9. Herbert Fales to the Secretary, Aug. 25, 1945, 800.24/8-2545, SDR; Williams, *Twilight of Empire*, p. 131; Northedge, *British Foreign Policy*, p. 35. The quote may be found in Donald Cameron Watt, *Personalities and Policies: Studies in the Formulation of British Foreign Policy in the Twentieth Century*, p. 64.

10. Churchill quote in *New York Times*, Aug. 25, 1945, p. 5; economist quote in *Washington Post*, Aug. 26, 1945, p. M10.

11. Summary of Current News Reports, Aug. 25, 26, 27, 1945, Subject File, Havlik Files, SDR; Editorial Summaries, Office of War Information, Sept. 13, 1945, Truman Papers; Gardner, *Sterling-Dollar Diplomacy*, p. 185.

12. OF 356-Miscel., Truman Papers.

13. Dalton, *High Tide*, pp. 69–70; "Our Overseas Financial Prospects," Keynes memorandum circulated to the Cabinet on Aug. 14, 1945, PREM 8/35.

14. Dilks, *Cadogan Diaries*, pp. 782, 786; "Our Overseas Financial Prospects," Keynes memorandum circulated to the Cabinet on Aug. 14, 1945, PREM 8/35.

15. Churchill to Truman, July 24, 1945, *FRUS. Potsdam*, 2:1180.

16. Winant to the Secretary, Aug. 17, 1945, *ibid.*, 1945, 6:100; Winant to the Secretary, Sept. 24, 1945, *ibid.*, p. 136. Also see Ted [Achilles] to Hickerson, Oct. 22, 1945, 711.41/10-2245, SDR.

17. Winant to the Secretary, Aug. 17, 1945, *FRUS*, 1945, 6:101.

18. *Ibid.*, Sept. 24, 1945, p. 135; *ibid.*, Nov. 3, 1945, p. 154.

19. *Ibid.*, Aug. 17, 1945, pp. 98–100; *ibid.*, Aug. 18, 1945, p. 104; Byrnes to Winant, Aug. 27, 1945, *ibid.*, p. 110; Memorandum for the President, Sept. 18, 1945, 841.51/9-1845, SDR; Gardner, *Sterling-Dollar Diplomacy*, p. 203.

20. Earley memorandum, Sept. 21, 1945, folder "Correspondence, 1945," Earley Papers. London was also being pressed by some of the Dominions, particularly Australia, not to dismantle imperial preferences without significant

concessions from the United States. Winant to the Secretary, Nov. 3, 1945, *FRUS*, 1945, 6:153.

21. Fales to the Secretary, Feb. 14, 1945, 841.51/2-1445, SDR; Earley memorandum, Sept. 7, 1945, folder "British," box 1, Clayton-Thorp Files.

22. Record of conversation, Aug. 20, 1945, 611.4131/5-146, SDR. Also see Keynes to Walter Lippmann, Oct. 6, 1945, Selected Correspondence, Walter Lippmann Papers, Yale University.

23. Reuters' quote is in Gardner, *Sterling-Dollar Diplomacy*, p. 183; *Financial News* quote in Winant to the Secretary, Feb. 6, 1945, 841.51/2-645, SDR.

24. Winant to the Secretary, Jan. 11, 1946, *FRUS*, 1945, 6:201; Winant to the Secretary, July 5, 1945, 841.51/7-545, SDR.

25. Combined Production and Resources Board, *Combined Production: United States, United Kingdom, and Canada as of October 1, 1945*, p. 19; Winant to the Secretary, Sept. 24, 1945, *FRUS*, 1945, 6:136.

26. This, of course, is exactly what Truman had said about lend-lease to Churchill at Potsdam. See chapter 9 above. For an expression of this idea by officials in the Foreign Office, see minute by Nevile Butler, Oct. 27, 1945, AN 3820/3121/45, F.O. 371. Bevin also employed this argument in talking with American diplomats. See record of conversation, Aug. 20, 1945, 611.4131/5-146, SDR.

27. Dalton, *High Tide*, pp. 73–74; newspaper headline reported in Earley memorandum, Sept. 18, 1945, folder "Correspondence, 1945," Earley Papers.

28. Minutes, U.S. Top Committee, Sept. 17, 1945, 611.4131/5-146, SDR.

29. Clayton to Vinson, June 25, 1945, *FRUS*, 1945, 6:54.

30. Briefing Book Paper, *ibid., Potsdam*, 1:810.

31. Random examples that such considerations were appreciated by the American negotiators include: Diary, Aug. 20, 1945, Leahy Papers; Fetter memorandum, Sept. 5, 1945, 800.24/9-545, SDR; Hawkins to Clayton, Nov. 21, 1945, 841.51/11-2145, *ibid.*; Truman to Eleanor Roosevelt, Nov. 26, 1945, OF 280, Truman Papers; U.S. House of Representatives, Special Committee on Postwar Economic Policy and Planning, *Economic Reconstruction in Europe*, H. Rept. 1205, 79th Cong., 1st sess., 1945, p. 9.

32. Hickerson to Clayton, Sept. 14, 1945, 711.41/10-2245, SDR.

33. Earley to Clayton and Collado, Sept. 14, 1945, folder "Correspondence, 1945," Earley Papers.

34. Quoted in Lloyd C. Gardner, *Architects of Illusion: Men and Ideas in American Foreign Policy 1941–1949*, p. 124.

35. Special Committee on Postwar Economic Policy and Planning, *Economic Reconstruction in Europe*, pp. 9, 13, 29.

36. *New York Herald Tribune*, Oct. 4, 1945, p. 25. In early September, according to Gallup, Americans disapproved of any loan to Britain by a margin of more than two to one. Gallup, *The Gallup Poll*, 1:530. Also see *ibid.*, pp. 535, 549, 550.

37. Keynes to Lippmann, Oct. 6, 1945, Selected Correspondence, Lippmann Papers.

38. See in particular Appendix, Raynor memorandum, Oct. 31, 1945, 611.4131/10-3145, SDR.

39. Raynor to Matthews, Oct. 22, 1945, Records of the Office of European Affairs, *ibid.*; Walstrom memorandum, Sept. 7, 1945, folder "Aviation," box 1, Clayton-Thorp Files; "British Export Subsidy of Refined Sugar," March 8, 1946, folder "Memoranda of Conversation," box 4, *ibid.*; Roger Kenney to Vinson, Sept. 15, 1945, General Correspondence, 1933–56, Office of the Secretary, TDR; Gardner, *Sterling-Dollar Diplomacy*, p. 197.

40. Editorial Summaries, Office of War Information, mid-September 1945, Truman Papers; Sen. Kenneth McKellar to Truman, Nov. 6, 1945, OF 48, *ibid.*; Herbert Hoover comment in American Press Summary, Sept. 18, 1945, box 240, Winant Papers; McNaughton Reports, Sept. 14, 1945, McNaughton Papers; Baruch to the President, Aug. 30, 1945, box 1, Rosenman Papers; Baruch to Rep. Albert Gore, Oct. 25, 1945, Washington File, box 37, Baruch Papers; Gardner, *Sterling-Dollar Diplomacy*, pp. 193–94. For indications that the American negotiators were actually influenced by these expressions of distrust and these demands for reciprocal benefits, see Hickerson to Clayton, Sept. 14, 1945, 711.41/10-2245, SDR; Wailes to Matthews, Oct. 2, 1945, 611.4131/10-245, *ibid.*; Raynor to Matthews and Hickerson, Nov. 15, 1945, Records of the Office of European Affairs, *ibid.*; Diary, Dec. 7, 1945, Dalton Papers.

41. Memorandum of conversation, n.d., folder 596, Byrnes Papers; aide-mémoire, Nov. 6, 1945, *FRUS*, 1945, 6:207–10.

42. Keynes to Dalton, Oct. 1, 1945, 47 O.F. 272/45, Keynes Papers, Trea. 247; "Washington Financial Talks," Memorandum by the Chancellor of the Exchequer, Nov. 22, 1945, PREM 8/35. Keynes' assessment of the situation bears repeating. There was "widespread goodwill and a desire to help" among the Americans, he reported. But in "this business country," it was "a moral duty and not merely a self-regarding act to make any money which the traffic will bear and the law allow." Consequently, "some imitation of a normal banking transaction is necessary if the moral principles of the country are not to be affronted." Keynes to Dalton, Oct. 18, 1945, PREM 8/35.

43. Earl of Birkenhead, *Halifax*, p. 555.

44. Harrod, *Life of Keynes*, pp. 611–13; Birkenhead, *Halifax*, p. 555. Keynes had originally sought to hold the talks in the United States in order to escape day-to-day meddling by the British Cabinet. Even the span of three thousand miles, however, did not spare him from close supervision by his superiors in London. Cf. Winant to the Secretary, Aug. 17, 1945, *FRUS*, 1945, 6:99.

45. Dalton, *High Tide*, pp. 74–75.

46. *Ibid.*, p. 75; Diary, Dec. 7, 1945, Dalton Papers. Although this entry is dated December 7, internal evidence makes it clear that it was written sometime earlier, probably during the first two weeks in November. For one quite re-

markable example of this "mutual incomprehension," see Jt. Staff Mission to Cabinet Office, Nov. 26, 1945, CAB 122/1471.

47. Dalton, *High Tide*, p. 84; Diary, Dec. 7, 1945, Dalton Papers. (This entry does appear to have been written on December 7. In Dalton's diary it is clearly separated from the other December 7 entry, mentioned above.)

48. Diary, Nov. 6, 1945, Dec. 7, 1945, Dalton Papers; C.M. (45) 50th Conclusions, Nov. 6, 1945, PREM 8/35; C.M. (45) 59th Conclusions, Dec. 5, 1945, *ibid.*

49. Gardner, *Sterling-Dollar Diplomacy*, p. 206; Lionel C. Robbins, *Autobiography of an Economist*, p. 207.

50. Raynor to Matthews, Nov. 7, 1945, 611.4131/11-745, SDR.

51. Birkenhead, *Halifax*, p. 555; minute by J. C. Donnelly, Oct. 23, 1945, AN 3224/4/45, F.O. 371.

52. Diary, Dec. 7, 1945, Dalton Papers. Also see Dalton, *High Tide*, p. 82; Birkenhead, *Halifax*, p. 555.

53. U.S. Dept. of State, *Anglo-American Financial and Commercial Agreements*; U.S. Dept. of State, *Proposals for Expansion of World Trade and Employment*. The text of these agreements may be found as well in U.S. Dept. of State, *Bulletin*, 13:907 ff. Also see Gardner, *Sterling-Dollar Diplomacy*, ch. 11; Statement by Secretary Vinson before the Senate Committee on Banking and Currency, March 5, 1946, General Correspondence, 1933–56, Office of the Secretary, TDR; Harrod, *Life of Keynes*, p. 605; Paterson, *Soviet-American Confrontation*, pp. 163–64. Although these arrangements are commonly referred to as the British loan, the money offered Britain was not strictly a loan, since the total amount was not immediately transferred to the British. Rather, the United States agreed to advance credit as it was needed by the United Kingdom. This method was chosen as a means of reducing the interest charges Britain would have to pay. McNeill, *America, Britain, and Russia*, p. 682.

54. Birkenhead, *Halifax*, p. 556; Halifax to Eden, Dec. 3, 1945, Halifax Papers.

55. Keynes to Dalton, Oct. 1, 1945, 47 O.F. 272/45, Keynes Papers, Trea. 247. Also see *The Economist*, Dec. 15, 1945, p. 850.

56. Diary, Dec. 7, 1945, Dalton Papers. Also see Dalton, *High Tide*, p. 86. By way of contrast, in the same week in which this settlement was reached, the United States also signed a loan agreement with French authorities. The interest charged the French was 2 ⅜ percent. Some months later the British negotiated a further loan from Canada, a nation with even closer ties to Great Britain than the United States enjoyed, and one from which the British expected particularly magnanimous treatment. It is indicative of the reasonableness of the American terms that the Canadian loan closely paralleled the Anglo-American agreement in its fundamentals, including the emphasis upon nondiscriminatory restrictions and exchange controls. Only in the size of the loan relative to the GNP of the lender did the American credit appear less than munificent.

57. Gabriel Kolko is perhaps the foremost proponent of this line of interpretation. The quoted phrase comes from Joyce Kolko and Gabriel Kolko, *The Limits of Power: The World and United States Foreign Policy, 1945–1954*, p. 66. Other scholars who stress the antagonistic nature of the talks include: Gardner, *Economic Aspects of New Deal Diplomacy*, p. 289; Bert Cochran, *Harry Truman and the Crisis Presidency*, p. 192; Richard M. Freeland, *The Truman Doctrine and the Origins of McCarthyism: Foreign Policy, Domestic Politics, and International Security 1946–1948*, pp. 47–48.

58. Fetter memorandum, Sept. 5, 1945, 800.24/9-545, SDR; Hawkins to Clayton, Nov. 21, 1945, 841.51/11-2145, *ibid.*; Eckes, *Search for Solvency*, pp. 203–4.

59. Harrod, *Life of Keynes*, p. 605; Raynor to Matthews, Nov. 16, 1945, Records of the Office of European Affairs, SDR.

60. Raynor to Matthews and Hickerson, Oct. 29, 1945, 611.4131/10-2945, SDR.

61. Harrod, *Life of Keynes*, p. 605; Dalton, *High Tide*, p. 72.

62. "Statistical Material Presented During Washington Negotiations," n.d., 611.4131/5-146, SDR.

63. Earley to Clayton, July 20, 1945, 841.51/7-2045, *ibid.*

64. This is a point which Lloyd Gardner argues in his *Architects of Illusion*, p. 125.

65. William L. Clayton, *Selected Papers*, p. 180. Also see Watt, *Personalities and Policies*, p. 54. W. J. Gallman, Counsellor in the American embassy in London during these months, has suggested the opposite idea, that a Tory government might have had a more difficult task during the Washington negotiations than the Socialists did, due to an American distaste for politicians and programs seen as excessively conservative. Gallman interview.

66. Henry A. Wallace, *The Price of Vision: The Diary of Henry A. Wallace, 1942–1946*, pp. 490, 492. The historian who has gone most thoroughly through Attlee's papers has also written that British warnings about Soviet intentions merely confirmed American suspicions that London's ideas on international affairs were hopelessly anachronistic. Cf. Williams, *Twilight of Empire*, p. 132.

11. AMERICAN DISENGAGEMENT—BRITISH DISENCHANTMENT

1. Attlee to Truman, Aug. 18, 1945, *FRUS*, 1945, 7:504.

2. Truman, *Year of Decisions*, pp. 237, 446. The Roosevelt comment was repeated to Truman in COMNAVGRP to the President, May 29, 1945, White House Map Room file, box 3, Truman Papers.

3. "Estimate of Conditions in Asia and the Pacific at the Close of the War in the Far East and the Objectives and Policies of the United States," State Department memorandum, June 28, 1945, Secretary of the Army TS Subject file, 1940–45, RG 107, MMRD.

4. Truman, *Year of Decisions*, pp. 446–48; Truman's message to Chiang is contained in Byrnes to Hurley, Aug. 21, 1945, *FRUS*, 1945, 7:509.

5. Truman, *Year of Decisions*, p. 244.

6. Thorne, "Indochina and Anglo-American Relations," p. 95; LaFeber, "Roosevelt, Churchill, and Indochina," p. 1294. For an early indication of this retreat from FDR's ardent anticolonialism, see Louis, *Imperialism At Bay*, pp. 537–40.

7. "Estimate of Conditions in Asia and the Pacific at the Close of the War in the Far East and the Objectives and Policies of the United States," June 28, 1945, Secretary of the Army TS Subject file, 1940–45, RG 107, MMRD. For apprehensions on the part of one State Department official that the administration was moving too much in the direction of aiding British imperialism, see Henry Wallace's account of a conversation with John Carter Vincent, the Director of the Office of Far Eastern Affairs, in Wallace, *Price of Vision*, p. 525.

8. At the Cairo conference in November 1943. See Senate Committee on Foreign Relations, *A Decade of American Foreign Policy*, p. 22.

9. See, for instance, Hull, *Memoirs*, 2:1596.

10. "US Post-War Military Policy in the Far East," n.d., OPD Exec. files, 1940–45, RG 165, MMRD. Many months earlier Leahy had written on behalf of the Joint Chiefs of Staff that "partial control" by another nation of even one of the Japanese mandated islands would endanger American control of the Pacific and, hence, the security of the United States. There appeared to Leahy "no valid reason why their future status should be the subject of discussion with any other nation." JCS to Secretary of State, March 11, 1944, *FRUS*, 1944, 5:1201. For an updated analysis with a similar conclusion, see Office of Strategic Services, "Problems and Objectives of United States Policy," April 2, 1945, folder "Chronological File," Truman Papers.

11. Memorandum of conversation, n.d., folder 596, Byrnes Papers.

12. Aide-mémoire, Nov. 6, 1945, *FRUS*, 1945, 6:207–10.

13. Minutes, C.O.S. meeting, Dec. 3, 1945, AN 3712/3121/45, F.O. 371; Gen. 117/2d meeting, Jan. 28, 1946, PREM 8/176.

14. Byrnes, *Speaking Frankly*, p. 210; McNeill, *America. Britain. and Russia*, pp. 638–39; Dilks, *Cadogan Diaries*, p. 781.

15. See U.S. Dept. of State, *Occupation of Japan: Policy and Progress*, p. 1; and Byrnes, *Speaking Frankly*, p. 213, for American assertions of the collaborative nature of the occupation. The United States by the Moscow, Tehran, and Cairo Declarations was committed to allied cooperation in all matters pertaining to the surrender and disarmament of Japan. See Appendix B, SWNCC 70/5, Aug. 11, 1945, *FRUS*, 1945, 6:607.

16. U.S. Dept. of State, *Occupation of Japan*, p. 75. Also consult Wheeler-Bennett and Nicholls, *The Semblance of Peace*, p. 489.

17. Truman, *Year of Decisions*, p. 412.

18. Appendix B, SWNCC 70/5, Aug. 11, 1945, *FRUS*, 1945, 6:608; Sumner Welles, *Where Are We Heading?* pp. 313–14.

19. Case 227, n.d., OPD dec. files, 1942–45; OPD 336TS, RG 165, MMRD; Truman, *Year of Decisions*, p. 519.

20. Appendix B, SWNCC 70/5, Aug. 11, 1945, *FRUS*, 1945, 6:608; Harriman to Secretary of State, Oct. 30, 1945, *ibid.*, p. 809.

21. British Embassy to Department of State, Aug. 20, 1945, *ibid.*, pp. 678–80; Byrnes, *Speaking Frankly*, p. 213. Truman later wrote that the British "raised no objections to the manner in which we handled the occupation in Japan." Truman, *Year of Decisions*, p. 519. The most charitable comment which might be made about this statement is that the President's memory seems to have been fading by this time.

22. Quoted in Thorne, *Allies of a Kind*, pp. 678–79.

23. "Excerpt from Committee of Three Minutes," Oct. 10, 1945, OPD dec. files,1942–45: OPD 334.8TS, RG 165, MMRD; Byrnes, *Speaking Frankly*, p. 215; U.S. Dept. of State, *The Far Eastern Commission*, pp. 13–14.

24. Hugh Borton, *Japan's Modern Century*, p. 405. The quotation comes from Edwin O. Reischauer, *The United States and Japan*, pp. 47–48. In addition to the Far Eastern Commission, a second body was created to advise MacArthur on the execution of his duties. This Allied Council for Japan proved even less effective in supervising American military authorities than was the FEC. See Wheeler-Bennett and Nicholls, *Semblance of Peace*, p. 492.

25. Memorandum of conversation, n.d., folder 596, Byrnes Papers. Support for this assertion of a perceived community of interests will be provided throughout the following pages, but for several good, concise illustrations, see minute by J. C. Donnelly, Sept. 11, 1945, AN 2767/4/45, F.O. 371; Halifax to Bevin, Dec. 12, 1945, AN 3853/35/45, *ibid.*; Sherwood, *Roosevelt and Hopkins*, pp. 921–22.

26. Hopkins quote in Sherwood, *Roosevelt and Hopkins*, p. 921; Wallace, *Price of Vision*, pp. 490, 523. For another illustration see Forrestal to Byrnes, Jan. 17, 1946, White House Map Room file, box 4, Truman Papers.

27. Henry Norweb to Matthews, Feb. 7, 1946, 711.41/2-746, SDR. Harold Laski, the chairman of the British Labour Party, seemed to possess an uncanny ability to create American ill-feeling toward the British by his strident, sometimes irresponsible, public statements, which were invariably circulated throughout the United States by Anglophobic journalists. See Bureau of the Budget, Editorial Summaries, early Dec. 1945, Truman Papers; Knights of Columbus to Representative John Taber, Oct. 24, 1945, copy in 711.41/11-245, SDR; *Chicago Tribune*, Dec. 10, 1945, p. 16; Williams, *Twilight of Empire*, p. 169; Sir John Balfour, "Diadems Askew: A Diplomatic Cavalcade," p. 252; Arnold A. Rogow, *James Forrestal: A Study of Personality, Politics, and Policy*, pp. 145–47.

28. This assertion, of course, is the point of heated historical contention. But if the sentiments expressed by Washington policy makers at the time, in private as well as public settings, mean anything at all, then one is extremely hard pressed to defend the opposite viewpoint. For random illustrations of this feeling, see Truman's October 27, 1945 address in U.S. Dept. of State, *Bulletin*, 13:655;

State Department memorandum, Dec. 1, 1945, *FRUS*, 1946, 1:1136–39; memorandum of meeting of the Secretaries of State, War, and Navy, Nov. 6, 1945, *ibid.*, 1945, 6:833; memorandum of conversation, Nov. 29, 1945, *ibid.*, 2:591; Pool to Wailes and Hickerson, Oct. 11, 1945, 711.41/10-1145, SDR; Hull to Assistant Secretary of War, Aug. 22, 1945, OPD dec. files, 1942–45: OPD 334.8TS, RG 165, MMRD.

29. In a survey which appeared in the December 1945 issue of *Fortune*, more than 50 percent of the respondents thought that there was a good chance to avoid another big war for at least twenty-five to thirty years, while only one person in six felt that there would be a large war started by the Soviet Union. Early the following year Gallup found that only 26 percent of his interviewees believed that Russia sought to dominate the world. (Twelve percent thought Britain desired to do so.) "The Fortune Survey," p. 303; Gallup, *The Gallup Poll*, 1:564.

30. Attlee to Smuts, Aug. 31, 1945, PREM 3, 430/13. Eden late in November assured the Commons that Soviet actions in Eastern Europe were directed solely against a German resurgence and not at the western democracies. *New York Times*, Nov. 23, 1945, p. 10. For a representative editorial from The *Times* see Dec. 4, 1945, p. 5.

31. Gallman to Secretary of State, Oct. 18, 1945, *FRUS*, 1945, 5:897; Halifax to Bevin, Dec. 12, 1945, AN 3853/35/45, F.O. 371.

32. Harriman and Abel, *Special Envoy*, p. 509. Many other observers at the time commented on British unhappiness at the American habit of unilateral action without prior coordination between London and Washington. Winant to Secretary of State, Nov. 26, 1945, *FRUS*, 1945, 2:581; Bohlen, *Witness to History*, p. 248; George F. Kennan, *Memoirs: 1925–1950*, pp. 286–87; James B. Conant, *My Several Lives: Memoirs of a Social Inventor*, p. 480; *New York Times*, Oct. 16, 1945, p. 8.

33. Minute by J. C. Donnelly, Jan. 2, 1946, AN 3768/763/45, F.O. 371.

34. Attlee to Truman, July 31, 1945, *FRUS, Potsdam*, 2:1205–6; Truman to Attlee, Oct. 24, 1945, Records of the JCS, Leahy Files, RG 218, MMRD.

35. Davis, *Postwar Defense Policy and the U.S. Navy*, p. 178; Arnold, *Global Mission*, p. 607. The quotation is from Byrnes to Stimson, Aug. 9, 1945, OPD dec. file, 1942–45: OPD 475, RG 165, MMRD.

36. Gen. Hull to Assistant Secretary of War, Aug. 22, 1945, OPD dec. files, 1942–45: OPD 334.8TS, RG 165, MMRD. Also J.P.S. 765/1, "Desirability and Priority of Providing U.S. Military Supplies and Equipment to Foreign Nations," Dec. 11, 1945, CCS dec. file, 1942–45: CCS 400.3, RG 218, *ibid.*

37. McNeill, *America, Britain, and Russia*, p. 679. It was not until the formation of NATO in 1949 that the CCS was actually terminated.

38. Acheson to Truman, Sept. 25, 1945, *FRUS*, 1945, 2:48.

39. Gordon Dean quoted in P.M.S. Blackett, "America's Atomic Dilemma," in *The Shaping of American Diplomacy*, p. 987. It should perhaps be observed

that the American military was never as sanguine in its assessment of the bomb's immediate usefulness as were most civilians associated with the discovery.

40. Williams, *Twilight of Empire*, pp. 95, 101. In a similar vein, Eden warned in the House of Commons that each new scientific discovery made greater nonsense of old-time conceptions of national sovereignty. U.K., Parliament, *Parliamentary Debates* (Commons), 5th series, 416 (1945):612. If new inventions and ever more deadly horrors have today appreciably lessened the world's dread of atomic energy, we should nonetheless avoid underestimating the impact which the first explosions had on an earlier generation.

41. Special Message to the Congress on Atomic Energy, Oct. 3, 1945, in *Harry S. Truman, 1945* of *Public Papers of the Presidents of the United States*, p. 365.

42. Basil Collier, *The Lion and the Eagle: British and Anglo-American Strategy, 1900–1950*, p. 417; Leslie R. Groves, *Now It Can Be Told*, pp. 129–36; Barton J. Bernstein, "The Uneasy Alliance: Roosevelt, Churchill, and the Atomic Bomb, 1940–1945," pp. 202–30. In the early months of the war, however, it had been the British who rebuffed American interest in closer collaboration. On this see Bernstein, pp. 205–7.

43. Martin J. Sherwin, *A World Destroyed: The Atomic Bomb and the Grand Alliance*, p. 86. Churchill signed this agreement without consulting the Cabinet, and it was more than two years later before most of the senior policy makers in London were apprised of its existence. "An astounding sell-out," Dalton wrote when he first learned of these arrangements. If knowledge of this became public, he predicted, it "would indeed be an Atomic Bomb on W. C.'s reputation." Diary, Dec. 7, 1945, Dalton Papers.

44. Aide-mémoire, Sept. 19, 1944, *FRUS, Quebec*, 1944, 492–93; Bernstein, "The Uneasy Alliance," pp. 224–26. This time it was the Americans' turn to remain in the dark concerning the existence of an important international understanding. According to one British authority, not a single American knew of this document following Roosevelt's death until told by the British. Margaret Gowing, *Independence and Deterrence: Britain and Atomic Energy, 1945–1952*, 1:7. Also Groves, *Now It Can Be Told*, p. 401.

45. Leahy, *I Was There*, pp. 265, 433.

46. Bush memorandum, Sept. 22, 1944, *FRUS, Quebec*, 1944, 296.

47. Sherwin, *A World Destroyed*, p. 111.

48. Truman, *Year of Decisions*, p. 523; the quote is from a Truman press conference, Oct. 8, 1945, in *Harry S. Truman, 1945*, p. 382.

49. Truman, *Year of Decisions*, p. 539.

50. *Ibid.*, p. 536; Leahy, *I Was There*, p. 433; H. A. DeWeerd, "British-American Collaboration on the A-Bomb in World War II," in R. N. Rosecrance, ed., *The Dispersion of Nuclear Weapons: Strategy and Politics*, p. 43. Bush, for instance, opposed a close atomic partnership with Britain for fear that this would make the Russians unwilling to work for effective international control. Many

military officials, on the other hand, sought to retain an American monopoly in atomic weapons solely for national security justifications. See Raymond Dawson and Richard Rosecrance, "Theory and Reality in the Anglo-American Alliance," p. 22.

51. For examples of congressional sentiment along these lines, see Bailey to Tom Connally, July 11, 1945, "Trade and Commerce, 1944," Bailey Papers; and Arthur H. Vandenberg, Jr., ed., *The Private Papers of Senator Vandenberg*, p. 226. Dalton recorded in his diary that "Truman is said to be terrified lest the decisions on all this should get into the hands of the Senate Foreign Affairs Committee." Diary, Oct. 17, 1945, Dalton Papers.

52. A copy of the Joint Declaration may be found in Senate Committee on Foreign Relations, *A Decade of American Foreign Policy*, pp. 1076–78. Attlee's ideas are summarized in "International Control of Atomic Energy," memorandum by the Prime Minister, Nov. 5, 1945, C. P. (45) 272, U 9660/6550/70, F. O. 371; Williams, *Twilight of Empire*, p. 104. Also see the helpful, at times comprehensive, Richard G. Hewlett and Oscar E. Anderson, Jr., *A History of the United States Atomic Energy Commission*, 1:462–66.

53. R. N. Rosecrance, "British Incentives to Become a Nuclear Power," in Rosecrance, *Dispersion of Nuclear Weapons*, pp. 55–61; Gowing, *Independence and Deterrence*, p. 72.

54. Truman, *Year of Decisions*, p. 544; Williams, *Twilight of Empire*, p. 109.

55. Memorandum by Groves and Anderson, Nov. 16, 1945, *FRUS*, 1945, 2:75–76; Hewlett and Anderson, *The New World*, pp. 466–68; Groves, *Now It Can Be Told*, pp. 403–5.

56. Achilles to Hickerson, July 30, 1945, 711.90F/7-3045, SDR. Also interesting is Henderson memorandum, Dec. 28, 1945, *FRUS*, 1946, 7:1.

57. James L. Gormly, "Keeping the Door Open in Saudi Arabia: The United States and the Dhahran Airfield, 1945–46," p. 202.

58. Memorandum by Sir Ronald J. Campbell, June 9, 1945, cited in John A. DeNovo, "The Culbertson Economic Mission and Anglo-American Tensions in the Middle East, 1944–1945," pp. 933–34. I am indebted to Professor DeNovo for sharing with me a prepublication draft of this article. For a desire to use a more active American presence as a counterbalance to the Soviet Union, see draft of P. H. P. (44) 16 (0), Jan. 5, 1945, U 181/36/70, F. O. 371; and a year later, Jock Balfour to Paul Mason, Jan. 11, 1946, AN 205/5/45, *ibid.*

59. Clayton to McCloy, Nov. 8, 1945, Reading File, Clayton-Thorp Files. Other examples from the American side include Report #L57092, June 2, 1945, Office of Strategic Services, RG 226, MMRD; Report #XL22754, Oct. 24, 1945, *ibid.*; Gen. Giles to War Department, Nov. 19, 1945, Secretary of the Army Subject File, 1945–47, RG 335, *ibid.* For the British quote, see Campbell memorandum, June 9, 1945, cited in DeNovo, "Culbertson Economic Mission," p. 933.

60. Hickerson to Achilles, n.d., 711.90F/7-3045, SDR.

61. Memorandum for the President, May 1, 1945, Subject File 1945, folder

"Palestine," Papers of Samuel I. Rosenman, HSTL; Herbert Parzen, "The Roosevelt Palestine Policy, 1943–1945: An Exercise in Dual Diplomacy," pp. 31–65; Selig Adler, "American Policy vis-à-vis Palestine in the Second World War." For a revealing illustration of this approach, see Stettinius "Record," 1:21, SDR.

62. Examples include Grew to the President, May 1, 1945, Subject File 1945, folder "Palestine," Rosenman Papers, HSTL; Truman, *Year of Decisions*, p. 69; Harry S. Truman, *Memoirs*, 2:134; Report #XL18072, Aug. 24, 1945, Office of Strategic Services, RG 226, MMRD. John Snetsinger, *Truman, the Jewish Vote, and the Creation of Israel*, pp. 13–15, amplifies this.

63. "S." to "Roberta," n.d., OF 204, Truman Papers.

64. Copy found in *ibid.* Also consult Richard P. Stevens, *American Zionism and U.S. Foreign Policy, 1942–1947*, pp. 129–30.

65. For Truman's own views, see Truman, *Year of Decisions*, p. 69; Truman, *Years of Trial and Hope*, pp. 132, 140. Also Acheson, *Present at the Creation*, p. 169. Arab spokesmen and some circles in Great Britain saw American policy toward Palestine as part of a larger pattern of economic imperialism. But the economic merits of a pro-Jewish and anti-Arab stance would have been at best only very mixed. Equally important, Truman was not particularly moved by narrowly economic considerations of this sort. Nor, for that matter, were Samuel Rosenman and David Niles, the key aides who influenced the President most heavily on questions involving Palestine. See Report #XL22754, Oct. 24, 1945, Office of Strategic Services, RG 226, MMRD.

66. Truman to Churchill, July 24, 1945, *FRUS, Potsdam*, 2:1402.

67. The 1944 Foreign Office study is summarized in "Estimate of British Post-War Capabilities and Intentions," Feb. 13, 1946, CCS geog. files, 1942–45: CCS 000.1 Gr. Britain, RG 218, MMRD. Also helpful are Eden to War Cabinet, W. P. (45) 229, April 10, 1945, PREM 4, 52/1; "The Anglo-American Problem in Palestine," R&A No. 2263, July 20, 1944, Research Analysis Branch, Office of Strategic Services, RG 59.

68. U.K. Parliament, *Parliamentary Debates* (Commons), 5th series, 408 (1945):1289.

69. Williams, *Twilight of Empire*, p. 181. In this discussion I am not particularly concerned with the merits of the Zionist case or the relative justice or fairness of the respective Arab and Jewish positions (not that there was a single Arab or Jewish position). Rather, I intend to focus only on the American and British perspectives on the issue. Hence, Jewish protests that the question of "absorptive capacity" was never rasied at the time of the constant Arab immigration into Palestine throughout the twenties and thirties, though important within a larger context, are no more relevant to this study than are many possibly justifiable Arab complaints against the Jews.

70. Press conference, Aug. 16, 1945, in *Harry S. Truman, 1945*, p. 106; Truman, *Years of Trial and Hope*, pp. 137–39; Harrison Report in U.S. Dept. of State, *Bulletin*, 13:456–63; Truman to Attlee, Aug. 31, 1945, *FRUS, 1945*, 8:737–39.

71. Attlee to Truman, Oct. 5, 1945, Records of the JCS, Leahy Files, RG 218, MMRD; the quote is from Attlee to Truman, Sept. 16, 1945, in Williams, *Twilight of Empire*, pp. 189–91.

72. Truman, *Years of Trial and Hope*, p. 137.

73. Williams, *Twilight of Empire*, p. 181; Laski to Judge Stanley Mosk, Oct. 10, 1945, copy found in OF 204, Truman Papers.

74. Williams, *Twilight of Empire*, pp. 181, 185; Laski to Felix Frankfurter, Oct. 21, 1945, General Correspondence, box 75, Frankfurter Papers; Nicholas Bethell, *The Palestine Triangle: The Struggle for the Holy Land, 1935–48*, p. 213.

75. Minute by J. C. Donnelly, Oct. 11, 1945, AN 3069/4/45, F.O. 371.

76. Bethell, *The Palestine Triangle*, pp. 198, 201, 292.

77. *Ibid.*, p. 202.

78. Rosenman to the President, Oct. 23, 1945, Subject File 1945, folder "Palestine," Rosenman Papers, HSTL; Truman, *Years of Trial and Hope*, pp. 143–44.

79. Rosenman to the President, Nov. 1, 1945, Subject File 1945, folder "Palestine," Rosenman Papers, HSTL; Truman, *Years of Trial and Hope*, p. 142.

80. Statement by the President, Nov. 13, 1945, in *Harry S. Truman, 1945*, pp. 467–69; Truman to Roosevelt, Nov. 26, 1945, OF 280, Truman Papers; Miriam J. Haron, "Anglo-American Relations and the Question of Palestine, 1945–1947," pp. 42–43. Also see Truman to Wagner, Dec. 10, 1945, OF 204, Truman Papers.

81. Stettinius, *Diaries*, p. 409; Dwight D. Eisenhower, *The Papers of Dwight David Eisenhower*, 6:494. Truman had appointed Stettinius United States Representative on the United Nations Preparatory Commission following the latter's resignation as Secretary of State.

82. Harriman and Abel, *Special Envoy*, p. 509. Also consult Daniel Yergin, *Shattered Peace: The Origins of the Cold War and the National Security State*, p. 131. Of course this is the exact complaint lodged by the Americans over British actions in Greece and Italy the previous year.

83. Teletype conference, Nov. 27, 1945, *FRUS*, 1945, 2:584; Byrnes to Winant, Nov. 29, 1945, *ibid.*, p. 588. And again, Byrnes memorandum, Dec. 4, 1945, *ibid.*, pp. 593–95.

84. Dilks, *Cadogan Diaries*, p. 786.

85. Halifax to Bevin, Dec. 12, 1945, AN 3853/35/45, F.O. 371. For another example of this comparison of the two Presidents, see Keynes to Dalton, Oct. 18, 1945, PREM 8/35.

86. Cadogan to Halifax, Dec. 30, 1945, Halifax Papers. George Kennan recorded in his diary that Bevin felt much the same way about Byrnes. See Kennan, *Memoirs*, p. 286.

87. Mrs. Herbert Agar to Winant, Jan. 19, 1946, box 180, Winant Papers.

88. Keynes to Lippmann, Jan. 29, 1946, Selected Correspondence, Lippmann Papers.

89. Halifax to Foreign Office, Nov. 3, 1945, AN 3373/4/45, F.O. 371. Also Balfour to Bevin, Sept. 8, 1945, AN 2851/763/45, *ibid.*; Halifax to Bevin, Dec. 12, 1945, AN 3853/35/45, *ibid.*
90. Frank Roberts to Sargent, Oct. 23, 1945, N 14846/165/38, *ibid.*
91. Roberts to Bevin, Oct. 31, 1945, N 15702/165/38, *ibid.*
92. Williams, *Twilight of Empire*, p. 118. Also see R. N. Rosecrance, *Defense of the Realm: British Strategy in the Nuclear Epoch*, pp. 38–42.
93. Minute by J. C. Donnelly, Dec. 5, 1945, AN 2851/763/45, F.O. 371. Also see minute by Paul Mason, Dec. 6, 1945, *ibid.*; and Mason to Michael Wright, Dec. 22, 1945, AN 205/5/45, *ibid.*

12. FINANCIAL AID AND FRATERNAL ASSOCIATION

1. U.K., Parliament, *Parliamentary Debates* (Lords), 5th series, 138 (1945):778.
2. *The Times*, Dec. 12, 1945, p. 5; *The Economist*, Dec. 8, 1945, p. 821.
3. London Embassy to Secretary, Dec. 13, 1945, 611.4131/5-146, SDR.
4. Gardner, *Sterling-Dollar Diplomacy*, p. 226.
5. Bedford quote in U.K. Parliament, *Parliamentary Debates* (Lords), 5th series, 138 (1945):769; Simon cited in Gardner, *Sterling-Dollar Diplomacy*, p. 226.
6. Harrod, *Life of Keynes*, p. 617. For other comment, see Richard P. Hedlund, "Congress and the British Loan, 1945–1946: A Congressional Study," pp. 40–41.
7. *The Economist*, Dec. 15, 1945, p. 850; Keynes quote in U.K. Parliament, *Parliamentary Debates* (Lords), 5th series, 138 (1945):782; *Manchester Guardian*, Dec. 27, 1945, copy filed with London Embassy to Secretary, Dec. 31, 1945, 711.41/12-3145, SDR. The irritable British reaction to the aid package is helpfully analyzed in Winant to Secretary, Jan. 3, 1946, 841.51/1-346, *ibid.* Also see Gardner, *Sterling-Dollar Diplomacy*, pp. 225–36.
8. *The Times*, Dec. 7, 1945, p. 5; Dec. 12, 1945, p. 5; *The Economist*, Dec. 15, 1945, p. 850. Also see quote by Sir Hubert Henderson, cited in Gardner, *Sterling-Dollar Diplomacy*, p. 227.
9. Diary, Dec. 19, 1945, Dalton Papers.
10. See *The Economist*, Dec. 15, 1945, p. 849, for an illustration of this.
11. Harrod, *Life of Keynes*, p. 618; Keynes to Lippmann, Jan. 3, 1946, Selected Correspondence, Lippmann Papers; Paterson, *Soviet-American Confrontation*, p. 164; quote by G. D. H. Cole in Gardner, *Sterling-Dollar Diplomacy*, p. 229.
12. Winant to Secretary, Dec. 14, 1945, *FRUS*, 1945, 6:199; Eden to Halifax, Jan. 17, 1946, Halifax Papers; Macmillan, *Tides of Fortune*, pp. 77–78; Bevin quip in Winant to Secretary, Dec. 14, 1945, 841.51/12-1445, SDR.
13. Birkenhead, *Halifax*, p. 557.
14. Gardner, *Sterling-Dollar Diplomacy*, p. 235; copy of *London Daily Telegraph*, Dec. 14, 1945, in box 240, Winant Papers.

15. Gardner, *Sterling-Dollar Diplomacy*, p. 232; *The Times*, Dec. 8, 1945, p. 7; *Daily Telegraph* quote in Winant to Secretary, Dec. 8, 1945, 841.51/12-845, SDR.

16. U.K. Parliament, *Parliamentary Debates* (Lords), 5th series, 138 (1945):790.

17. *The Economist*, Dec. 8, 1945, p. 821.

18. Vandenberg, *Private Papers*, p. 231; Lippmann to Keynes, Jan. 2, 1946, Selected Correspondence, Lippmann Papers.

19. *Chicago Tribune*, Dec. 20, 1945, p. 1; also see *ibid.*, Dec. 10, 1945, p. 16; Dec. 19, 1945, p. 18.

20. White to Truman, Dec. 13, 1945, OF 212A, Truman Papers.

21. U.S. House of Representatives, *Congressional Record*, 79th Cong., 2d sess., 1946, vol. 92, pt. 9, pp. A660–661.

22. *Ibid.*, pp. A556–557.

23. *Daily Jefferson County* (Wisc.) *Union*, June 25, 1946, reprinted in *ibid.*, pt. 12, p. A3765.

24. Bunn memorandum, April 18, 1946, 841.51/10-1145, SDR.

25. C. H. Schlaeger to Truman, July 15, 1946, OF 212A, Truman Papers.

26. Dulles to Vandenberg, Dec. 17, 1945, Selected Correspondence, box 27, Dulles Papers. Also cf. Josiah Bailey to P. W. Garland, March 22, 1946, "Lend Lease, 1941–1946," Bailey Papers.

27. Wallace, *Price of Vision*, p. 526; Vandenberg, *Private Papers*, p. 231.

28. Roosevelt to Truman, Nov. 20, 1945, OF 280, Truman Papers. The information in these above paragraphs may be supplemented by a memorandum by Margaret Carter, Jan. 15, 1946, 841.51/1-1546, SDR; Halifax to Foreign Office, Dec. 15, 1945, AN 3804/4/45, F.O. 371; Gardner, *Sterling-Dollar Diplomacy*, pp. 236–42; Paterson, *Soviet-American Confrontation*, pp. 169–71; Hedlund, "Congress and the British Loan," pp. 45–59.

29. Carter memorandum, Jan. 5, 1946, 841.51/1-546, SDR; Carter memorandum, Jan. 15, 1946, 841.51/1-1546, *ibid.*; U.S. Board of Governors of the Federal Reserve System, *Federal Reserve Bulletin* (January 1946), 32:1–13; (March 1946), 32:232–35.

30. "Statement by Secretary Vinson before the House Committee on Banking and Currency," May 14, 1946, General Correspondence, 1933–56, Office of the Secretary, TDR.

31. Fred M. Vinson and Dean Acheson, "The British Loan—What it Means to Us," in U.S. Dept. of State, *Bulletin*, 14:53.

32. *Ibid.*, p. 55.

33. "Statement by Secretary Vinson before the Senate Committee on Banking and Currency," March 5, 1946, General Correspondence, 1933–56, Office of the Secretary, TDR. Also see speech by Harry Hawkins, enclosed in Winant to Secretary, Feb. 19, 1946, 611.4131/2-1946, SDR.

34. Press Release, March 4, 1946, OF 48, Truman Papers. Also "Conference with the President," Dec. 19, 1945, box 15, Harold Smith papers.

35. U.S. Dept. of State, *Why Lend to Britain?* pp. 18–19; U.S. Senate, Com-

mittee on Banking and Currency, *Anglo-American Financial Agreement, Hearings before the Committee on Banking and Currency on S. J. Res. 138*, 79th Cong., 2d sess., 1946, *passim*; U.S. Dept. of the Treasury, *The Loan to Britain—A Sound Economic Step*, address by Fred M. Vinson, Philadelphia, Pa., Jan. 9, 1946, p. 1; draft letter, Acheson to Representative Margaret C. Smith, May 2, 1946, 711.41/4-1746, SDR.

36. A long, though by no means complete list of the national organizations which publicly endorsed the British credit may be found in U.S. House of Representatives, Committee on Banking and Currency, *Anglo-American Financial Agreement. Hearings on H. J. Res. 311*, 79th Cong., 2d sess., 1946, pp. 44–45.

37. William Benton to Jesse Jones, Nov. 1, 1945, 841.51/11-145, SDR; "Public Attitudes Toward Great Britain, 1940–1947," June 25, 1947, 711.41/6-2547, *ibid.*, p. 25; Gallup, *The Gallup Poll*, 1:561; *Public Opinion Quarterly* (Summer 1946), 10:262; Gardner, *Sterling-Dollar Diplomacy*, p. 248.

38. Vardaman to Truman, Feb. 13, 1946, OF 212A, Truman Papers. Also see Vandenberg's comment in Vandenberg, *Private Papers*, p. 231.

39. Williams, *Twilight of Empire*, pp. 162–63. In an earlier cable Churchill reported Byrnes' approval of the speech and added that the Secretary had said that he had no objections to a "special friendship" within the U.N.O., since the United States had already established similar relationships with some of the Latin American states. Halifax to Foreign Office, Feb. 21, 1946, PREM 8/197. The story of Churchill's mishaps at the poker table is in Birkenhead, *Halifax*, p. 559. Such a trifling sum, Churchill told Halifax, was a small price to pay for the closer relations with Truman he had established, adding that the President and he were now on first-name terms.

40. Diary, March 5, 1946, Leahy Papers.

41. U.S. Congress, *Congressional Record*, 79th Cong., 2d sess., 1946, vol. 92, pt. 9, pp. A1145–47.

42. William Henry Chamberlin in *Wall Street Journal*, March 8, 1946, p. 6.

43. Jeremy K. Ward, "Winston Churchill and the 'Iron Curtain' Speech," p. 57.

44. *The Economist*, March 9, 1946, p. 361; Roosevelt quoted in Wallace, *Price of Vision*, p. 561.

45. Ward, "Winston Churchill and the 'Iron Curtain' Speech," p. 57.

46. Both letters may be found in OF 48, Truman Papers.

47. Forrestal, *Diaries*, p. 154. One memo prepared by a White House clerk listed 134 telegrams protesting the Fulton speech and Truman's presence there, against only three supporting the address. See memorandum by M. C. Latta, March 8, 1946, OF 48, Truman Papers. Strangely enough, Whitehall anticipated this negative reaction to the Fulton address with a great deal more accuracy than had the rather nonchalant Truman and his top aides. Hence, the immediate response in the Foreign Office to the speech was one of consternation, due not so much to the content of Churchill's remarks as to fears of their possible repercussion in the United States. The former Prime Minister, Bevin com-

plained, had demonstrated poor judgment by saying the "right thing at the wrong time." Anderson, "Britain, the United States, and the Cold War," p. 176. Also Williams, *Twilight of Empire*, p. 162.

48. Halifax to Bevin, March 8, 1946, AN 649/4/45, F. O. 371. Halifax's overly sanguine reading of the American mood following the Fulton address led Foreign Office officials, once they recovered from their initial dismay, to expect a greater willingness in the United States to coordinate political and military strategy than actually existed. For example, see minute by J. C. Donnelly, March 9, 1946, *ibid.*; minute by B. E. F. Gage, March 11, 1946, AN 674/4/45, *ibid.*; minute by Nevile Butler, March 12, 1946, *ibid.* The British unhappiness when this heightened collaboration failed to materialize will be illustrated in the following chapter.

49. *Public Opinion Quarterly* (Summer 1946), 10:264; *New York Times*, March 7, 1946, p. 1; broadcast of March 7, 1946, box 29, Swing Papers.

50. Unidentified editorial found in General Correspondence, 1933–56, Office of the Secretary, TDR. Copy of the letter is in OF 280, Truman Papers.

51. OF 48, Truman Papers.

52. Broadcast of March 7, 1946, box 29, Swing Papers.

53. Wallace, *Price of Vision*, pp. 558–59.

54. McNeill, *America, Britain, and Russia*, p. 658; Dean Acheson, *Sketches from Life of Men I Have Known*, p. 62; Byrnes' speech is in U.S. Dept. of State, *Bulletin* 14:483.

55. *New York Times*, March 9, 1946, p. 3.

56. London Embassy to Secretary, March 8, 1946, 711.41/3-846, SDR.

57. Minutes, meeting of the Secretaries of State, Army, and Navy, Feb. 28, 1946, Secretary of the Army Subject File, 1945–47, RG 107, MMRD; Williams, *Twilight of Empire*, p. 164. Also see Keynes' satisfaction at Churchill's efforts on behalf of the credit in Harrod, *Life of Keynes*, p. 620.

58. Byrnes to Halifax, April 19, 1946, *FRUS*, 1946, 5:28; memorandum of conversation, May 2, 1946, *ibid.*, p. 39.

59. Hickerson to Acheson, May 23, 1946, *ibid.*, p. 46.

60. Lincoln to Hull, May 2, 1946, *ibid.*, p. 36; memorandum of conversation, May 2, 1946, *ibid.*, p. 39; Hickerson to Acheson, May 23, 1946, *ibid.*, p. 46; Cabinet Conclusions, May 6, 1946, CAB 128/5.

61. Memorandum by Holden Furber, Mar. 19, 1946, *FRUS*, 1946, 5:23.

62. U.S. Senate, *Congressional Record*, 79th Cong., 2d sess., 1946, vol. 92, pt. 3, p. 4079.

63. *Public Opinion Quarterly*, 10:262; Gardner, *Sterling-Dollar Diplomacy*, p. 236; McNaughton Reports, April 19, 1946, McNaughton Papers.

64. Halifax quote in Birkenhead, *Halifax*, p. 558; "Washington Loan Prospects," D. P. T. Jay to Attlee, May 7, 1946, PREM 8/195; Cabinet Conclusions, May 9, 1946, CAB 128/5. For a prediction by a former Chancellor of the Exchequer of what rejection would mean to Britain and to Anglo-American relations, see Harold Nicolson, *Diaries and Letters*, 3:53.

65. Herter quoted in Gardner, *Sterling-Dollar Diplomacy*, p. 250. For the State Department's reluctance to defend the credit by appealing to fears concerning Soviet actions, see *Atlanta Constitution*, July 5, 1946, p. 10.

66. But the crucial ballot had been considerably closer, with administration forces defeating McFarland's amendment demanding extensive rights at British military installations around the world by a scant five votes. For this see Hedlund, "Congress and the British Loan," pp. 117–20.

67. *New York Times*, June 13, 1946, p. 1.

68. Gardner, *Sterling-Dollar Diplomacy*, p. 251; Stevens, *American Zionism*, p. 117.

69. McNaughton Reports, July 5, 1946, McNaughton Papers. Also see Stewart Alsop's column in the *Atlanta Constitution*, July 5, 1946, p. 10.

70. McCormack remark in McNaughton Reports, July 13, 1946, McNaughton Papers; Robertson quote in U.S. House of Representatives, *Congressional Record*, 79th Cong., 2d sess., 1946, vol. 92, pt. 11, pp. A2868–69.

71. *New York Times*, July 14, 1946, p. 3. For further discussion of the importance of the Russian factor in passing the credit, see Gardner, *Sterling-Dollar Diplomacy*, p. 252; Hedlund, "Congress and the British Loan," pp. 160–164, 173–74; Halifax to Foreign Office, March 23, 1946, AN 840/1/45, F.O. 371.

72. Hedlund, "Congress and the British Loan," pp. 123–25, 171–73. Celler quote in *ibid.*, p. 148.

13. THE REIGN OF AMBIVALENCE

1. For contemporary assessments of Byrnes' thinking along these lines, see *U.S. News*, March 1, 1946, p. 64; Diary, Jan. 1, 1946, Leahy Papers; undated notes [Jan. 1946] in Davies Papers, cited in Messer, "Making of a Cold Warrior," p. 390; *The Economist*, Jan. 5, 1946, pp. 3–4.

2. Patricia Dawson Ward, *The Threat of Peace: James F. Byrnes and the Council of Foreign Ministers, 1945–1946*, p. 85.

3. Anderson, "Britain, the United States, and the Cold War," p. 206. Translating these twin objectives into concrete policy proved difficult at times. In June, for instance, the State Department directed the American ambassador in Iran to discourage any joint Anglo-American action in that troubled country. But then in the very next sentence this cable acknowledged the fact that Great Britain and the United States had similar interests in Iran and urged the embassy staff to remain in close contact with British officials there. See Acheson to George V. Allen, June 20, 1946, *FRUS*, 1946, 7:502.

4. George Kennan's "Long Telegram" is usually credited with a prominent role in this transition in United States policy in the direction of a stronger stand toward the Soviet Union. Still unexamined, however, are the striking similarities between Kennan's dispatch and those being cabled to London at the same time by Frank Roberts, Kennan's close friend and opposite number in the British embassy in Moscow. Compare, for instance, the Long Telegram with Roberts'

wires to Bevin of March 14, 17, and 18, 1946, N 4065, N 4156, and N 4157/ 97/38 respectively, F.O. 371. One recent study has briefly hinted at the significance of this collaboration between the two diplomats, but an extended analysis of their relationship may show that this British official had a far greater impact on the Washington decision-making process—and on the movement toward cold war—than anyone has heretofore imagined. Kennan's telegram is in *FRUS*, 1946, 6:696–709. For its impact see Kennan, *Memoirs*, pp. 308–10; and Gaddis, *The United States and the Origins of the Cold War*, pp. 302–4. For the Kennan-Roberts association, Anderson, "Britain, the United States, and the Cold War," p. 166; Peter G. Boyle, "The British Foreign Office View of Soviet-American Relations, 1945–46," p. 310; Roberts to D. F. A. Warner, March 2, 1946, N 3369/97/38, F.O. 371; Warner to Roberts, May 4, 1946, N 4157/97/38, *ibid.*

5. Minute by B. E. F. Gage, May 17, 1946, AN 1515/1/45, F.O. 371; Balfour to Christopher Warner, June 24, 1946, N 8694/97/38, *ibid.* Also cf. Boyle, "The British Foreign Office View of Soviet-American Relations," pp. 309–10.

6. *New York Times*, May 31, 1946, p. 8; D. D. Maclean to Paul Mason, June 4, 1946, AN 1827/15/45, F.O. 371.

7. Inverchapel to Foreign Office, Sept. 30, 1946, AN 3065/1/45, F.O. 371; Halifax cable in Anderson, "Britain, the United States, and the Cold War," p. 201; C. M. Woodhouse, *British Foreign Policy Since the Second World War*, p. 18.

8. Unidentified minute, April 16, 1946, AN 3509/5/45, F.O. 371.

9. Minute by Gage, May 24, 1946, AN 1566/1/45, *ibid.*; minute by Donnelly, April 30, 1946, AN 1269/1/45, *ibid.*

10. *Washington Post*, Feb. 13, 1947, p. 13.

11. *The Economist*, Feb. 23, 1946, p. 282.

12. Somerville's proposal is in JIS 232, Feb. 13, 1946, CCS dec. files, 1946–47: CCS 350.05, RG 218, MMRD. Also Diary, Feb. 8, 1946, March 7, 1946, Leahy Papers; Forrestal, *Diaries*, p. 183.

13. Alfred Goldberg, "The Military Origins of the British Nuclear Deterrent," p. 601; R. M. Rosecrance, "British Defense Strategy: 1945–1952," in Rosecrance, *Dispersion of Nuclear Weapons*, pp. 68–70; Christopher John Bartlett, *The Long Retreat: A Short History of British Defence Policy, 1945–70*, p. 20. A further consideration also pushed the British in the direction of military collaboration with the United States. If they failed to achieve agreement regarding standardization of arms with the Americans, this would adversely affect not only Anglo-American strategic coordination, but also Anglo-Canadian, for senior military officers in Ottawa had indicated that they were likely to adopt equipment of United States rather than British design if forced to choose between the two. See minute by J. E. Stephenson, Oct. 25, 1945, D.O. 35/1746.

14. "Foreign Policy of Great Britain—Anglo-American Relations," Feb. 18, 1947, 711.41/2-2047, SDR. In circulating this document, the Navy requested that particular care be exercised to safeguard its contents because of "the unorthodox manner" in which it was obtained, a warning which arouses but hardly satisfies the curiosity.

15. Quoted in Winant to Secretary, March 8, 1946, 711.41/3-846, *ibid.* For similar sentiments later in the year, see Harriman to Secretary, June 4, 1946, 711.41/6-446, *ibid.*; *The Economist*, Sept. 21, 1946, p. 442.

16. Gowing, *Independence and Deterrence*, p. 91.

17. *New York Times*, Jan. 11, 1946, p. 3.

18. Diary, Dec. 7, 1945, Dalton Papers.

19. Hickerson memorandum, March 13, 1946, *FRUS*, 1946, 5:14, 16; memorandum of conversation, March 19, 1946, *ibid.*, p. 21; "U.S. Military Bases in Countries Dealt with by the Office of European Affairs," Jan. 16, 1947, Records of the Office of European Affairs, SDR.

20. See Halifax to Bevin, Dec. 12, 1945, AN 3853/35/45, F.O. 371 for an expression of this.

21. Minute by G. O. B. Davies, Oct. 14, 1946, D.O. 35/2044; Robert L. Smyth, Counselor of Embassy, Nanking, to Secretary, July 15, 1946, 711.41/7-1546, SDR; Iriye, *The Cold War in Asia*, p. 126.

22. Hickerson memorandum, May 24, 1946, Records of the Office of European Affairs, SDR.

23. John Russell Minter, American Chargé, Canberra, to Secretary, April 13, 1946, *FRUS*, 1946, 5:28; Gallman to Secretary, April 25, 1946, *ibid.*, p. 33; Matthews memorandum, May 2, 1946, *ibid.*, pp. 38–39; Acheson to Truman, May 7, 1946, *ibid.*, p. 41.

24. Winant to the Secretary, Feb. 20, 1946, 611.11B31/2-2046, SDR; Gardner, *Sterling-Dollar Diplomacy*, p. 353.

25. Diary, Aug. 1, 1946, Dalton Papers; *The Economist*, Nov. 23, 1946, p. 818.

26. Quoted in Gardner, *Sterling-Dollar Diplomacy*, p. 267. For Keynes' discouragement, see "The Savannah Conference on the Bretton Woods Final Act," March 27, 1946, CAB 78/37. Even a ranking American official, Harry Dexter White, protested that the American insistence upon dominating the Bretton Woods institutions "resembles much too closely the operation of power politics rather than of international cooperation." See Gardner, *Economic Aspects of New Deal Diplomacy*, p. 290.

27. Memorandum for the files, Dec. 31, 1946, folder "United Kingdom— trade, 1946–48," John W. Snyder Papers, HSTL. Also see O'Connell and Overby to Snyder, Dec. 10, 1946, *ibid.*

28. Clair Wilcox to the Secretary, Dec. 27, 1946, *FRUS*, 1946, 1:1363.

29. Dalton, *High Tide*, p. 166; "Germany: Memorandum by the Chancellor of the Exchequer," Oct. 18, 1946, C.P. (46) 385, CAB 129/13.

30. Williams, *Twilight of Empire*, p. 148; Woodhouse, *British Foreign Policy*, p. 17.

31. See, for example, "Pooling of Food Supplies between the Occupied Zones of Western Germany," April 2, 1946, folder "Memoranda of Conversation," box 4, Clayton-Thorp Files. At least one Washington official recognized the incongruity of abruptly terminating lend-lease to the British in August 1945

and subsequently conducting what was in effect a large-scale lend-lease operation in Germany for the benefit of America's principal enemy. See Raynor to Matthews, March 6, 1946, Records of the Office of European Affairs, SDR.

32. Lucius D. Clay, *Decision in Germany*, p. 78.

33. Memorandum of conversation, Nov. 29, 1946, *FRUS*, 1946, 5:644–46.

34. Diary, Oct. 3, 1946, Dalton Papers.

35. Memorandum of conversation, Nov. 19, 1946, folder "Memoranda of Conversation," box 4, Clayton-Thorp Files.

36. Draft letter, Patterson to Byrnes, Nov. 19, 1946, Office of the Assistant Secretary of War, dec. files 1940–47: ASW 091.31, RG 107, MMRD; Byrnes, *Speaking Frankly*, pp. 195–97; Bevin to Foreign Office, Nov. 17, 1946, C 14102/13325/18, F.O. 371. Byrnes' sympathies on this issue may also have been tempered by the fact that London authorities had been so insistent, over strenuous objections from Roosevelt, on retaining the northwestern zone for themselves in the first place.

37. Memorandum of conversation, Nov. 19, 1946, folder "Memoranda of Conversation," box 4, Clayton-Thorp Files.

38. Memorandum for the Files, Dec. 2, 1946, folder "United Kingdom—general, 1946–49," box 34, Snyder Papers.

39. See chapter 11 above.

40. "Atomic Energy," memorandum by Byrnes, n.d., folder 596, Byrnes Papers; Truman to Attlee, April 20, 1946, *FRUS*, 1946, 1:1235–37.

41. See David E. Lilienthal, *Journals*, vol. 2: *The Atomic Energy Years, 1945–1950*, p. 26.

42. Groves to Byrnes, Feb. 13, 1946, *FRUS*, 1946, 1:1205; Acheson, *Present at the Creation*, p. 166; Schnabel, *Joint Chiefs of Staff*, pp. 296–97. For American dismay over the Canadian espionage case, see *Newsweek*, March 4, 1946, p. 46.

43. Gowing, *Independence and Deterrence*, p. 109.

44. Some years later, when Churchill informed Senator McMahon of the Hyde Park agreement, the American responded that had he known of its existence in 1946, he would never have sponsored the legislation bearing his name. Normanbrook, *Action This Day*, p. 122.

45. Attlee to Truman, April 16, 1946, *FRUS*, 1946, 1:1231–32; Attlee to Truman, June 7, 1946, *ibid.*, pp. 1249–53; Gowing, *Independence and Deterrence*, pp. 105–7. Acheson realized that the McMahon Act violated previous American pledges to the British but does not seem to have fought very hard to secure a more liberal policy. Harriman privately thought the act "shameful" and later claimed that he did what he could to continue atomic sharing between the two nations, but he, too, was unsuccessful in interesting any of his superiors in this. Acheson, *Present at the Creation*, pp. 164–65; Harriman and Abel, *Special Envoy*, p. 551.

46. See, for example, "Estimate of British Post-War Capabilities and Intentions," Feb. 13, 1946, CCS geog. files, 1942–45: CCS 000.1 Gr. Britain, RG 218, MMRD; JLC 400/2, Aug. 14, 1946, CCS 004.3, *ibid.*; "Comments of the

Embassy at Moscow with respect to the Policy and Information Statement on Great Britain on March 15, 1946," April 22, 1946, 711.41/4-2346, SDR; Matthews memorandum, April 1, 1946, *FRUS*, 1946, 1:1170.

47. C.O.S. (45) 670 (0), Nov. 22, 1945, CAB 80/98.

48. Memorandum for the Chief of Staff, Feb. 8, 1946, ABC 381 United Nations, RG 165, MMRD.

49. Yergin, *Shattered Peace*, p. 445, n. 36.

50. J. S. M. Washington to Cabinet Offices, Jan. 11, 1946 and Feb. 9, 1946, CAB 105/51.

51. J. S. M. Washington to Cabinet Offices, Feb. 9, 1946, *ibid.* Also consult Eisenhower, *Papers*, 7:1158.

52. J. S. M. Washington to Cabinet Offices, Feb. 14, 1946, CAB 105/51; C.O.S. (46) 81st Meeting, May 22, 1946, CAB 79/48; C.O.S. (46) 91st Meeting, June 11, 1946, CAB 79/49.

53. J. S. M. Washington to Cabinet Offices, Feb. 14, 1946, CAB 105/51; Memorandum for Col. Bonesteel, April 27, 1946, ABC 381 United Nations, RG 165, MMRD.

54. Eisenhower, *Papers*, 7:1157–58; Leahy quoted in J. S. M. Washington to Cabinet Offices, March 16, 1946, CAB 105/52.

55. SWNCC 206/40, Jan. 30, 1947, CCS dec. files, 1946–47: CCS 350.05, RG 218, MMRD.

56. SWNCC 206/9, Jan. 31, 1946, *ibid.*; JCS 927/26, Feb. 22, 1946, *ibid.*; JIC 370/1, Nov. 31, 1946, *ibid.*

57. "Report on the British Army Staff (Washington) by Lieutenant-General Sir Gordon N. Macready. . . ," Jan. 17, 1946, W.O. 32/12178.

58. C.O.S. (46) 110 (0), April 9, 1946, CAB 80/101. Also "Situation Report on Collaboration U.K.-U.S.A. Defence Field—Air Technical," Notes by Air Vice-Marshal L. M. Iles, May 29, 1946, CAB 122/1378.

59. D.C.O.S. (46) 15th Meeting, May 8, 1946, CAB 122/1378.

60. C.O.S. (46) 91st Meeting, June 11, 1946, CAB 79/49.

61. "B.A.S. Notes on Exchange of Information U.S.A. to U.K.," June 28, 1946, CAB 122/1378.

62. Inverchapel to Foreign Office, Sept. 17, 1946, AN 2857/7/45, F.O. 371; Montgomery, *Memoirs*, pp. 440–41.

63. Montgomery spent only fifteen minutes with Truman during his September 11 appointment. This would hardly have given him sufficient time to make an appeal for collaboration except on the most general and innocuous terms. Moreover, at their meeting on October 30, the British Chiefs of Staff were still discussing ways to persuade the Americans of the desirability of a policy of cooperation. On this see C.O.S. (46) 159th Meeting, Oct. 30, 1946, CAB 79/52.

64. American naval authorities also initiated similar arrangements with Canada, Australia, New Zealand, and South Africa.

65. For these developments, see J. S. M. Washington to Cabinet Offices,

Dec. 20, 1946, CAB 105/52; Gowing, *Independence and Deterrence*, p. 117; Rosecrance, *Defense of the Realm*, p. 49.

66. For other details on this domestic challenge to Attlee's foreign policies, see Bernard Donoughue and G. W. Jones, *Herbert Morrison: Portrait of a Politician*, p. 387; Elaine Windrich, *British Labour's Foreign Policy*, p. 187; Watt, *Personalities and Policies*, p. 66. The October 29 letter to Attlee may be found in N 14755/97/38, F.O. 371.

67. C. M. (46) 97th Conclusions, Nov. 18, 1946, CAB 128/8; Prime Minister's Office to J.P.E.C. Henniker, Nov. 24, 1946, AN 3938/101/45, F.O. 371; Eisenhower, *Papers*, 7:1345.

68. Montgomery to Eisenhower, March 6, 1947, Personal Files, 1916–52: Principal Files, box 75, Dwight D. Eisenhower Papers, Dwight D. Eisenhower Library; Inverchapel to Foreign Office, Nov. 20, 1946, AN 3641/15/45, F.O. 371; minute to Brigadier Price, JSM, Nov. 20, 1946, CAB 122/1378.

69. Clifford's memorandum has been reprinted in Arthur Krock, *Memoirs: Sixty Years on the Firing Line*, pp. 419–82. Truman, fearing the consequences of a leak, quietly buried the report.

70. Minute by Paul Mason, Jan. 8, 1946, AN 3853/35/45, F.O. 371; diary, Feb. 18, 1946, Dalton Papers. For Foreign Office worries about a Republican-dominated Congress, see minute by F. B. A. Rundall, Oct. 15, 1946, AN 3114/1/45, F.O. 371; and minute by Nevile Butler, Nov. 13, 1946, AN 3389/1/45, *ibid.*

71. Princeton Seminars, July 2, 1953, Dean Acheson Papers, HSTL; Bohlen, *Witness to History*, p. 248.

72. "The Savannah Conference on the Bretton Woods Final Act," March 27, 1946, CAB 78/37; Forrestal, *Diaries*, p. 267. For a similar complaint from within the State Department, see Coordinating Committee minutes, Sept. 7, 1945, folder 584, Byrnes Papers.

73. For illustrations of this continued distrust at the popular level, see Gallup, *The Gallup Poll*, 1:601; Robert G. Kaiser, *Cold Winter, Cold War*, p. 183; *Chicago Daily Tribune* editorial, quoted in Eisenhower, *Papers*, 7:1155.

74. Consult Eisenhower, *Papers*, 7:1121–22 for a striking example of this.

14. MIDDLE EAST MORASS

1. For a recent examination of the committee's work, see Leonard Dinnerstein, "America, Britain, and Palestine: The Anglo-American Committee of Inquiry and the Displaced Persons, 1945–46." A copy of its report is in the *New York Times*, May 1, 1946, pp. 15–21. This may also be found in OF 204-B, Truman Papers. Two members of the committee have published accounts of the investigation. For the perspective of one of the Americans, see Bartley C. Crum, *Behind the Silken Curtain*. A British colleague's recollections are in Richard Crossman, *Palestine Mission: A Personal Record*. Crum emphasizes the friction within the committee between nationals of the two countries much more than

Crossman does. While at Lausanne writing the final report, Crum even convinced himself that his telephone was being tapped by unknown or unspecified persons. See Niles to Connelly, April 16, 1946, OF 204, Truman Papers. Also helpful is Halifax to Foreign Office, April 23, 1946, E 3634/4/31, F.O. 371.

2. Byrnes memorandum to Truman, April 19, 1946, *FRUS*, 1946, 7:585; Statement by the President, April 30, 1946, in *Public Papers of the Presidents: Harry S. Truman, 1946*, pp. 218–19.

3. Francis Williams, *Ernest Bevin: Portrait of a Great Englishman*, p. 260; Bevin to Attlee, April 30, 1946, E 3921/4/31, F.O. 371; Bevin to Foreign Office, May 1, 1946, E 3967/4/31, *ibid*.

4. D. O. (46) 14th Meeting, April 24, 1946, E 3839/4/31, F.O. 371; Dinnerstein, "America, Britain, and Palestine," p. 297; Attlee's statement in the House is reported in Harriman to Secretary, May 1, 1946, *FRUS*, 1946, 7:589–90. Also see British Embassy, Jedda, to Foreign Office, April 23, 1946, E 3663/4/31, F.O. 371.

5. Matthews memorandum, April 27, 1946, *FRUS*, 1946, 7:587–88; Byrnes to the President, May 9, 1946, *ibid*., pp. 601–2.

6. See chapter 12 above.

7. Bethell, *The Palestine Triangle*, pp. 234, 238; Dinnerstein, "America, Britain, and Palestine," p. 298.

8. Leo R. Sack to Charles Ross, Oct. 25, 1945, OF 204, Truman Papers.

9. Truman to Myron C. Taylor, May 27, 1946, *ibid*. Also see memorandum by Maj. Gen. John H. Hilldring, Assistant Secretary of State for Occupied Areas, May 3, 1946, *FRUS*, 1946, 7:591; Acheson, *Present at the Creation*, p. 173.

10. Notes on Cabinet Meeting, Feb. 1, 1946, folder "Cabinet Meetings, Agenda, Notes," Secretary of the Army Subject File, 1945–47, RG 107, MMRD.

11. Intelligence estimate on Palestine, May 18, 1946, CCS geog. files, 1946–47: CCS 092, RG 218, *ibid*.

12. Truman, *Years of Trial and Hope*, p. 149; SWNCC 311, June 21, 1946, *FRUS*, 1946, 7:631–33. For public disapproval of the idea of sending troops to Palestine, see Cantril and Strunk, *Public Opinion*, p. 370.

13. Ismay to Attlee, May 8, 1946, E 4623/4/31, F.O. 371.

14. Attlee to Truman, June 14, 1946, *FRUS*, 1946, 7:627.

15. A copy of these recommendations is in *ibid*., pp. 652–67.

16. For one particularly stormy session between Truman and several Zionist supporters over this matter, see James G. McDonald, *My Mission in Israel, 1948–1951*, p. 11.

17. Truman, *Years of Trial and Hope*, p. 152; Wallace, *Price of Vision*, pp. 603–7.

18. Wallace, *Price of Vision*, pp. 604, 606.

19. Byrnes to the President, July 30, 1946, *FRUS*, 1946, 7:675. Also see Diary, July 31, 1946, Leahy Papers.

20. Acheson memorandum, July 30, 1946, *FRUS*, 1946, 7:673–74; Truman to Attlee, Aug. 12, 1946, *ibid*., p. 682.

21. Paul E. Fitzpatrick to Truman, Aug. 2, 1946, folder "Political—1946 Campaign," White House file, Papers of Philleo Nash, HSTL.

22. Connelly to the President, July 30, 1946, OF 204-C, Truman Papers; Acheson, *Present at the Creation*, p. 175; McDonald, *My Mission in Israel*, p. 11.

23. Truman, *Years of Trial and Hope*, p. 153.

24. Wallace, *Price of Vision*, p. 607.

25. Byrnes to the President, July 31, 1946, *FRUS*, 1946, 7:675.

26. Gallup, *The Gallup Poll*, 1:604; Kaiser, *Cold Winter, Cold War*, p. 43; Robert J. Donovan, *Conflict and Crisis: The Presidency of Harry S. Truman, 1945–1948*, p. 229.

27. Truman's appointments calendar may be found in Matthew J. Connelly Office Files, HSTL. Byrnes himself later attributed Truman's subsequent actions to this fear of a Republican victory in New York. See Forrestal, *Diaries*, p. 347.

28. Wallace R. Deuel in *Miami Herald*, Feb. 28, 1947, clipping found in OF 204, Truman Papers.

29. Forrestal, *Diaries*, pp. 309–10.

30. Niles has only within the past few years begun to receive the intense scrutiny which historians have accorded other members of the Truman administration. Cf. Snetsinger, *Truman, the Jewish Vote, and the Creation of Israel*, pp. 35–39; and Francis H. Heller, ed., *The Truman White House: The Administration of the Presidency, 1945–1953*, pp. 53–54. The title of a 1949 magazine article, "Mr. Truman's Mystery Man," conveys a sense of his preference for operating behind the scenes. See Alfred Steinberg's portrait in *The Saturday Evening Post*, pp. 24ff. Of particular help in documenting Niles' influence on the Palestinian issue is a letter from Eliahu Epstein, a representative of the Jewish Agency for Palestine, to Dr. Nahum Goldman, an important Zionist leader. Epstein does not call Niles by name, referring to him only as "our friend," but the content of the letter leaves little doubt that it is Niles about whom he is writing. See Epstein to Goldman, Oct. 9, 1946, Chaim Weizmann Archives, copy deposited in HSTL.

31. Attlee to Truman, Oct. 3, 1946, *FRUS*, 1946, 7:704.

32. Bevin to Attlee, Oct. 4, 1946, E 9966/4/31, F.O. 371; Bevin to Attlee, Oct. 4, 1946, E 9999/4/31, *ibid.*

33. A copy of this may be found in U.S. Dept. of State, *Bulletin*, 15:669–70.

34. Aide mémoire for General of the Army Eisenhower, Oct. 10, 1946, P&O dec. file 1946–48, 337, RG 319, MMRD; Attlee to Truman, Oct. 4, 1946, *FRUS*, 1946, 7:705.

35. Celler to Truman, Oct. 7, 1946, OF 204, Truman Papers. In this regard Celler proved to be a very poor forecaster. As a political gambit Truman's statement was notoriously ineffectual. Dewey merely responded with a demand for the immediate immigration "not of 100,000, but of several hundreds of thousands." See *New York Times*, Oct. 7, 1946, p. 1. The November elections were as disastrous for the Democrats, both nationally and in New York state, as the most pessimistic White House officials had feared. Dewey was returned

to the governor's mansion for another term by an overwhelming majority, carrying with him practically the entire statewide ticket, including New York's first Republican United States senator in twenty years.

36. *New York Herald Tribune*, Oct. 6, 1946, 2:6; Reston in *New York Times*, Oct. 7, 1946, p. 4; *Washington Post*, Oct. 7, 1946, p. 8.

37. Truman, *Years of Trial and Hope*, p. 154; Truman to Attlee, Oct. 10, 1946, *FRUS*, 1946, 7:706–7.

38. Haron, "Anglo-American Relations and the Question of Palestine," p. 96. In his memoirs Acheson supports Truman in rejecting these charges of political expediency, but in 1946 he was more candid, informing the British embassy that the President had yielded to pressure from Democratic party officials and New York Jews, and specifically mentioning the threat posed by Dewey's anticipated speech backing the Zionists. See Acheson, *Present at the Creation*, p. 176; Inverchapel to Foreign Office, Oct. 3, 1946, E 9938/4/31, F.O. 371; Inverchapel to Foreign Office, Oct. 4, 1946, E 9987/4/31, *ibid.* In May of the following year, Truman himself wrote Niles: "We could have settled this Palestine thing if U.S. politics had been kept out of it." Donovan, *Conflict and Crisis*, p. 319.

39. British embassy, Bucharest, to Foreign Office, May 8, 1946, E 4266/4/31, F.O. 371; Diary, Aug. 1, 1946, Dalton Papers; C.O.S. (46) 97th Meeting, June 24, 1946, CAB 79/49.

40. "British Proposals in connection with the Inquiry Report," June 18, 1946, CCS geog. files, 1946–47, CCS 092, RG 218, MMRD. Also Report XL38002, Jan. 5, 1946, Office of Strategic Services, RG 226, *ibid.*; Schnabel, *Joint Chiefs of Staff*, p. 151.

41. Crum, *Silken Curtain*, pp. 8, 33. Also see Crossman, *Palestine Mission*, p. 18.

42. Memorandum by Fraser Wilkins, Jan. 14, 1947, *FRUS*, 1947, 5:1004. Of course there is some question as to how much of this reflected sincere apprehensions about an expanded Soviet presence in the Middle East and how much was simply one more rationale dredged up to defend the pro-Arab sentiments held by most of the State Department's Near East specialists. Undoubtedly the two were tightly entwined. It is worth noting, however, that other officials, particularly in the military, who had never before expressed any sort of a commitment to the Arabs also voiced a concern over Russian intentions in the area.

43. C.O.S. (46) 169th Meeting, Nov. 20, 1946, CAB 79/53.

44. Acheson memorandum, Jan. 28, 1947, Records of the Office of European Affairs, SDR; London embassy to Department of State, April 16, 1947, 711.41/4-1647, *ibid.*; Williams, *Twilight of Empire*, p. 197.

45. D.O. (46) 14th Meeting, April 24, 1946, E 3839/4/31, F.O. 371; "Palestine," minute by R. G. Howe, Dec. 18, 1946, E 12394/4/31, *ibid.*

46. Acheson memorandum, Jan. 21, 1947, *FRUS*, 1947, 5:1008–11; Acheson, *Present at the Creation*, p. 179.

47. See Department of State to the British Embassy, Jan. 27, 1947, *FRUS*, 1947, 5:1014–15.

48. Marshall to Bevin, Feb. 21, 1947, *ibid.*, pp. 1054–55; *New York Times*, Feb. 25, 1947, p. 1.

49. U.K., Parliament, *Parliamentary Debates* (Commons), 5th series, 433 (1947):1906.

50. *Ibid.*, col. 1908. According to the London correspondent of the *New York Times*, Bevin's strong words were not extemporaneous charges uttered in the heat of debate, but had received Attlee's advance approval. See *New York Times*, Feb. 27, 1947, p. 4; Snetsinger, *Truman, the Jewish Vote, and the Creation of Israel*, p. 48.

51. U.S. Dept. of State, *Bulletin* (March 9, 1947), 16:449; *New York Times*, Feb. 27, 1947, p. 1; Bloom and Celler quotes in *ibid.*, Feb. 26, 1947, p. 1; examples of Republican support are in *ibid.*, Feb. 27, 1947, p. 4; *Washington Post*, Feb. 27, 1947. p. 10.

52. *The Economist*, March 1, 1947, p. 310; *Manchester Guardian* quoted in *Newsweek*, March 10, 1947, pp. 25–26.

53. Hickerson memorandum, March 28, 1947, Records of the Office of European Affairs, SDR.

54. William A. Eddy, American minister in Saudi Arabia, first reported this comment. It is quoted in Stevens, *American Zionism and U.S. Foreign Policy*, p. 138.

55. Merriam memorandum, Dec. 27, 1946, *FRUS*, 1946, 7:732–33.

56. Niles memorandum, May 27, 1946, OF 204, Truman Papers (my italics). Public opinion polls backed Niles in this assessment. In December 1945, only 5 percent of the Americans questioned thought the United States should permit more European immigrants than it had before the war. Another 32 percent felt the same number should be admitted, while 37 percent wanted fewer and 14 percent desired to see an end to all European immigration. Gallup, *The Gallup Poll*, 1:555. This survey, however, does not necessarily indicate that forceful leadership playing to American humanitarian instincts could not have persuaded Congress and the country to make an exception for the Jewish DPs.

57. For amplification of these points, see memorandum by G. L. Warren, Feb. 1, 1946, Records of the Office of European Affairs, SDR; memorandum by Gordon Merriam, Dec. 27, 1946, *FRUS*, 1946, 7:733.

58. Truman, *Year of Decisions*, p. 293.

59. Truman, *Years of Trial and Hope*, p. 56. Ernest R. May in his *"Lessons" of the Past: The Use and Misuse of History in American Foreign Policy*, p. 29, first drew my attention to this passage and its significance.

60. Acheson, *Present at the Creation*, p. 177.

61. On this see Bethell, *The Palestine Triangle*, p. 204; Haron, "Anglo-American Relations and the Question of Palestine," pp. 116–17.

62. Haron, "Anglo-American Relations and the Question of Palestine," p. 54.

15. INDEPENDENCE AND INTERDEPENDENCE

1. U.K., Parliament, *Parliamentary Debates* (Lords), 5th series, 145 (1947):1017.

2. For brief summaries of the British financial plight at the end of 1946, see Hickerson to Acheson, Feb. 19, 1947, 841.50/2-1947, SDR; Gardner, *Sterling-Dollar Diplomacy*, pp. 306–8; Mallalieu, *British Reconstruction*, p. 39. American assessments earlier in the year, particularly in the Treasury Department, had been considerably more optimistic and probably contributed to the slowness with which many Washington officials appreciated the extent of Britain's troubles. See William H. Taylor to Snyder, Aug. 1, 1946, folder "United Kingdom—trade, 1946–48," Snyder Papers; "British Export Drive," Taylor memorandum, Aug. 22, 1946, *ibid.*

3. "Rate of Exhaustion of the Dollar Credit," March 1947, Dalton Papers; quote in Dalton, *High Tide*, p. 5.

4. Secretary of State to Embassy in London, Jan. 18, 1947, *FRUS*, 1947, 3:2.

5. "Conservative Attack on British Export Drive," memorandum by F. Lisle Widman, Dec. 16, 1946, folder "United Kingdom—trade, 1946–48," Snyder Papers.

6. Rosecrance, "British Defense Strategy," p. 69; Bartlett, *The Long Retreat*, p. 12.

7. Goldberg, "The Military Origins of the British Nuclear Deterrent," p. 601.

8. Bryant, *Triumph in the West*, p. 383; Diary, March 22, 1946, Dalton Papers.

9. Bartlett, *The Long Retreat*, p. 16; Montgomery, *Memoirs*, p. 436.

10. U.K., *Statement Relating to Defence*, Cmd. 7042, p. 4.

11. Attlee, *As It Happened*, p. 238.

12. These events have been described in Dalton, *High Tide*, pp. 204–5; Kaiser, *Cold Winter, Cold War*, p. 29; Joseph M. Jones, *The Fifteen Weeks*, p. 79.

13. U.K., *Economic Survey for 1947*, Cmd. 7046, p. 16; *The Times*, Feb. 22, 1947, p. 5.

14. Dalton to Snyder, Feb. 19, 1947, folder "United Kingdom—general, 1946–49," Snyder Papers.

15. Acheson to Marshall, Feb. 24, 1947, *FRUS*, 1947, 5:45.

16. British Embassy to Department of State, Feb. 21, 1947, *ibid.*, pp. 32–37.

17. Kaiser, *Cold Winter, Cold War*, pp. 106–7; quote in Dalton, *High Tide*, p. 206.

18. Dalton, *High Tide*, pp. 194, 197.

19. U.S. Senate, Committee on Foreign Relations, *Assistance to Greece and Turkey, hearings on S. 938*, 80th Cong., 1st sess., 1947, pp. 3–4; Byrnes, *Speaking Frankly*, p. 300.

20. Truman, *Years of Trial and Hope*, pp. 97, 99.

21. Byrnes to Acheson, Sept. 24, 1946, *FRUS*, 1946, 7:223–24. Also see Forrestal, *Diaries*, p. 210.

22. Meeting of the three Secretaries, Nov. 6, 1946, Office of the Secretary of the Army, subject file, 1945–47, RG 107, MMRD; Forrestal, *Diaries*, pp. 216–17; Acheson to MacVeagh, Nov. 8, 1946, *FRUS*, 1946, 7:263.

23. Truman, *Years of Trial and Hope*, p. 99; *FRUS*, 1947, 5:14–28 *passim*.

24. Jones, *Fifteen Weeks*, p. 131. Also consult David S. McLellan, *Dean Acheson: The State Department Years*, pp. 110–14. For numerous other public indications of official concern for the deteriorating situations in Greece and Turkey during these months, see Stephen G. Xydis, "America, Britain, and the USSR in the Greek Arena, 1944–1947," p. 590.

25. Gardner, *Sterling-Dollar Diplomacy*, p. 300; Durham to John A. Buchanan, March 25, 1947, folder 733, Carl T. Durham Papers, Southern Historical Collection, University of North Carolina.

26. Jones, *Fifteen Weeks*, p. 130.

27. Kaiser, *Cold Winter, Cold War*, p. 203; Marshall opinion in *ibid.*, p. 193.

28. Jones, *Fifteen Weeks*, p. 130.

29. Diary, March 7, 1947, Leahy Papers.

30. Dalton, *High Tide*, p. 209.

31. Jones, *Fifteen Weeks*, p. 151.

32. *Ibid.*, p. 139; "Questions regarding the request of Greece and Turkey for financial aid for rehabilitation," Sen. H. Alexander Smith to Vandenberg, March 17, 1947, folder: Aid to Greece and Turkey, box 91, H. Alexander Smith Papers, Princeton University; Committee on Foreign Relations, *Assistance to Greece and Turkey, Hearings*, pp. 12, 193, 221.

33. For an amplification of this, see Nicholas, *Britain and the U.S.A.*, p. 41.

34. U.K., Parliament, *Parliamentary Debates* (Commons), 5th series, 433 (1947):2304.

35. *New York Times*, Feb. 25, 1947, p. 1; Russell's proposal is in Kaiser, *Cold Winter, Cold War*, p. 187.

36. *New York Times*, March 12, 1947, p. 24.

37. "U.S. Relations With Greece," n.d., folder: Aid to Greece and Turkey, box 91, H. Alexander Smith Papers.

38. McNeill, *America, Britain, and Russia*, p. 757; memorandum by L. Berry, n.d. [March 1946], Records of the Office of European Affairs, SDR.

39. Thorne, "Indochina and Anglo-American Relations," p. 96; Leahy to Byrnes, March 13, 1946, Leahy files, Records of the JCS, RG 218, MMRD. Years later Loy Henderson, the State Department's Director of the Office of Near Eastern and African Affairs, was to recall that he never allowed any of the people working under him to press the British for independence for the empire—greater self-government, yes; but not independence. Conversation with the author, Washington, D.C., Aug. 15, 1975.

40. Truman, *Year of Decisions*, pp. 242–43.

41. Minute by Alan Dudley, Aug. 16, 1944, AN 3260/16/45, F.O. 371. State Department surveys indicated that the burning resentment over British impe-

rialism harbored by a relatively small proportion of the American public was accompanied by a much more extensive ignorance or apathy. See "A Pilot Study of American Sentiment Toward the British," March 29, 1943, 711.41/584, SDR; "Public Attitudes Toward Great Britain, 1940–1947," June 1947, 711.41/6-2547, *ibid.*

42. Minute by Sir Orme Sargent, Oct. 1, 1945, AN 2560/22/45, F.O. 371; Frank Roberts to Sargent, Oct. 23, 1945, N 14846/165/38, *ibid.*

43. U.K., Parliament, *Parliamentary Debates* (Commons), 5th series, 427 (1946):1521.

44. See Dilks, *Cadogan Diaries*, p. 674, for one expression of this.

45. Minute by J. C. Donnelly, March 23, 1945, AN 929/22/45, F.O. 371.

46. "Notes on a Visit to Washington," memorandum by R. A. Gallop, March 8, 1944, AS 1538/901/51, *ibid.*

47. On the minimal influence of public opinion on British foreign policy, see Kaiser, *Cold Winter. Cold War*, p. 100. Still, there were sufficient occasions—such as the backbench revolt in late 1946—to place in doubt the smug assumption that London's policy was largely impervious to undisciplined, emotional public outcry. As to the systemized fashion in devising policy with which Gallop credited Whitehall, a casual glance through Sir Alexander Cadogan's diary provides an arresting antidote to any tendency to overestimate the orderliness of this process. See Dilks, *Cadogan Diaries*, esp. pp. 653, 670, 684, 687, 693.

48. Minutes, Secretary's Staff Committee, March 1, 1945, box 235, Stettinius Papers.

49. Transcript of telephone conversation, Dec. 5, 1944, box 243, *ibid.* For similar expressions of admiration for British policy-making procedures, see Tony Satterthwaite, civil air attaché in London, to Hickerson, Feb. 7, 1945, Records of the Office of European Affairs, SDR; minutes, Secretary's Staff Committee, Feb. 24, 1945, box 235, Stettinius Papers; Gallman interview; Handy Oral History, interview IV, p. 19; Eisenhower, *Papers*, 7:657.

50. Moran, *Churchill*, p. 239.

51. Hull, *Memoirs*, 2:1472–73.

52. Davies to Ralph Blummenfeld, April 24, 1945, Chronological File, Davies Papers.

53. Hickerson to Stettinius, Nov. 2, 1944, *FRUS*, 1944, 3:70.

54. Minutes, Coordinating Committee, July 26, 1945, folder 584, Byrnes Papers.

55. Truman memorandum, May 21, 1945, quoted in Truman, *Harry S. Truman*, p. 253.

56. "Estimate of British Post-War Capabilities and Intentions," Feb. 13, 1946, CCS geog. files, 1942–45: CCS 000.1 Gr. Britain, RG 218, MMRD.

57. *The Economist*, Sept. 21, 1946, p. 442.

58. Memorandum of conversation, Aug. 20, 1945, 611.4131/5-146, SDR;

remarks by Redvers Opie, University of Cincinnati's 25th Annual Business and Professional Men's Group, March 29, 1946, box 157, Charles Taft Papers, Library of Congress.

59. *Aide-mémoire*, Feb. 6, 1947, *FRUS*, 1947, 4:528; Matthews memorandum, Feb. 7, 1947, Records of the Office of European Affairs, SDR. For a similar message on the military side, see Montgomery to Eisenhower, Feb. 1, 1947, Personal Files, 1916–1952: Principal Files, box 75, Eisenhower Papers. For concern in Washington that these talks might lead to a loosening of Anglo-American ties, see Hickerson to Matthews, Feb. 17, 1947, *FRUS*, 1947, 1:715–17; Raynor to Hickerson, April 25, 1947, 741.61/4-2547, SDR.

60. U.K. Parliament, *Parliamentary Debates* (Commons), 5th series, 433 (1947):2303.

61. John S. Fischer to Lauchlin Currie, July 20, 1944, folder "Phase Two," box 5, Clayton-Thorp Files.

Bibliography

The following is by no means designed to be an inclusive bibliography of all the published works relevant to this study, but is simply a listing of those volumes I found most useful in my researches.

GOVERNMENT ARCHIVES

United Kingdom. Public Record Office.
    Cabinet Office.
    Dominions Office.
    Foreign Office.
    Prime Minister's Office.
    Treasury.
    War Office.
United States. National Archives.
    Modern Military Records Division. RG 107, 165, 218, 319, 335.
    Office of Strategic Services. RG 59, 226.
    State Department. RG 59.
    State-War-Navy Coordinating Committee. RG 353.
    Treasury Department. RG 56.

MANUSCRIPT COLLECTIONS

Acheson, Dean. Truman Library, Independence, Mo.
Bailey, Josiah W. Duke University, Durham, N.C.

Balfour, Sir John. "Diadems Askew: A Diplomatic Cavalcade." Unpublished Manuscript. Foreign and Commonwealth Office Library, London.

Baruch, Bernard M. Princeton University, Princeton, N.J.

Berle, Adolf A. Roosevelt Library, Hyde Park, N.Y.

Byrnes, James F. Clemson University, Clemson, S.C.

Clapper, Raymond. Library of Congress, Washington, D.C.

Clay, Lucius D. Oral History Interview. U.S. Military History Institute, Carlisle Barracks, Pa.

Clayton-Thorp Files. Truman Library.

Connelly, Matthew J. Office Files. Truman Library.

Cox, Oscar. Roosevelt Library.

Dalton, Hugh. British Library of Political and Economic Science, London.

Davies, Joseph E. Library of Congress.

Dulles, John Foster. Princeton University.

Durham, Carl T. University of North Carolina, Chapel Hill, N.C.

Earley, James S. Truman Library.

Eisenhower, Dwight D. Eisenhower Library, Abilene, Kan.

Fischer, Louis. Roosevelt Library.

Frankfurter, Felix. Library of Congress.

Halifax, 1st Earl of. Churchill College, Cambridge, England.

Handy, Thomas T. Oral History Interview. U.S. Army Military History Institute.

Hassett, William D. Roosevelt Library.

Hopkins, Harry L. Roosevelt Library.

Hull, Cordell. Library of Congress.

Krock, Arthur. Princeton University.

Leahy, William D. Library of Congress.

Lippmann, Walter. Yale University, New Haven, Conn.

McNaughton, Frank. Truman Library.

Morgenthau, Henry M., Jr. Roosevelt Library.

Nash, Philleo. Truman Library.

Pettengill, Samuel. University of Vermont, Burlington, Vt.

Roosevelt, Eleanor. Roosevelt Library.

Roosevelt, Franklin D. Roosevelt Library.

Rosenman, Samuel I. Roosevelt Library.

Rosenman, Samuel I. Truman Library.

Smith, H. Alexander. Princeton University.

Smith, Harold D. Roosevelt Library.

Snyder, John W. Truman Library.

Spaatz, Carl. Library of Congress.
Stettinius, Edward R., Jr. University of Virginia, Charlottesville, Va.
Stevenson, Adlai E. Princeton University.
Stimson, Henry L. Yale University.
Swing, Raymond Gram. Library of Congress.
Taft, Charles. Library of Congress.
Truman, Harry S. Truman Library.
Weizmann, Chaim. Photocopies in Truman Library.
White, Harry Dexter. Princeton University.
Winant, John G. Roosevelt Library.

GOVERNMENT PUBLICATIONS

U.K. *Economic Survey for 1947*, Cmd. 7046. London, 1947.
U.K. Parliament. *Parliamentary Debates.* 5th series. Annual volumes, 1941–1947.
U.K. *Statement Relating to Defence*, Cmd. 7042. London, 1947.
U.K. *Statistics Relating to the War Effort of the United Kingdom*, Cmd. 6564. London, 1944.
U.S. Board of Governors of the Federal Reserve System. *Federal Reserve Bulletin* (1946), vol. 32.
U.S. Commerce Department. Bureau of the Census. *Historical Statistics of the United States, Colonial Times to 1970.* Washington, 1975.
U.S. Congress. *Congressional Record.* Annual volumes, 1943–47, 1952.
U.S. House of Representatives. Committee on Banking and Currency. *Anglo-American Financial Agreement. Hearings on H.J. Res. 311.* 79th Cong., 2d sess., 1946.
——Special Committee on Postwar Economic Policy and Planning. *Economic Reconstruction in Europe.* H.R. 1205, 79th Cong., 1st sess., 1945.
U.S. Senate. Committee on Banking and Currency. *Anglo-American Financial Agreement. Hearings on S.J. Res. 138.* 79th Cong., 2d sess., 1946.
——Committee on Foreign Relations. *Assistance to Greece and Turkey. Hearings on S. 938.* 80th Cong., 1st sess., 1973.
——*A Decade of American Foreign Policy: Basic Documents, 1941–49.* S. Doc. 123, 81st Cong., 1st sess., 1950.
U.S. *Public Papers of the Presidents: Harry S. Truman, 1945–1946.* Washington, 1961, 1962.
——*Seventeenth Report to Congress on Lend-Lease Operations: Reverse Lend-Lease Aid from the British Commonwealth of Nations.* Washington, 1944.

U.S. State Department. *Anglo-American Financial and Commercial Agreements.* Commercial Policy Series Pubn. No. 2439 (1945).

——*Bulletin.* Vols. 6, 11–16 (1942–47).

——*The Far Eastern Commission,* by George H. Blakeslee. Far Eastern Series Pubn. No. 5138 (1953).

——*Foreign Relations of the United States.* Annual volumes, 1944–47.

——*Occupation of Japan: Policy and Progress.* Far Eastern Series Pubn. No. 267 (1946).

——*Proposals for Expansion of World Trade and Employment.* Commercial Policy Series Pubn. No. 2411 (1945).

——*Why Lend to Britain?* Commercial Policy Series Pubn. No. 2468 (1946).

U.S. Treasury Department. *The Loan to Britain—A Sound Economic Step.* Address by Fred M. Vinson, Philadelphia, Pa., Jan. 9, 1946. Washington, 1946.

U.S. War Production Board. *Wartime Production Achievements and the Reconversion Outlook: Report of the Chairman.* Washington, 1945.

U.S., U.K., and Canada. Combined Production and Resources Board. *Combined Production: United States, United Kingdom, and Canada as of October 1, 1945.* Washington, 1946.

PRINTED SOURCES

Acheson, Dean. *Among Friends: Personal Letters of Dean Acheson.* Edited by David S. McLellan and David C. Acheson. New York: Dodd, Mead, 1980.

——*Present at the Creation: My Years in the State Department.* New York: Norton, 1969.

——*Sketches from Life of Men I Have Know.* New York: Harper, 1959.

Adams, Henry H. *Harry Hopkins: A Biography.* New York: Putnam, 1977.

Adler, Selig. "American Policy vis-á-vis Palestine in the Second World War." In James E. O'Neill and Robert W. Krauskopf, eds., *World War II: An Account of Its Documents.* Washington, D.C.: Howard University Press, 1976.

Agar, Herbert. "Our Last Great Chance." *Survey Graphic* (May 1945), 34:153–57.

Aldcroft, Derek H. and Harry W. Richardson. *The British Economy, 1870–1939.* London: Macmillan, 1969.

Allen, Harry C. *Great Britain and the United States.* London: Odhams Press, 1954.

Ambrose, Stephen E. *The Supreme Commander: The War Years of General Dwight D. Eisenhower.* Garden City, N.Y.: Doubleday, 1970.

Anderson, Terry H. "Britain, the United States, and the Cold War, 1944–1947." Ph.D. dissertation, Indiana University, 1978.

Arnold, Henry H. *Global Mission.* New York: Harper, 1949.

Attlee, Clement R. *As It Happened.* New York: Viking Press, 1954.

——*The Labour Party in Perspective.* London: Victor Gollancz, 1937.

Baram, Phillip J. *The Department of State in the Middle East, 1919–1945.* Philadelphia: University of Pennsylvania Press, 1978.

Bartlett, Christopher John. *The Long Retreat: A Short History of British Defence Policy, 1945–70.* London: Macmillan, 1972.

Baruch, Bernard M. *Baruch: The Public Years.* New York: Holt, Rinehart & Winston, 1960.

Batt, William L. "British and American Opinion." *Vital Speeches* (February 15, 1945), 11:286–88.

Bellush, Bernard. *He Walked Alone: A Biography of John Gilbert Winant.* Foreword by Allan Nevins. The Hague: Mouton, 1968.

Beloff, Max. *New Dimensions in Foreign Policy: A Study in British Administrative Experience, 1947–59.* New York: Macmillan, 1961.

——"The Special Relationship: An Anglo-American Myth." In Martin Gilbert, ed., *A Century of Conflict, 1850–1950: Essays for A. J. P. Taylor.* New York: Atheneum, 1967.

Berle, Adolf A. *Navigating the Rapids, 1918–1971: From the Papers of Adolf A. Berle.* Edited by Beatrice Bishop Berle and Travis Beal Jacobs. New York: Harcourt Brace Jovanovich, 1973.

Bernstein, Barton J. "The Quest for Security: American Foreign Policy and International Control of Atomic Energy, 1942–1946." *Journal of American History* (March 1974), 60:1003–44.

——"The Uneasy Alliance: Roosevelt, Churchill, and the Atomic Bomb, 1940–1945." *Western Political Quarterly* (June 1976), 29:202–30.

Bernstein, Barton J., ed. *Politics and Policies of the Truman Administration.* Chicago: Quadrangle Books, 1970.

Bethell, Nicholas. *The Palestine Triangle: The Struggle for the Holy Land, 1935–48.* New York: Putnam, 1979.

Birkenhead, The Earl of. *Halifax.* London: Hamish Hamilton, 1965.

Birse, A. H. *Memoirs of an Interpreter.* New York: Coward-McCann, 1967.

Blackett, P. M. S. "America's Atomic Dilemma." In William Appleman Williams, ed., *The Shaping of American Diplomacy*. Chicago: Rand McNally, 1956.

Blum, John Morton. *From the Morgenthau Diaries: Years of War, 1941–1945*. Boston: Houghton Mifflin, 1967.

Bohlen, Charles E. *The Transformation of American Foreign Policy*. New York: Norton, 1969.

——*Witness to History, 1929–1969*. New York: Norton, 1973.

Borton, Hugh. *Japan's Modern Century*. New York: Ronald Press, 1955.

Boyle, Peter G. "The British Foreign Office View of Soviet-American Relations, 1945–46." *Diplomatic History* (Summer 1979), 3:307–20.

Brinton, Crane. *The United States and Britain*. Rev. ed. Cambridge: Harvard University Press, 1948.

Bryant, Arthur. *Triumph in the West, 1943–46*. London: The Reprint Society, 1959.

Buchan, Alastair. "Mothers and Daughters (or Greeks and Romans)." *Foreign Affairs*, (July 1976), 54:645–69.

Burns, James MacGregor. *Roosevelt: The Soldier of Freedom*. New York: Harcourt Brace Jovanovich, 1970.

Bush, Vannevar. *Pieces of the Action*. New York: William Morrow, 1970.

Byrnes, James F. *All in One Lifetime*. New York: Harper, 1958.

——"Byrnes Answers Truman." *Collier's* (April 26, 1952), 129:15.

——*Speaking Frankly*. New York: Harper, 1947.

Campbell, A. E. "The United States and Great Britain: Uneasy Allies." In John Braeman, Robert H. Bremner, and David Brody, eds., *Twentieth-Century American Foreign Policy*. Columbus: Ohio State University Press, 1971.

Campbell, Thomas M. *Masquerade Peace: America's UN Policy, 1944–1945*. Tallahassee: Florida State University Press, 1973.

Cantril, Hadley and Mildred Strunk. *Public Opinion, 1935–1946*. Princeton: Princeton University Press, 1951.

Churchill, Winston S. *The End of the Beginning: War Speeches*. Compiled by Charles Eade. Boston: Little, Brown, 1943.

——*The Second World War*. Vol. 6: *Triumph and Tragedy*. Boston: Houghton Mifflin, 1953.

Clark, William. *Less Than Kin: A Study of Anglo-American Relations*. Boston: Houghton Mifflin, 1957.

Clay, Lucius D. *Decision in Germany*. Garden City, N.Y.: Doubleday, 1950.

Clayton, William L. *Selected Papers*. Edited by Fredrick J. Dobney. Baltimore: Johns Hopkins University Press, 1971.

Clemens, Diane Shaver. *Yalta*. New York: Oxford University Press, 1970.

Coakley, Robert W. and Richard M. Leighton. *Global Logistics and Strategy, 1943–1945*. United States Army in World War II: The War Department. Washington: United States Army, 1968.

Cochran, Bert. *Harry Truman and the Crisis Presidency*. New York: Funk & Wagnalls, 1973.

Collier, Basil. *The Lion and the Eagle: British and Anglo-American Strategy, 1900–1950*. New York: Putnam, 1972.

Commager, Henry Steele, ed. *Britain Through American Eyes*. New York: McGraw-Hill, 1974.

Conant, James B. *My Several Lives: Memoirs of a Social Inventor*. New York: Harper & Row, 1970.

Cooke, Colin. *The Life of Richard Stafford Cripps*. London: Hodder & Stoughton, 1957.

Crossman, Richard. *Palestine Mission: A Personal Record*. New York: Harper, 1947.

Crum, Bartley C. *Behind the Silken Curtain*. New York: Simon & Schuster, 1947.

Cunningham, Sir Andrew. *A Sailor's Odyssey*. New York: Dutton, 1951.

Curry, George. *James F. Byrnes*. The American Secretaries of State and Their Diplomacy. Edited by Robert H. Ferrell. Vol. 14. New York: Cooper Square, 1965.

Dallek, Robert. *Franklin D. Roosevelt and American Foreign Policy, 1932–1945*. New York: Oxford University Press, 1979.

Dalton, Hugh. *High Tide and After: Memoirs, 1945–1960*. London: Frederick Muller, 1962.

Davis, Lynn Etheridge. *The Cold War Begins: Soviet-American Conflict over Eastern Europe*. Princeton: Princeton University Press, 1974.

Davis, Vincent. *Postwar Defense Policy and the U.S. Navy, 1943–1946*. Chapel Hill: University of North Carolina Press, 1962.

Dawson, Raymond and Richard Rosecrance. "Theory and Reality in the Anglo-American Alliance." *World Politics* (October 1966), 19:21–51.

DeNovo, John A. "The Culbertson Economic Mission and Anglo-American Tensions in the Middle East, 1944–1945." *Journal of American History* (March 1977), 63:913–36.

Dilks, David, ed. *The Diaries of Sir Alexander Cadogan, 1938–1945*. New York: Putnam, 1971.

Dinnerstein, Leonard. "America, Britain, and Palestine: The Anglo-American Committee of Inquiry and the Displaced Persons, 1945–46." *Diplomatic History* (Summer 1980), 4:283–301.

Divine, Robert A. *Second Chance: The Triumph of Internationalism in America During World War II.* New York: Atheneum, 1967.

Dixon, Piers. *The Life of Sir Pierson Dixon.* London: Hutchinson, 1968.

Donoughue, Bernard and G. W. Jones. *Herbert Morrison: Portrait of a Politician.* London: Weidenfeld & Nicolson, 1973.

Donovan, Robert J. *Conflict and Crisis: The Presidency of Harry S. Truman, 1945–1948.* New York: Norton, 1977.

Drury, Allen. *A Senate Journal, 1943–1945.* New York: McGraw-Hill, 1963.

Eckes, Alfred E., Jr. *A Search for Solvency: Bretton Woods and the International Monetary System, 1941–1971.* Austin: University of Texas Press, 1975.

Eden, Anthony. *The Reckoning: The Memoirs of Anthony Eden.* Boston: Houghton Mifflin, 1965.

Ehrman, John. *Grand Strategy, August 1943–September 1944.* Vol. 5, History of the Second World War. Edited by J. R. M. Butler. London: Her Majesty's Stationery Office, 1956.

——*Grand Strategy, October 1944–August 1945.* Vol. 6, History of the Second World War. Edited by J. R. M. Butler. London: Her Majesty's Stationery Office, 1956.

Eisenhower, Dwight D. *Crusade in Europe.* Garden City, N.Y.: Doubleday, 1948.

——*The Papers of Dwight David Eisenhower.* Edited by Alfred D. Chandler, Jr. et al. 9 vols. Baltimore: Johns Hopkins University Press, 1970–78.

Epstein, Leon D. *Britain—Uneasy Ally.* Chicago: University of Chicago Press, 1954.

Feis, Herbert. *Between War and Peace: The Potsdam Conference.* Princeton: Princeton University Press, 1960.

——*The Birth of Israel: The Tousled Diplomatic Bed.* New York: Norton, 1969.

——*Churchill—Roosevelt—Stalin: The War They Waged and the Peace They Sought.* Princeton: Princeton University Press, 1957.

——*From Trust to Terror: The Onset of the Cold War, 1945–1950.* New York: Norton, 1970.

——"On Our Economic Relations with Britain." *Foreign Affairs* (April 1943), 21:462–75.

——*Seen from E.A.: Three International Episodes.* New York: Knopf, 1947.

Ferrell, Robert H., ed. "Truman at Potsdam." *American Heritage* (June/July 1980), 31:36–47.

Forrestal, James V. *The Forrestal Diaries.* Edited by Walter Millis with the collaboration of E. S. Duffield. New York: Viking Press, 1951.

"The Fortune Survey." *Fortune* (Dec. 1945), 32:303.

Franklin, William M. "Zonal Boundaries and Access to Berlin." *World Politics* (October 1963), 16:1–31.

Freeland, Richard M. *The Truman Doctrine and the Origins of McCarthyism: Foreign Policy, Domestic Politics, and Internal Security, 1946–1948.* New York: Knopf, 1972.

Gaddis, John Lewis. *The United States and the Origins of the Cold War, 1941–1947.* New York: Columbia University Press, 1972.

Gallup, George H. *The Gallup Poll: Public Opinion, 1935–1971.* Vol. 1. New York: Random House, 1972.

Gardner, Lloyd C. *Architects of Illusion: Men and Ideas in American Foreign Policy, 1941–1949.* Chicago: Quadrangle, 1970.

——*Economic Aspects of New Deal Diplomacy.* Madison: University of Wisconsin Press, 1964.

Gardner, Richard H. *Sterling-Dollar Diplomacy.* Expanded ed. New York: McGraw-Hill, 1969.

Gladwyn, Lord. *The Memoirs of Lord Gladwyn.* New York: Weybright & Talley, 1972.

Goldberg, Alfred. "The Military Origins of the British Nuclear Deterrent." *International Affairs* (October 1964), 40:600–618.

Gore-Booth, Paul. *With Great Truth and Respect.* London: Constable, 1974.

Gormly, James L. "Keeping the Door Open in Saudi Arabia: The United States and the Dhahran Airfield, 1945–46." *Diplomatic History* (Spring 1980), 4:189–205.

——"Secretary of State James F. Byrnes: An Initial British Evaluation." *South Carolina Historical Magazine* (July 1978), 79:198–205.

Gosnell, Harold F. *Truman's Crises: A Political Biography of Harry S. Truman.* Westport, Conn.: Greenwood Press, 1980.

Gowing, Margaret. *Independence and Deterrence: Britain and Atomic Energy, 1945–1952.* Assisted by Lorna Arnold. Vol. 1: *Policy Making.* New York: St. Martin's Press, 1974.

Green, David. *The Containment of Latin America: A History of the Myths and Realities of the Good Neighbor Policy.* Chicago: Quadrangle, 1971.

Grew, Joseph C. *Turbulent Era: A Diplomatic Record of Forty Years,*

1904–1945. Edited by Walter Johnson. Vol. 2. Boston: Houghton Mifflin, 1952.

Groves, Leslie R. *Now It Can Be Told.* New York: Harper & Row, 1962.

Halifax, Lord. *Fullness of Days.* New York: Dodd, Mead, 1957.

Hancock, W. K. and M. M. Gowing. *British War Economy.* History of the Second World War. London: His Majesty's Stationery Office, 1949.

Haron, Miriam J. "Anglo-American Relations and the Question of Palestine, 1945–1947." Ph.D. dissertation, Fordham University, 1979.

Harriman, W. Averell and Elie Abel. *Special Envoy.* New York: Random House, 1975.

Harrod, Roy Forbes. *The Life of John Maynard Keynes.* New York: Harcourt, Brace, 1951.

Hedlund, Richard P. "Congress and the British Loan, 1945–1946: A Congressional Study." Ph.D. dissertation, University of Kentucky, 1976.

Heim, Keith M. "Hope Without Power: Truman and the Russians, 1945." Ph.D. dissertation, University of North Carolina, 1973.

Heller, Francis H., ed. *The Truman White House: The Administration of the Presidency, 1945–1953.* Lawrence: Regents Press of Kansas, 1980.

Herring, George C., Jr. *Aid to Russia, 1941–1946: Strategy, Diplomacy, the Origins of the Cold War.* New York: Columbia University Press, 1973.

——"The United States and British Bankruptcy, 1944–1945: Responsibilities Deferred." *Political Science Quarterly* (June 1971), 86:260–80.

Hewlett, Richard G. and Oscar E. Anderson, Jr. *A History of the United States Atomic Energy Commission.* Vol. 1: *The New World, 1939/1946.* University Park: Pennsylvania State University Press, 1962.

Hull, Cordell. *The Memoirs of Cordell Hull.* 2 vols. New York: Macmillan, 1948.

Iriye, Akira. *The Cold War in Asia: A Historical Introduction.* Englewood Cliffs, N.J.: Prentice-Hall, 1974.

Ismay, Hastings. *The Memoirs of General Lord Ismay.* New York: Viking Press, 1960.

Jones, Joseph M. *The Fifteen Weeks.* New York: Viking, 1955.

Kaiser, Robert G. *Cold Winter, Cold War.* New York: Stein and Day, 1974.

Kennan, George F. *Memoirs: 1925–1950.* Boston: Little, Brown, 1967.

Kimball, Warren F. "Churchill and Roosevelt: The Personal Equation." *Prologue* (Fall 1974), 6:169–82.

——"Lend-Lease and the Open Door: The Temptation of British Opulence, 1937–1942." *Political Science Quarterly* (June 1971), 86:232–59.

——*Swords or Ploughshares? The Morgenthau Plan for Defeated Nazi Germany, 1943–1946.* The America's Alternatives Series. Edited by Harold M. Hyman. Philadelphia: Lippincott, 1976.

King, Ernest Joseph and Walter Muir Whitehill. *Fleet Admiral King: A Naval Record.* New York: 1952.

Kirkendall, Richard S., ed. *The Truman Period as a Research Field: A Reappraisal, 1972.* Columbia: University of Missouri Press, 1974.

Kolko, Gabriel. *The Politics of War: The World and United States Foreign Policy, 1943–1945.* New York: Vintage Books, 1968.

Kolko, Joyce and Gabriel Kolko. *The Limits of Power: The World and United States Foreign Policy, 1945–1954.* New York: Harper & Row, 1972.

Koppes, Clayton R. and Gregory D. Black. "What to Show the World: The Office of War Information and Hollywood, 1942–1945." *Journal of American History* (June 1977), 64:87–105.

Krock, Arthur. *Memoirs: Sixty Years on the Firing Line.* New York: Funk & Wagnalls, 1968.

Kuklick, Bruce. *American Policy and the Division of Germany: The Clash with Russia over Reparations.* Ithaca N.Y.: Cornell University Press, 1972.

LaFeber, Walter. "Roosevelt, Churchill, and Indochina: 1942–45." *American Historical Review* (December 1975), 80:1277–95.

Langer, William L. and S. Everett Gleason. *The Challenge to Isolation, 1937–1940.* New York: Harper, 1952.

——*The Undeclared War, 1940–1941.* New York: Harper, 1953.

Lash, Joseph P. *Roosevelt and Churchill, 1939–1941: The Partnership That Saved the West.* New York: Norton, 1976.

Leahy, William D. *I Was There.* New York: Whittlesey House, 1950.

Leigh, Michael. *Mobilizing Consent: Public Opinion and American Foreign Policy, 1937–1947.* Westport, Conn.: Greenwood Press, 1976.

Lilienthal, David E. *Journals.* Vol. 2: *The Atomic Energy Years, 1945–1950.* New York: Harper & Row, 1964.

Loewenheim, Francis L., Harold D. Langley, and Manfred Jonas, eds. *Roosevelt and Churchill: Their Secret Wartime Correspondence.* New York: Saturday Review Press, 1975.

Louis, William Roger. *Imperialism At Bay: The United States and the Decolonization of the British Empire, 1941–1945.* New York: Oxford University Press, 1978.

McDonald, James G. *My Mission in Israel, 1948–1951.* New York: Simon & Schuster, 1951.

McIver, Honora Bruere. "American Invasion." *Survey Graphic* (May 1945), 34:165–66 ff.

McLellan, David S. *Dean Acheson: The State Department Years.* New York: Dodd, Mead, 1976.

Macmillan, Harold. *The Blast of War, 1939–1945.* New York: Harper & Row, 1967.

——*Tides of Fortune, 1945–1955.* New York: Harper & Row, 1969.

McNeill, William Hardy. *America, Britain, and Russia: Their Co-Operation and Conflict, 1941–1946.* Survey of International Affairs, 1939–1946. Edited by Arnold Toynbee. London: Oxford University Press, 1953.

Mallaby, George. *From My Level.* New York: Atheneum, 1965.

Mallalieu, William C. *British Reconstruction and American Policy, 1945–1955.* New York: Scarecrow Press, 1956.

Martel, Leon. *Lend-Lease, Loans, and the Coming of the Cold War: A Study of the Implementation of Foreign Policy.* Boulder, Colo.: Westview Press, 1979.

Martin, Edwin M. *The Allied Occupation of Japan.* Stanford: Stanford University Press, 1948.

Marwick, Arthur. "The British Elite in the Inter-War Years." In Gerhard L. Weinberg, ed., *Transformation of a Continent: Europe in the Twentieth Century.* Minneapolis, Minn.: Burgess, 1975.

Mastny, Vojtech. *Russia's Road to the Cold War: Diplomacy, Warfare, and the Politics of Communism, 1941–1945.* New York: Columbia University Press, 1979.

Matloff, Maurice. *Strategic Planning for Coalition Warfare, 1943–1944.* United States Army in World War II: The War Department. Washington: United States Army, 1959.

May, Ernest R. "The 'Bureaucratic Politics' Approach: U.S.-Argentine Relations, 1942–47." In Julio Cotler and Richard R. Fagen, eds., *Latin America and the United States: The Changing Political Realities.* Stanford: Stanford University Press, 1974.

——*"Lessons" of the Past: The Use and Misuse of History in American Foreign Policy.* New York: Oxford University Press, 1973.

Mee, Charles L., Jr. *Meeting at Potsdam.* New York: M. Evans, 1975.

Messer, Robert L. "The Making of a Cold Warrior: James F. Byrnes and American-Soviet Relations, 1945–1946." Ph.D. dissertation, University of California, Berkeley, 1975.

Miller, John Andrew. "Air Diplomacy: The Chicago Civil Aviation Conference of 1944 in Anglo-American Wartime Relations and Post-War Planning." Ph.D. dissertation, Yale University, 1971.

Millis, Walter. "American Choices." *Survey Graphic* (May 1945), 34:241–44.

Milward, Alan S. *War, Economy and Society, 1939–1945.* Berkeley: University of California Press, 1977.

Montgomery, Bernard Law. *Memoirs.* London: Collins, 1958.

Moran, Lord Charles. *Churchill: Taken from the Diaries of Lord Moran.* Boston: Houghton Mifflin Co., 1966.

Morgenthau, Henry, Jr. *Germany is Our Problem.* New York: Harper, 1945.

Morrison, Herbert. *An Autobiography.* London: Odhams Press, 1960.

Nicholas, Herbert. *Britain and the U.S.A.* Baltimore: Johns Hopkins University Press, 1963.

——*The United States and Britain.* Chicago: University of Chicago Press, 1975.

Nicolson, Harold. *Diaries and Letters.* Edited by Nigel Nicolson. Vol. 3: *The Later Years, 1945–1962.* New York: Atheneum, 1968.

——*Diaries and Letters.* Edited by Nigel Nicolson. Vol. 2: *The War Years, 1939–1945.* New York: Atheneum, 1967.

Normanbrook, Lord, John Colville, Sir John Martin, Sir Ian Jacob, Lord Bridges, and Sir Leslie Rowan. *Action This Day: Working with Churchill.* Edited with an introduction by Sir John Wheeler-Bennett. New York: St. Martin's Press, 1969.

Northedge, Frederick S. *British Foreign Policy: The Process of Readjustment, 1945–1961.* London: Allen and Unwin, 1962.

Offner, Arnold A. *The Origins of the Second World War: American Foreign Policy and World Politics, 1917–1941.* New York: Praeger, 1975.

Pachter, Henry. "Revisionist Historians & the Cold War." *Dissent* (November–December 1968), 15:505–18.

Parkinson, Roger. *A Day's March Nearer Home.* New York: McKay, 1974.

Parks, Wallace Judson. *United States Administration of Its International Economic Affairs.* Baltimore: Johns Hopkins University Press, 1951.

Parzen, Herbert. "The Roosevelt Palestine Policy, 1943–1945: An Exercise in Dual Diplomacy." *American Jewish Archives* (April 1974), 26:31–65.

Paterson, Thomas G. *On Every Front: The Making of the Cold War.* New York: Norton, 1979.

——*Soviet-American Confrontation: Postwar Reconstruction and the Origins of the Cold War.* Baltimore: Johns Hopkins University Press, 1973.

Peffer, E. Louise. "Cordell Hull's Argentine Policy and Britain's Meat Supply." *Inter-American Economic Affairs* (Autumn 1956), 10:3–21.

Penrose, E. F. *Economic Planning For The Peace.* Princeton: Princeton University Press, 1953.

Pickersgill, J. W. and D. F. Forster. *The Mackenzie King Record.* Vol. 2: *1944–1945.* Toronto: University of Toronto Press, 1968.

Pogue, Forrest C. *George C. Marshall: Organizer of Victory, 1943–1945.* New York: Viking Press, 1973.

——"SHAEF—A Retrospect on Coalition Command," *Journal of Modern History,* (December 1951), 23:329–35.

——*The Supreme Command.* United States Army in World War II: The European Theater of Operations. Washington: United States Army, 1954.

Potter, Elmer Belmont. *Nimitz.* Annapolis: Naval Institute Press, 1976.

Reischauer, Edwin O. *The United States and Japan.* 3d ed. Cambridge, Mass.: Harvard University Press, 1965.

Robbins, Lionel C. *Autobiography of an Economist.* London: Macmillan, 1971.

Rogow, Arnold A. *James Forrestal: A Study of Personality, Politics, and Policy.* New York: Macmillan, 1963.

Roosevelt, Franklin D. *The Public Papers and Addresses of Franklin D. Roosevelt.* Compiled by Samuel I. Rosenman. Vol. 13: *Victory and the Threshold of Peace.* New York: Harper, 1950.

Rose, Lisle A. *Dubious Victory: The United States and the End of World War II.* The Coming of the American Age, 1945–1946. Kent, Ohio: Kent State University Press, 1973.

Rosecrance, R. N. *Defense of the Realm: British Strategy in the Nuclear Epoch.* New York: Columbia University Press, 1968.

Rosecrance, R. N., ed. *The Dispersion of Nuclear Weapons: Strategy and Politics.* New York: Columbia University Press, 1964.

Rosenman, Samuel I. *Working With Roosevelt.* New York: Harper, 1952.

Rosenman, Samuel and Dorothy Rosenman. *Presidential Style: Some Giants and a Pygmy in the White House.* New York: Harper & Row, 1976.

Russett, Bruce M. *Community and Contention: Britain and America in the Twentieth Century.* Cambridge: M.I.T. Press, 1963.

Sayre, Francis Bowes. *The Way Forward: The American Trade Agreements Program.* New York: Macmillan, 1939.

Schatz, Arthur W. "The Anglo-American Trade Agreement and Cordell Hull's Search for Peace, 1936–1938." *Journal of American History* (June 1970), 57:85–103.

Schnabel, James F. *The Joint Chiefs of Staff and National Policy*. Vol. 1: *1945–1947*. The History of the Joint Chiefs of Staff. Wilmington, Del.: Michael Glazier, 1979.

Sherry, Michael S. *Preparing for the Next War: American Plans for Postwar Defense, 1941–45*. New Haven: Yale University Press, 1977.

Sherwin, Martin J. *A World Destroyed: The Atomic Bomb and the Grand Alliance*. New York: Knopf, 1975.

Sherwood, Robert E. *Roosevelt and Hopkins: An Intimate History*. New York: Harper, 1948.

Smith, Gaddis. *American Diplomacy During the Second World War*. New York: Wiley, 1965.

Smith, Perry McCoy. *The Air Force Plans for Peace, 1943–1945*. Baltimore: Johns Hopkins University Press, 1970.

Smith, Walter Bedell. *My Three Years in Moscow*. Philadelphia: Lippincott, 1950.

Snell, John, ed. *The Meaning of Yalta*. Baton Rouge: Louisiana State University Press, 1956.

Snetsinger, John. *Truman, the Jewish Vote, and the Creation of Israel*. Stanford: Hoover Institution Press, 1974.

Snowman, Daniel. *Britain and America: An Interpretation of Their Culture, 1945–1975*. New York: Harper, 1977.

Steinberg, Alfred. "Mr. Truman's Mystery Man." *The Saturday Evening Post* (December 24, 1949), 222:24ff.

Stettinius, Edward Reilly, Jr. *The Diaries of Edward R. Stettinius, Jr., 1943–1946*. Edited by Thomas M. Campbell and George C. Herring. New York: New Viewpoints, 1975.

——*Roosevelt and the Russians: The Yalta Conference*. Edited by Walter Johnson. Garden City, N.Y.: Doubleday, 1949.

Stevens, Richard P. *American Zionism and U.S. Foreign Policy, 1942–1947*. New York: Pageant Press, 1962.

Stevenson, William. *A Man Called Intrepid*. New York: Harcourt Brace Jovanovich, 1976.

Stimson, Henry L. and McGeorge Bundy. *On Active Service in Peace and War*. New York: Harper, 1947.

Stoff, Michael B. *Oil, War, and American Security: The Search for a National Policy on Foreign Oil, 1941–1947*. New Haven: Yale University Press, 1980.

Stoler, Mark A. *The Politics of the Second Front: American Military Planning and Diplomacy in Coalition Warfare, 1941–1943.* Westport, Conn.: Greenwood Press, 1977.

Stuart, Graham H. *The Department of State: A History of Its Organization, Procedure, and Personnel.* New York: Macmillan, 1949.

Sulzberger, Cyrus L. *A Long Row of Candles.* New York: Macmillan, 1969.

Taylor, A. J. P. *Beaverbrook.* London: Hamish Hamilton, 1972.

Theoharis, Athan G. *The Yalta Myths: An Issue in U.S. Politics, 1945–1955.* Columbia: University of Missouri Press, 1970.

Thorne, Christopher. *Allies of a Kind: The United States, Britain, and the War Against Japan, 1941–1945.* New York: Oxford University Press, 1978.

——"Indochina and Anglo-American Relations, 1942–1945." *Pacific Historical Review* (February 1976), 45:73–96.

Tompkins, C. David. *Senator Arthur H. Vandenberg: The Evolution of a Modern Republican, 1884–1945.* East Lansing: Michigan State University Press, 1970.

Truman, Harry S. *Memoirs.* Vol. 1: *Year of Decisions.* Garden City, N.Y.: Doubleday, 1955.

——*Memoirs.* Vol. 2: *Years of Trial and Hope.* Garden City, N.Y.: Doubleday, 1956.

Truman, Margaret. *Harry S. Truman.* New York: Morrow, 1973.

Turner, Arthur Campbell. *The Unique Partnership: Britain and the United States.* New York: Pegasus, 1971.

Vandenberg, Arthur H., Jr., ed. *The Private Papers of Senator Vandenberg.* With the collaboration of Joe Alex Morris. Boston: Houghton Mifflin, 1952.

Varga, Eugene. "Anglo-American Rivalry and Partnership: A Marxist View." *Foreign Affairs* (July 1947), 25:583–95.

Wallace, Henry A. *The Price of Vision: The Diary of Henry A. Wallace, 1942–1946.* Edited by John Morton Blum. Boston: Houghton Mifflin, 1973.

Waltz, Kenneth N. *Foreign Policy and Democratic Politics: The American and British Experience.* Boston: Little, Brown, 1967.

Ward, Jeremy K. "Winston Churchill and the 'Iron Curtain' Speech." *The History Teacher* (January 1968), 1:5–13.

Ward, Patricia Dawson. *The Threat of Peace: James F. Byrnes and the Council of Foreign Ministers, 1945–1946.* Kent, Ohio: Kent State University Press, 1979.

Watt, Donald Cameron. *Personalities and Policies: Studies in the Formulation of British Policy in the Twentieth Century.* Notre Dame, Ind.: University of Notre Dame Press, 1965.

Welles, Sumner. *Where Are We Heading?* New York: Harper, 1946.

Wheeler-Bennett, John W., and Anthony Nicholls. *The Semblance of Peace: The Political Settlement After the Second World War.* New York: Norton, 1972.

Williams, Francis. *Ernest Bevin: Portrait of a Great Englishman.* Foreword by Clement Attlee. London: Hutchinson, 1952.

——*Twilight of Empire: Memoirs of Prime Minister Clement Attlee.* New York: Barnes, 1962.

Wilmot, Chester. *The Struggle for Europe.* New York: Harper, Brothers, 1952.

Wilson, Henry Maitland. *Eight Years Overseas, 1939–1947.* London: Hutchinson, 1950.

Wilson, Theodore A. *The First Summit: Roosevelt and Churchill at Placentia Bay 1941.* Boston: Houghton Mifflin, 1969.

Winant, John Gilbert. *Letter from Grosvenor Square.* Boston: Houghton Mifflin, 1947.

Windrich, Elaine. *British Labour's Foreign Policy.* Stanford: Stanford University Press, 1952.

Winocour, Jack and Michael Young. "British Labor in Power." *The New Republic* (October 7, 1946), 115:436–45.

Wittner, Lawrence S. "American Policy Toward Greece During World War II." *Diplomatic History* (Spring 1979), 3:129–49.

Woodhouse, C. M. *British Foreign Policy Since the Second World War.* New York: Praeger, 1960.

Woods, Randall B. "Hull and Argentina: Wilsonian Diplomacy in the Age of Roosevelt." *Journal of Interamerican Studies and World Affairs* (August 1974), 16:350–71.

Woodward, Sir Llewellyn. *British Foreign Policy in the Second World War.* History of the Second World War. London: Her Majesty's Stationery Office, 1962.

Xydis, Stephen G. "America, Britain, and the USSR in the Greek Arena, 1944–1947." *Political Science Quarterly* (December 1963), 78:581–96.

Yergin, Daniel. *Shattered Peace: The Origins of the Cold War and the National Security State.* Boston: Houghton Mifflin, 1977.

Youngson, A. J. *The British Economy, 1920–1957.* London: Allen & Unwin, 1960.

Ziemke, Earl F. *The U.S. Army in the Occupation of Germany, 1944–1946.* Army Historical Series. Washington: United States Army, 1975.

NEWSPAPERS AND MAGAZINES

Atlanta Constitution
Barron's
Business Week
Chicago Tribune
Denver Post
Detroit Free Press
The *Economist*
Houston Post
Kansas City Star
Life
Los Angeles Times
New York Herald Tribune
New York Times
Newsweek
Public Opinion Quarterly
St. Louis Post-Dispatch
Time
The *Times* (London)
U.S. News
Wall Street Journal
Washington Post

Index